A Preface to

MARKETING MANAGEMENT

THE IRWIN SERIES IN MARKETING

GILBERT A. CHURCHILL, JR., CONSULTING EDITOR
University of Wisconsin, Madison

Alreck & Settle
The Survey Research Handbook, 2/E

Arens
Contemporary Advertising, 6/E

Belch & Belch
Introduction to Advertising and Promotion: An Integrated Marketing Communications Approach, 3/E

Bearden, Ingram & LaForge
Marketing: Principles & Perspectives, 1/E

Bernhardt & Kinnear
Cases in Marketing Management, 7/E

Berkowitz, Kerin, Hartley & Rudelius
Marketing, 5/E

Boyd, Walker & Larreche
Marketing Management: A Strategic Approach with a Global Orientation, 2/E

Cateora
International Marketing, 9/E

Churchill, Ford & Walker
Sales Force Management, 5/E

Cole & Mishler
Consumer and Business Credit Management, 10/E

Cravens
Strategic Marketing, 5/E

Cravens, Lamb & Crittenden
Strategic Marketing Management Cases, 5/E

Crawford
New Products Management, 5/E

Dillon, Madden & Firtle
Essentials of Marketing Research, 2/E

Dillon, Madden, & Firtle
Marketing Research in a Marketing Environment, 3/E

Faria, Nulsen & Roussos
Compete, 4/E

Futrell
ABC's of Selling, 5/E

Futrell
Fundamentals of Selling, 5/E

Gretz, Drozdeck, & Weisenhutter
Professional Selling: A Consultative Approach, 1/E

Hawkins, Best & Coney
Consumer Behavior, 6/E

Hayes, Jenster, & Aaby
Business to Business Marketing, 1/E

Johansson
Global Marketing, 1/E

Lambert & Stock
Strategic Logistics Management, 3/E

Lehmann & Winer
Analysis for Marketing Planning, 4/e

Lehmann & Winer
Product Management, 2/E

Levy & Weitz
Retailing Management, 2/E

Levy & Weitz
Essentials of Retailing, 1/E

Mason, Mayer & Ezell
Retailing, 5/E

Mason & Perreault
The Marketing Game!, 2/E

Meloan & Graham
International and Global Marketing Concepts and Cases, 1/E

Patton
Sales Force: A Sales Management Simulation Game, 1/E

Pelton, Strutton, & Lumpkin
Marketing Channels: A Relationship Management Approach, 1/E

Perreault & McCarthy
Basic Marketing: A Global Managerial Approach, 12/E

Perreault & McCarthy
Essentials of Marketing: A Global Managerial Approach, 7/E

Peter & Donnelly
Marketing Management: Knowledge and Skills, 4/E

Peter & Olson
Consumer Behavior and Marketing Strategy, 4/E

Peter & Olson
Understanding Consumer Behavior, 1/E

Quelch
Cases in Product Management, 1/E

Quelch, Dolan & Kosnik
Marketing Management: Text & Cases, 1/E

Quelch & Farris
Cases in Advertising and Promotional Management, 4/E

Quelch, Kashani & Vandermerwe
European Cases in Marketing Management, 1/E

Rangan, Shapiro, & Moriarty
Business Marketing Strategy: Cases, Concepts & Applications, 1/E

Rangan, Shapiro, & Moriarty
Business Marketing Strategy: Concepts & Applications, 1/E

Smith & Quelch
Ethics in Marketing, 1/E

Stanton, Buskirk & Spiro
Management of a Sales Force, 9/E

Thompson & Stappenbeck
The Marketing Strategy Game, 1/E

Walker, Boyd & Larreche
Marketing Strategy: Planning and Implementation, 2/E

Weitz, Castleberry & Tanner
Selling: Building Partnerships, 2/E

A Preface to

MARKETING MANAGEMENT

7TH EDITION

J. PAUL PETER
MC MANUS-BASCOM PROFESSOR OF MARKETING
UNIVERSITY OF WISCONSIN—MADISON

JAMES H. DONNELLY, JR.
THOMAS C. SIMONS PROFESSOR OF BUSINESS
GATTON COLLEGE OF BUSINESS AND ECONOMICS
UNIVERSITY OF KENTUCKY

IRWIN

Burr Ridge, Illinois
Boston, Massachusetts
Sydney, Australia

Irwin Book Team

Publisher: *Rob Zwettler*
Senior sponsoring editor: *Stephen M. Patterson*
Developmental editor: *Tricia Howland*
Marketing manager: *Colleen Suljic*
Project editor: *Jim Labeots*
Production supervisor: *Dina L. Genovese*
Art Director: *Keith J. McPherson*
Assistant manager, desktop services: *Jon Christopher*
Cover and interior design: *Randy Scott*
Cover illustration: *Communigrafix Inc.*
Compositor: *Carlisle Communications, Ltd.*
Typeface: *10/12 New Baskerville*
Printer: *R. R. Donnelley & Sons Company*

**Times Mirror
Higher Education Group**

Library of Congress Cataloging-in-Publication Data

Peter J. Paul.
    A preface to marketing management / J. Paul Peter, James H.
Donnelly, Jr. — 7th ed.
        p. cm. — (The Irwin series in marketing)
    Includes bibliographical references and indexes.
    ISBN 0-256-20281-8
I. Marketing—Management.   I. Donnelly, James H. II. Title.
III. Series
HF5415.13.P388 1996
658.8—dc20   95-51535

Printed in the United States of America
1 2 3 4 5 6 7 8 9 0 DO 3 2 1 0 9 8 7

Preface

Throughout its history, *A Preface to Marketing Management* has been used successfully in a variety of situations. This was our intention—we developed it with several potential uses in mind—and as the title indicates, it is intended to serve as an overview of the critical aspects of marketing management.

As we introduce the seventh edition, we are pleased to find that yet another important use has been found for our book. During the past several years there has been increasing demand from business students, the organizations that hire business school graduates, and from the American Assembly of Collegiate Schools of Business for cross-functional emphasis in business school programs. Obviously, most real business problems span functional disciplines in real organizations. For example, product quality and service quality problems usually have production and operations implications.

Consequently, many business schools have undertaken efforts to integrate their curricula. At the undergraduate level, one means has been to integrate several core curriculum courses into one multidisciplinary 9- to 12-hour course, which is usually team taught. These institutions are finding our book perfectly suited for this innovative course. Thus, one of the many goals of this edition has been, wherever possible, to reinforce the cross-functional nature of many marketing problems. This change will also be of assistance to those who continue to use our book

- As a supplement in undergraduate and MBA-level marketing management courses that focus on case problems.
- In short courses, executive development programs, and continuing education seminars.
- As a primary introductory test. Perhaps because of the rising prices of introductory marketing texts, our book has been used successfully as an introductory text. In fact one reviewer commented that our book is "pound for pound, the best introductory marketing text available."

We encourage you to review this new edition. It is a major revision with significant amounts of new material. The book has five major sections:

Section I. Essentials of Marketing Management

This section consists of 14 chapters that present what we believe to be the essentials of marketing. The objective of this section is to present material that can be useful in analyzing a marketing problem or case. Readers are also directed to relevant sources in the discussion as well as additional sources of information at the end of each chapter.

Important new topics have been added to this edition including relationship marketing, total quality management, globalization, measuring customer satisfaction, value disciplines, relationship selling, competitive advantage, brand equity, and strategic marketing. In addition, a great deal of material has been reorganized, replaced, revised, and rewritten. For example, the discussion of organizational strategies has been totally reorganized. We now present three approaches: strategies based on products and markets, strategies based on competitive advantage, and strategies based on value disciplines. Important changes such as this one have been made throughout the book.

A popular feature of our book that has received very positive feedback from both students and teachers is the occasional "highlight" that appears throughout. Not the usual "new items" found in other texts, this feature emphasizes important information and handy tools for analyzing marketing cases and problems. We have revised and replaced many in this edition.

Section II. Analyzing Marketing Problems and Cases

This section presents an approach to analyzing, writing, and presenting case analyses. It has received widespread praise from both faculty and students and we believe it is the best presentation available on the topic.

It is important to note that this section could have been placed at the beginning of the book because it is designed to be read at the start of a course using cases. However, since it is usually referred to throughout the semester, it was placed after the text material for convenience. Also, for those courses or training seminars that do not employ cases, the text may be used without reference to this section.

Section III. Financial Analysis for Marketing Decisions

The ultimate objectives of marketing activities are usually expressed in financial terms. This section presents some important financial calculations that can be useful in evaluating the financial position of a firm and the financial impact of various marketing strategies.

Section IV. Developing Marketing Plans

This section contains an approach to developing marketing plans. In keeping with our concept of this book and the needs of intended users, the purpose of the section is to help readers develop practical planning skills by providing a general format for structuring actual marketing plans.

Section V. Secondary Data Sources

A new section "On-Line Marketing Information Services" has been added to this section and includes discussions of the marketing uses of Internet and other on-line information services. We believe this addition adds significant value to our book as a resource. This section also contains an annotated bibliography of numerous relevant secondary sources that can be used as a resource for the analysis of many types of marketing problems. We have found this section to be extremely valuable. It can increase the depth of case analysis as well as expose readers to important secondary sources that will be useful to them in their careers. Nine specific classifications of secondary sources are presented: selected periodicals, general marketing information sources, selected marketing information services, selected retail trade publications, financial information sources, basic U.S. statistical sources, general business and industry sources, indexes and abstracts, and on-line marketing information services.

Throughout this edition we have implemented the suggestions and ideas of those individuals who have served as reviewers of this and previous editions. We would like to publicly acknowledge their assistance.

Reviewers of previous editions:

Catherine Axinn, Syracuse University
Linda M. Delene, Western Michigan University
Robert Finney, California State University, Hayward
Stephen Goldberg, Fordham University
David Horne, Wayne State University
Sol Klein, Northeastern University
Edward J. Mayo, Western Michigan University
Johannah Jones Nolan, University of Alabama, Birmingham
Debu Purohit, Duke University
Matthew H. Sauber, Eastern Michigan University
Ronald L. Schill, Brigham Young University
Vernon R. Stauble, California State Polytechnic University
Ann Marie Thompson, Northern Illinois University
John R. Thompson, Memphis State University
Kathleen R. Whitney, Central Michigan University
J. B. Wilkinson, University of Akron

Reviewers of the present edition:

Roger D. Absmire, Sam Houston State University
Reid P. Claxton, East Carolina University
Franklyn Manu, Morgan State University
Gary K. Rhoads, Brigham Young University
R. Stephen Parker, Southwest Missouri State University

Finally, we acknowledge Andrew Policano, Dean of the School of Business at the University of Wisconsin, and Richard Furst, Dean of the Gatton College of Business and Economics, University of Kentucky, who have always supported our efforts. We would also like to thank Steve Patterson, Senior Sponsoring Editor; Tricia Howland, Developmental Editor; and Jim Labeots, Project Editor, for their contributions in bringing this new edition to print.

Finally, we wish to thank Dr. Geoffrey Gordon of Northern Illinois University who deserves special recognition for his many contributions to the book and for his strong belief in the concept of the book. Thank you Geoff.

J. Paul Peter
James H. Donnelly, Jr.

Contents

Section I
ESSENTIALS OF MARKETING MANAGEMENT

Part A

INTRODUCTION

CHAPTER 1
STRATEGIC PLANNING AND THE MARKETING MANAGEMENT PROCESS

Chapter 1
STRATEGIC PLANNING AND THE MARKETING MANAGEMENT PROCESS

The purpose of this introductory chapter is to present the marketing management process and outline what marketing managers must *manage* if they are to be effective. In doing so, it will also present a framework around which the remaining chapters are organized. Our first task is to review the organizational philosophy known as the marketing concept, since it underlies much of the thinking presented in this book. The remainder of this chapter will focus on the process of strategic planning and its relationship to the process of marketing planning.

THE MARKETING CONCEPT

Simply stated, the marketing concept means that *an organization should seek to make a profit by serving the needs of customer groups.* The concept is very straightforward and has a great deal of common sense validity. Perhaps this is why it is often misunderstood, forgotten, or overlooked.

The purpose of the marketing concept is to rivet the attention of marketing managers on serving broad classes of customer needs (customer orientation), rather than on the firm's current products (production orientation) or on devising methods to attract customers to current products (selling orientation). Thus, effective marketing starts with the recognition of customer needs and then works backward to devise products and services to satisfy these needs. In this way, marketing managers can satisfy customers more efficiently in the present and anticipate changes in customer needs more accurately in the future. This means that organizations should focus on building long-term customer relationships in which the initial sale is viewed as a beginning step in the process, not as an end goal. As a result, the customer will be more satisfied and the firm will be more profitable.

HIGHLIGHT 1–1

Basic Elements of the Marketing Concept

1. Companywide managerial awareness and appreciation of the consumer's role as it is related to the firm's existence, growth, and stability. As Drucker has noted, business enterprise is an organ of society; thus, its basic purpose lies outside the business itself. And the valid definition of business purpose is the creation of customers.

2. Active, company wide managerial awareness of, and concern with, interdepartmental implications of decisions and actions of an individual department. That is, the firm is viewed as a network of forces focused on meeting defined customer needs, and comprising a system within which actions taken in one department or area frequently result in significant repercussions in other areas of the firm. Also, it is recognized that such actions may affect the company's equilibrium with its external environment, for example, its customers, its competitors.

3. Active, companywide managerial concern with innovation of products and services designed to solve selected consumer problems.

Source: Robert L. King, "The Marketing Concept: Fact or Intelligent Platitude," *The Marketing Concept in Action,* Proceedings of the 47th National Conference (Chicago: American Marketing Association, 1964), p. 657. For an up-to-date discussion of the marketing concept, see Frederick E. Webster, Jr., "Defining the New Marketing Concept," *Marketing Management* 2, no. 4 (1994), pp. 22–31.

4. General managerial concern with the effect of new products and service introduction on the firm's profit position, both present and future, and recognition of the potential rewards that may accrue from new product planning, including profits and profit stability.

5. General managerial appreciation of the role of marketing intelligence and other fact-finding and -reporting units within and adjacent to the firm in translating the general statements presented above into detailed statements of profitable market potentials, targets, and action. Implicit in this statement is not only an expansion of the traditional function and scope of formal marketing research, but also assimilation of other sources of marketing data, such as the firm's distribution system and its advertising agency counsel, into a potential marketing intelligence service.

6. Companywide managerial effort, based on participation and interaction of company officers, in establishing corporate and departmental objectives that are understood by and acceptable to these officers, and that are consistent with enhancement of the firm's profit position.

The principal task of the marketing function operating under the marketing concept is not to manipulate customers to do what suits the interests of the firm, but rather to find effective and efficient means of making the business do what suits the interests of customers. This is not to say that all firms practice marketing in this way. Clearly, many firms still emphasize only production and sales. However, effective marketing, as defined in this text, requires that consumer needs come first in organizational decision making.

One qualification to this statement deals with the question of a conflict between consumer wants and societal needs and wants. For example, if society deems clean air and water as necessary for survival, this need may well take precedence over a consumer's want for goods and services that pollute the environment.

WHAT IS MARKETING?

One of the most persistent conceptual problems in marketing is its definition.[1] The American Marketing Association has recently defined *marketing* as "the process of planning and executing conception, pricing, promotion, and distribution of ideas, goods, and services to create exchanges that satisfy individual and organizational goals."[2] This definition takes into account all parties involved in the marketing effort: members of the producing organization, resellers of goods and services, and customer or clients.[3] While the broadness of the definition allows the inclusion of nonbusiness exchange processes, the primary emphasis in this text is on marketing in the business environment. However, this emphasis is not meant to imply that marketing concepts, principles, and techniques cannot be fruitfully employed in other areas of exchange. In fact, some discussions of nonbusiness marketing take place later in the text.

WHAT IS STRATEGIC PLANNING?

Before a production manager, marketing manager, and personnel manager can develop plans for their individual departments, hopefully some larger plan or blueprint for the *entire* organization has been developed. Otherwise, on what would the individual departmental plans be based?

In other words, there is a larger context for planning activities. Let us assume that we are dealing with a large business organization that has several business divisions and several product lines within each division (e.g., General Electric, Philip Morris). Before any marketing planning can be done by individual divisions or departments, a plan has to be developed for the *entire* organization.[4] This means that senior managers must look toward the future and evaluate their ability to shape their organization's destiny in the years and decades to come.[5] The output of this process is objectives and strategies designed to give the organization a chance to compete effectively in the future. The objectives and strategies established at the top level provide the context for planning in each of the divisions and departments by divisional and departmental managers. It is worth noting that, depending on the environmental challenges faced by the organization, different planning approaches may be called for.[6]

Strategic Planning and Marketing Management

Some of the most successful business organizations are here today because many years ago they offered the right product at the right time to a rapidly growing market. The same can also be said for nonprofit and governmen-

---

HIGHLIGHT 1–2

Fifteen Guidelines for the Market-Driven Manager

1. Create customer focus throughout the business.
2. Listen to the customer.
3. Define and nurture your distinctive competence.
4. Define marketing as marketing intelligence.
5. Target customers precisely.
6. Manage for profitability, not sales volume.

Source: Frederick E. Webster, Jr., "Executing the New Marketing Concept," *Marketing Management* 3, no. 1 (1994), pp. 8–16.

7. Make customer value the guiding star.
8. Let the customer define quality.
9. Measure and manage customer expectations.
10. Build customer relationships and loyalty.
11. Define the business as a service business.
12. Commit to continuous improvement and innovation.
13. Manage culture along with strategy and structure.
14. Grow with partners and alliances.
15. Destroy marketing bureaucracy.

---

tal organizations. Many of the critical decisions of the past were made without the benefit of strategic thinking or planning. Whether these decisions were based on wisdom or were just luck is not important; they worked for these organizations. However, a worse fate befell countless other organizations. Over three quarters of the 100 largest U.S. corporations of 70 years ago have fallen from the list.[7] These corporations at one time dominated their markets, controlled vast resources, and had the best-trained workers. In the end, they all made the same critical mistake. Their managements failed to recognize that business strategies need to reflect changing environments and emphasis must be placed on developing business systems that allow for continuous improvement.[8] Instead, they attempted to carry on business as usual.

Present-day managers are increasingly recognizing that wisdom and innovation alone are no longer sufficient to guide the destinies of organizations, both large and small. These same managers also realize that the true mission of the organization is to provide value for three key constituencies: customers, employees, and investors. Without this type outlook, no one, including shareholders, will profit in the long run.[9] Indeed, this focus can be seen in the mission statements contained in Highlight 1–3. Over the course of the past decade, markets have become increasingly global, technology has evolved at an accelerated pace, novel forms of distributing products and services have proliferated, and firms have continually invented new organizational forms—all occurring as customer needs and preferences continually shift in sometimes unpredictable ways.[10] Indeed, today's challenge is to respond to rapid changes happening in almost every sector of commercial life.[11] To be 21st century winners, most current organizations will

---

HIGHLIGHT 1–3
Mission Statements

mOrganization	Mission
Goodyear	Our mission is constant improvement in products and services to meet our customers' needs. This is the only means to business success for Goodyear and prosperity for its investors and employees.
Intel Corporation	Do a great job for our customers, employees, and stockholders by being the preeminent building block supplier to the computing industry.
Levi Strauss & Co.	The mission of Levi Strauss & Co. is to sustain responsible commercial success as a global marketing company of branded casual apparel. We must balance goals of superior profitability and return on investment, leadership market positions, and superior products and service. We will conduct our business ethically and demonstrate leadership in satisfying our responsibilities to our communities and to society. Our work environment will be safe and productive and characterized by fair treatment, teamwork, open communications, personal accountability, and opportunities for growth and development.
Merck & Co., Inc.	The mission of Merck & Co., Inc., is to provide society with superior products and services—innovations and solutions that satisfy customer needs and improve their quality of life—to provide employees with meaningful work and advancement opportunities and investors with a superior rate of return.
Marriott	Grow a worldwide lodging business using total quality management (TQM) principles to continuously improve preference and profitability. Our commitment is that *every guest leaves satisfied*.

Source: Patricia Jones and Larry Kahaner, *Say It And Live It: The 50 Corporate Mission Statements That Hit the Mark* (New York: Doubleday, 1995).

---

need to remake themselves fundamentally. How to change is relatively easy to identify, but difficult to pull off.

For example, 15 years ago, few would have predicted that Sears, the world's largest retailer for half a century, would have to shed its catalog operations and develop freestanding hardware and furniture stores to retain a fighting chance to remain a top retailer. Further, five years ago, no one could guess that Kmart would be fighting for its very survival while two relative newcomers, Wal-Mart and Target, would become market leaders.[12]

Change is not solely limited to the retail sector. For example, few would have thought that IBM would have to link up with Lotus to compete for market supremacy against Microsoft, and that Digital Equipment Company (DEC) would be undertaking massive change in the hopes of surviving as merely a middle-tier player in the computer industry.[13] Organizations today need not only function in a competitive and hostile environment but must also be able to cooperate with other companies, perhaps even with ones that in other respects are competitors.[14] For these and other countless reasons, strategic planning remains valuable to ensure competitive viability.

Figure 1–1   *The Strategic Planning Process*

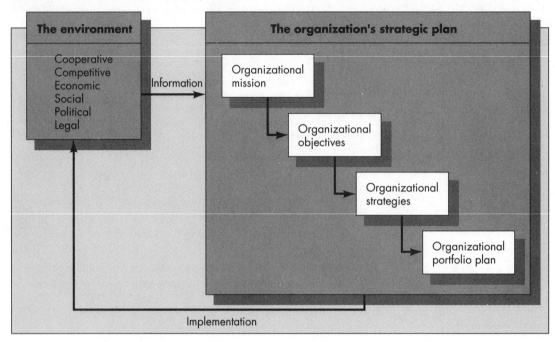

Strategic planning includes all the activities that lead to the development of a clear organizational mission, organizational objectives, and appropriate strategies to achieve the objectives for the entire organization. While the form of the process itself has come under criticism in some quarters for being too structured; strategic planning, if performed successfully, plays a key role in achieving an equilibrium between the short and the long term by balancing acceptable financial performance with preparation for inevitable changes in markets, technology, and competition, as well as in economic and political arenas.[15] Managing principally for current cash flows, market share gains, and earnings trends can mortgage the firm's future. An intense focus on the near term can produce an aversion to risk that dooms a business to stagnation. Conversely, an overemphasis on the long run is just as inappropriate. Companies that overextend themselves betting on the future may penalize short-term profitability and other operating results to such an extent that the company is vulnerable to takeover and other threatening actions.

The strategic planning process is depicted in Figure 1–1. In the strategic planning process the organization gathers information about the changing elements of its environment. Managers from all functional areas in the organization assist in this information-gathering process. This information is useful in aiding the organization to adapt better to these changes

through the process of strategic planning. The strategic plan(s)[16]
porting plan are then implemented in the environment. The en
of this implementation are fed back as new information so that continuous
adaptation and improvement can take place.

The Strategic Planning Process

The output of the strategic planning process is the development of a strategic plan. Figure 1–1 indicates four components of a strategic plan: mission,
objectives, strategies, and portfolio plan. Let us carefully examine each one.

Organizational mission

The organization's environment provides the resources that sustain the
organization, whether it is a business, a college or university, or a government agency. In exchange for these resources, the organization must supply the environment with quality goods and services at an acceptable price.
In other words, every organization exists to accomplish something in the
larger environment and that purpose, vision, or mission usually is clear at
the organization's inception. As time passes, however, the organization expands, and the environment and managerial personnel change. As a result, one or more things are likely to occur. First, the organization's original purpose may become irrelevant as the organization expands into new
products, new markets, and even new industries. For example, Levi Strauss
began as a manufacturer of work clothes. Second, the original mission may
remain relevant, but managers begin to lose interest in it. Finally, changes
in the environment may make the original mission inappropriate. The result of any or all three of these conditions is a "drifting" organization, without a clear mission, vision, or purpose to guide critical decisions. When this
occurs, management must search for a purpose or emphatically restate and
reinforce the original purpose.

The mission statement, or purpose, of an organization is the description
of its reason for existence.[17] It is the long-run vision of what the organization strives to be, the unique aim that differentiates the organization from
similar ones and the means by which this differentiation will take place. In
essence, the mission statement defines the direction in which the organization is heading and how it will succeed in reaching its desired goal. While
some argue that vision and mission statements differ in their purpose, the
perspective we will take is that both reflect the organization's attempt to
guide behavior, create a culture, and inspire commitment.[18] However, it is
more important that the mission statement must come from the heart, and
be practical, easy to identify with, and easy to remember so that it will provide direction and significance to all members of the organization regardless of their organizational level.[19]

The basic questions that must be answered when an organization decides to examine and restate its mission are What is our business?, Who is

the customer?, What do customers value?, and What will our business be?[20] The answers are, in a sense, the assumptions on which the organization is being run and from which future decisions will evolve.[21] While such questions may seem simplistic, they are such difficult and critical ones that the major responsibility for answering them must lie with top management, not planning gurus.[22] In fact, the mission statement remains the most widely used management tool in business today. In developing a statement of mission, management must take into account three key elements: the organization's history, its distinctive competencies, and its environment.[23]

1. *The organization's history.* Every organization—large or small, profit or non-profit—has a history of objectives, accomplishments, mistakes, and policies. In formulating a mission, the critical characteristics and events of the past must be considered.

2. *The organization's distinctive competencies.* While there are many things an organization may be able to do, it should seek to do what it can do best. Distinctive competencies are things that an organization does well: so well in fact that they give it an advantage over similar organizations. For Honeywell, it's their ability to design, manufacture, and distribute a superior line of thermostats.[24] Similarly, Procter & Gamble's distinctive competence is its knowledge of the market for low-priced, repetitively purchased consumer products. No matter how appealing an opportunity may be, to gain advantage over competitors, the organization must formulate strategy based on distinctive competencies.[25]

3. *The organization's environment.* The organization's environment dictates the opportunities, constraints, and threats that must be identified before a mission statement is developed. For example, managers in any industry that is affected by technology breakthroughs should continually be asking, How will the changes in technology affect my customers' behavior and the means by which we need to conduct our business?[26]

However, it is extremely difficult to write a useful and effective mission statement. It is not uncommon for an organization to spend one or two years developing a useful mission statement. When completed, an effective mission statement will be: *focused on markets rather than products, achievable, motivating, and specific.*[27]

Focused on markets rather than products. The customers or clients of an organization are critical in determining its mission. Traditionally, many organizations defined their business in terms of what they made, "our business is glass," and in many cases they named the organization for the product or service (e.g., National Cash Register, Harbor View Savings and Loan Association). Many of these organizations have found that, when products and technologies become obsolete, their mission is no longer relevant and the name of the organization may no longer describe what it does. Thus, a more enduring way of defining the mission is needed. In recent years, therefore, a key feature of mission statements has been an *external* rather than *internal* focus. In other words, the mission statement should focus on the broad class of needs that the organization is seeking to satisfy (external focus), *not* on the physical product or service that the organization is offering at present (internal focus). These market-driven firms stand out in their ability to continuously anticipate market opportunities and respond before their competitors.[28] This has been clearly stated by Peter Drucker:

> A business is not defined by the company's name, statutes, or articles of incorporation. It is defined by the want the customer satisfies when he buys a product or service. To satisfy the customer is the mission and purpose of every business. The question "What is our business?" can, therefore, be answered only by looking at the business from the outside, from the point of view of customer and market.[29]

While Drucker was referring to business organizations, the same necessity exists for both nonprofit and governmental organizations. That necessity is to state the mission in terms of serving a particular group of clients or customers and meeting a particular class of need.

Achievable. While the mission statement should "stretch" the organization toward more effective performance, it should, at the same time, be realistic and achievable. In other words, it should open a vision of new opportunities but should not lead the organization into unrealistic ventures far beyond its competencies.

Motivational. One of the side (but very important) benefits of a well-defined mission is the guidance it provides employees and managers working in geographically dispersed units and on independent tasks. It provides a shared sense of purpose outside the various activities taking place within the organization. Therefore, such end results as sales, patients cared for, and reduction in violent crimes can then be viewed as the result of careful pursuit and accomplishment of the mission and not as the mission itself.

Specific. As we mentioned earlier, public relations should not be the primary purpose of a statement of mission. It must be specific to provide direction and guidelines to management when they are choosing between alternative courses of action. In other words, "to produce the highest quality products at the lowest possible cost" sounds very good, but it does not provide direction for management.

Organizational objectives

Organizational objectives are the end points of an organization's mission and are what it seeks through the ongoing, long-run operations of the organization. The organizational mission is distilled into a finer set of specific and achievable organizational objectives. These objectives must be *specific, measurable, action commitments* by which the mission of the organization is to be achieved.

As with the statement of mission, organizational objectives are more than good intentions. In fact, if formulated properly, they can accomplish the following:

1. They can be converted into specific action.
2. They will provide direction. That is, they can serve as a starting point for more specific and detailed objectives at lower levels in the organization. Each manager will then know how his or her objectives relate to those at higher levels.
3. They can establish long-run priorities for the organization.
4. They can facilitate management control because they serve as standards against which overall organizational performance can be evaluated.

Organizational objectives are necessary in all areas that may influence the performance and long-run survival of the organization. As shown in Figure 1–2, objectives can be established in and across many areas of the organization. The list provided in Figure 1–2 is by no means exhaustive. For example, some organizations are specifying the primary objective as the attainment of a specific level of quality, either in the marketing of a product or the providing of a service. These organizations believe that objectives should reflect an organization's commitment to the customer rather than its own finances.[30] The important point is that management must translate the organizational mission into specific objectives that support the realization of the mission. The objectives may flow directly from the mission or be considered subordinate necessities for carrying out the mission. As discussed earlier, the objectives are specific, measurable, action commitments on the part of the organization. Because of these traits, well-formulated objectives also greatly facilitate the process of performance measurement.[31]

Organizational strategies

Hopefully, when an organization has formulated its mission and developed its objectives, it knows where it wants to go. The next managerial task is to develop a "grand design" to get there. This grand design constitutes the organizational strategies. The role of strategy in strategic planning is to provide a clear, realistic articulation of a desired competitive position and the underlying core strategic goals and objectives related to achieving this position and enhancing it over time.[32] Strategy involves the choice of major directions the organization will take in pursuing its objectives. Toward this end, it is critical that strategies are consistent with goals and objectives and that top management ensures strategies are implemented effectively.[33] As many as 60 percent of strategic plans have failed because the strategies in them were not well defined and, thus, were unable to be implemented effectively.[34] What follows is a discussion of various strategies organizations can pursue.

Figure 1–2   *Sample Organizational Objectives* (manufacturing firm)

Area of Performance	Possible Objective
1. Market standing	To make our brands number one in their field in terms of market share.
2. Innovations	To be a leader in introducing new products by spending no less than 7 percent of sales for research and development.
3. Productivity	To manufacture all products efficiently as measured by the productivity of the work force.
4. Physical and financial resources	To protect and maintain all resources—equipment, buildings, inventory, and funds.
5. Profitability	To achieve an annual rate of return on investment of at least 15 percent.
6. Manager performance and responsibility	To identify critical areas of management depth and succession.
7. Worker performance and attitude	To maintain levels of employee satisfaction consistent with our own and similar industries.
8. Social responsibility	To respond appropriately whenever possible to societal expectations and environmental needs.

Organizational strategies based on products/markets

One means to develop organizational strategies is to focus on products offered and markets served. Using this focus, organizations can achieve their objectives in two ways. They can better manage what they are presently doing and/or find new things to do. In choosing either or both of these paths, the organization then must decide whether to concentrate on present customers or to seek new ones, or both. Figure 1–3 presents the available strategic choices. This figure is known as a product-market matrix and indicates the strategic alternatives available to an organization for achieving its objectives. It indicates that an organization can grow in a variety of ways by concentrating on present or new products and on present or new customers.[35]

Market penetration strategies. These organizational strategies focus on improving the position of the organization's present products with its present customers. For example:

— A snack products company concentrates on getting its present customers to purchase more of its products.

—A charity seeks ways to increase donations from present supporters.

Figure 1–3   *Organizational Growth Strategies*

Products Markets	Present Products	New Products
Present customers	Market penetration	Product development
New customers	Market development	Diversification

—A bank concentrates on getting present credit card customers to use their cards more frequently.

A market penetration strategy might involve devising a marketing plan to encourage customers to purchase more of a product. Tactics used to carry out the strategy could include price reductions, advertising that stresses the many benefits of the product, packaging the product in different-sized packages, or making the product available at more locations. For example, Procter & Gamble recently decided to implement an everyday low pricing strategy, slashing prices on over 40 percent of its product offerings, in order to stimulate consumer demand. Likewise, a production plan might be developed to produce more efficiently what is being produced at present. Implementation of such a plan could include increased production runs, the substitution of pre-assembled components for individual product parts, or the automation of a process that previously was performed manually. In other words, market penetration strategies concentrate on improving the efficiency of various functional areas in the organization.

Market development strategies. Following this strategy, an organization would seek to find new customers for its present products. For example:

—A manufacturer of industrial products may decide to develop products for entrance into consumer markets.
—A governmental social service agency may seek individuals and families who have never utilized the agency's services.
—A manufacturer of automobiles decides to sell automobiles in Eastern Europe because of the recent transition to a free market system.
—An athletic clothing and footwear company decides to develop a line of fitness clothing for children.

Market development strategies involve much more than simply getting the product to a new market. Before considering marketing techniques such as packaging and promotion, companies often find they must establish a foothold in the market, sometimes spending millions of dollars simply to educate consumers as to why they should consider purchase of the product. ***Product development strategies.*** In choosing either of the remaining two strategies, the organization in effect seeks new things to do. With this particular strategy, the new products developed would be directed to present customers. For example:

—A candy manufacturer may decide to offer a fat-free candy.
—A social service agency may offer additional services to present clients.
—A college or university may develop programs for nontraditional students.
—A soft drink manufacturer may develop a mid-calorie or clear cola.

Diversification. An organization diversifies when it seeks new products for customers it is not serving at present. For example:

—A discount store purchases a savings and loan association.
—A cigarette manufacturer diversifies into real estate development.
—A college or university establishes a corporation to find commercial uses for the results of faculty research efforts.
—A cosmetics manufacturer acquires a baby-care products company.

Organizational strategies based on competitive advantage

Michael Porter developed a model for formulating organizational strategy that is applicable across a wide variety of industries.[36] The focus of the model is on organizations devising means to gain competitive advantage. Porter's generic strategy model suggests that firms should first analyze their industry and then develop either a cost leadership strategy or a strategy based on differentiation. These strategies can be utilized on a marketwide basis or in a niche (segment) contained within the total market. Businesses using a cost leadership strategy focus on being the low-cost company in their industry. They attempt to be efficient and offer a standard, no-frills product. They can accomplish this through efficiencies in production, product design, manufacturing, distribution, technology, or some other means. To succeed, the organization must continually strive to be the cost leader in the industry or market segment they compete in. However, even a cost leader must offer products and/or services that are acceptable to customers when compared to competitors' offerings. Wal-Mart, Southwest Airlines, Timex Group Ltd., and Toys R Us are examples of companies that have succeeded with this approach.

Second, an organization may pursue a competitive advantage through differentiation. With a differentiation strategy, a company attempts to be unique in its industry or market segment along some dimension(s) that customers value. These dimensions might pertain to design, quality, service, variety of offerings, brand name, or some other factor. Because of the uniqueness of the product or service, companies can charge a premium price. L. L. Bean, Rolex, Coca-Cola, and Microsoft are all examples of companies that have successfully employed this strategy.

Organizational strategies based on value disciplines

More recently, Michael Treacy and Fred Wiersma developed a model for devising organizational strategy that is based on three core value disciplines that organizations can strive to achieve.[37] Their contention is that no firm in today's complex environment can succeed by trying to be all things to all people. Instead, the firm must find the unique value that it alone can deliver to a given market. The first value discipline, *operational excellence*, is pursued by companies that are not product or service innovators, nor do they cultivate deep, one-to-one relationships with customers. Instead, operationally excellent companies provide middle-of-the-road products (in terms of quality) at the best price with the least inconvenience. Their proposition to customers is simple: low price or hassle-free service or both. Price/Costco and Dell Computer are examples of this type of company.

The second value discipline, *product leadership*, is pursued by companies that push performance boundaries. Their proposition to customers is that they offer the best product or service, period. These companies continually innovate year after year. For these product leaders, competition is not about price or customer service (although those can't be ignored), it's about product performance. Johnson & Johnson, Nike, and Rubbermaid are examples of companies following this discipline. The final value discipline, *customer intimacy*, is adhered to by companies not interested in what the entire market wants; rather, the focus is on providing what specific customers want. Customer-intimate companies do not pursue one-time transactions; they cultivate relationships. These companies specialize in satisfying unique needs that are often only recognized by developing close relationships with and intimate knowledge of select customers. Their proposition to customers is that we have the best products for you, and we provide all the support you need to achieve optimum results. Airborne Express, Roadway, and Cott Corp. are examples of companies pursuing this final discipline.

Choosing an appropriate strategy

On what basis does an organization choose one (or all) of its strategies? Of extreme importance are the directions set by the mission statement. Management should select those strategies consistent with its mission and capitalize on the organization's distinctive competencies that will lead to a sustainable competitive advantage.[38] A sustainable competitive advantage can be based on either the assets or skills of the organization. Technical superiority, low-cost production, customer service/product support, location, financial resources, continuing product innovation, and overall marketing skills are all examples of distinctive competencies that can lead to a sustainable competitive advantage.[39] For example, Honda is known for providing quality automobiles at a reasonable price. Each succeeding generation of Honda automobiles has shown marked quality improvements over previous generations. Likewise, VF Corporation, manufacturer of Wrangler and Lee jeans, has formed "quick response" partnerships with both discounters and department stores to ensure the efficiency of product flow.[40] The key to sustaining a competitive advantage is to continually focus and build on the assets and skills that will lead to long-term performance gains.

Organizational portfolio plan

The final phase of the strategic planning process is the formulation of the organizational portfolio plan. In reality, most organizations at a particular time are a portfolio of businesses, that is, product lines, divisions, schools. To illustrate, an appliance manufacturer may have several product lines (e.g., televisions, washers and dryers, refrigerators, stereos) as well as two divisions, consumer appliances and industrial appliances. A college or university will have numerous schools (e.g., education, business, law, architecture) and several programs within each school. Some widely diversified organizations such as Philip Morris are in numerous unrelated businesses, such as cigarettes, food products, land development, industrial paper products, and a brewery.

Managing such groups of businesses is made a little easier if resources are plentiful, cash is plentiful, and each is experiencing growth and profits. Unfortunately, providing larger and larger budgets each year to all businesses is seldom feasible. Many are not experiencing growth, and profits and resources (financial and nonfinancial) are becoming more and more scarce. In such a situation, choices must be made, and some method is necessary to help management make the choices. Management must decide which businesses to build, maintain, or eliminate, or which new businesses to add.[41] Indeed, much of the recent activity in corporate restructuring has centered around decisions relating to which groups of businesses management should focus on.

Obviously, the first step in this approach is to identify the various division's product lines and so on that can be considered a "business." When identified, these are referred to as *strategic business units* (SBUs) and have the following characteristics:

—They have a distinct mission.
—They have their own competitors.
—They are a single business or collection of related businesses.
—They can be planned independently of the other businesses of the
  total organization.

Thus, depending on the type of organization, an SBU could be a single product, product line, or division; a department of business administration; or a state mental health agency. Once the organization has identified and classified all of its SBUs, some method must be established to determine how resources should be allocated among the various SBUs. These methods are known as *portfolio models*. For those readers interested, the appendix of this chapter presents two of the most popular portfolio models, the Boston Consulting Group model and the General Electric model.

The SBU concept is a powerful tool because SBUs partition a company according to the principal markets served.[42] A critical element of successful planning involves an organization possessing an outward orientation. However, such an orientation must remain flexible. Last year's SBU may not be the best unit for planning next year's strategy. It is all too common for larger companies to overlook an important new competitor, technology, or customer segment for several planning cycles, simply because it does not show up clearly in the company's reports. Managers must be aware that the optimal form of any individual SBU is likely to change over time and, as a result, companies must have flexible organizational structures in place.[43]

The Complete Strategic Plan

Figure 1–1 indicates that at this point the strategic planning process is complete, and the organization has a time-phased blueprint that outlines its mission, objectives, and strategies. Completion of the strategic plan facilitates the development of marketing plans for each product, product line, or division of the organization. The marketing plan serves as a subset of the strategic plan in that it allows for detailed planning at a target market level. Several marketing plans, each one targeted toward a specific market, will evolve from the strategic plan. For example, separate marketing plans would be developed for the various markets that a firm that produces consumer appliances and industrial electrical products competes in. Given a completed strategic plan, each area knows exactly where the organization wishes to go and can then develop objectives, strategies, and programs that are consistent with the strategic plan.[44] This important relationship between strategic planning and marketing planning is the subject of the final section of this chapter.

THE MARKETING MANAGEMENT PROCESS

Marketing management can be defined as "the process of planning and executing the conception, pricing, promotion, and distribution of goods, services, and ideas to create exchanges with target groups that satisfy customer and organizational objectives."[45] It should be noted that this

Figure 1–4   *Strategic Planning and Marketing Planning*

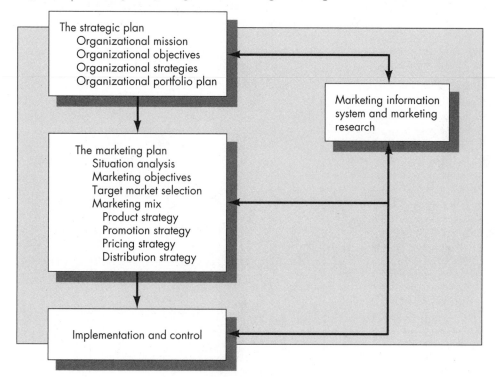

definition is entirely consistent with the marketing concept, since it emphasizes the serving of target market needs as the key to achieving organizational objectives. The remainder of this section will be devoted to a discussion of the marketing management process in terms of the model in Figure 1–4.

Relating Marketing Activities to the Organizational Mission and Objectives

Marketing activities should start with a clear understanding of the organization's mission and objectives. These factors provide marketing management direction by specifying the industry, the desired role of the firm in the industry (such as research-oriented innovator, custom-batch specialist, or mass producer), and, hopefully, a precise statement of what the firm is trying to accomplish. However, since written mission statements and objectives are often ambiguous or ill-defined, the marketing manager may have to consult with other members of top management to determine precisely what the firm is trying to accomplish, both overall and during a specific planning period. For example, a commonly stated organizational objective is growth. Obviously, this objective is so general that it is practically

---

HIGHLIGHT 1–4

Some Commonly Used Performance Standards

Effectiveness Standards

A. Sales criteria.
1. Total sales.
2. Sales by product or product line.
3. Sales by geographic region.
4. Sales by salesperson
5. Sales by customer type.
6. Sales by market segment.
7. Sales by size of order.
8. Sales by sales territory.
9. Sales by intermediary.
10. Market share.
11. Percentage change in sales.

B. Customer satisfaction.
1. Quantity purchased.
2. Degree of brand loyalty.
3. Repeat purchase rates.
4. Perceived product quality.
5. Brand equity.
6. Number of letters of complaint.

Source: Charles D. Schewe, *Marketing: Principles and Strategies* © *1987,* New York, McGraw-Hill, Inc., p. 593. Reproduced by The McGraw-Hill Companies.

Efficiency Standards

C. Costs.
1. Total costs.
2. Costs by product or product line.
3. Costs by geographic region.
4. Costs by salesperson.
5. Costs by customer type.
6. Costs by market segment.
7. Costs by size of order.
8. Costs by sales territory.
9. Costs by intermediary.
10. Percentage change in costs.

Effectiveness–Efficiency Standards

D. Profits.
1. Total profits.
2. Profits by product or product line.
3. Profits by geographic region.
4. Profits by salesperson.
5. Profits by customer type.
6. Profits by market segment.
7. Profits by size of order.
8. Profits by sales territory.
9. Profits by intermediary.

---

useless. On the other hand, a statement such as "sustained growth of 14 percent in profits before taxes" provides a quantitative goal that the marketing manager can use for determining desired sales levels and the marketing strategies to achieve them. In addition, the marketing manager must monitor any changes in mission or objectives and adapt marketing strategies to meet them.

Increasingly, organizations are also developing customer service mission statements. These statements can outline which dimensions of customer service are important, how customers are and should be served, define customer service performance standards, and describe the extent of the organization's commitment to customer service.[46] In effect, a customer service mission statement serves to direct management attention toward the all-important goal of serving the customer.

Situation Analysis

With a clear understanding of organizational objectives and mission, the marketing manager must then analyze and monitor the position of the firm and, specifically, the marketing department, in terms of its past, present, and future situation. Of course, the future situation is of primary concern. However, analyses of past trends and the current situation are most useful for predicting the future situation.

The situation analysis can be divided into six major areas of concern: (1) the cooperative environment; (2) the competitive environment; (3) the economic environment; (4) the social environment; (5) the political environment; and (6) the legal environment. In analyzing each of these environments, the marketing executive must search both for opportunities and for constraints or threats to achieving objectives. Opportunities for profitable marketing often arise from changes in these environments that bring about new sets of needs to be satisfied. Constraints on marketing activities, such as limited supplies of scarce resources, also arise from these environments.

The cooperative environment. The cooperative environment includes all firms and individuals who have a vested interest in the firm accomplishing its objectives. Parties of primary interest to the marketing executive in this environment are (1) suppliers; (2) resellers; (3) other departments in the firm; and (4) subdepartments and employees of the marketing department. Opportunities in this environment are primarily related to methods of increasing efficiency. For example, a company might decide to switch from a competitive bid process of obtaining materials to a single source that is located near the company's plant. Likewise, members of the marketing, engineering, and manufacturing functions may utilize a teamwork approach to developing new products versus a sequential approach. Constraints consist of such things as unresolved conflicts and shortages of materials. For example, a company manager may believe that a distributor is doing an insufficient job of promoting and selling the product, or a marketing manager may feel that manufacturing is not taking the steps needed to produce a quality product.

The competitive environment. The competitive environment includes primarily other firms in the industry that rival the organization for both resources and sales. Opportunities in this environment include such things as (1) acquiring competing firms; (2) offering demonstrably better value to consumers and attracting them away from competitors; and (3) in some cases, driving competitors out of the industry. For example, one airline purchases another airline, a bank offers depositors a free checking account with no minimum balance requirements, or a grocery chain engages in an everyday low-price strategy that competitors can't meet. The primary constraints in these environments are the demand stimulation activities of competing firms and the number of consumers who cannot be lured away from competition.

The economic environment. The state of the macroeconomy and changes in it also bring about marketing opportunities and constraints. For example, such factors as high inflation and unemployment levels can limit the size of the market that can afford to purchase a firm's top-of-the-line product. At the same time, these factors may offer a profitable opportunity to develop rental services for such products or to develop less expensive models of the product. In addition, changes in technology can provide significant threats and opportunities. For example, in the communications industry, technology has developed to a level where it is now possible to provide cable television using phone lines. Obviously such a system poses a severe threat to the existence of the cable industry as it exists today.

The social environment. This environment includes general cultural and social traditions, norms, and attitudes. While these values change slowly, such changes often bring about the need for new products and services. For example, a change in values concerning the desirability of large families brought about an opportunity to market better methods of birth control. On the other hand, cultural and social values also place constraints on marketing activities. As a rule, business practices that are contrary to social values become political issues, which are often resolved by legal constraints. For example, public demand for a cleaner environment has caused the government to require that automobile manufacturers' products meet certain average gas mileage and emission standards.

The political environment. The political environment includes the attitudes and reactions of the general public, social and business critics, and other organizations, such as the Better Business Bureau. Dissatisfaction with such business and marketing practices as unsafe products, products that waste resources, and unethical sales procedures can have adverse effects on corporation image and customer loyalty. However, adapting business and marketing practices to these attitudes can be an opportunity. For example, these attitudes have brought about markets for such products as unbreakable children's toys, high-efficiency air conditioners, and more economical automobiles.

The legal environment. This environment includes a host of federal, state, and local legislation directed at protecting both business competition and consumer rights. In past years legislation reflected social and political attitudes and has been primarily directed at constraining business practices. Such legislation usually acts as a constraint on business behavior, but again can be viewed as providing opportunities for marketing safer and more efficient products. In recent years, there has been less emphasis on creating new laws for constraining business practices. As an example, deregulation has become more common as evidenced by recent events in the airlines, financial services, and telecommunications industries.

In addition, political leaders are increasingly going to bat for their own multinational organizations.[47] For example, the U.S. vice president

HIGHLIGHT 1–5

Key Issues in the Marketing Planning Process That Need to be Addressed

Issue

The Speed of the Process. There is the problem of either being so slow that the process seems to go on forever or so fast that there is an extreme burst of activity to rush out a plan.

The Amount of Data Collected. Sufficient data are needed to properly estimate customer needs and competitive trends. However, the law of diminishing returns quickly sets in on the data-collection process.

Responsibility for Developing the Plan. If planning is delegated to professional planners, valuable line management input may be ignored. If the process is left to line managers, planning may be relegated to secondary status.

The Structure. Many executives believe the most important part of planning is not the plan itself but the structure of thought about the strategic issues facing the business. However, the structure should not take precedence over the content so that planning becomes merely filling out forms or crunching numbers.

The Length of the Plan. The length of a marketing plan must be balanced between being so long it is ignored by both staff and line managers and so brief that it ignores key details.

Frequency of Planning. Too frequent reevaluation of strategies can lead to erratic firm behavior. However, when plans are not revised frequently enough, the business may not adapt quickly enough to environmental changes and thus suffer a deterioration in its competitive position.

Number of Alternative Strategies Considered. Discussing too few alternatives raises the likelihood of failure, while discussing too many increases the time and cost of the planning effort.

Cross-Functional Acceptance. A common mistake is to view the plan as the proprietary possession of marketing. Successful implementation requires a broad consensus including other functional areas.

Using the Plan as a Sales Document. A major but often overlooked purpose of a plan and its presentation is to generate funds from either internal or external sources. Therefore, the better the plan, the better the chance of gaining desired funding.

Source: Donald R. Lehmann and Russell S. Winer, *Analysis for Marketing Planning,* 3rd ed., pp. 5-7. © Richard D. Irwin, Inc., 1988, 1991, 1994.

recently lobbied on behalf of such organizations as AT&T and Guardian Industries, trying to get foreign countries to open their markets to American companies.

Marketing Planning

In the previous sections it was emphasized that (1) marketing activities must be aligned with organizational objectives; and (2) marketing opportunities are often found by systematically analyzing situational environments. Once an opportunity is recognized, the marketing executive must

---

HIGHLIGHT 1–6

Criteria for Setting Marketing Objectives

Criteria	Poor Goal	Good Goal
Overall marketing objectives are clearly stated.	To get people to buy our new Betty Crocker Microwave Bread Shop products.	To obtain 5 percent of the fresh-baked bread market in 12 months.
Behavioral objectives are clearly stated.	To have sales increase.	To stimulate 30 percent of all U.S. households to try one loaf of Betty Crocker Microwave bread.
Expectations are realistic.	To obtain half the fresh-baked bread market.	Given the strong name of Betty Crocker in the baked bread goods market and that Americans consume 50 lbs. of bread a year, we hope to achieve an 18 percent share of the fresh-baked bread market.
Adequate support exists for the program.	No mention of budget dollars in the program statement. No check to make sure the program meshes with corporate goals.	Given the commitment by General Mills to grow in the baked goods market, the budget for Betty Crocker's Microwave Bread Shop over the next three years is $45 million, $41 million, and $35 million, respectively.

Source: Reproduced from *Principles of Marketing,* by Charles W. Lamb, Jr., Joseph F. Hair, Jr., and Carl McDaniel, p. 27 with the permission of the South-Western Publishing Co. © 1992, Cincinnati, by South-Western Publishing Co. All rights reserved.

---

then plan an appropriate strategy for taking advantage of the opportunity. This process can be viewed in terms of three interrelated tasks: (1) establishing marketing objectives; (2) selecting the target market; and (3) developing the marketing mix.

Establishing objectives. Marketing objectives usually are derived from organizational objectives; in some cases where the firm is totally marketing-oriented, the two are identical. In either case, objectives must be specified and performance in achieving them should be measurable. Marketing objectives are usually stated as standards of performance (e.g., a certain percentage of market share or sales volume) or as tasks to be achieved by given dates. While such objectives are useful, the marketing concept emphasizes that profits rather than sales should be the overriding objective of the firm and marketing department. In any case, these objectives provide the framework for the marketing plan.

Selecting the target market. The success of any marketing plan hinges on how well it can identify customer needs and organize its resources to satisfy them profitably. Thus, a crucial element of the marketing plan is selecting the groups or segments of potential customers the firm is going to serve with each of its products. Four important questions must be answered:

1. What do customers want and/or need?
2. What must be done to satisfy these wants and/or needs?
3. What is the size of the market?
4. What is its growth profile?

Present target markets and potential target markets are then ranked according to (*a*) profitability; (*b*) present and future sales volume; and (*c*) the match between what it takes to appeal successfully to the segment and the organization's capabilities. Those that appear to offer the greatest potential are selected. One cautionary note on this process involves the importance of not neglecting present customers when developing market share and sales strategies. In a recent study, it was found that for every 10 companies who develop strategies aimed at increasing the number of first-time customers, only 4 made any serious effort to develop strategies geared towards retaining present customers and increasing their purchases.[48] Chapters 3, 4, and 5 are devoted to discussing consumer behavior, industrial buyers, and market segmentation.

Developing the marketing mix. The marketing mix is the set of controllable variables that must be managed to satisfy the target market and achieve organizational objectives. These controllable variables are usually classified according to four major decision areas: product, price, promotion, and place (or channels of distribution). The importance of these decision

areas cannot be overstated and, in fact, the major portion of this text is devoted to analyzing them. Chapters 6 and 7 are devoted to product and new product strategies; Chapters 8 and 9 to promotion strategies in terms of both nonpersonal and personal selling; Chapter 10 to distribution strategies; and Chapter 11 to pricing strategies. In addition, marketing mix variables are the focus of analysis in two chapters on marketing in special fields, that is, the marketing of services (Chapter 12) and international marketing (Chapter 13). Thus, it should be clear to the reader that the marketing mix is the core of the marketing management process.

The output of the foregoing process is the marketing plan. It is a formal statement of decisions that have been made on marketing activities; it is a blueprint of the objectives, strategies, and tasks to be performed.

Implementation and Control of the Marketing Plan

Implementing the marketing plan involves putting the plan into action and performing marketing tasks according to the predefined schedule. Even the most carefully developed plans often cannot be executed with perfect timing. Thus, the marketing executive must closely monitor and coordinate implementation of the plan. In some cases, adjustments may have to be made in the basic plan because of changes in any of the situational environments. For example, competitors may introduce a new product. In this event, it may be desirable to speed up or delay implementation of the plan. In almost all cases, some minor adjustments or "fine tuning" will be necessary in implementation.

Controlling the marketing plan involves three basic steps. First, the results of the implemented marketing plan are measured. Second, these results are compared with objectives. Third, decisions are made on whether the plan is achieving objectives. If serious deviations exist between actual and planned results, adjustments may have to be made to redirect the plan toward achieving objectives.

Marketing Information Systems and Marketing Research

Throughout the marketing management process, current, reliable, and valid information is needed to make effective marketing decisions. Providing this information is the task of the marketing decision support system (MDSS) and marketing research. These topics are discussed in detail in Chapter 2.

THE RELATIONSHIP BETWEEN THE STRATEGIC PLAN AND THE MARKETING PLAN

Strategic planning is clearly a top-management responsibility. However, there has been an increasing shift towards more active participation of marketing professionals in corporate strategic analysis and planning.[49] Management is finding that a key strategic challenge is deciding how to best position a company in a market to gain the greatest advantage over the competition. A critical prerequisite to making successful decisions is gaining the necessary information regarding each market opportunity. Toward this end, marketing managers are involved in the strategic planning process in two important ways: (1) they often influence the strategic planning process by providing inputs in the form of information and suggestions relating to their particular products, product lines, and areas of responsibility; and (2) they must be aware of what the process of strategic planning involves as well as the results because everything they do, the marketing objectives and strategies they develop, must be derived from the strategic plan. There is rarely a strategic planning question or decision that does not have marketing implications.

Thus, if strategic planning is done properly, it will result in a clearly defined blueprint for managerial action at all levels in the organization. Figure 1–5 illustrates the hierarchy of objectives and strategies using one possible objective and two strategies from the strategic plan (above the dotted line) and illustrating how these relate to elements of the marketing and

Figure 1–5   *Relating the Marketing Plan to the Strategic Plan and the Production Plan*

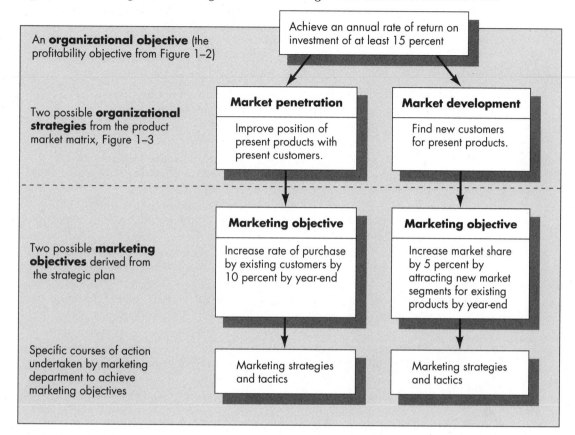

production plans (below the dotted line). The production plan is included to illustrate the interdependencies existing between marketing and other functional areas (i.e., production, finance, human resources) in the achievement of the strategic plan. Indeed, the ability that marketers have as cross-functional experts is one that allows the melding of marketing vision with the financial goals and manufacturing capabilities of the firm. The greater this ability, the better the likelihood is that the firm will be able to achieve and sustain a competitive advantage, an important aim of the strategic planning process.[50]

CONCLUSION

This chapter has described the marketing management process and provided an outline for many of the remaining chapters in this text. At this point it would be useful for the reader to review Figure 1–4 as well as the Table of Contents. This review will enable you to relate the content and progression of material to the marketing management process.

ADDITIONAL READINGS

Dunn, Dan T., Jr., and Claude A. Thomas. "Partnering with Customers." *Journal of Business & Industrial Marketing* (1994), pp. 34–40.

Dreilinger, Craig. "Why Management Fads Fizzle." *Business Horizons,* November/December 1994, pp. 11–15.

Evans, Joel R., and Richard L. Laskin. "The Relationship Marketing Process: A Conceptualization and Application." *Industrial Marketing Management,* 1994, pp. 439–52.

Fraering, J. Martin, and Michael S. Minor. "The Industry-Specific Basis of the Market Share–Profitability Relationship." *Journal of Consumer Marketing,* 1994, pp. 27–37.

Hutt, Michael D.; Beth A. Walker; and Gary L. Frankwick. "Hurdle the Cross-Functional Barriers to Strategic Change." *Sloan Management Review,* Spring 1994, pp. 22–30.

Lancaster, Geoff. "Marketing and Engineering Revisited." *Journal of Business & Industrial Marketing,* 1995, pp. 6–15.

McGahan, A. M., and Pankaj Ghemawat. "Competition to Retain Customers." *Marketing Science,* Spring 1994, pp. 165–76.

Meyer, Christopher. "How the Right Measures Help Teams Excel." *Harvard Business Review,* May/June 1994, pp. 95–97.

Mintzberg, Henry. "Diversification and Diversifact." *California Management Review,* Fall 1994, pp. 8–27.

————. *The Rise and Fall of Strategic Planning.* New York: Free Press, 1994.

Rayport, Jeffrey F., and John J. Sviokala. "Managing in the Marketspace." *Harvard Business Review,* November/December 1994, pp. 141–50.

Redman, Thomas C. "Improve Data Quality for Competitive Advantage." *Sloan Management Review,* Winter 1995, pp. 99–107.

Reichheld, Fredrick F. G. "Loyalty and the Renaissance of Marketing." *Marketing Management,* 1994, pp. 10–21.

Slater, Stanley F., and John C. Narver. "Does Competitive Environment Moderate the Market Orientation-Performance Relationship?" *Journal of Marketing,* January 1994, pp. 46–55.

PORTFOLIO MODELS

Wright, Peter; Mark Kroll; Bevalee Pray; and Augustine Lado. "Strategic Orientation, Competitive Advantage, and Business Performance." *Journal of Business Research,* 1995, pp. 143–51.

Portfolio models remain a valuable aid to marketing managers in their efforts to develop effective marketing plans. The use of these models can aid managers who face situations that can best be described as "more products, less time, and less money." More specifically, (1) as the number of products a firm produces expands, the time available for developing marketing plans for each product decreases; (2) at a strategic level, management must make resource allocation decisions across lines of products and, in diversified organizations, across different lines of business; and (3) when resources are limited (which they usually are), the process of deciding which strategic business units (SBUs) to emphasize becomes very complex. In such situations, portfolio models can be very useful.

Portfolio analysis is not a new idea. Banks manage loan portfolios seeking to balance risks and yields. Individuals who are serious investors usually have a portfolio of various kinds of investments (common stocks, preferred stocks, bank accounts, and the like), each with different characteristics of risk, growth, and rate of return. The investor seeks to manage the portfolio to maximize whatever objectives he or she might have. Applying this same idea, most organizations have a wide range of products, product lines, and businesses, each with different growth rates and returns. Similar to the investor, managers should seek a desirable balance among alternative SBUs. Specifically, management should seek to develop a business portfolio that will assure long-run profits and cash flow.

Portfolio models can be used to classify SBUs to determine the future cash contributions that can be expected from each SBU as well as the future resource requirement that each will require. Remember, depending on the organization, an SBU could be a single product, product line, division, or a distinct business. While there are many different types of portfolio models, they generally examine the competitive position of the SBU and the chances for improving the SBU's contribution to profitability and cash flow.

There are several portfolio analysis techniques. Two of the most widely used are discussed in this appendix. To truly appreciate the concept of portfolio analysis, however, we must briefly review the development of portfolio theory.

A REVIEW OF PORTFOLIO THEORY

The interest in developing aids for managers in the selection of strategy was spurred by an organization known as the Boston Consulting Group over 25 years ago. Its ideas, which will be discussed shortly, and many of those that followed were based on the concept of experience curves.

Experience curves are similar in concept to learning curves. Learning curves were developed to express the idea that the number of labor hours it takes to produce one unit of a particular product declines in a predictable manner as the number of units produced increases. Hence, an accurate estimation of how long it takes to produce the 100th unit is possible if the production time for the 1st and 10th units are known.

The concept of experience curves was derived from the concept of learning curves. Experience curves were first widely discussed in the on-going Profit Impact of Marketing Strategies (PIMS) study conducted by the Strategic Planning Institute. The PIMS project studies 150 firms with more than 1,000 individual business units. Its major focus is on determining which environmental and internal firm variables influence the firm's return on investment (ROI) and cash flow. The researchers have concluded that seven categories of variables appear to influence the return on investment: (1) competitive position; (2) industry/market environment; (3) budget allocation; (4) capital structure; (5) production processes; (6) company characteristics; and (7) "change action" factors.[51]

The experience curve includes all costs associated with a product and implies that the per-unit costs of a product should fall, due to cumulative experience, as production volume increases. In a given industry, therefore, the producer with the largest volume and corresponding market share should have the lowest marginal cost. This leader in market share should be able to underprice competitors, discourage entry into the market by potential competitors, and, as a result, achieve an acceptable return on investment. The linkage of experience to cost to price to market share to ROI is exhibited in Figure A–1. The Boston Consulting Group's view of the experience curve led the members to develop what has become known as the BCG Portfolio Model.

THE BCG MODEL

The BCG is based on the assumption that profitability and cash flow will be closely related to sales volume. Thus, in this model, SBUs are classified in terms of their relative market share and the growth rate of the market the SBU is in. Using these dimensions, products are either classified as stars, cash cows, dogs, or question marks. The BCG model is presented in Figure A–2.

Figure A–1 *Experience Curve and Resulting Profit Curve*

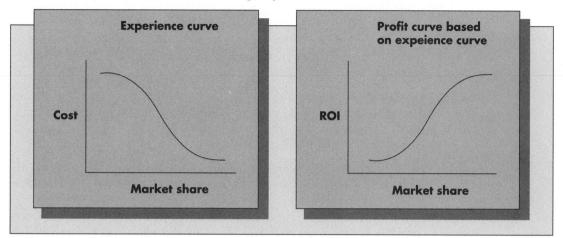

Figure A–2 *The Boston Consulting Group Portfolio Model*

—*Stars* are SBUs with a high share or a high-growth market. Because high-growth markets attract competition, such SBUs are usually cash users because they are growing and because the firm needs to protect their market share position.

—*Cash cows* are often market leaders, but the market they are in is not growing rapidly. Because these SBUs have a high share of a low-growth market, they are cash generators for the firm.

—*Dogs* are SBUs that have a low share of a low-growth market. If the SBU has a very loyal group of customers, it may be a source of profits and cash. Usually, dogs are not large sources of cash.

—*Question marks* are SBUs with a low share of a high-growth market. They have great potential but require great resources if the firm is to successfully build market share.

As you can see, a firm with 10 SBUs will usually have a portfolio that includes some of each of the above. Having developed this analysis, management must determine what role each SBU should assume. Four basic objectives are possible:

1. *Build share.* This objective sacrifices immediate earnings to improve market share. It is appropriate for promising question marks whose share has to grow if they are ever to become stars.
2. *Hold share.* This objective seeks to preserve the SBU's market share. It is very appropriate for strong cash cows to ensure that they can continue to yield a large cash flow.
3. *Harvest.* Here, the objective seeks to increase the product's short-term cash flow without concern for the long-run impact. It allows market share to decline in order to maximize earnings and cash flow. It is an appropriate objective for weak cash cows, weak question marks, and dogs.
4. *Divest.* This objective involves selling or divesting the SBU because better investment opportunities exist elsewhere. It is very appropriate for dogs and those question marks the firm cannot afford to finance for growth.

There have been several major criticisms of the BCG Portfolio Model, revolving around its focus on market share and market growth as the primary indicators of preference. First, the BCG model assumes market growth is uncontrollable.[52] As a result, managers can become preoccupied with setting market share objectives, instead of trying to grow the market. Second, assumptions regarding market share as a critical factor affecting firm performance may not hold true, especially in international markets.[53] Third, the BCG model assumes that the major source of SBU financing comes from internal means. Fourth, the BCG matrix does not take into account any interdependencies that may exist between SBUs, such as shared distribution.[54] Fifth, the BCG matrix does not take into account any measures of profits and customer satisfaction.[55] Sixth, and perhaps most important, the thrust of the BCG matrix is based on the underlying assumption that corporate strategy begins with an analysis of competitive position. By its very nature, a strategy developed entirely on competitive analysis will always be a reactive one.[56] While the above criticisms are certainly valid ones, managers (especially of large firms) across all industries continue to find the BCG matrix useful in assessing the strategic position of SBUs.[57]

Figure A–3   *The General Electric Portfolio Model*

Business Strength

		Strong	Average	Weak
Industry Attractiveness	**High**	A	A	B
	Medium	A	B	C
	Low	B	C	C

Figure A–4   *Components of Industry Attractiveness and Business Strength at*

Industry Attractiveness	Business Strength
Market size	Market position:
Market growth	Domestic market share
Profitability	World market share
Cyclicality	Share growth
Ability to recover from inflation	Share compared with leading competitor
World scope	
	Competitive strengths:
	Quality leadership
	Technology
	Marketing
	Relative profitability

THE GENERAL ELECTRIC MODEL

Although the BCG model can be useful, it does assume that market share is the sole determinant of an SBU's profitability. Also, in projecting market growth rates, a manager should carefully analyze the factors that influence sales and any opportunities for influencing industry sales.

Some firms have developed alternative portfolio models to incorporate more information about market opportunities and competitive positions. The GE model is one of these. The GE model emphasizes all the potential sources of strength, not just market share, and all of the factors that influence the long-term attractiveness of a market, not just its growth rate. As Figure A–3 indicates, all SBUs are classified in terms of *business strength and industry attractiveness*. Figure A–4 presents a list of items that can be used to position SBUs in the matrix.

Industry attractiveness is a composite index made up of such factors as those listed in Figure A–4. For example: *market size*—the larger the market, the more attractive it would be; *market growth*—high-growth markets are more attractive than low-growth markets; *profitability*—high-profit-margin markets are more attractive than low-profit margin industries.

Business strength is a composite index made up of such factors as those listed in Figure A–4. For example: *market share*—the higher the SBU's share of market, the greater its business strength; *quality leadership*—the higher the SBU's quality compared to competitors, the greater its business strength; *share compared with leading competitor*—the closer the SBU's share to the market leader, the greater its business strength.

Once the SBUs are classified, they are placed on the grid (Figure A–3). Priority "A" SBUs (often called *the green zone*) are those in the three cells at the upper left, indicating that these are SBUs high in both industry attractiveness and business strength, and that the firm should "build share." Priority "B" SBUs (often called *the yellow zone*) are those medium in both industry attractiveness and business strength. The firm will usually decide to "hold share" on these SBUs. Priority "C" SBUs are those in the three cells at the lower right (often called *the red zone*). These SBUs are low in both industry attractiveness and business strength. The firm will usually decide to *harvest* or *divest* these SBUs.

Part B

MARKETING INFORMATION, RESEARCH, AND UNDERSTANDING THE TARGET MARKET

Chapter 2
MARKETING DECISION SUPPORT SYSTEMS AND MARKETING RESEARCH

It is obvious that the American business system has been capable of producing a vast quantity of goods and services. However, in the past two decades the American business system has also become extremely capable of producing massive amounts of information and data. In fact, the last few decades have been referred to as the "Information Era" and the "Age of Information."

This situation is a complete reversal from what previously existed. In the past, marketing executives did not have to deal with an oversupply of information for decision-making purposes. In most cases they gathered what little data they could and hoped that their decisions would be reasonably good. In fact, it was for this reason that marketing research came to be recognized as an extremely valuable staff function. It provided marketing management with information where previously there had been little or none and, thereby, alleviated to a great extent the paucity of information for marketing decision making. However, marketing management in many companies has failed to store marketing information, and much valuable marketing information is lost when marketing personnel change jobs or companies.

Today, some marketing managers feel buried by the deluge of information and data that comes across their desks. How can it be, then, that marketing managers complain that they have insufficient or inappropriate information on which to base their everyday operating decisions? Specifically, managers complain that:

1. There is too much marketing information of the wrong kind and not enough of the right kind.
2. Marketing information is so dispersed throughout the company that great effort is usually needed to locate simple facts.
3. Vital information is sometimes suppressed by other executives or subordinates for personal reasons.

Figure 2–1 *The Marketing Decision Support System*

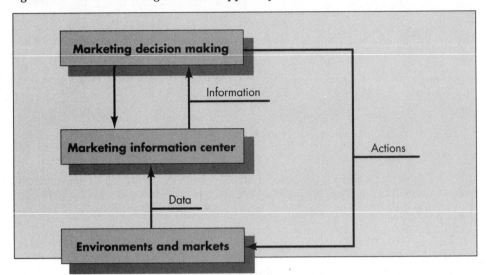

4. Vital information often arrives too late to be useful.
5. Information often arrives in a form that provides no idea of its accuracy, and there is no one to turn to for confirmation.

Marketing management requires current, reliable information before it can function efficiently. Because of this need, and the information explosion of the past decades, many large corporations have banked their total marketing knowledge in computers. Well-designed marketing decision support systems (MDSS) can eliminate corporate losses of millions of dollars from lost information and lost opportunities.

This chapter is concerned with marketing decision support systems and marketing research. Since the two concepts are easily confused, it is important initially to distinguish one from the other. In general terms, a marketing decision support system is concerned with the continuous gathering, processing, and utilization of pertinent information for decision-making purposes. The primary objective of the MDSS is to ensure that the right information is available to the right decision maker at the right time. Marketing research, on the other hand, usually focuses on a specific marketing problem with the objective of providing information for a particular decision. As such, marketing research is an integral part of the overall marketing decision support system but usually is project oriented rather than a continuous process.

MARKETING DECISION SUPPORT SYSTEMS

A marketing decision support system is a new type of marketing information system. This type of information system is designed to support all phases of marketing decision making—from problem identification to

---

HIGHLIGHT 2–1

Suggestions for Developing an MDSS

The following is a list of suggestions to aid in the effective implementation of an MDSS.

1. Develop small systems first before coordinating them into an overall system.
2. Develop systems relevant to current management practices and organizational structures.
3. Develop decision support system skills internally and do not rely too heavily on outside experts.

4. Involve users of the system in its design and implementation.
5. Build a flexible system to meet the information needs of various levels of management and types of managers.
6. Monitor early usage of the system to ensure success and make sure future users of the system are aware of the success.
7. Build the system in an evolutionary manner, adding complex models only after data storage and retrieval systems are successfully in place.

Source: From *Principles of Marketing,* 3rd ed., pp. 218–19 by Thomas C. Kinnear and Kenneth L. Bernhardt. Copyright © 1990, 1986 by Scott, Foresman and Company. Reprinted by permission of HarperCollins Publishers.

---

choosing the relevant data to work with, picking the approach to be used in making the decision, and evaluating alternative courses of action. This type of information system can be defined as:

> a coordinated collection of data, system tools, and techniques with supporting software and hardware by which an organization gathers and interprets relevant information from business and the environment and turns it into a basis for making management decisions.[1]

Figure 2–1 illustrates the concept of an MDSS. There are two main changes depicted in this figure: (1) the conversion of data to information; and (2) the conversion of information to action. The first conversion is the task of the marketing information center, while the second is the major purpose of marketing decision making.

The Marketing Information Center

Although the growth of the concept of a marketing decision support system has been fairly recent, most experts agree that a single, separate marketing information center must exist to centralize responsibility for marketing information within the firm. This is necessary because both the users and suppliers of such information are widely scattered throughout the organization, and some unit is needed to oversee the entire operation.

The general purpose of this organizational unit is to maintain, as well as to improve and upgrade, the accuracy, completeness, and timeliness of information for marketing management decisions. Operationally, this means that the information center must gather raw data from various environments and

Figure 2–2 *Examples of MISs and MDSSs*

A Marketing Information System (MIS) at Savin Corporation

Savin Corporation has installed a computer terminal in each of its warehouses to keep track of every item in its inventory. The system identifies the quantity on hand, the location and movement of stock, and the status of all orders. The system is used to plan shipments, locate single items in inventory, and locate customer records.

A Marketing Information System (MIS) at United Services Automobile Association

The United Services Automobile Association, the nation's eighth largest insurer of passenger cars, purchased a $4 million system that now contains virtually all of the company's written records. When a customer reports an accident, an adjuster can call up the customer's file, check the coverage, and keep track of all the paperwork through the final settlement of the claim. The company figures that it used to take five people a day-and-a-half to perform tasks that one person now handles in 20 minutes.

A Marketing Decision Support System (MDSS) at Crocker National Bank

The Crocker National Bank in San Francisco has purchased desktop terminals for most of its top-level executives. Each terminal is tapped into the huge computers that record all bank transactions. The executives are able to make comparisons, analyze problems, and prepare charts and tables in response to simple commands. For example, they can analyze emerging trends in deposits and loans and monitor the influence of various interest rates and loan maturities.

A Marketing Decision Support System (MDSS) at Gould, Inc.

Gould, Inc., has developed a decision support system to help managers retrieve, manipulate, and display information needed for making decisions. The system combines large visual display and video terminals with a computerized information system. The system is designed solely to assist managers to make comparisons and analyze problems for decision-making purposes. The MDSS instantly prepares tables and color charts in response to simple commands.

markets and process them so they can be obtained and analyzed by marketing executives. Data must be gathered from both internal and external sources. Internally, such data as sales, costs, and profits, as well as other company reports, need to be converted to information and stored in the computer. Externally, data from trade journals, magazines, newspapers, government publications, and other sources of pertinent information used by marketing executives for decision making also must be converted and stored.

A critical point here is that the MDSS converts raw data into information that marketing management can actually use for making intelligent decisions. An MDSS must produce information in a form marketing executives can understand when it is needed and have it under the manager's control. In other words, a key distinction that separates an MDSS from other types of marketing information systems is that an MDSS has the directed and primary objective of supporting marketing management decision making.[2]

Figure 2–2 provides examples of two firms with conventional MISs and two firms with MDSSs to illustrate this important difference.

Marketing Decision Making

Earlier we stated that the main purpose of marketing executives is to convert information to actions through the process of decision making. Note that, in Figure 2–1, two up-and-down arrows connect marketing decision making with the marketing information center. These arrows represent an important aspect of the MDSS (i.e., it is an *interactive system* in which marketing executives sit at computer terminals and actively analyze information and convert it to actions).

In previous types of marketing information systems, the information center often attempted to prepare reports to meet the individual needs of different marketing executives at different levels in the organization. More often than not, such attempts provided too much information of the wrong kind and not enough information of the right kind. However, in addition to the flexibility, timeliness, and detail provided by an MDSS, such problems do not occur because marketing executives themselves retrieve and manipulate the information.

Many experts believe that, in a few years, most marketing executives will be sharing their desk space with a personal computer. Personal computers have the capability of increasing both the productivity of marketing managers and the quality of their decisions. First, the capacity of the computers to extract, process, and analyze data swiftly and accurately is awesome. Second, computers have gotten smaller, faster, and smarter in a shorter time than any other technological innovation in history. A desktop personal computer can solve ordinary arithmetic problems 18 times faster than the world's first large-scale computer built less than 50 years ago (weighing 30 tons). Finally, computers have become extremely inexpensive in comparison to earlier models. Just 30 years ago a medium-sized computer cost a quarter of a million dollars. A firm can now buy a desktop computer with three times the memory capacity for less than $2,000. While it may take some time for marketing executives to learn to use the equipment, the potential for better, more profitable decision making may outweigh the brief inconvenience.

MARKETING RESEARCH

Marketing research should be an integral part of a marketing decision support system. In essence, marketing research combines insights and intuition with the research process to provide information for making marketing decisions. In general, marketing research can be defined as:

> the function that links the consumer, customer, and public to the marketer through information—information used to identify and define marketing op-

portunities and problems; generate, refine, and evaluate marketing actions; monitor marketing performance; and improve understanding of marketing as a process. Marketing research specifies the information required to address these issues; designs the method for collecting information; manages and implements the data collection process; analyzes the results; and communicates the findings and their implications.[3]

Today's marketing managers should understand the role of research in decision making. It cannot be overstated that *marketing research is an aid to decision making and not a substitute for it.* In other words, marketing research does not make decisions but it can substantially increase the probability that the best decision will be made. Unfortunately, too often marketing managers view marketing research reports as the final answer to their problems. Instead, marketing managers should recognize that (1) even the most carefully controlled research projects can be fraught with pitfalls and (2) decisions should be made in the light of their own knowledge and experience and other factors that are not explicitly considered in the research project. The problems that the Coca-Cola Company faced when it dropped its original formula and introduced New Coke were brought about by both faulty marketing research and failure of Coke executives to use sound judgment in interpreting the research results.[4]

Although marketing research does not make decisions, it is a direct means of reducing risks associated with managing the marketing mix and long-term marketing planning. In fact, a company's return on investment from marketing research is a function of the extent to which research output reduces the risk inherent in decision making. For example, marketing research can play an important role in reducing new product failure costs by evaluating consumer acceptance of a product prior to full-scale introduction.

In a highly competitive economy, a firm's survival depends on the marketing manager's ability to make sound decisions, to outguess competitors, to anticipate consumer needs, to forecast business conditions, and to plan for company growth. Marketing research is one tool to help accomplish these tasks. Research is also vital for managerial control, because without appropriate data, the validity of past decisions on the performance of certain elements in the marketing system (e.g., the performance of the sales force or advertising) cannot be evaluated reliably.

Although many of the technical aspects of marketing research, such as sampling design or statistical analysis, can be delegated to experts, the process of marketing research begins and ends with the marketing manager. In the beginning of a research project, it is the marketing manager's responsibility to work with researchers to define the problem carefully. When the research project is completed, the application of the results in terms of decision alternatives rests primarily with the marketing manager. For these reasons, and since the marketing manager must be able to communicate with researchers throughout the course of the project, it is vital for managers to understand the research process from the researcher's point of view.[5]

HIGHLIGHT 2–2

Marketing Research that Influenced Marketing Strategies

Marketing research can be a useful aid in decision making. Below are several examples of marketing research that helped firms develop their marketing strategies.

Kraft USA

Kraft USA, realizing the growing importance of using research for store-specific marketing, staged an experiment combining a demographic profile of cream cheese buyers with data showing which supermarkets drew most of those shoppers. Kraft pinpointed 30 stores where people frequently bought items from special displays and installed coolers in them, tailoring the types of cream cheese in each to the tastes of the store's shoppers. Shoppers in a big Midwestern city found extra rows of strawberry-flavored cream cheese at one supermarket. Just miles away, another store had almost no strawberry cream cheese but lots of diet versions. Still another had mostly large, 12-ounce cartons of Philadelphia cream cheese. Sales in these supermarkets jumped 147 percent over the previous year. Such experiments are possible due to the new insights provided by checkout scanners, which are generating more sophisticated data on consumers' buying habits.

Chrysler Corporation

Chrysler Corporation, as part of the introduction of its new LH lines of cars, spent $30 million to reeducate the more than 100,000 employees in its dealerships. Chrysler wants to win back younger, more affluent buyers with the Chrysler Concorde, Dodge Intrepid, and Eagle Vision. In simulated test drives, Chrysler will use microphones to see how salespeople treat different types of customers (played by trainers). Chrysler trainers will coach the dealership staffers on better ways to present both the new cars and older models. The company is offering cash incentives to dealers with high customer satisfaction scores.

Quaker Oats

Quaker Direct, a direct-marketing program established by Quaker Oats, sent out packets of coupons to some 18 million homes. A household identification number was embedded in the bar code of each coupon. Within four months, Quaker's research department was able to understand how well the promotion worked by tracking exactly which coupons each household redeemed. All of the information gathered by household is appended to a database recording specific transactions. Quaker executives call this "household management" because they know exactly which coupons were redeemed by which household. Using this information, the company is able to target future mailings, offering higher incentives to resistant shoppers or dropping from the packet products consumers are not interested in.

Source: Gilbert A. Churchill, Jr., *Marketing Research: Methodological Foundations,* 6th ed. (Fort Worth, TX: Dryden Press, 1995), pp. 3–4.

The Research Process

Marketing research can be viewed as a systematic process for obtaining information to aid in decision making. Although there are many different types of marketing research, the framework illustrated in Figure 2–3 represents a general approach to defining the research process. Each element of this process will be briefly discussed.

Figure 2–3 *The Five Ps of the Research Process*

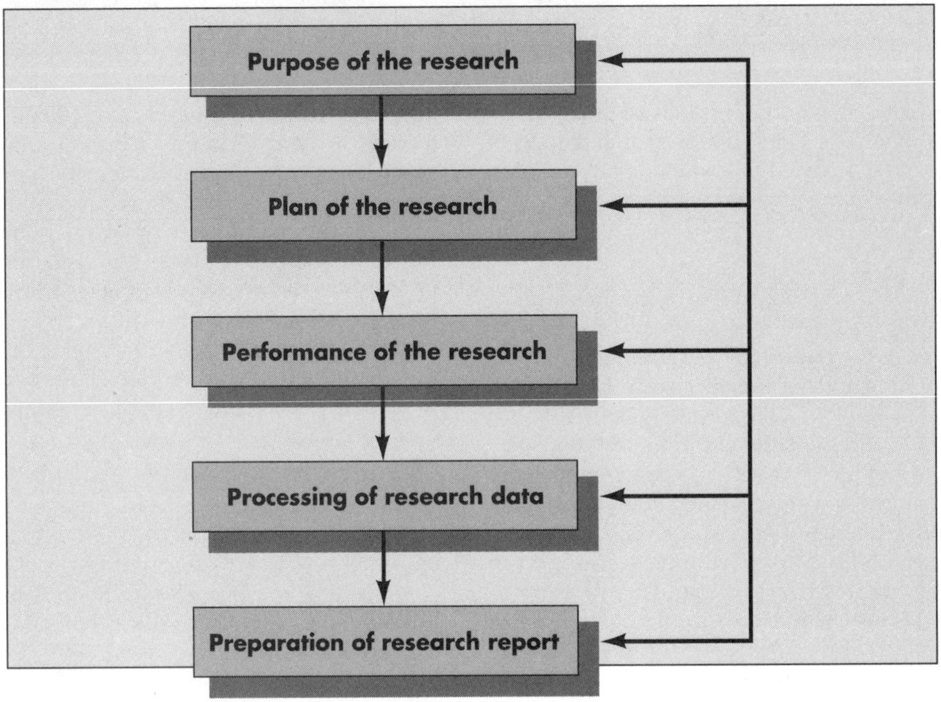

Purpose of the research

The first step in the research process is to determine explicitly the purpose of the research. This may well be much more difficult than it sounds. Quite often a situation or problem is recognized as needing research, yet the nature of the problem is not clear or well defined. Thus, an investigation is required to clarify the problem or situation. This investigation includes such things as interviewing corporate executives, reviewing records, and studying existing information related to the problem. At the end of this stage the researcher should know (1) the current situation: (2) the nature of the problem: and (3) the specific question or questions the research is to find answer to— that is, why the research is being conducted.

Plan of the research

The first step in the research plan is to formalize the specific purpose of the study. Once this is accomplished, the sequencing of tasks and responsibilities for accomplishing the research are spelled out in detail. This stage is critical since decisions are made that determine the who, what, when, where, and how of the research study.

An initial decision in this stage of the process is the type of data that will be required. The two major types of data are primary and secondary.

HIGHLIGHT 2–3
External Sources of Information

Source	Examples
Business and industry publications	*Million Dollar Directory* (details about companies with assets over $500,000); *Directory of Mailing List Houses* (sources of mailing lists); *Sales & Marketing Management; The Wall Street Journal; Encyclopedia of Associations*
Research services	A. C. Nielson Co., Arbitron Co., IMS International, Information Resources, Inc.
Trade groups	American Medical Association; National Association of Realtors; National Association of Retail Dealers of America
Customer surveys	Mail surveys, telephone surveys, personal surveys (including mall intercepts, focus group interviews, and in-home interviews)
Government reports	*Statistical Abstract of the United States; Survey of Current Business;* state employment and economic data; *United Nations Statistical Yearbook* (worldwide data)
Computer databases	NEXIS (full text of articles from 125 periodicals); LEXIS (legal cases and documents); PATSEARCH (U.S. patents filed since 1975); CompuServe; Dow Jones News/Retrieval; Dialog; The Source; Mead Data Central

Source: Gilbert A. Churchill, Jr. and J. Paul Peter, *Marketing: Creating Value for Customers,* (Burr Ridge, IL: Austen Press/Irwin, 1995), p. 199.

Primary data is data that must be collected from original sources for the purposes of the study. Secondary data is information that has been previously collected for some other purpose but can be used for the purposes of the study.

If the research project requires primary data, decisions have to be made concerning the following issues:

1. How will the data be collected? Personal interviews? Mail questionnaires? Telephone interviews?
2. How much data is needed?
3. What measures will be used, and how will they be checked for reliability and validity?
4. Who will design the measures and collect the data?
5. Where will the data be collected? Nationally? Regionally? Locally? At home? At work?
6. When and for how long will data be collected?

If secondary data will suffice for the research question(s), similar decisions have to be made. However, since the data are already in existence, the task is much simpler (and cheaper). For example, most of the sources of secondary data listed in Section 5 of this text are available in a public or university library.

In addition to determining data requirements, the research plan also specifies the method of data analysis, procedures for processing and interpreting the data, and the structure of the final report. In other words, the

---

HIGHLIGHT 2–4

Types of Questions that Marketing Research Can Help Answer

I. Planning.
  A. What kinds of people buy our product? Where do they live? How much do they earn? How many of them are there?
  B. Is the market for our product increasing or decreasing? Are there promising markets that we have not yet reached?
  C. Are there markets for our products in other countries?

II. Problem Solving.
  A. Product
    1. Which, of various product designs, is likely to be the most successful.
    2. As production costs decline, should we lower our prices or try to develop a higher-quality product.
  B. Price
    1. What price should we charge for our new product?
    2. As production costs decline, should we lower our prices or try to develop a higher-quality product?
  C. Place
    1. Where, and by whom, should our product be sold?

  2. What kinds of incentives should we offer to induce the trade to push our product?
  D. Promotion
    1. How effective is our advertising? Are the right people seeing it? How does it compare with the competition's advertising?
    2. What kinds of sales promotional devices—coupons, contests, rebates, and so forth—should we employ?
    3. What combination of media—newspapers, radio, television, magazines—should we use?

III. Control.
  A. What is our market share overall? In each geographic area? By each customer type?
  B. Are customers satisfied with our product? How is our record for service? Are there many returns?
  C. How does the public perceive our company? What is our reputation with the trade?

Source: Table from *Marketing Research: Methodological Foundations,* 6th ed. by Gilbert A. Churchill, Jr. © 1995, Fort Worth, TX. The Dryden Press, reproduced by permission of the publisher.

---

entire research project is sequenced, and responsibility for the various tasks is assigned. Thus, the research plan provides the framework for the coordination and control of the entire project.

When the research plan is fully specified, the time and money costs of the project are estimated. If management views the benefits of the research as worth the costs, the project proceeds to the next phase. A sample research plan is presented in Figure 2–4.

Performance of the research

Performance is used here in the narrow sense: of preparing for data collection and actually collecting the data. It is at this point that the research plan is put into action.

Figure 2–4   *Sample Research Plan*

I. **Tentative projective title.**
II. **Statement of the problem.**
   One or two sentences to outline or to describe the general problem under consideration.
III. **Define and delimit the problem.**
   Here the writer states the purpose(s) and scope of the problem. *Purpose* refers to goals or objectives. Closely related to this is *justification*. Sometimes this is a separate step, depending on the urgency of the task. *Scope* refers to the actual limitations of the research effort; in other words, what is *not* going to be investigated. Here is the point where the writer spells out the various hypotheses to be investigated or the questions to be answered.
IV. **Outline.**
   Generally, this is a tentative framework for the entire project by topics. It should be flexible enough to accommodate unforeseen difficulties, show statistical tables in outline form, and also show graphs planned. Tables should reflect the hypotheses.
V. **Method and data sources.**
   The types of data to be sought (primary, secondary) are briefly identified. A brief explanation of how the necessary information or data will be gathered (e.g., surveys, experiments, library sources) is given. *Sources* refer to the actual depositories for the information, whether from government publications, company records, actual people, and so forth. If measurements are involved, such as consumers' attitudes, the techniques for making such measurements are stated. All of the techniques (statistical and nonstatistical) should be mentioned and discussed about their relevance for the task at hand. The nature of the problem will probably indicate the types of techniques to be employed, such as factor analysis, depth interviews, or focus groups.
VI. **Sample design.**
   This provides the limits of the universe or population to be studied and how it will be listed (or prepared). The writer specifies the population, states the sample size, whether sample stratification will be employed, and how. If a nonrandom sample is to be used, the justification and type of sampling strategy to be employed, such as convenience sample, are stated.
VII. **Data collection forms.**
   The forms to be employed in gathering the data should be discussed and, if possible, included in the plan. For surveys, this will involve either a questionnaire or an interview schedule. For other types of methods, the forms could include IBM cards, inventory forms, psychological tests, and so forth. The plan should state how these instruments have been or will be validated, and the reader should be given some indication of their reliability and validity.
VIII. **Personnel requirements.**
   This provides a complete list of all personnel who will be required, indicating exact jobs, time duration, and expected rate of pay. Assignments should be made indicating each person's responsibility and authority.
IX. **Phases of the study with a time schedule.**
   This is a detailed outline of the plan to complete the study. The entire study should be broken into workable pieces. Then, considering the person who will be employed in each phase, their qualifications and experience, and so forth, the time in months for the job is estimated. Some jobs may overlap. This plan will help in estimating the work months required. The overall time for the project should allow for time overlaps on some jobs.

The preparations obviously depend on the type of data desired and method of data collection. For primary research, questions and questionnaire items must be pretested and validated. In addition, preparations for mail surveys include such things as sample selection, questionnaire printing, and envelope and postage considerations. For telephone or personal interviews, such things as interviewer scoring forms, instructions, and

Figure 2–4   *(continued)*

IX. Phases of the study with a time schedule.
  Illustration:
  1. Preliminary investigation—two months.
  2. Final test of questionnaire—one month.
  3. Sample selection—one month.
  4. Mail questionnaires, field follow-up, and so forth—four months.
  5. Additional phases.
X. Tabulation plans.
  This is a discussion of editing and proof of questionnaires, card punching, and the type of computer analysis. An outline of some of the major tables required is very important.
XI. Cost estimate for doing the study.
  Personnel requirements are combined with time on different phases to estimate total personnel costs. Estimates on travel, materials, supplies, drafting, computer charges, and printing and mailing costs must also be included. If an overhead charge is required by the administration, it should be calculated and added to the subtotal of the above items.

HIGHLIGHT 2–5

A Comparison of Survey Data Collection Techniques

Basis of Comparison	Mail Surveys	Telephone Surveys	Personal Interview Surveys
Cost per completed survey	Usually the least expensive, assuming adequate return rate	Moderately expensive, assuming reasonable completion rate	Most expensive because of interviewer's time and travel expenses
Ability to probe and ask complex questions	Little, since self-administered format must be short and simple	Some, since interviewer can probe and elaborate on questions to a degree	Much, since interviewer can show visual materials, gain rapport, and probe
Opportunity for interviewer to bias results	None, since form is completed without interviewer	Some because of voice inflection of interviewer	Significant because of voice and facial expressions of interviewer
Anonymity given respondent	Complete, since no signature is required	Some because of telephone contact	Little because of face-to-face contact

Source: Eric N. Berkowitz, Roger A. Kerin, Steven W. Hartley, and William Rudelius, *Marketing*, 4th ed. (Burr Ridge, IL: Richard D. Irwin, 1994), p. 216.

scheduling must be taken care of. For secondary data, such things as data recording procedures and instructions need attention.

In terms of actual data collection, a cardinal rule is to obtain and record the maximal amount of useful information, subject to the constraints of time, money, and interviewee privacy. Failure to obtain and record data clearly can obviously lead to a poor research study, while failure to consider the rights of

Figure 2–5 *Six Criteria for Evaluating Marketing Research Reports*

1. Under what conditions was the study made? The report should provide:
   a. Full statement of the problems to be investigated by the study.
   b. Source of financing for the study.
   c. Names of organizations participating in the study, together with their qualifications and vested interests.
   d. Exact time period covered in data collection.
   e. Definitions of terms employed.
   f. Copies of data collection instruments.
   g. Source of collateral data.
   h. Complete statement of method.

2. Has the questionnaire been well designed?

3. Has the interviewing been adequately and reliably done?

4. Has the best sampling plan been followed, or has the best experimental design been used?

5. Was there adequate supervision and control over the editing, coding, and tabulating?

subjects or interviewees raises both ethical and practical questions. Thus, both the objectives and constraints of data collection must be closely monitored.

Processing research data

Processing research data includes the preparation of data for analysis and the actual analysis of the data. Preparations include such things as editing and structuring the data, and perhaps coding and preparing it for computer analysis. Data sets should be clearly labeled to ensure that they are not misinterpreted or misplaced. The data are then analyzed according to the procedure specified in the research plan and are interpreted according to standard norms of the analysis.

Preparation of research report

The research report is a complete statement of everything accomplished relative to the research project and includes a writeup of each of the previous stages. Figure 2–5 illustrates the types of questions the researcher should ask prior to submitting the report to the appropriate decision maker.

The importance of clear and unambiguous report writing cannot be overstressed, since the research is meaningless if it cannot be communicated. Often the researcher must trade off the apparent precision of scientific jargon for everyday language that the decision maker can understand. It should always be remembered that research is an aid for decision making and not a substitute for it.

Problems in the research process

Although the foregoing discussion presented the research process in a simplified framework, this does not mean that conducting research is a simple task. There are many problems and difficulties that must be overcome if a research study is to be of value. For example, consider the difficulties in one type of marketing research, *test marketing*.

The major goal of most test marketing is to measure new product sales on a limited basis where competitive retaliation and other factors are allowed to operate freely. In this way, future sales potential can be estimated. Test market research is a vital element in new product marketing. Listed below are a number of problem areas that can invalidate test market study results.[6]

1. Representative test areas are improperly selected from the standpoint of size, geographical location, population characteristics, and promotional facilities.
2. Sample size and design are incorrectly formulated because of ignorance, budget constraints, or an improper understanding of the test problem.
3. Pretest measurements of competitive brand's sales are not made, which means that the researcher has no realistic base to use for comparison purposes.
4. Attempts are not made to control the cooperation and support of test stores. Consequently, certain package sizes might not be carried, or pricing policies might not be adhered to.
5. Test market products are overadvertised or overpromoted during the test.
6. The full effect of such sales-influencing factors as sales force, season, weather conditions, competitive retaliation, shelf space, and so forth are not fully evaluated.
7. Market test periods are too short to determine whether the product is fully accepted by consumers or only tried on a limited basis.

Similar problems could be listed for almost any type of marketing research. However, the important point to be recognized is that careful planning, coordination, and control are imperative if the research study is to accomplish its objective.

CONCLUSION

This chapter has been concerned with marketing decision support systems and with marketing research. In terms of marketing decision support systems, one of the major reasons for increased interest has been the rapid growth in information-handling technology. However, as we have seen in this chapter, the study of MDSSs is not the study of computers. The study of MDSSs is part of a much larger task: the study of more efficient methods for marketing management decision making.

In terms of marketing research, this chapter has emphasized the importance of research as an aid for marketing decision making. Just as planning is integral for marketing management, the research plan is critical for marketing research. A research plan not only formalizes the objectives of the study but also details the tasks and responsibilities of the research team as well as cost estimates. Conducting research is a matter of following the research plan and reporting the events of each stage clearly and unambiguously. Finally, emphasis was placed on the extreme care that must be taken to avoid research difficulties and pitfalls.

ADDITIONAL READINGS

Aaker, David A.; V. Kumar; and George S. Day. *Marketing Research.* 5th ed. New York: John Wiley, 1995.

Burns, Alvin C., and Ronald F. Bush. *Marketing Research.* Englewood Cliffs, NJ: Prentice Hall, 1995.

Churchill, Gilbert A., Jr. *Basic Marketing Research.* 2nd ed. Ft. Worth, TX: Dryden Press, 1992.

————. *Marketing Research: Methodological Foundations.* 6th ed. Fort Worth, TX: Dryden Press, 1995.

Crask, Melvin; Richard J. Fox; and Roy G. Stout. *Marketing Research: Principles and Applications.* Englewood Cliffs, NJ: Prentice Hall, 1995.

Dillon, William R.; Thomas J. Madden; and Neil H. Firtle. *Marketing Research in a Marketing Environment.* 3rd ed. Burr Ridge, IL: Richard D. Irwin, 1994.

Malhotra, Naresh K. *Marketing Research: An Applied Orientation.* Englewood Cliffs, NJ: Prentice Hall, 1993.

O'Brien, James A. *Management Information Systems.* Homewood, IL: Richard D. Irwin, 1993.

Zikmund, William G. *Explore Marketing Research.* 5th ed. Forth Worth, TX: Dryden Press, 1994.

Chapter 3

CONSUMER BEHAVIOR

The marketing concept emphasizes that profitable marketing begins with the discovery and understanding of consumer needs and then develops a marketing mix to satisfy these needs. Thus, an understanding of consumers and their needs and purchasing behavior is integral to successful marketing.

Unfortunately, there is no single theory of consumer behavior that can totally explain why consumers behave as they do. Instead, there are numerous theories, models, and concepts making up the field. In addition, the majority of these notions have been borrowed from a variety of other disciplines, such as sociology, psychology, social psychology, and economics, and must be integrated to understand consumer behavior.

In this chapter some of the many influences on consumer behavior will be examined in terms of the buying process. The reader may wish to examine Figure 3–1 closely, since it provides the basis for this discussion.

The chapter will proceed by first examining the buying process and then discussing the group, product class, and situational influences on this process.

THE BUYING PROCESS

The buying process can be viewed as a series of five stages: need recognition, alternative search, alternative evaluation, purchase decision, and postpurchase feelings. In this section, each of these stages will be discussed. It should be noted at the outset that this is a general model for depicting a logical sequence of buying behavior. Clearly, individuals will vary from this model because of personal differences in such things as personality, self-concept, subjective perceptions of information, the product, and the purchasing situation. However, the model provides a useful framework for organizing our discussion of consumer behavior.

Need Recognition

The starting point for this model of the buying process is the recognition of an unsatisfied need by the consumer. Any number of either internal or external stimuli may activate needs or wants and recognition of them. Internal stimuli are such things as feeling hungry and wanting some food,

Figure 3–1   *An Overview of the Buying Process*

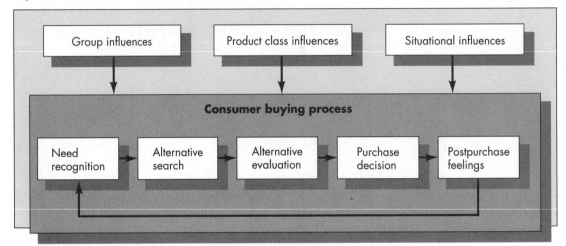

feeling a headache coming on and wanting some Excedrin, or feeling bored and looking for a movie to go to. External stimuli are such things as seeing a McDonald's sign and then feeling hungry or seeing a sale sign for winter parkas and remembering that last year's coat is worn out.

It is the task of marketing managers to find out what needs and wants a particular product can and does satisfy and what unsatisfied needs and wants consumers have for which a new product could be developed. In order to do so, marketing managers should understand what types of needs consumers may have. A well-known classification of needs was developed many years ago by Abraham Maslow and includes five types.[1] Maslow's view is that lower-level needs, starting with physiological and safety, must be attended to before higher-level needs can be satisfied. Maslow's hierarchy is described below.

Physiological needs. This category consists of the primary needs of the human body, such as food, water, and sex. Physiological needs will dominate when all needs are unsatisfied. In such a case, none of the other needs will serve as a basis for motivation.

Safety needs. With the physiological needs met, the next higher level assumes importance. Safety needs consist of such things as protection from physical harm, ill health, economic disaster, and avoidance of the unexpected.

Belongingness and love needs. These needs are related to the social and gregarious nature of humans and the need for companionship. This level in the hierarchy is the point of departure from the physical or quasi-physical needs of the two previous levels. Nonsatisfaction of this level of need may affect the mental health of the individual.

Esteem needs. These needs consist of both the need for the self-aware-ness of importance to others (self-esteem) and actual esteem from oth-ers. Satisfaction of these needs leads to feelings of self-confidence and prestige.

Self-actualization needs. This need can be defined as the desire to be-come more and more what one is, to become everything one is capable of becoming. This means that the individual will fully realize the potentiali-ties of given talents and capabilities. Maslow assumes that satisfaction of these needs is only possible after the satisfaction of all the needs lower in the

hierarchy.

While the hierarchy arrangement of Maslow presents a convenient ex-planation, it is probably more realistic to assume that the various need cat-egories overlap. Thus, in affluent societies, many products may satisfy more than one of these needs. For example, gourmet foods may satisfy both the basic physiological need of hunger as well as esteem and status needs for those who serve gourmet foods to their guests.

Alternative Search

Once a need is recognized, the individual then searches for alternatives for satisfying the need. There are five basic sources from which the individual can collect information for a particular purchase decision.

1. *Internal sources.* In most cases the individual has had some previous experi-ence in dealing with a particular need. Thus, the individual will usually "search" through whatever stored information and experience is in his or her mind for dealing with the need. If a previously acceptable product for satisfying the need is remembered, the individual may purchase with little or no additional information search or evaluation. This is quite common for routine or habitual purchases.

2. *Group sources.* A common source of information for purchase decisions comes from communication with other people, such as family, friends, neighbors, and acquaintances. Generally, some of these (i.e., relevant oth-ers) are selected that the individual views as having particular expertise for the purchase decision. Although it may be quite difficult for the marketing manager to determine the exact nature of this source of information, group sources of information often are considered to be the most powerful influ-ence on purchase decisions.

3. *Marketing sources.* Marketing sources of information include such factors as advertising, salespeople, dealers, packaging, and displays. Generally, this is the primary source of information about a particular product. These sources of information will be discussed in detail in the promotion chapters of this text.

HIGHLIGHT 3-1

Getting Close and Staying Close to Customers

A number of leading companies have recognized that understanding consumers and offering them the products and services that they want is the key to success. Below are several examples

Nike

While there are many strong competitors in the sports shoe market, Nike is at the top. In 1990, sales jumped 31 percent to $2.2 billion, about $75 million higher than archrival Reebok International. Nike's profits were $243 million compared to $177 million for Reebok. The company sells over 800 models for use in about 25 sports. It makes three lines of basketball shoes, each expressing what Nike calls a different attitude. The Air Jordan (retail price $125) is for consumers who want to follow in the footsteps of the Chicago Bulls superstar. The Flight (up to

Source: J. Paul Peter and Jerry C. Olson, *Consumer Behavior and Marketing Strategy,* 4th ed. (Burr Ridge, IL: Richard D. Irwin, 1996), p. 8.

$115) is for players who value the lightest Nikes, while the Force (up to $150) incorporates the latest designs, such as a custom air bladder, for consumers who want a snug fit. The company updates its shoes at least every six months to tempt new customers to lace on new pairs before last year's wear out. By carefully segmenting the market, coming out with frequent innovations and style changes, and continually researching to develop the most effective and stylish athletic shoes, Nike offers quality products that consumers want.

Harley-Davidson, Inc.

By the early 1980s, Japanese motorcycle manufacturers dominated the U.S. market. The Japanese bikes were more sophisticated, of better quality, and cheaper than Harleys. Harley-Davidson was days away from filing for bankruptcy by the end of 1985. However, it got refinanced and continued to work hard to improve the quality of its motorcycles through bettering the design, getting em-

4. *Public sources.* Public sources of information include publicity, such as a newspaper article about the product, and independent ratings of the product, such as *Consumer Reports.* Here product quality is a highly important marketing management consideration, since such articles and reports often discuss such features as dependability and service requirements.
5. *Experiential sources.* Experiential sources refer to handling, examining, and perhaps trying the product while shopping. This usually requires an actual shopping trip by the individual and may be the final source consulted before purchase.

Information collected from these sources is then processed by the consumer.[2] However, the exact nature of how individuals process information to form evaluations of products is not fully understood. In general, information processing is viewed as a four-step process in which the individual

ployees more committed to quality, working with dealers, and interacting continuously with consumers to get feedback on its products and ideas for improvements. By 1990, Harley-Davidson dominated the super-heavyweight motorcycle market with a market share of over 62 percent.

Monroe Auto Equipment

In the past decade, nine companies from Japan and Europe stormed the U.S. market for shock absorbers and struts—under-the-body parts that give cars a smooth ride. Monroe Auto Equipment recognized that to survive in this mature market, it had to increase the quality of its products and reduce costs. Since 1986, productivity in its 36 plants increased 26 percent, annual sales increased 70 percent to $900 million, and profits increased 20 percent. In the $1.5 billion-a-year market, Monroe sells more than half of all the replacement shocks and close to one-third of those put on new cars. Monroe learned how to build

better quality products by studying Japanese methods and focused on having zero defects, which satisfies both organizational and consumer buyers.

Wal-Mart

Sam Walton, founder of Wal-Mart, had a simple idea on how to be a successful retailer: be an agent for consumers, find out what they want, and sell it to them for the lowest possible price. To do so effectively, Wal-Mart has developed a corporate culture focused on consumers. The company has a sophisticated computerized warehouse and inventory system that carefully tracks sales and communicates sales data with manufacturers to ensure stores remain well stocked with high-demand merchandise. Wal-Mart bargains hard with manufacturers to get the lowest possible price and keeps overhead low, in fact, the lowest in the industry. Wal-Mart stays close to customers. Is it any wonder that in 1991 it became the number one retailer in the United States, with sales of

is (1) exposed to information; (2) becomes attentive to the information; (3) understands the information; and (4) retains the information.[3]

Alternative Evaluation

During the process of collecting information or, in some cases, after information is acquired, the consumer then evaluates alternatives based on what has been learned. One approach to describing the evaluation process can be found in the logic of attitude modeling.[4] The basic logic can be described as follows:

1. The consumer has information about a number of brands in a product class.
2. The consumer perceives that at least some of the brands in a product class are viable alternatives for satisfying a recognized need.

HIGHLIGHT 3–2

Factors Affecting Information Search by Consumers

Influencing Factor	Increasing the Influencing Factor Causes Search to:
I. Market characteristics	
A. Number of alternatives	Increase
B. Price range	Increase
C. Store concentration	Increase
D. Information availability	Increase
1. Advertising	
2. Point-of-purchase	
3. Sales personnel	
4. Packaging	
5. Experienced consumers	
6. Independent sources	
II. Product characteristics	
A. Price	Increase
B. Differentiation	Increase
C. Positive products	Increase
III. Consumer characteristics	
A. Learning and experience	Decrease
B. Shopping orientation	Mixed
C. Social status	Increase
D. Age, gender, and household life cycle	Mixed
E. Perceived risk	Increase
IV. Situational characteristics	
A. Time availability	Increase
B. Purchase for self	Decrease
C. Pleasant surroundings	Increase
D. Social surroundings	Mixed
E. Physical/mental energy	Increase

Source: Del I. Hawkins, Kenneth A. Coney, and Roger Best, Jr., *Consumer Behavior: Implications for Marketing Strategy,* 6th ed. (Burr Ridge, IL: Richard D. Irwin, 1995), p. 454.

3. Each of these brands has a set of attributes (color, quality, size, and so forth).

4. A set of these attributes is relevant to the consumer, and the consumer perceives that different brands vary in terms of how much of each attribute they possess.

5. The brand that is perceived as offering the greatest number of desired attributes in the desired amounts and desired order will be the brand the consumer will like best.
6. The brand the consumer likes best is the brand the consumer will intend to purchase.

Purchase Decision

If no other factors intervene after the consumer has decided on the brand that is intended for purchase, the actual purchase is a common result of search and evaluation. Actually, a purchase involves many decisions, which include product type, brand, model, dealer selection, and method of payment, among other factors. In addition, rather than purchasing, the consumer may make a decision to modify, postpone, or avoid purchase based on an inhibitor to purchase or a perceived risk.

Traditional risk theorists believe that consumers tend to make risk-minimizing decisions based on their *perceived* definition of the particular purchase. The perception of risk is based upon the possible consequences and uncertainties involved. Consequences may range from economic loss, to embarrassment if a new food product does not turn out well, to actual physical harm. Perceived risk may be either functional (related to financial and performance considerations) or psychosocial (related to whether the product will further one's self- or reference group image). That amount of risk a consumer perceives in a particular product depends on such things as the price of the product and whether other people will see the individual using the product.

The perceived risk literature emphasizes that consumers generally try to reduce risk in their decision making. This can be done by either reducing the possible negative consequences or by reducing the uncertainty. The possible consequences of a purchase might be minimized by purchasing in small quantities or by lowering the individual's aspiration level to expect less in the way of results from the product. However, this cannot always be done. Thus, reducing risk by attempting to increase the certainty of the purchase outcome may be the more widely used strategy. This can be done by seeking additional information regarding the proposed purchase. In general, the more information the consumer collects prior to purchase, the less likely postpurchase dissonance is to occur.

Postpurchase Feelings

In general, if the individual finds that a certain response achieves a desired goal or satisfies a need, the success of this cue-response pattern will be remembered. The probability of responding in a like manner to the same or similar situation in the future is increased. In other words, the response has a higher probability of being repeated when the need and cue appear together again, and thus it can be said that learning has taken place. Frequent reinforcement increases the habit potential of the particular response. Likewise, if a response does not satisfy the need adequately, the probability that the same response will be repeated is reduced.

For some marketers this means that if an individual finds a particular product fulfills the need for which it was purchased, the probability is high that the product will be repurchased the next time the need arises. The firm's promotional efforts often act as the cue. If an individual repeatedly purchases a product with favorable results, loyalty may develop toward the particular product or brand. This loyalty can result in habitual purchases, and such habits are often extremely difficult for competing firms to alter.

Although many studies in the area of buyer behavior center around the buyer's attitudes, motives, and behavior before and during the purchase decision, emphasis has also been given to study of behavior after the purchase. Specifically, studies have been undertaken to investigate postpurchase dissonance, as well as postpurchase satisfaction.

The occurrence of postdecision dissonance is related to the concept of cognitive dissonance. This theory states that there is often a lack of consistency or harmony among an individual's various cognitions, or attitudes and beliefs, after a decision has been made—that is, the individual has doubts and second thoughts about the choice made. Further, it is more likely that the intensity of the anxiety will be greater when any of the following conditions exist:

1. The decision is an important one psychologically or financially, or both.
2. There are a number of forgone alternatives.
3. The forgone alternatives have many favorable features.

These factors can relate to many buying decisions. For example, postpurchase dissonance might be expected to be present among many purchasers of such products as automobiles, major appliances, and homes. In these cases, the decision to purchase is usually an important one both financially and psychologically, and there are usually a number of favorable alternatives available.

These findings have much relevance for the marketer. In a buying situation, when a purchaser becomes dissonant it is reasonable to predict such a person would be highly receptive to advertising and sales promotion that support the purchase decision. Such communication presents favorable aspects of the product and can be useful in reinforcing the buyer's wish to believe that a wise purchase decision was made. For example, purchasers of major appliances or automobiles might be given a phone call or sent a letter reassuring them that they have made a wise purchase.

As noted, researchers have also studied postpurchase consumer satisfaction. Much of this work has been based on what is called the "disconfirmation paradigm." Basically, this approach views satisfaction with products and brands as a result of two other variables. The first variable is the expectations a consumer has about a product before purchase. These expectations concern the beliefs the consumer has about the product's performance.

The second variable is the difference between expectations and postpurchase perceptions of how the product actually performed. If the product performed as well as expected or better than expected, the consumer will be satisfied with the product. If the product performed worse than expected, the consumer will be dissatisfied with it.

One implication of this view for marketers is that care must be taken not to raise prepurchase expectations to such a level that the product cannot possibly meet them. Rather, it is important to create positive expectations consistent with the product's likely performance.[5]

GROUP INFLUENCES ON CONSUMER BEHAVIOR

Behavioral scientists have become increasingly aware of the powerful effects of the social environment and personal interactions on human behavior. In terms of consumer behavior, culture, social class, and reference group influences have been related to purchase and consumption decisions. It should be noted that these influences can have both direct and indirect effects on the buying process. By direct effects we mean direct communication between the individual and other members of society concerning a particular decision. By indirect effects we mean the influence of society on an individual's basic values and attitudes as well as the important role that groups play in structuring an individual's personality.

Cultural and Subcultural Influences

Culture is one of the most basic influences on an individual's needs, wants, and behavior, since all facets of life are carried out against the background of the society in which an individual lives. Cultural antecedents affect everyday behavior, and there is empirical support for the notion that culture is a determinant of certain aspects of consumer behavior.

Cultural values are transmitted through three basic organizations; the family, religious organizations, and educational institutions, and, in today's society, educational institutions are playing an increasingly greater role in this regard. Marketing managers should adapt the marketing mix to cultural values and constantly monitor value changes and differences in both domestic and international markets. To illustrate, one of the changing values in America is the increasing emphasis on achievement and career success. This change in values has been recognized by many business firms that have expanded their emphasis on time-saving, convenience-oriented products.

In a nation as large as the United States the population is bound to lose a significant amount of its homogeneity, and thus subcultures arise. In other words, there are subcultures in the American culture where people have more frequent interactions than with the population at large and thus

It is important for marketers to understand cultural values and to create and adapt products to the values held by consumers. Below is a description of American cultural values and their relevance to marketing.

Value	General Features	Relevance to Marketing
Achievement and success	Hard work is good; success flows from hard work	Acts as a justification for acquisition of goods ("You deserve it")
Activity	Keeping busy is healthy and natural	Stimulates interest in products that are time-savers and enhance leisure-time activities
Efficiency and practicality	Admiration of things that solve problems (e.g., save time and effort)	Stimulates purchase of products that function well and save time
Progress	People can improve themselves; tomorrow should be better	Stimulates desire for new products that fulfill unsatisfied needs; acceptance of products that claim to be "new" or "improved"
Material comfort	"The good life"	Fosters acceptance of convenience and luxury products

Source: Consumer Behavior, 5th ed., p. 437 by Leon G. Schiffman and Leslie Lazar Kanuck, © 1994. Reprinted by permission of Prentice-Hall, Inc., Upper Saddle River, NJ.

tend to think and act alike in some respects. Subcultures are based on such things as geographic areas, religions, nationalities, ethnic groups, and age. Many subcultural barriers are decreasing because of mass communication, mass transit, and a decline in the influence of religious values. However, age groups, such as the teen market, baby boomers, and the mature market, have become increasingly important for marketing strategy. For example, since baby boomers (those born between 1946 and 1962) make up about a third of the U.S. population and soon will account for about half of discretionary spending, many marketers are repositioning products to serve them. Snickers candy bars, for instance, used to be promoted to children as a treat but are now promoted to adults as a wholesome, between-meals snack.

Social Class

While one likes to think of America as a land of equality, a class structure can be observed. Social classes develop on the basis of such things as

Value	General Features	Relevance to Marketing
Individualism	Being one's self (e.g., self-reliance, self-interest, and self-esteem)	Stimulates acceptance of customized or unique products that enable a person to "express his or her own personality"
Freedom	Freedom of choice	Fosters interest in wide product lines and differentiated products
External conformity	Uniformity of observable behavior; desire to be accepted	Stimulates interest in products that are used or owned by others in the same social group
Humanitarianism	Caring for others, particularly the underdog	Stimulates patronage of firms that compete with market leaders
Youthfulness	A state of mind that stresses being young at heart or appearing young	Stimulates acceptance of products that provide the illusion of maintaining or fostering youth
Fitness and health	Caring about one's body, including the desire to be physically fit and healthy	Stimulates acceptance of food products, activities, and equipment perceived to maintain or increase physical fitness

wealth, skill, and power. The single best indicator of social class is occupation. However, interest at this point is in the influence of social class on the individual's behavior. What is important here is that different social classes tend to have different attitudinal configurations and values, which influence the behavior of individual members. Figure 3–2 presents a social class hierarchy developed specifically for marketing analysis and describes some of these important differences in attitudes and values.

For the marketing manager, social class offers some insights into consumer behavior and is potentially useful as a market segmentation variable. However, there is considerable controversy as to whether social class is superior to income for the purpose of market segmentation.

Reference Groups

Groups that an individual looks to (uses as a reference) when forming attitudes and opinions are described as reference groups.[6] Primary reference groups include family and close friends, while secondary reference

Figure 3–2   *Social Class Groups for Marketing Analysis*

Upper Americans (14 percent of population). This group consists of the upper-upper, lower-upper, an upper-middle classes. They have common goals and are differentiated mainly by income. This group has many different lifestyles, which might be labeled postpreppy, conventional, intellectual, and political, among others. The class remains the segment of our society in which quality merchandise is most prized, special attention is paid to prestige brands, and the self-image is "spending with good taste." Self-expression is more prized than in previous generations, and neighborhood remains important. Depending on income and priorities, theater, books, investment in art, European travel, household help, club memberships for tennis, golf, and swimming, and prestige schooling for children remain high consumption priorities.

Middle class (32 percent of population). These consumers definitely want to "do the right thing" and buy "what's popular." They have always been concerned with fashion and following recommendations of "experts" in print media. Increased earnings result in better living, which means a "nicer neighborhood on the better side of town with good schools." It also means spending more on "worthwhile experiences" for children, including winter ski trips, college educations, and shopping for better brands of clothes at more expensive stores. Appearance of home is important, because guests may visit and pass judgment. This group emulates upper Americans, which distinguishes it from the working class. It also enjoys trips to Las Vegas and physical activity. Deferred gratification may still be an ideal, but it is not often practiced.

Working class (38 percent of population). Working-class Americans are "family folk" depending heavily on relatives for economic and emotional support (e.g., tips on job opportunities, advice on purchases, help in times of trouble). The emphasis on family ties is only one sign of how much more limited and different working-class horizons are socially, psychologically, and geographically compared to those of the middle class. In almost every respect, a parochial view characterizes this blue-collar world. This group has changed little in values and behaviors in spite of rising incomes in some cases. For them, "keeping up with the times" focuses on the mechanical and recreational, and thus, ease of labor and leisure is what they continue to pursue.

Lower Americans (16 percent of population). The men and women of lower America are no exception to the rule that diversities and uniformities in values and consumption goals are to be found at each social level. Some members of this world, as has been publicized, are prone to every form of instant gratification known to humankind when the money is available. But others are dedicated to resisting worldly temptations as they struggle toward what some believe will be a "heavenly reward" for their earthly sacrifices.

Source: Reprinted with permission of the University of Chicago Press from *Journal of Consumer Research* (December 1983), "The Continuing Significance of Social Class to Marketing," by Richard P. Coleman, pp. 265–80. © 1983 by the University of Chicago.

groups include fraternal organizations and professional associations. A buyer may also consult a single individual about decisions, and this individual would be considered a reference individual.

A person normally has several reference groups or reference individuals for various subjects or different decisions. For example, a woman may consult one reference group when she is purchasing a car and a different reference group for lingerie. In other words, the nature of the product and the role the individual is playing during the purchasing process influence which reference group will be consulted. Reference group influence is generally considered to be stronger for products that are "public" or conspicuous—that is, products that other people see the individual using such as clothes or automobiles.

As noted, the family is generally recognized to be an important reference group, and it has been suggested that the household, rather than the individual, is the relevant unit for studying consumer behavior.[7] This is because within a household the purchaser of goods and services is not always the user of these goods and services. Thus, it is important for marketing managers to determine not only who makes the actual purchase but also who makes the decision to purchase. In addition, it has been recognized that the needs, income, assets, debts, and expenditure patterns change over the course of what is called the *family life cycle*. Basic stages in the family life cycle include:

1. Bachelor stage: young, single people not living at home.
2. Newly married couples: young, no children.
3. Full nest I: young married couples with youngest child under six.
4. Full nest II: young married couples with youngest child six or over.
5. Full nest III: older married couples with dependent children.
6. Empty nest I: older married couples, no children living with them, household head(s) in labor force.
7. Empty nest II: older married couples, no children living at home, household head(s) retired.
8. Solitary survivor in labor force.
9. Solitary survivor, retired.

Because the life cycle combines trends in earning power with demands placed on income, it is a useful way of classifying and segmenting individuals and families.[8]

PRODUCT CLASS INFLUENCES

The nature of the product class selected by the consumer to satisfy an aroused need plays an important role in the decision-making process. Basically, the nature of the product class and the brands within it determine (1) the amount of information the consumer will require before making a decision, and, consequently (2) the time it takes to move through the buying process. In general, product classes in which there are many alternatives that are expensive, complex, or new will require the consumer to collect more information and take longer to make a purchase decision. As illustration, buying an automobile is probably one of the most difficult purchase decisions most consumers make. An automobile is expensive,

HIGHLIGHT 3–4

Some Common Verbal Tools Used by Reference Groups

Below are a number of verbal tools used by reference groups to influence consumer behavior. If the statements listed below were made to you by a close friend or someone you admired or respected, do you think that they might change your behavior?

Tools	Definitions	Examples
Reporting	Talking about preferences and behaviors.	"All of us drink Budweiser."
Recommendations	Suggesting appropriate behaviors.	"You should get a Schwinn High Sierra."
Invitations	Asking for participation in events.	"Do you want to go to the Michael Jackson concert with us?"
Requests	Asking for behavior performance.	"Would you run down to the corner and get me a newspaper?"
Prompts	Suggesting desired behaviors.	"It sure would be nice if someone would buy us a pizza!"
Commands	Telling someone what to do.	"Get me some Kleenex, and be quick about it!"
Promises	Offering a reward for performing a behavior.	"If you'll go to Penney's with me, I'll take you to lunch later."
Coercion	Threatening to punish for inappropriate behavior.	"If you don't shut up, I'm going to stuff a sock in your mouth!"
Criticism	Saying something negative about a behavior.	"Quit hassling the salesclerk. You're acting like a jerk."
Compliments	Saying something positive about a behavior.	"You really know how to shop. I bet you got every bargain in the store!"
Teasing	Good-natured bantering about behavior or appearance.	"Man, that shirt makes you look like Bozo the clown!"

complex, and there are many new styles and models to choose from. Such a decision will usually require extensive information search and time before a decision is made.

A second possibility is referred to as limited decision making. For these purchases a lesser amount of information is collected and less time is devoted to shopping. For example, in purchasing a new pair of jeans the consumer may already have considerable experience, and price and complexity are somewhat limited. However, since there are many alternative styles and brands, some information processing and decision making is generally needed.

Finally, some product classes require what is called "routinized decision making." For these product classes, such as candy bars or other food products, the consumer has faced the decision many times before and has found an acceptable alternative. Thus, little or no information is collected, and the consumer purchases in a habitual, automatic manner.

SITUATIONAL INFLUENCES

Situational influences can be defined as all those factors particular to a time and place of observation that have a demonstrable and systematic effect on current behavior. In terms of purchasing situations, five groups of situational influences have been identified.[9] These influences may be perceived either consciously or subconsciously and may have considerable effect on product and brand choice.

1. *Physical surroundings* are the most readily apparent features of a situation. These features include geographical and institutional location, decor, sounds, aromas, lighting, weather, and visible configurations of merchandise or other material surrounding the stimulus object.
2. *Social surroundings* provide additional depth to a description of a situation. Other persons present, their characteristics, their apparent roles and interpersonal interactions are potentially relevant examples.
3. *Temporal perspective* is a dimension of situations that may be specified in units ranging from time of day to season of the year. Time also may be measured relative to some past or future event for the situational participant. This allows such conceptions as time since last purchase, time since or until meals or paydays, and time constraints imposed by prior or standing commitments.
4. *Task definition* features of a situation include an intent or requirement to select, shop for, or obtain information about a general or specific purchase. In addition, task may reflect different buyer and user roles anticipated by the individual. For instance, a person shopping for a small appliance as a wedding gift for a friend is in a different situation than when shopping for a small appliance for personal use.
5. *Antecedent states* make up a final feature that characterizes a situation. These are momentary moods (such as acute anxiety, pleasantness, hostility, and excitation) or momentary conditions (such as cash on hand, fatigue, and illness) rather than chronic individual traits. These conditions are further stipulated to be immediately antecedent to the current situation to distinguish the states the individual brings to the situation from states of the individual resulting from the situation. For instance, people may select a certain motion picture because they feel depressed (an antecedent state and a part of the choice situation), but the fact that the movie causes them to feel happier is a response to the consumption situation. This altered state then may become antecedent for behavior in the next choice situation encountered, such as passing a street vendor on the way out of the theater.

CONCLUSION

The purpose of this chapter was to present an overview of consumer behavior in terms of an analysis of the buying process. The buying process is viewed as a series of five stages: need recognition, alternative search, alternative evaluation, purchase decision, and postpurchase feelings. This process is influenced by group, product class, and situational factors. Clearly, marketing managers must understand consumer behavior to formulate effective marketing strategies.

ADDITIONAL READINGS

Assael, Henry. *Consumer Behavior and Marketing Action.* 5th ed. Cincinnati: South-Western College Publishing, 1995.

Engel, James F.; Roger D. Blackwell; and Paul W. Miniard. *Consumer Behavior.* 8th ed. Fort Worth, TX: Dryden Press, 1995.

Hawkins, Del; Kenneth A. Coney; and Roger Best, Jr. *Consumer Behavior: Implications for Marketing Strategy.* 6th ed. Burr Ridge, IL: Richard D. Irwin, 1995.

Mowen, John C. *Consumer Behavior.* 4th ed. New York: Macmillan Publishing, 1995.

Onkvisit, Sak, and John J. Shaw. *Consumer Behavior: Strategy and Analysis.* New York: Macmillan Publishing, 1994.

Peter, J. Paul, and Jerry C. Olson. *Consumer Behavior and Marketing Strategy.* 4th ed. Burr Ridge, IL: Richard D. Irwin, 1996.

_____. *Understanding Consumer Behavior.* Burr Ridge, IL: Richard D. Irwin, 1994.

Schiffman, Leon G., and Leslie Kanuck. *Consumer Behavior.* 5th ed. Englewood Cliffs, NJ: Prentice Hall, 1994.

Solomon, Michael R. *Consumer Behavior.* 2nd ed. Boston: Allyn & Bacon, 1994.

Wilkie, William L. *Consumer Behavior.* New York: John Wiley & Sons, 1994.

Appendix
SELECTED CONSUMER BEHAVIOR DATA SOURCES

1. **Demographic information:**
   U.S. Census of Population.
   Marketing Information Guide.
   A Guide to Consumer Markets.
   State and city governments.
   Media (newspapers, magazines, television, and radio stations) make demographic data about their readers or audiences available.

2. **Consumer Research Findings:**

Journal of Consumer Research	*Journal of Advertising Research*
Journal of Marketing	*Journal of Consumer Marketing*
Journal of Marketing Research	*Journal of Applied Psychology*
Journal of Advertising	*Advances in Consumer Research*

3. **Marketing Applications:**

Advertising Age	*Nation's Business*
Marketing Communications	*Fortune*
Sales Management	*Forbes*
Business Week	Industry and trade magazines

Chapter 4
ORGANIZATIONAL BUYER BEHAVIOR

Organizational buyers include individuals involved in purchasing products for businesses, government agencies, and other institutions and agencies. Those who purchase for businesses include industrial buyers who purchase goods and services to aid them in producing other goods and services for sale, and resellers who purchase goods and services to resell at a profit. Government agencies purchase products and services to carry out their responsibilities to society, and other institutions and agencies, such as churches and schools, purchase to fulfill their organizational missions.

The purpose of this chapter is to examine the organizational buying process and the factors that influence it. Figure 4–1 provides a model of the organizational buying process that will be used as a framework for discussion in this chapter.

Figure 4–1 *A Model of the Organizational Buying Process*

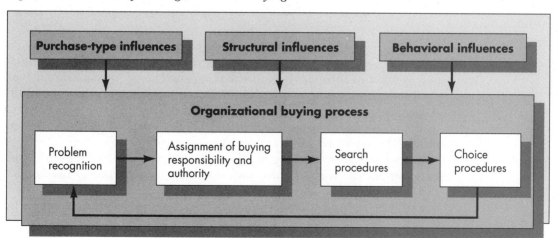

PURCHASE-TYPE INFLUENCES ON ORGANIZATIONAL BUYING

A major consideration that affects the organizational buying process is the complexity of the purchase that is to be made. Three types of organizational purchase based on their degree of complexity include the straight rebuy, modified rebuy, and new task purchase.[1]

Straight Rebuy

The simplest and most common type of purchase is called a *straight rebuy*. This type of purchase involves routinely reordering from the same supplier a product that has been purchased in the past. Organizations use a straight rebuy when they are experienced at buying the product, have an ongoing need for it, and have regular suppliers of it. In many cases, organizations have computer systems that automatically reorder certain commonly used products. Organizations use this simple approach to purchasing because it is fast and requires relatively few employees.

Straight rebuys are common among organizations that practice just-in-time inventory, which is a system of replenishing parts or goods for resale just before they are needed. Such buyers do not have time to hunt around for potential suppliers and solicit bids. Instead they regularly place their orders with a supplier whose quality and timely delivery can be counted on. If a supplier delivers items that are late or of unacceptable quality, these buyers will not have a reserve in inventory to draw on. Therefore, organizations that use just-in-time inventory tend to favor suppliers with a strong commitment to quality.

To retain customers who use straight rebuys, the marketer needs to maintain high-quality products and reliable service so that the customers will continue to be satisfied with their purchases.

Modified Rebuy

When some aspects of the buying situation are unfamiliar, the organization will use a modified rebuy. This type of purchase involves considering a limited number of alternatives before making a selection. Organizational buyers follow this approach rather than a straight rebuy when a routine purchase changes in some way; for example, a supplier discontinues a product or stops satisfying the customer, the price of a usual product rises, or a new product becomes available to meet the same need.

In such situations, the organizational buyer considers the new information and decides what changes to make. If the change proves satisfactory and the product is one needed routinely, the buyer may then make it part of a straight rebuy. Marketers seek to win new organizational customers by giving them reasons to change from a straight rebuy to a modified rebuy in which they consider the marketer's products.

Figure 4–2 *Differences in Types of Organizational Purchases*

Purchase Type	Complexity	Time Frame	Number of Suppliers	Applications
Straight rebuy	Simple	Short	One	Frequently purchased, routine products, such as printer ribbons
Modified rebuy	Moderate	Medium	Few	Routine purchase that has changed in some way, such as air travel (new fares, flights, destinations)
New task purchase	Complex	Long	Many	Expensive, seldom-purchased products, such as new location for a department store

New Task Purchase

Organizations purchase some products only occasionally, especially in the case of large investments such as machinery, equipment, and real estate. In these cases, the organization may use a new task purchase. This type of purchase involves an extensive search for information and a formal decision process.

New task purchases are most often used for big-ticket items, so the cost of a mistake is great. Therefore, a new task purchase is time consuming and involves a relatively large number of decision makers, who consider many alternatives. This is the type of purchase decision that is most likely to involve joint decision making because many kinds of expertise are required to make the best decision.

A new task purchase is an opportunity for the marketer to learn about the needs of the organizations in its target market and to discuss with the organization ways to meet its needs, such as through the use of new products and technology. Figure 4–2 summarizes the differences in the three types of purchases.

STRUCTURAL INFLUENCES ON ORGANIZATIONAL BUYING

The term *structural influences* refers to the design of the organizational environment and how it affects the purchasing process. Two important structural influences on organizational buying are joint decision making and organization-specific factors.

Joint Decision Making

It is common in organizational buying for more than one department and several persons to be involved in the purchasing process. These people may also play a variety of different roles in arriving at a purchase decision. These roles include:

HIGHLIGHT 4–1

Major Differences between Organizational Buyers and Final Consumers

Differences in Purchases

1. Organizational buyers acquire for further production, use in operations, or resale to other consumers. Final consumers acquire only for personal, family, or household use.
2. Organizational buyers commonly purchase installations, raw materials, and semifinished materials. Final consumers rarely purchase these goods.
3. Organizational buyers purchase on the basis of specifications and technical data. Final consumers frequently purchase on the basis of description, fashion, and style.
4. Organizational buyers utilize multiple-buying and team-based decisions more often than final consumers.
5. Organizational buyers are more likely to apply value and vendor analysis.
6. Organizational buyers more commonly lease equipment.

Source: Marketing, 5th ed., p. 174 by Joel R. Evans and Barry Berman, © 1992. Reprinted by permission of Prentice-Hall, Inc., Upper Saddle River, NJ.

7. Organizational buyers more frequently employ competitive bidding and negotiation.

Differences in the Market

1. The demand of organizational buyers is derived from the demand of final consumers.
2. The demand of organizational buyers is more subject to cyclical fluctuations than final-consumer demand.
3. Organizational buyers are fewer in number and more geographically concentrated than final consumers.
4. Organizational buyers often employ buying specialists.
5. The distribution channel for organizational buyers is shorter than for final consumers.
6. Organizational buyers may require special services.
7. Organizational buyers are more likely than final consumers to be able to make goods and services as alternatives to purchasing them.

1. *Users,* who are the people in the organization who actually use the product, for example, a secretary who would use a new word processor.
2. *Influencers,* who affect the buying decision, usually by helping define the specifications for what is bought. For example, an information systems manager would be a key influencer in the purchase of a new mainframe computer.
3. *Buyers,* who have the formal authority and responsibility to select the supplier and negotiate the terms of the contract. For example, in the purchase of a mainframe computer, the purchasing manager would likely perform this role.
4. *Deciders,* who have the formal or informal power to select or approve the supplier that receives the contract. For important technical purchases, deciders may come from R&D, engineering, or quality control.
5. *Gatekeepers,* who control the flow of information in the buying center. Purchasing personnel, technical experts, and secretaries can all keep marketers and their information from reaching people performing the other four roles.[2]

When several persons are involved in the organizational purchase decision, marketers may need to use a variety of means to reach each individual or group. Fortunately, it is often easy to find which individuals in organizations are involved in a purchase because such information is provided to suppliers. Organizations do this because it makes suppliers more knowledgeable about purchasing practices, thus making the purchasing process more efficient.[3] Also a number of firms have developed closer channel relationships that facilitate these transactions, as discussed in Chapter 10.

Organization-Specific Factors

There are three primary organization-specific factors that influence the purchasing process: orientation, size, and degree of centralization. First, in terms of orientation, the dominant function in an organization may control purchasing decisions. For example, if the organization is technology oriented, it is likely to be dominated by engineering personnel, and buying decisions will be made by them. Similarly, if the organization is production oriented, production personnel may dominate buying decisions.

Second, the size of the organization may influence the purchasing process. If the organization is large, it will likely have a high degree of joint decision making for other than straight rebuys. Smaller organizations are likely to have more autonomous decision making.

Finally, the degree of centralization of an organization influences whether decisions are made individually or jointly with others. Organizations that are highly centralized are less likely to have joint decision making. Thus, a privately owned, small company with technology or production orientations will tend toward autonomous decision making, while a large-scale, public corporation with considerable decentralization will tend to have greater joint decision making.

BEHAVIORAL INFLUENCES ON ORGANIZATIONAL BUYING

Organizational buyers are influenced by a variety of psychological and social factors. We will discuss two of these, personal motivations and role perceptions.

Personal Motivations

Organizational buyers are, of course, subject to the same personal motives or motivational forces as other individuals. Although these buyers may emphasize nonpersonal motives in their buying activities, it has been found that organizational buyers often are influenced by such personal factors as friendship, professional pride, fear and uncertainty (risk), and personal ambitions in their buying activities.

HIGHLIGHT 4–2

Functional Areas and Their Key Concerns in Purchasing

Functional Area	Key Concerns in Purchase Decision Making
Design and development engineering	Name, reputation of vendor; ability of vendors to meet design specifications
Production	Delivery and reliability of purchases such that interruption of production schedules is minimized
Sales/marketing	Impact of purchased items on marketability of the company's products
Maintenance	Degree to which purchased items are compatible with existing facilities and equipment; maintenance services offered by vendor; installation arrangements offered by vendor
Finance/accounting	Effects of purchases on cash flow, balance sheet, and income statement positions; variances in costs of materials over estimates; feasibility of make-or-buy and lease options to purchasing
Purchasing	Obtaining lowest possible price at acceptable quality levels; maintaining good relations with vendors
Quality control	Assurance that purchased items meet prescribed specifications and tolerances, governmental regulations, and customer requirements

Source: *Industrial and Organizational Marketing,* by Michael H. Morris (Columbus, OH: Merrill Publishing, 1989), p. 81. © 1988. Reprinted by permission of Prentice-Hall, Inc., Upper Saddle River, NJ.

For example, professional pride often expresses itself through efforts to attain status in the firm. One way to achieve this might be to initiate or influence the purchase of goods that will demonstrate a buyer's value to the organization. If new materials, equipment, or components result in cost savings or increased profits, the individuals initiating the changes have demonstrated their value at the same time. Fear and uncertainty are strong motivational forces on organizational buyers, and reduction of risk is often important to them. This can have a strong influence on purchase behavior. Marketers should understand the relative strength of personal gain versus risk-reducing motives and emphasize the more important motives when dealing with buyers.

Thus, in examining buyer motivations, it is necessary to consider both personal and nonpersonal motivational forces and to recognize that the relative importance of each is not a fixed quantity. It will vary with the nature of the product, the climate within the organization, and the relative strength of the two forces in the particular buyer.

Role Perception

A final factor that influences organizational buyers is their own perception of their role. The manner in which individuals behave depends on their perception of their role, their commitment to what they believe is expected of their role, the "maturity" of the role type, and the extent to which the institution is committed to the role type.

HIGHLIGHT 4–3
Twenty Potential Decisions Facing Organizational Buyers

1. Is the need or problem pressing enough that it must be acted upon now? If not, how long can action be deferred?
2. What types of products or services could conceivably be used to solve our need or problem?
3. Should we make the item ourselves?
4. Must a new product be designed, or has a vendor already developed an acceptable product?
5. Should a value analysis be performed?
6. What is the highest price we can afford to pay?
7. What trade-offs are we prepared to make between price and other product/vendor attributes?
8. Which information sources will we rely on?

9. How many vendors should be considered?
10. Which attributes will be stressed in evaluating vendors?
11. Should bids be solicited?
12. Should the item be leased or purchased outright?
13. How far can a given vendor be pushed in negotiations? On what issues will that vendor bend the most?
14. How much inventory should a vendor be willing to keep on hand?
15. Should we split our order among several vendors?
16. Is a long-term contract in our interest?
17. What contractual guarantees will we require?
18. How shall we establish our order routine?
19. After the purchase, how will vendor performance be evaluated?
20. How will we deal with inadequate product or vendor performance?

Source: Industrial and Organizational Marketing, by Michael H. Morris (Columbus, OH: Charles E. Merrill Publishing, 1988), p. 87. © 1988. Reprinted by permission of Prentice-Hall, Inc., Upper Saddle River, NJ.

Different buyers will have different degrees of commitment to their buying role, which will cause variations in role behavior from one buyer to the next. By *commitment* we mean willingness to perform their job in the manner expected by the organization. For example, some buyers seek to take charge in their role as buyer and have little commitment to company expectations. The implication for marketers is that such buyers expect, even demand, that they be kept constantly advised of all new developments to enable them to more effectively shape their own role. On the other hand, other buyers may have no interest in prescribing their role activities and accept their role as given to them. Such a buyer is most concerned with merely implementing prescribed company activities and buying policies with sanctioned products. Thus, some buyers will be highly committed to play the role the firm dictates (i.e., the formal organization's perception of their role) while others might be extremely innovative and uncommitted to the expected role performance. Obviously, roles may be heavily influenced by the organizational climate existing in the particular organization.[4]

Organizations can be divided into three groups based on differences in degree of employee commitment. These groups include innovative, adaptive, and lethargic firms. In *innovative firms,* individuals approach their occupational roles with a weak commitment to expected norms of behavior.

HIGHLIGHT 4–4

An Operational View of the Organizational Buying Process

Although there is no single format dictating how organizations actually purchase goods and services, a relatively standard process is followed in most cases:

1. A department discovers or anticipates a problem in its operation that it believes can be overcome with the addition of a certain product or service.
2. The department head draws up a requisition form describing the desired specifications he or she believes the product or service must have to solve the problem.
3. The department head sends the requisition form to the firm's purchasing department.
4. Based on the specifications required, the purchasing department conducts a search for qualified sources of supply.
5. Once sources have been located, proposals based on the specifications are solicited, received, and analyzed for price, delivery, service, and so on.

6. Proposals are compared with the cost of producing the product in-house in a make-or-buy decision: if it is decided that the buying firm can produce the product more economically, the buying process for the product in question is terminated; however, if the inverse is true, the process continues.
7. A source or sources of supply is selected from those who have submitted proposals.
8. The order is placed, and copies of the purchase order are sent to the originating department, accounting, credit, and any other interested departments within the company.
9. After the product is shipped, received, and used, a follow-up with the originating department is conducted to determine if the purchased product solved the department's problem.

Although there are many variations of this process in actual operation, this is typical of the process by which organizational goods and services are purchased. It must be understood that in actual practice these steps are combined, not separate.

Source: Reproduced from *Business Marketing Management,* Robert W. Hass, 5th ed., p. 174. Reproduced with the permission of South-Western College Publishing. © 1992 PWS-Kent Publishing Co. All rights reserved.

In an *adaptive organization,* there is a moderate commitment, while in a *lethargic organization,* individuals express a strong commitment to traditionally accepted behavior and behave accordingly. Thus, a buyer in a lethargic firm would probably be less innovative in order to maintain acceptance and status within the organization and would keep conflict within the firm to a minimum.

Buyers' perception of their role may differ from the perception of their role held by others in the organization. This difference can result in variance in perception of the proper and the actual purchase responsibility to be held by the buyer. One study involving purchasing agents revealed that, in every firm included in the study, the purchasing agents believed they had more responsibility and control over certain decisions than the other influential purchase decision makers in the firm perceived them as having. The decisions were (1) design of the product, (2) cost of the product, (3) performance life, (4) naming of the specific supplier, (5) assessing the amount of engineering help available from the supplier, and (6) reduction of rejects. This variance in role perception held true regardless of the size of the firm or the significance of the item purchased to the overall success of the firm. It is important, therefore, that the marketer be aware that such perceptual differences may exist and to determine as accurately as possible the amount of control and responsibility over purchasing decisions held by each purchase decision influencer in the firm.

STAGES IN THE BUYING PROCESS

As with consumer buying, most organizational purchases are made in response to a particular need or problem faced by the firm. Recognition of the need, however, is only the first step in the organizational buying process. The following four stages represent one model of the industrial buying process:

1. Problem recognition.
2. Organizational assignment of buying responsibility and authority.
3. Search procedures for identifying product offerings and for establishing selection criteria.
4. Choice procedures for evaluating and selecting among alternatives.

Problem Recognition

As mentioned previously, most organizational purchases are made in response to a particular need or problem. The product purchased is hopefully the means to solve the particular problem. Buyers must be concerned with budgets and profits since the firm cannot put forth a great amount of financial resources if it does not have sufficient funds, regardless of the benefits that might be derived from the purchase. However, as was mentioned, there is more subjective buying and persuasion in the organizational buying process than some earlier writers indicated.

Assignment of Buying Authority

The influence of individuals on the buying decision will be determined in part by their responsibility as defined by the formal organization. An individual's responsibility in a given buying situation will be a function of (1) the technical complexity of the product, (2) the importance of the product to the firm either in dollar terms or in terms of its relationship with the process or system that will use the product, (3) the product-specific technical knowledge that the individual has, and (4) the individual's centrality in the process or system that will use the product.

In some organizations the responsibility for the purchasing decision is assigned to a centralized purchasing unit. When centralization of the buying function occurs, it is usually based on the assumption that knowledge of the market and not knowledge of the physical product itself is the major consideration in the buying decision. Therefore, the purchasing agent will concentrate on such market variables as price, delivery, and seller performance, rather than on the technical aspects of the product.

Search Procedures

This stage involves the search procedures for identifying product offerings and for establishing selection criteria. Basically, buyers perform two key tasks related to the collection and analysis of information. First, the criteria against which to evaluate potential sellers have to be developed. These are usually based on a judgment about what is needed compared to what is available. Second, alternative product candidates must be located in the market. The important point here is that buyers seek sellers just as sellers seek buyers.

Choice Procedures

The final stage in the organizational buying process involves establishing choice procedures for evaluating and selecting among alternatives. Once alternative products and alternative suppliers have been identified, the buyer must choose from among the alternatives. The choice process is guided by the use of decision rules and specific criteria for evaluating the product offering. These decision rules evolve from objectives, policies, and procedures established for buying actions by management. Often some type of rating scheme or value index is used.

These stages in the organizational buying process have particular significance for marketers in their method of approach to potential buyers. This is not to say that these stages are the only activities organizational buyers go through before making a purchase, or that they are even aware that they are going through them. The stages are presented here only as a convenient way to examine the organizational buying process and the importance of certain activities during particular stages.

CONCLUSION

Organizational buying has long been regarded as the stepchild of marketing in terms of the amount of research effort devoted to its problems. However, considerable recent research has been conducted and in this chapter an overview of the organizational buying process has been presented. Basically, the model viewed organizational buying as a process of problem recognition, assignment of buying authority, search procedures, and choice procedures. Purchase-type structural, and behavioral influences were recognized as playing important roles in terms of the speed and complexity of this process.

ADDITIONAL READING

Bingham, Frank G., and Barney T. Raffield III. *Business to Business Marketing Management.*, Homewood, IL: Richard D. Irwin, 1990.

Bunn, Michele. "Taxonomy of Buying Decision Approaches." *Journal of Marketing,* January 1993, pp. 38–56.

Corey, E. Raymond. *Industrial Marketing: Cases and Concepts.*, 4th ed. Englewood Cliffs, NJ: Prentice Hall, 1991.

Drumwright, Minette E. "Socially Responsible Organizational Buying: Environmental Concern as a Noneconomic Buying Criterion." *Journal of Marketing,* July 1994, pp. 1–19.

Eckles, Robert W. *Business Marketing Management,* Englewood Cliffs, NJ: Prentice Hall, 1990.

Perdue, Barbara C., and John O. Summers. "Purchasing Agents' Use of Negotiation Strategies." *Journal of Marketing Research,* May 1991, pp. 175–89.

Ramaswamy, Venkatram; Hubert Gatignon; and David J. Reibstein, "Competitive Marketing Behavior in Industrial Markets." *Journal of Marketing,* April 1994, pp. 45–55.

Sherlock, Paul, *Rethinking Business to Business Marketing.* New York: Free Press, 1991.

Ward, Scott, and Frederick E. Webster, Jr. "Organizational Buying Behavior." In *Handbook of Consumer Behavior,* ed. T. S. Robertson and H. H. Kassarjian. Englewood Cliffs, NJ: Prentice Hall, 1991, pp. 419–58.

Weiss, Allen M., and Jan B. Heide. "The Nature of Organizational Search in High Technology Markets." *Journal of Marketing Research,* May 1993, pp. 220–33.

Wilson, Elizabeth J.; Gary L. Lilien; and David T. Wilson. "Developing and Testing a Contingency Paradigm of Group Choice in Organizational Buying." *Journal of Marketing Research,* November 1991, pp. 452–66.

Chapter 5
MARKET SEGMENTATION

Market segmentation is one of the most important concepts in the marketing literature. In fact, a primary reason for studying consumer and organizational buyer behavior is to provide bases for effective segmentation, and a large portion of marketing research is concerned with segmentation. From a marketing management point of view, selection of the appropriate target market is paramount to developing successful marketing programs.

The logic of market segmentation is quite simple and is based on the idea that a single product item can seldom meet the needs and wants of *all* consumers. Typically, consumers vary as to their needs, wants, and preferences for products and services, and successful marketers adapt their marketing programs to fulfill these preference patterns. For example, even a simple product like chewing gum has multiple flavors, package sizes, sugar contents, calories, consistencies (e.g., liquid centers), and colors to meet the preferences of various consumers. While a single product item cannot meet the needs of all consumers, it can almost always serve more than one consumer. Thus, there are usually *groups of consumers* who can be served well by a single item. If a particular group can be served *profitably* by a firm, it is a viable market segment. In other words, the firm should develop a marketing mix to serve the group or market segment.

In this chapter we consider the process of market segmentation. We define *market segmentation* as the process of dividing a market into groups of similar consumers and selecting the most appropriate group(s) for the firm to serve. We break down the process of market segmentation into six steps, as shown in Figure 5–1. While we recognize that the order of these steps may vary, depending on the firm and situation, there are few if any times when market segmentation analysis can be ignored. In fact, even if the final decision is to "mass market" and not segment at all, this decision should be reached only *after* a market segmentation analysis has been conducted. Thus, market segmentation analysis is a cornerstone of sound marketing planning and decision making.

DELINEATE THE FIRM'S CURRENT SITUATION

As emphasized in Chapter 1, a firm must do a complete situational analysis when embarking on a new or modified marketing program. At the marketing planning level, such an analysis aids in determining objectives, oppor-

Figure 5–1   *A Model of the Market Segmentation Process*

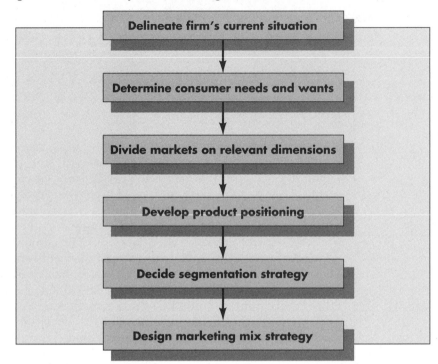

tunities, and constraints to be considered when selecting target markets and developing marketing mixes. In addition, marketing managers must have a clear idea of the amount of financial and other resources that will be available for developing and executing a marketing plan. Thus, the inclusion of this first step in the market segmentation process is intended to be a reminder of tasks to be performed prior to marketing planning.

DETERMINE CONSUMER NEEDS AND WANTS

As emphasized throughout this text, successful marketing strategies depend on discovering and satisfying consumer needs and wants. In some cases, this idea is quite operational. To illustrate, suppose a firm has a good deal of venture capital and is seeking to diversify its interest into new markets. A firm in this situation may seek to discover a broad variety of unsatisfied needs. However, in most situations, the industry in which the firm operates specifies the boundaries of a firm's need satisfaction activities. For example, a firm in the communication industry may seek more efficient methods for serving consumers' long-distance telephone needs.

As a practical matter, new technology often brings about an investigation of consumer needs and wants for new or modified products and services. In these situations, the firm is seeking the group of consumers whose needs could best be satisfied by the new or modified product. Further, at a strategic level, consumer needs and wants usually are translated into more operational concepts. For instance, consumer attitudes, preferences, and benefits sought, which are determined through marketing research, are commonly used for segmentation purposes.

DIVIDE MARKETS ON RELEVANT DIMENSIONS

In a narrow sense, this step is often considered to be the whole of market segmentation (i.e., consumers are grouped on the basis of one or more similarities and treated as a homogeneous segment of a heterogeneous total market). There are three important questions to be considered here:

1. Should the segmentation be a priori or post hoc?
2. How does one determine the relevant dimensions or bases to use for segmentation?
3. What are some bases for segmenting consumer and industrial buyer markets?

A Priori versus Post Hoc Segmentation

Real-world segmentation has followed one of two general patterns. An *a priori segmentation* approach is one in which the marketing manager has decided on the appropriate basis for segmentation in advance of doing any research on a market. For example, a manager may decide that a market should be divided on the basis of whether people are nonusers, light users, or heavy users of a particular product. Segmentation research is then conducted to determine the size of each of these groups and their demographic or psychographic profiles.

Post hoc segmentation is an approach in which people are grouped into segments on the basis of research findings. For example, people interviewed concerning their attitudes or benefits sought in a particular product category are grouped according to their responses. The size of each of these groups and their demographic and psychographic profiles are then determined.

Both of these approaches are valuable, and the question of which to use depends in part on how well the firm knows the market for a particular product class. If through previous research and experience a marketing manager has successfully isolated a number of key market dimensions, then an a priori approach based on them may provide more useful information. In the case of segmentation for entirely new products, a post hoc approach may be useful for determining key market dimensions. However, even when using a post hoc approach, some consideration must be given to the variables to be included in the research design. Thus, some consideration must be given to the relevant segmentation dimensions regardless of which approach is used.

Hitting Target Markets in the 1990s

By combining data from several sources, a company can have extensive information on its target markets and where they shop. Below are examples of the target market profiles for three products and the stores in the New York area where they are most likely to purchase them. Marketers could design special promotions in these stores to further increase the probability of purchase.

Brand	Heavy User Profile	Lifestyle and Media Profile	Top Stores
Peter Pan peanut butter	Households with kids headed by 18–54 year olds, in suburban and rural areas	Heavy video renters Go to theme parks Below average TV viewers Above average radio listeners	Foodtown Super Market Levittown, N.Y. Pathmark Supermarket Levittown, N.Y. King Kullen Market Bethpage, N.Y.
Stouffers Red Box frozen entrees	Households headed by people 55 and older, and up-scale suburban households headed by 35–54 year olds	Go to gambling casinos Give parties Involved in public activities Travel frequently Heavy newspaper readers Above average TV viewers	Dan's Supreme Super Market Flushing, N.Y. Food Emporium New York City Waldbaum Super Market Flushing, N.Y.
Coors Light beer	Head of household, 21–34, middle to upper income, suburban and urban	Belong to a health club Buy rock music Travel by plane Give parties, cookouts Rent videos Heavy TV sports viewers	Food Emporium New York City Gristades Supermarket New York City

Source: The Wall Street Journal, "Marketers Zero in on Their Customers," by Michael J. McCarthy, March 18, 1991, p. B1. © 1991 Dow Jones & Company, Inc. All rights reserved worldwide.

Relevance of Segmentation Dimensions

Unfortunately, there is no simple solution for determining the relevant dimensions for segmenting markets. Certainly, managerial expertise and experience are needed for selecting the appropriate dimensions or bases on which to segment particular markets. In most cases, however, at least some initial dimensions can be determined from previous research, purchase trends, and managerial judgment. For instance, suppose we wish to segment the market for all-terrain vehicles. Clearly, several dimensions come to mind for initial consideration, including sex (male), age (18 to 35 years), lifestyle (outdoorsman), and income level (perhaps $25,000 to $40,000). At a minimum, these variables should be included in subsequent segmentation research. Of course, the most market-oriented approach to segmentation is on the basis of what benefits the potential consumer is seeking. Thus, consideration and research of sought benefits is a strongly recommended approach in the marketing literature. This approach will be considered in some detail in the following section.

Bases for Segmentation

A number of useful bases for segmenting consumer and organizational markets are presented in Figure 5–2. This is by no means a complete list of possible segmentation variables but represents some useful bases and categories. Two commonly used approaches for segmenting markets include benefit segmentation and psychographic segmentation. We will discuss these two in some detail.

Benefit segmentation

The belief underlying this segmentation approach is that the benefits people are seeking in consuming a given product are the basic reasons for the existence of true market segments.[1] Thus, this approach attempts to measure consumer value systems and consumer perceptions of various

Figure 5–2   *Useful Segmentation Bases for Consumer and Organizational Buyer Markets*

Consumer Markets	
Segmentation Base	**Examples of Base Categories**
Geographic:	
Region	Pacific, Mountain, West North Central, West South Central, East North Central, East South Central, South Atlantic, Middle Atlantic, New England
City, county, or SMSA size	Under 5,000; 5,000–19,999; 20,000–49,999; 50,000–99,999; 100,000–249,999; 250,000–499,999; 500,000–999,999; 1,000,000–3,999,999; 4,000,000 or over
Population density	Urban, suburban, rural
Climate	Warm, cold
Demographic:	
Age	Under 6; 6–12; 13–19; 20–29; 30–39; 40–49; 50–59; 60+
Sex	Male, female
Family size	1–2; 3–4; 5+
Family life cycle	Young, single; young, married, no children; young, married, youngest child under 6; young, married, youngest child 6 or over; older married, with children; older, married, no children under 18; older, single; other
Income	Under $10,000; $10,000–$14,999; $15,000–$24,999; $25,000–$34,999; $35,000 or over

Figure 5–2   *(continued)*

	Organizational Buyer Markets
Segmentation Base	**Examples of Base Categories**
Occupation	Professional and technical; managers, officials, and proprietors; clerical, sales; craftsmen, foremen; operatives; farmers; retired; students; housewives, unemployed
Education	Grade school or less; some high school; graduated high school; some college; graduated college; some graduate work; graduate degree
Religion	Catholic, Protestant, Jewish, other
Race	White, black, oriental, other
Nationality	American, British, German, Italian, Japanese, other
Psychographic:	
Social class	Upper Americans, middle class, working class, lower Americans
Lifestyle	Traditionalist, sophisticate, swinger
Personality	Compliant, aggressive, detached
Cognitive and behavioral:	
Attitudes	Positive, neutral, negative
Benefits sought	Convenience, economy, prestige
Readiness stage	Unaware, aware, informed, interested, desirous, intention to purchase
Perceived risk	High, moderate, low
Innovativeness	Innovator, early adopter, early majority, late majority, laggard
Involvement	Low, high
Loyalty status	None, some, total
Usage rate	None, light, medium, heavy
User status	Nonuser, ex-user, potential user, current user
Source loyalty	Purchase from one, two, three, four, or more suppliers
Size of company	Small, medium, large relative to industry
Average size of purchase	Small, medium, large
Usage rate	Light, medium, heavy
Product application	Maintenance, production, final product component, administration
Type of organization	Manufacturer, wholesaler, retailer, government agency
Location	North, East, South, West sales territories
Purchase status	New customer, occasional purchaser, frequent purchaser, nonpurchaser
Attribute importance	Reliability of supply, price, service, durability, convenience, reputation of supplier

brands in a product class. To illustrate, the classic example of a benefit segmentation was provided by Russell Haley and concerned the toothpaste market. Haley identified five basic segments, which are presented in Figure 5–3. Haley argued that this segmentation could be very useful for selecting advertising copy, media, commercial length, packaging, and new product design. For example, colorful packages might be appropriate for the

Figure 5–3   *Toothpaste Market Benefit Segments*

	Sensory Segment	Sociable Segment	Worrier Segment	Independent Segment
Principal benefit sought	Flavor and product appearance	Brightness of teeth	Decay prevention	Price
Demographic strengths	Children	Teens, young people	Large families	Men
Special behavioral characteristics	Users of spearmint-flavored toothpaste	Smokers	Heavy users	Heavy users
Brands disproportionately favored	Colgate	Macleans, Ultra Brite	Crest	Cheapest brand
Lifestyle characteristics	Hedonistic	Active	Conservative	Value-oriented

Source: Adapted from Russell I. Haley, "Benefit Segmentation: A Decision-Oriented Research Tool." *Journal of Marketing,* July 1968, pp. 30–35.

Sensory Segment, perhaps aqua (to indicate fluoride) for the Worrier Group, and gleaming white for the Social Segment because of this segment's interest in white teeth.

Calantone and Sawyer also used a benefit segmentation approach to segment the market for bank services.[2] Their research was concerned with the question of whether benefit segments remain stable across time. While they found some stability in segments, there were some differences in attribute importance, size, and demographics at different times. Thus, they argue for ongoing benefit segmentation research to keep track of any changes in a market that might affect marketing strategy.

Benefit segmentation is clearly a market-oriented approach to segmentation that seeks to identify consumer needs and wants and to satisfy them by providing products and services with the desired benefits. It is clearly very consistent with the approach to marketing suggested by the marketing concept.

Psychographic segmentation

Whereas benefit segmentation focuses on the benefits sought by the consumer, psychographic segmentation focuses on the personal attributes of the consumer. The psychographic or lifestyle approach typically follows a post hoc model of segmentation. Generally, a large number of questions are asked concerning consumers' activities, interests, and opinions, and then consumers are grouped together empirically based on their responses. Although questions have been raised about the validity of this segmentation approach, it provides much useful information about markets.[3]

HIGHLIGHT 5–2

Market Segmentation at Campbell Soup Company

Campbell Soup Company cooked up its own version of market segmentation, which it calls regionalization. Basically, the company divided the United States into 22 regions, each with its own marketing and sales force. Each regional staff studies marketing strategies and media buying and has its own ad and trade-promotion budget.

Regional staffs came up with a number of innovative methods to sell Campbell's products, including:

- In Texas and California, where consumers like their food with a bit of a kick.

Campbell's nacho cheese soup is spicier than in other parts of the country.

- In New York, when the Giants were bound for the Super Bowl, a local sales manager used part of her ad budget to arrange a football-related radio promotion for Swanson frozen dinners.
- In Nevada, Campbell treats skiers at Ski Incline resort to hot samples of its soup of the day.
- In the South, Campbell has experimented with a Creole soup and a red-bean soup for the Hispanic market.

A well-known psychographic segmentation was developed at SRI International in California. The original segmentation divided consumers in the United States into nine groups and was called VALS,™ which stands for "values and lifestyles." However, while this segmentation was commercially successful, it tended to place the majority of consumers into only one or two groups, and SRI felt it needed to be updated to reflect changes in society. Thus, SRI developed a new typology called VALS 2.™[4]

VALS 2 is based on two national surveys of 2,500 consumers who responded to 43 lifestyle questions. The first survey developed the segmentation, and the second validated it and linked it to buying and media behavior. The questionnaire asked consumers to respond to whether they agreed or disagreed with statements such as "My idea of fun at a national park would be to stay at an expensive lodge and dress up for dinner" and "I could stand to skin a dead animal." Consumers were then clustered into the eight groups shown and described in Figure 5–4.

The VALS 2 groups are arranged in a rectangle and are based on two dimensions. The vertical dimension represents resources, which include income, education, self-confidence, health, eagerness to buy, intelligence, and energy level. The horizontal dimension represents self-orientations, and includes three different types. *Principle-oriented consumers* are guided by their views of how the world is or should be; *status-oriented consumers* by the action and opinions of others; and *action-oriented consumers* by a desire for social or physical activity, variety, and risk taking.

Each of the VALS 2 groups represents from 9 to 17 percent of the U.S. adult population. Marketers can buy VALS 2 information for a va-

HIGHLIGHT 5–3

Examples of Items Used in Psychographic Segmentation Research

1. I often watch the newspaper advertisements for announcements of department store sales.
2. I like to watch or listen to baseball or football games.
3. I often try new stores before my friends and neighbors do.
4. I like to work on community projects.

(These items are scored on an "agree strongly" to "disagree strongly" scale.)

5. My children are the most important thing in my life.
6. I will probably have more money to spend next year than I have now.
7. I often seek out the advice of my friends regarding which store to buy from.
8. I think I have more self-confidence than most people.
9. I enjoy going to symphony concerts.
10. It is good to have charge accounts.

riety of products and can have it tied to a number of other consumer databases.

DEVELOP PRODUCT POSITIONING

By this time the firm should have a good idea of the basic segments of the market that could potentially be satisfied with its product. The current step is concerned with positioning the product in the minds of consumers relative to competing products. Undoubtedly, the classic example of positioning is the 7UP "Uncola" campaign. Prior to this campaign, 7UP had difficulty convincing consumers that the product could be enjoyed as a soft drink and not just as a mixer. Consumers believed that colas were soft drinks but apparently did not perceive 7UP in this way. However, by positioning 7UP as the "Uncola" the company was capable of positioning the product (1) as a soft drink that could be consumed in the same situations as colas and (2) as an alternative to colas. This positioning was very successful.

In determining the appropriate positioning of the product, the firm must consider its offering relative to competition. Some experts argue that different positioning strategies should be used depending on whether the firm is the market leader or a follower, and that followers usually should not attempt positioning directly against the industry leader.[5] While there are many sophisticated research tools available for investigating positioning, they are beyond the scope of this text. The main point here is that, in segmenting markets, some segments otherwise appearing to be approachable might be forgone, since competitive products may already dominate that segment in sales and in the minds of consumers. Product positioning studies are useful for giving the marketing manager a clearer idea of consumer perceptions of market offerings and for selecting appropriate attributes for positioning products or stores.

Figure 5–4   *VALS 2™ Eight American Lifestyles*

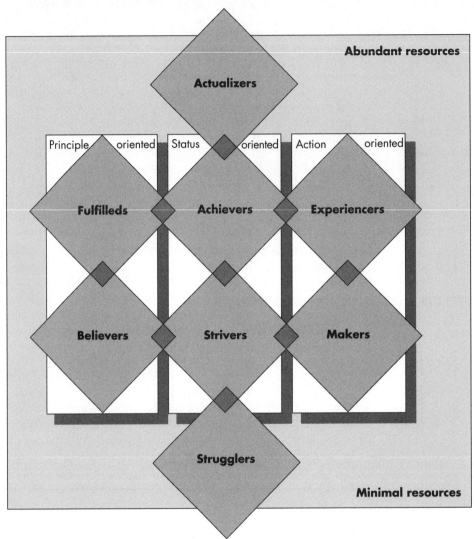

DECIDE SEGMENTATION STRATEGY

The firm is now ready to select its segmentation strategy. There are four basic alternatives. First, the firm may decide not to enter the market. For example, analysis to this stage may reveal there is no viable market niche for the firm's offering. Second, the firm may decide not to segment but to be a mass marketer. There are at least three situations when this may be the appropriate decision for the firm:

HIGHLIGHT 5–4

Target Markets for Three Chrysler Corporation Cars

Marketers often use a variety of segmentation dimensions to understand and describe their target markets. Below is a description of a profile of the most likely buyers Chrysler Corporation found for three of its models, the Chrysler Concorde, Eagle Vision, and Dodge Intrepid. The Concorde is the most expensive model and the Intrepid is the least expensive.

Targets for the Concorde

Family status: Married, two children between the ages of 20 and 25.
Education: Four-year college.
Income and occupation: $52,000 (median). He is a commodities broker who has worked 25 years for the same firm. She is a homemaker.
Media habits: Lots of prime-time TV. Read *House and Garden, TV Guide.* Got VCR two years ago, but still can't program it.

First important car:
His: '57 Chevy; **Hers:** '60 Impala

Vacation habits: Winter at Florida time-share, summer at friends' home on the lake.

Habitat: Colonial home in a suburban subdivision outside Philadelphia.
Leisure time: He has a wood shop; she gardens. They dance to oldies or big band music at least once a month.

. . . For the Vision

Family status: Married, two children under the age of 10.
Education: Graduate school.
Income and occupation: $50,000 (median). He sells commercial real estate. She develops computer software.
Media habits: Critical of most TV. Read *Vanity Fair.* Car radio preselects are jazz, classical, public radio.

First important car:
His: BMW 2002; **Hers:** Alfa Romeo Spider

Vacation habits: Three annually, one at family resort; one without kids at a semi-obscure location; third at home catching up on projects.
Habitat: Renovated 1930s home in northern Chicago suburb.
Leisure time: Work out twice a week at health club, rent videos, collect Art Deco objects and furniture.

. . . For the Intrepid

Family status: Married, up to three kids ranging in age from 6 to 16.
Education: 2 to 4 years of college.
Income and occupation: $35,000 to $75,000 range. He installs computer systems. She is a nurse, paralegal, or homemaker.
Media habits: Moderate TV, family shows and sports. Read how-to, investing magazines, and about participant sports like golf or fishing.

First important car:
His and Hers: Mustangs.

Vacation habits: Two family-centered vacations, one to destinations like Disney World or big cities, the other for camping and backpacking.
Habitat: Split-level home in newer suburbs around the country.
Leisure time: Split between participant sports like softball, and family activities like Boy or Girl Scouts.

Source: Doron P. Levin, "Chrysler's New L/H, as in Last Hope," *The New York Times,* July 12, 1992, p. 6F.

1. The market is so small that marketing to a portion of it is not profitable.
2. Heavy users make up such a large proportion of the sales volume that they are the only relevant target.
3. The brand is the dominant brand in the market, and targeting to a few segments would not benefit sales and profits.

Third, the firm may decide to market to one segment. And fourth, the firm may decide to market to more than one segment and design a separate marketing mix for each. In any case, the firm must have some criteria on which to base its segmentation strategy decisions. Three important criteria on which to base such decisions are that a viable segment must be (1) measurable, (2) meaningful, and (3) marketable.

1. *Measurable.* For a segment to be selected, the firm must be capable of measuring its size and characteristics. For instance, one of the difficulties with segmenting on the basis of social class is that the concept and its divisions are not clearly defined and measured. Alternatively, income is a much easier concept to measure.
2. *Meaningful.* A meaningful segment is one that is large enough to have sufficient sales potential and growth potential to offer long-run profits for the firm.
3. *Marketable.* A marketable segment is one that can be reached and served by the firm in an efficient manner.

Segments that meet these criteria are viable markets for the firm's offering. The firm must now give further attention to completing its marketing mix offering.

HIGHLIGHT 5–5

Segmentation Bases for Particular Marketing Decision Areas

For general understanding of the market:
Benefits sought
Product purchase and usage patterns
Needs
Brand loyalty and switching patterns
A hybrid of the variables above

For positioning studies:
Product usage
Product preference
Benefits sought
A hybrid of the variables above

For new product concepts (and new product introduction):
Reaction to new concepts (intention to buy, preference over current brand, and so on)
Benefits sought

For pricing decisions:
Price sensitivity
Deal proneness
Price sensitivity by purchase/usage patterns

For advertising decisions:
Benefits sought
Media usage
Psychographic/lifestyle
A hybrid (of the variables above or purchase/usage pattern, or both)

For distribution decisions:
Store loyalty and patronage
Benefits sought in store selection

Source: Yoram Wind, "Issues and Advances in Segmentation Research," *Journal of Marketing Research,* August 1978, p. 320.

			Multiple
Strategy Elements	**Mass Marketing**	**Single Market Segmentation**	**Market Segmentation**
Market definition	Broad range of consumers	One well-defined consumer group	Two or more well-defined consumer groups
Product strategy	Limited number of products under one brand for many types of consumers	One brand tailored to one consumer group	Distinct brand for each consumer group
Pricing strategy	One "popular" price range	One price range tailored to the consumer group	Distinct price range for each consumer group
Distribution strategy	All possible outlets	All suitable outlets	All suitable outlets—differs by segment
Promotion strategy	Mass media	All suitable media	All suitable media—differs by segment
Strategy emphasis	Appeal to various types of consumers through a uniform, broad-based marketing program	Appeal to one specific consumer group through a highly specialized, but uniform, marketing program	Appeal to two or more distinct market segments through different marketing plans catering to each segment

HIGHLIGHT 5–6
Differences in Marketing Strategy for Three Segmentation Alternatives

Source: Marketing, 5th ed., by Joel R. Evans and Barry Berman (New York: Macmillan, 1992), p. 219. © 1992. Reprinted by permission of Prentice-Hall, Inc., Upper Saddle River, NJ.

DESIGN MARKETING MIX STRATEGY

The firm is now in a position to complete its marketing plan by finalizing the marketing mix or mixes to be used for each segment. Clearly, selection of the target market and designing the marketing mix go hand in hand, and thus many marketing mix decisions should have already been carefully considered. To illustrate, the target market selected may be price sensitive, so some consideration has already been given to price levels, and clearly product positioning has many implications for promotion and channel decisions. Thus, while we place marketing mix design at the end of the model, many of these decisions are clearly made in *conjunction* with target market selection. In the next six chapters of this text, marketing mix decisions will be discussed in detail.

CONCLUSION

The purpose of this chapter was to provide an overview of market segmentation. Market segmentation was defined as the process of dividing a market into groups of similar consumers and selecting the most appropriate group(s) for the firm to serve. Market segmentation was analyzed as a six-stage process: (1) to delineate the firm's current situation; (2) to determine consumer needs and wants; (3) to divide the market on relevant dimensions; (4) to develop product positioning; (5) to decide segmentation strategy; (6) to design marketing mix strategy.

ADDITIONAL READINGS

Anderson, Eugene W., and Steven M. Shugan. "Repositioning for Changing Preferences: The Case of Beef versus Poultry." *Journal of Consumer Research,* September 1991, pp. 219–32.

Chintagunta, Pradeep K. "Heterogeneous Logit Model Implications for Brand Positioning." *Journal of Marketing Research,* May 1994, pp. 304–11.

Dickson, Peter R., and James L. Ginter. "Market Segmentation, Product Differentiation, and Marketing Strategy." *Journal of Marketing,* April 1987, pp. 1–10.

Green, Paul E., and Abba M. Krieger. "Segmenting Markets with Conjoint Analysis." *Journal of Marketing,* October 1991, pp. 20–31.

Gupta, Sachin, and Pradeep K. Chintagunta. "On Using Demographic Variables to Determine Segment Membership in Logit Mixture Models." *Journal of Marketing Research,* February 1994, pp. 128–36.

Kamakura, Wagner A., and Thomas P. Kovak. "Value-System Segmentation: Exploring the Meaning of LOV." *Journal of Consumer Research,* June 1992, pp. 119–32.

Novak, Thomas P.; Jan de Leeuw; and Bruce MacEvoy. "Richness Curves for Evaluating Market Segmentation." *Journal of Marketing Research,* May 1992, pp. 254–67.

Pechmann, Cornelia, and S. Ratneshwar. "The Use of Comparative Advertising for Brand Positioning: Association versus Differentiation." *Journal of Consumer Research,* September 1991, pp. 145–60.

Rangan, V. Kasturi; Rowland T. Moriarty; and Gordon S. Swartz. "Segmenting Customers in Mature Industrial Markets." *Journal of Marketing,* October 1992, pp. 72–82.

Part C

THE MARKETING MIX

Chapter 6
PRODUCT STRATEGY

Product strategy is a critical element of marketing and business strategy, since it is through the sale of products and services that companies survive and grow. This chapter discusses four important areas of concern in developing product strategies. First, some basic issues are discussed, including product definition, product classification, product quality and value, product mix and product line, branding and brand equity, and packaging. Second, the product life cycle and its implications for product strategy are explained. Third, the product audit is reviewed, and finally, five ways to organize for product management are outlined. These include the marketing manager system, product (brand) manager system, product planning committee, new product manager system, and venture team approaches.

BASIC ISSUES IN PRODUCT MANAGEMENT

Successful marketing depends on understanding the nature of products and basic decision areas in product management. In this section, we discuss the definition and classification of products, the importance of product quality and value, and the nature of a product mix and product lines. Also considered is the role of branding and packaging.

Product Definition

The way in which the product variable is defined can have important implications for the survival, profitability, and long-run growth of the firm. For example, the same product can be viewed at least three different ways. First, it can be viewed in terms of the tangible product—the physical entity or service that is offered to the buyer. Second, it can be viewed in terms of the extended product—the tangible product along with the whole cluster of services that accompany it. For example, a manufacturer of computer software may offer a 24-hour hotline to answer questions users may have, free or reduced-cost software updates, free replacement of damaged software, and a subscription to a newsletter that documents new applications of the software. Third, it can be viewed in terms of the generic product—the essential benefits the buyer expects to receive from the product. For example, many personal care products bring to the purchaser feelings of self-enhancement and security in addition to the tangible benefits they offer.

HIGHLIGHT 6–1

Elements of Product Strategy

1. *An audit of the firm's actual and potential resources*
   a. Financial strength
   b. Access to raw materials
   c. Plant and equipment
   d. Operating personnel
   e. Management
   f. Engineering and technical skills
   g. Patents and licenses
2. *Approaches to current markets*
   a. More of the same products
   b. Variations of present products in terms of grades, sizes, and packages

   c. New products to replace or supplement current lines
   d. Product deletions
3. *Approaches to new or potential markets*
   a. Geographical expansion of domestic sales
   b. New socioeconomic or ethnic groups
   c. Overseas markets
   d. New uses of present products
   e. Complementary goods
   f. Mergers and acquisitions
4. *State of competition*
   a. New entries into the industry
   b. Product imitation

From the standpoint of the marketing manager, to define the product solely in terms of the tangible product is to fall into the error of "marketing myopia." Executives who are guilty of committing this error define their company's product too narrowly, since they overemphasize the physical object itself. The classic example of this mistake can be found in railroad passenger service. Although no amount of product improvement could have staved off its decline, if the industry had defined itself as being in the transportation business, rather than the railroad business, it might still be profitable today. On the positive side, toothpaste manufacturers have been willing to exercise flexibility in defining their product. For years toothpaste was an oral hygiene product where emphasis was placed solely on fighting tooth decay and bad breath (e.g., Crest with fluoride). More recently, many manufacturers have recognized the need to market toothpaste as a cosmetic item (to clean teeth of stains), as a defense against gum disease (to reduce the buildup of tartar above the gumline), as an aid for denture wearers, and as a breath freshener. As a result, special purpose brands have been designed to serve these particular needs, such as Ultra Brite, Close-Up, Aqua-Fresh, Aim, Dental Care, and the wide variety of baking soda, tartar-control formula, and gel toothpastes offered under existing brand names.

In line with the marketing concept philosophy, a reasonable definition of product is that it is *the sum of the physical, psychological, and sociological satisfactions the buyer derives from purchase, ownership, and consumption.* From this standpoint, products are consumer-satisfying objects that include such things as accessories, packaging, and service.

Product Classification

A product classification scheme can be useful to the marketing manager as an analytical device to assist in planning marketing strategy and programs. A basic assumption underlying such classifications is that products with common attributes can be marketed in a similar fashion. In general, products are classed according to two basic criteria: (1) end use or market; and (2) degree of processing or physical transformation.

1. *Agricultural products and raw materials.* These are goods grown or extracted from the land or sea, such as iron ore, wheat, sand. In general these products are fairly homogeneous, sold in large volume, and have low value per unit or bulk weight.

2. *Organizational goods.* Such products are purchased by business firms for the purpose of producing other goods or for running the business. This category includes the following:
    a. Raw materials and semifinished goods
    b. Major and minor equipment, such as basic machinery, tools, and other processing facilities.
    c. Parts or components, which become an integral element of some other finished good.
    d. Supplies or items used to operate the business but that do not become part of the final product.

3. *Consumer goods.* Consumer goods can be divided into three classes:
    a. Convenience goods, such as food, which are purchased frequently with minimum effort. Impulse goods would also fall into this category.
    b. Shopping goods, such as appliances, which are purchased after some time and energy are spent comparing the various offerings.
    c. Specialty goods, which are unique in some way so the consumer will make a special purchase effort to obtain them.

In general, the buying motive, buying habits, and character of the market are different for organizational goods vis-à-vis consumer goods. A primary purchasing motive for organizational goods is, of course, profit. As mentioned in a previous chapter, organizational goods are usually purchased as means to an end, and not as an end in themselves. This is another way of saying that the demand for goods is a derived demand. Organizational goods are often purchased directly from the original source with few middlemen, because many of these goods can be bought in large quantities; they have high unit value; technical advice on installation and use is required; and the product is ordered according to the user's specifications. Many organizational goods are subject to multiple-purchase influence and a long period of negotiation is often required.

The market for organizational goods has certain attributes that distinguish it from the consumer goods market. Much of the market is concentrated geographically, as in the case of steel, auto, or shoe manufacturing.

A. Classes of Consumer Goods—Some Characteristics and Marketing Considerations

Characteristics and Marketing Considerations	Type of Product		
	Convenience	Shopping	Specialty
Characteristics:			
Time and effort devoted by consumer to shopping	Very little	Considerable	Cannot generalize; consumer may go to nearby store and buy with minimum effort or may have to go to distant store and spend much time and effort
Time spent planning the purchase	Very little	Considerable	Considerable
How soon want is satisfied after it arises	Immediately	Relatively long time	Relatively long time
Are price and quality compared?	No	Yes	No
Price	Usually low	High	High
Frequency of purchase	Usually frequent	Infrequent	Infrequent
Importance	Unimportant	Often very important	Cannot generalize
Marketing considerations:			
Length of channel	Long	Short	Short to very short
Importance of retailer	Any single store is relatively unimportant	Important	Very important
Number of outlets	As many as possible	Few	Few; often only one in a market
Stock turnover	High	Lower	Lower
Gross margin	Low	High	High
Responsibility for advertising	Producer's	Retailer's	Joint responsibility
Importance of point-of-purchase display	Very important	Less important	Less important
Brand or store name important	Brand name	Store name	Both
Importance of packaging	Very important	Less important	Less important

Source: William J. Stanton, Michael J. Etzel, and Bruce J. Walker, *Fundamentals of Marketing,* 9th ed. © 1991, New York, McGraw-Hill, Inc., pp. 171, 174. Reproduced by permission of The McGraw-Hill Companies.

Type of Product

Characteristics and Marketing Considerations	Raw Materials	Fabricating Parts and Materials	Installations	Accessory Equipment	Operating Supplies
Example:	Iron ore	Engine blocks	Blast furnaces	Storage racks	Paper clips
Characteristics:					
Unit price	Very low	Low	Very high	Medium	Low
Length of life	Very short	Depends on final product	Very long	Long	Short
Quantities purchased	Large	Large	Very small	Small	Small
Frequency of purchase	Frequent delivery; long-term purchase contract	Infrequent purchase, but frequent delivery	Very infrequent	Medium frequency	Frequent
Standardization of competitive products	Very much; grading is important	Very much	Very little; custom-made	Little	Much
Quantity of supply	Limited; supply can be increased slowly or not at all	Usually no problem	No problem	Usually no problem	Usually no problem
Marketing considerations:					
Nature of channel	Short; no middlemen	Short; middlemen for small buyers	Short; no middlemen	Middlemen used	Middlemen used
Negotiation period	Hard to generalize	Medium	Long	Medium	Short
Price competition	Important	Important	Not important	Not main factor	Important
Presale/postsale service	Not important	Important	Very important	Important	Very little
Promotional activity	Very little	Moderate	Sales people very important	Important	Not too important
Brand preference	None	Generally low	High	High	Low
Advance buying contract	Important; long-term contracts used	Important; long-term contracts used	Not usually used	Not usually used	Not usually used

For certain products there are a limited number of buyers; this is known as a *vertical market,* which means that *(a)* it is narrow, because customers are restricted to a few industries; and *(b)* it is deep, in that a large percentage of the producers in the market use the product. Some products, such as office supplies, have a *horizontal market,* which means that the goods are purchased by all types of firms in many different industries. In general, buyers of organizational goods are reasonably well informed. As noted previously, heavy reliance is often placed on price, quality control, and reliability of supply source.

In terms of consumer products, many marketing scholars have found the convenience, shopping, and specialty classification inadequate and have attempted to either refine it or to derive an entirely new typology. None of these attempts appears to have met with complete success. Perhaps there is no "best" way to deal with this problem. From the standpoint of the marketing manager, product classification is useful to the extent that it assists in providing guidelines for developing an appropriate marketing mix. For example, convenience goods generally require broadcast promotion and long channels of distribution as opposed to shopping goods, which generally require more targeted promotion and somewhat shorter channels of distribution.

Product Quality and Value

Quality can be defined as the degree of excellence or superiority that an organization's product possesses.[1] Quality can encompass both the tangible and intangible aspects of a firm's products and/or services. In a technical sense, quality can refer to physical traits such as features, performance, reliability, durability, aesthetics, serviceability, and conformance to specifications. Although quality can be evaluated from many perspectives, the customer is the key perceiver of quality because his/her purchase decision determines the success of the organization's product or service and often the fate of the organization itself.

Many organizations have formalized their interest in providing quality products by undertaking Total Quality Management (TQM) programs. TQM is an organizationwide commitment to satisfying customers by continuously improving every business process involved in delivering products or services. Instead of merely correcting defects when they occur, organizations that practice TQM train and commit employees to continually look for ways to do things better so defects and problems don't arise in the first place. The result of this process is higher quality products being produced at a lower cost.[2] Indeed, the emphasis on quality has risen to such a level that over 70 countries have adopted the ISO 9000 quality system of standards, a standardized approach for evaluating a supplier's quality system, which can be applied to virtually any business.[3]

The term quality is often confused with the concept of value. Value encompasses not only quality but also price. Value can be defined as what the customer gets in exchange for what the customer gives. In other words, a customer, in most cases, receives a product in exchange for having paid the supplier for the product. A customer's perception of the value associated with a product is generally based both on the degree to which the product meets his or her specifications and the price that the customer will have to pay to acquire the product. Some organizations are beginning to shift their primary focus from one that solely emphasizes quality to one that also equally encompasses the customer's viewpoint of the price/quality tradeoff. Organizations that are successful at this process derive their competitive advantage from the provision of customer value. In other words, they offer goods and services that meet or exceed customer needs at a fair price. Recall that Chapter 1 described various strategies based on value disciplines.

Product Mix and Product Line

The *product mix* is the composite of products offered for sale by the firm; *product line* refers to a group of products that are closely related, either because they satisfy a class of need, are used together, are sold to the same customer groups, are marketed through the same types of outlets, or fall within given price ranges. There are three primary dimensions of a firm's product mix: (1) width of the product mix, which refers to the number of product lines the firm handles; (2) depth of the product mix, which refers to the average number of products in each line; and (3) consistency of the product mix, which refers to the similarity of product lines. Thus, McDonald's hamburgers represent a product item in its line of sandwiches, whereas hotcakes or Egg McMuffins represent items in a different line, namely, breakfast foods.

Development of a plan for the existing product line has been called the most critical element of a company's product planning activity.[4] In designing such plans, management needs accurate information on the current and anticipated performance of its products, which should encompass:

1. Consumer evaluation of the company's products, particularly their strengths and weaknesses vis-à-vis competition (i.e., product positioning by market segment information).
2. Objective information on actual and anticipated product performance on relevant criteria, such as sales, profits, and market share.[5]

An integral component of product line planning revolves around the question of how many product variants should be included in the line.[6] Manufacturing costs are usually minimized through large-volume production runs, and distribution costs tend to be lower if only one product is sold, stocked, and serviced. At a given level of sales, profits will usually be highest if those sales have been achieved with a single product. However, many product variants are offered by many firms.

There are three reasons why organizations offer varying products within a given product line. First, potential customers rarely agree on a single set of specifications regarding their "ideal product," differing greatly in the importance and value they place on specific attributes. For example, in the laundry detergent market, there is a marked split between preferences for powder versus liquid detergent. Second, customers prefer variety. For example, a person may like Italian food, but does not want to only eat spaghetti. Therefore, an Italian restaurant will offer the customer a wide variety of Italian dishes to choose from. Third, the dynamics of competition lead to multiproduct lines. As competitors seek to increase market share, they find it advantageous to introduce new products that subsegment an existing market segment by offering benefits more precisely tailored to the specific needs of a portion of that segment. For example, Proctor & Gamble offers Jif peanut butter in a low-salt version to target a specific subsegment of the peanut butter market.

All too often, organizations pursue product line additions with little regard for consequences.[7] However, in reaching a decision on product line additions, organizations need to evaluate whether (1) total profits will decrease and/or (2) the quality/value associated with current products will suffer. If the answer to either of the above is yes, then the organization should not proceed with the addition. Closely related to product line additions are issues associated with branding. These are covered next.

Branding and Brand Equity

For some organizations, the primary focus of strategy development is placed on brand building, developing, and nurturing activities.[8] Many other companies use branding strategies in order to increase the strength of the product image. Factors that serve to increase the brand image strength include[9] (1) product quality when products do what they do very well (e.g., Windex and Easy-Off); (2) consistent advertising and other marketing communications in which brands tell their story often and well (e.g., Pepsi and Visa); (3) distribution intensity whereby customers see the brand wherever they shop (e.g., Marlboro); and (4) brand personality where the brand stands for something (e.g., Disney). The strength of the Coca-Cola brand, for example, is widely attributed to its universal availability, universal awareness, and trademark protection, which came as a result of strategic actions taken by the parent organization.[10]

The brand name is perhaps the single most important element on the package, serving as a unique identifier. Specifically, a *brand* is a name, term, design, symbol, or any other feature that identifies one seller's good or service as distinct from those of other sellers. The legal term for brand is *trade-*

mark.[11] A good brand name can evoke feelings of trust, confidence, security, strength, and many other desirable characteristics.[12] To illustrate, consider the case of Bayer Aspirin. Bayer can be sold at up to two times the price of generic aspirin due to the strength of its brand image.

Many companies make use of manufacturer branding strategies in carrying out market and product development strategies. The *line extension* approach uses a brand name to facilitate entry into a new market segment (e.g., Diet Coke and Liquid Tide). An alternative to line extension is brand extension. In *brand extension,* a current brand name is used to enter a completely different product class (e.g., Jello pudding pops, Ivory shampoo).[13]

A third form of branding is *franchise extension* or *family branding* whereby a company attaches the corporate name to a product either to enter a new market segment or a different product class (e.g., Honda lawnmower, Toyota Lexus). A final type of branding strategy that is becoming more and more common is dual branding. A *dual branding* (also known as joint or co-branding) strategy is one in which two or more branded products are integrated (e.g., Bacardi Rum and Coca-Cola, Archway cookies and Kellogg cereal, USAIR and Nationsbank Visa).[14] The logic behind this strategy is that if one brand name on a product gives a certain signal of quality, then the presence of a second brand name on the product should result in a signal that is at least as powerful, if not more powerful than, the signal in the case of the single brand name. Each of the above four approaches is an attempt by companies to gain a competitive advantage by making use of its and/or others' established reputation.

Companies may also choose to assign different or multiple brand names to related products. By doing so, the firm makes a conscious decision to allow the products to succeed or fail on their own merits. Major advantages of using multiple brand names are that 1) the firm can distance products from other offerings it markets; 2) the image of one product (or set of products) is not associated with other products the company markets; 3) the product(s) can be targeted at a specific market segment; and 4) should the product(s) fail, the probability of failure impacting on other company products is minimized. For example, many consumers are unaware that Dreft, Tide, Oxydol, Bold, Cheer, and Dash laundry detergents are all marketed by Proctor & Gamble. The major disadvantage of this strategy is that because new names are assigned, there is no consumer brand awareness and significant amounts of money must be spent familiarizing customers with new brands.

Increasingly, companies are finding that brand names are one of the most valuable assets they possess. Successful extensions of an existing brand can lead to additional loyalty and associated profits. Conversely, a wrong extension can cause damaging associations, as perceptions linked to the brand name are transferred back from one product to the other.[15] *Brand equity* can be viewed as the set of assets (or liabilities) linked to the brand that add (or subtract) value.[16] The value of these assets is dependent upon the consequences or results of the marketplace's relationship with a brand. Figure 6–1 lists the elements of brand equity. Brand equity is determined by the consumer and is the culmination of the consumer's assessment of the product, the company that manufactures and markets the product, and all other variables that impact on the product between manufacture and consumer consumption. Highlight 6–3 lists the 25 most valuable brands in the world.

Before leaving the topic of manufacturer brands, it is important to note that, as with consumer products, organizational products also can possess brand equity. However, several differences do exist between the two sectors.[17] First, organizational products are usually branded with firm names. As a result, loyalty (or disloyalty) to the brand tends to be of a more global nature, extending across all the firm's product lines. Second, because firm versus brand loyalty exists, attempts to position new products in a manner

Figure 6–1 *Elements of Brand Equity*

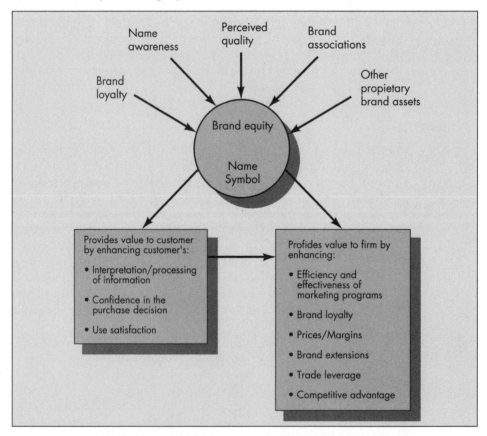

Source: Reprinted with the permission of The Free Press, a division of Simon & Schuster from *Managing Brand Equity* by David A. Aaker. © 1991, New York, by David A. Aaker.

HIGHLIGHT 6–3

25 Most Valuable Brands (Based on Quality)

Rank	Brand Name	Quality Score
1	Kodak photographic film	8.34
2	Disney World	8.26
3	Mercedes-Benz automobiles	8.21
4	Disneyland	8.13
5	Hallmark greeting cards	8.11
6	Fisher-Price toys	8.09
7	Levi's jeans	8.08
8	UPS	8.01
9	Arm & Hammer baking soda	7.99
10	Reynolds Wrap aluminum foil	7.97
11	Ziploc bags	7.95
12	Craftsman power tools	7.95
13	Duracell batteries	7.90
14	Lego toys	7.90
15	Lexus automobiles	7.89
16	IBM personal computers	7.87
17	AT&T Long Distance service	7.84
18	Hershey's Milk Chocolate candy bars	7.76
19	Rubbermaid household products	7.73
20	FedEx	7.72
21	Michelin automobile tires	7.69
22	Playskool toys	7.69
23	BMW automobiles	7.67
24	Tylenol pain reliever	7.67
25	Universal Studios Florida	7.66

Brand rankings are based on a large survey of U.S. consumers asked to rate each brand name according to their perception of brand quality. The survey uses a scale from 0 (poor quality) to 10 (exceptional quality). The total responses are then averaged to yield the quality score.

Source: T. L. Stanley, "How They Rate," *Brandweek*, April 3, 1995, pp. 45–48. © 1995 ASM Communications, Inc. Used with permission from *Brandweek*.

differing from existing products may prove to be difficult, if not impossible. Finally, loyalty to organizational products encompasses not only the firm and its products, but also the distribution channel members employed to distribute the product. Therefore, attempts to establish or change brand image must also take into account distributor image.

As a related branding strategy, many retail firms produce and/or market their products under a so-called private label.[18] For example, Kmart has phased in its own store-brand products to compete with the national brands. There's Nature's Classics, a line of fancy snacks and cookies; Oral Pure, a line of dental care products; Prevail house cleaners; B.E., a Gap-style line of weekend wear; and Benchmark, a line of "made in the U.S.A." tools. Such a strategy is highly important in industries where the middleman has

HIGHLIGHT 6-4

Top Five Brands in Major Product Categories

Potato Chips	Market Share	Pretzels	Market Share
Lay's	20.0%	Rold Gold	20.6%
Ruffles	18.8%	Snyder's of Hanover	15.1%
Pringles	8.7%	Private Label	8.2%
Private Label	7.4%	Eagle	6.3%
Eagle Thins	6.7%	Mister Salty	5.3%
Tortilla Chips		**Popcorn (unpopped)**	
Doritos	39.0%	Orville Redenbacher	42.2%
Tostitos	25.1%	Betty Crocker	29.6%
Eagle	5.5%	Private Label	12.4%
Private Labels	4.8%	Jolly Time	5.7%
Santitas	4.3%	Cousin Willies	1.6%

Source: "Snack Numbers," *Brandweek*, March 27, 1995, p. 40. © 1995 ASM Communications, Inc. Used with permission from *Brandweek*.

Soft Drinks	Market Share	Regular Coffee	Market Share
Coke Classic	20.4%	Folgers Regular	22.3%
Pepsi	17.8%	Maxwell House Regular	15.2%
Diet Coke	8.8%	Masterblend	7.6%
Dr. Pepper	6.4%	Hills Brothers	7.3%
Diet Pepsi	5.7%	Folgers Flakes	4.6%
Ready-to-Drink (RTD) Teas		**Instant Coffee**	
Lipton (Pepsi)	31.4%	Folgers Regular	19.6%
Snapple (Quaker Oats)	25.7%	Maxwell House Regular	16.1%
Nestea (Coke)	21.7%	Taster's Choice Regular	10.5%
Arizona	10.0%	Nescafe Regular	7.2%
All Others	11.2%	Folgers Decaf	6.6%

Source: Sam Bradley, "Beverage . . . by the Numbers," *Brandweek*, April 17, 1995, p. 48. © 1995 ASM Communications, Inc. Used with permission from *Brandweek*. John C. Maxwell, "Specialty Coffee Brews Gains as Total Sales Fall," *Advertising Age*, June 5, 1995, p. 43. Reprinted with permission from *Advertising Age*, June 5, 1995, © Crain Communications, Inc. All rights reserved.

gained control over distribution to the consumer. The growth of the large discount and specialty stores, such as Kmart, Wal-Mart, Target, The Gap, Limited, and others has accelerated the development of private brands. If a manufacturer refuses to supply certain middlemen with private branded merchandise, the alternative is for these middlemen to go into the manufacturing business, as in the case of Kroger supermarkets.

Private label products differ markedly from so-called generic products that sport labels such as "beer," "cigarettes," and "potato chips." Today's house brands are packaged in distinctively upscale containers. The quality of the products utilized as house brands equals and sometimes exceeds those offered by name brands. Indeed, the number of consumers who say that store brands are equal to or better than manufacturer brands has increased steadily in the last decade.[19] While generic products were positioned as a means for consumers to struggle through recessionary times, private label brands are being marketed as value brands, products that are equivalent to national brands but are priced much lower. Private brands are rapidly growing in popularity. For example, it only took J. C. Penney five years to nurture its private label jeans, the Arizona brand, into a powerhouse with annual sales surpassing $500 million. Recently, sales of private label grocery products in the United States exceeded $30 billion and are continuing to grow.[20] The popularity of private label products is not confined to the United States. In the United Kingdom, sales of private label products have claimed 31 percent of grocery store sales, while in Canada, 21 percent of all grocery products sold are marketed under a private label banner.[21]

Consolidation within the supermarket industry, growth of "super centers," and heightened product marketing are poised to strengthen private brands even further.[22] However, these gains will not come without a fight from national manufacturers who are undertaking aggressive actions to defend their brands' market share. Some have significantly rolled back prices while others have instituted increased promotional campaigns. The ultimate winner in this ongoing battle between private (store) and manufacturer (national) brands, not surprisingly, should be the consumer who is able to play off these store brands against national brands. By shopping at a mass merchandiser like Wal-Mart or Walgreens, consumers are exposed to and able to choose from a wide array of both national and store brands, thus giving them the best of both worlds: value and variety.

Packaging

Distinctive or unique packaging is one method of differentiating a relatively homogeneous product. To illustrate, shelf-stable microwave dinners, pumps rather than tubes of toothpaste or bars of soap, and different sizes and designs of tissue packages are attempts to differentiate a product through packaging and to satisfy consumer needs at the same time.

In some cases, companies have begun utilizing packaging strategies to strengthen their brands by updating the look. For example, in the cold pill product segment, there are over 240 varieties of products consumers can choose from.[23] SmithKline Beecham, the maker of Contac, saw its share of this market had been slipping steadily. To combat increasing competition, especially from private brands, SmithKline decided to radically redesign the package. The formerly white background is now blue, with the color growing darker from the bottom of the box to the top. A clock in the bottom right corner, indicating 12-hour relief was replaced by a globe, also meant to represent the passage of time. The Contac logo was maintained but underneath it was placed a yellow banner that indicated what cold symptoms each formula is for. There were two equally important net results of these changes. First, the new packaging made it very obvious to the consumer that they were purchasing the Contac brand. Second, due to all the color schemes, the package was very expensive to replicate, thus decreasing the likelihood of a look-alike private brand emerging.

In other cases, packaging changes have succeeded in creating new attributes of value in a brand. A growing number of manufacturers are using green labels or packaging their products totally in green wrap to signify low or no fat content.[24] Frito-Lay, Quaker Oats, ConAgra, Keebler, Pepperidge Farm, Nabisco, and Sunshine Biscuits are all examples of companies involved in this endeavor.

Finally, packaging changes can make products urgently salable to a targeted segment. For example, the products in the Gillette Series grooming line, including shave cream, razors, aftershave, and skin conditioner, come in ribbed, rounded, metallic-gray shapes, looking at once vaguely sexual and like precision engineering.[25]

Marketing managers must consider both the consumer and costs in making packaging decisions. On one hand, the package must be capable of protecting the product through the channel of distribution to the consumer. In addition, it is desirable for packages to have a convenient size and be easy to open for the consumer. For example, single-serving soups and zip-lock packaging in cereal boxes are attempts by manufacturers to serve consumers better. Hopefully, the package is also attractive and informative, capable of being used as a competitive weapon to project a product's image. However, maximizing these objectives may increase the cost of the product to such an extent that consumers are no longer willing to purchase it. Thus, the marketing manager must determine the optimal protection, convenience, positioning, and promotional strengths of packages, subject to cost constraints.

PRODUCT LIFE CYCLE

A firm's product strategy must take into account the fact that products have a life cycle. Figure 6-2 illustrates this life-cycle concept. Products are introduced, grow, mature, and decline. This cycle varies according to industry, product, technology, and market. Marketing executives need to be aware of the life-cycle concept because it can be a valuable aid in developing marketing strategies.

During the introduction phase of the cycle, there are usually high production and marketing costs, and, since sales are only beginning to materialize, profits are low or nonexistent. Profits increase and are positively correlated with sales during the growth stage as the market begins trying and adopting the product. As the product matures, profits for the initiating firm do not keep pace with sales because of competition. Here the

Figure 6–2 *The Product Life Cycle*

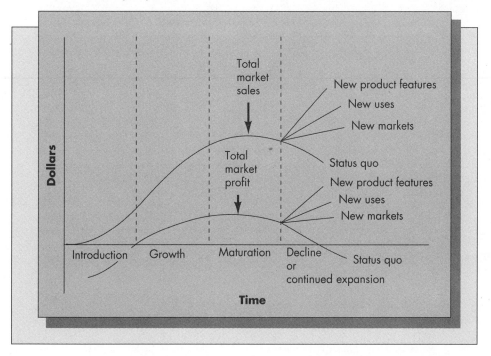

seller may be forced to "remarket" the product, which may involve making price concessions, increasing product quality, or expanding outlays on advertising and sales promotion just to maintain market share. At some time sales decline, and the seller must decide whether to (1) drop the product; (2) alter the product; (3) seek new uses for the product; (4) seek new markets; or (5) continue with more of the same.[26]

The usefulness of the product life-cycle concept is primarily that it forces management to take a long-range view of marketing planning. In doing so, it should become clear that shifts in phases of the life cycle correspond to changes in the market situation, competition, and demand. Thus, the astute marketing manager should recognize the necessity of altering the marketing mix to meet these changing conditions. It is possible for managers to undertake strategies that, in effect, can lead to a revitalized product life cycle. For example, past advancements in technology led to the replacement of rotary dial telephones by touch-tone, push-button phones. Today, newer technology is allowing the cordless and cellular phone to replace the traditional touch-tone, push-button phone. When applied with sound judgment, the life-cycle concept can aid in forecasting, pricing, advertising, product planning, and other aspects of marketing management.[27] However, the marketing manager must also recognize

HIGHLIGHT 6–5

Marketing Strategy Implications of the Product Life Cycle

Strategy Dimension	Life-Cycle Stage			
	Introduction	Growth	Maturity	Decline
Basic objectives	Establish a market for product type; persuade early adopters to buy	Build sales and market share; develop preference for brand	Defend brand's share of market; seek growth by luring customers from competitors	Limit costs or seek ways to revive sales and profits
Product	Provide high quality; select a good brand; get patent and/or trademark protection	Provide high quality; add services to enhance value	Improve quality; add features to distinguish brand from competitors	Continue providing high quality to maintain brand's reputation; seek ways to make the product new again
Pricing	Often high to recover development costs; sometimes low to build demand rapidly	Somewhat high because of heavy demand	Low, reflecting heavy competition	Low to sell off remaining inventory or high to serve a niche market
Channels	Limited number of channels	Greater number of channels to meet demand	Greater number of channels and more incentives to resellers	Limited number of channels
Communication	Aimed at early adopters; messages designed to educate about product type; incentives such as samples and coupons to induce trial	Aimed at wider audience; messages focus on brand benefits; for consumer products, emphasis on advertising	Messages focus on differentiating brand from its competitors; heavy use of incentives such as coupons to induce buyers to switch brands	Minimal, to keep costs down

Source: Gilbert A. Churchill, Jr., and J. Paul Peter, Marketing: Creating Value For Customers, 1st ed. (Burr Ridge, IL: Richard D. Irwin, 1995).

that the life cycle is purely a tool for assisting in strategy development and not let the life cycle dictate strategy development.[28]

THE PRODUCT AUDIT

The product audit is a marketing management technique whereby the company's current product offerings are reviewed to ascertain whether each product should be continued as is, improved, modified, or deleted. The audit is a task that should be carried out at regular intervals as a matter of policy. Product audits are the responsibility of the product manager unless specifically delegated to someone else.

Deletions

In today's environment, there are a growing number of products being introduced each year that are competing for limited shelf space. This growth is primarily due to: (1) new knowledge being applied faster, and (2) the decrease in time between product introductions (by a given organization).[29] In addition, companies are not consistently removing products from the market at the same time they are introducing new products.[30] The result is a situation in which too many products are fighting for too little shelf space. One of the main purposes of the product audit is to detect sick products and then bury them. Rather than let the retailer or distributor decide which products should remain, organizations themselves should take the lead in developing criteria for deciding which products should stay and which should be deleted. Some of the more obvious factors to be considered are:

Sales trends. How have sales moved over time? What has happened to market share? Why have sales declined? What changes in sales have occurred in competitive products both in our line and in those of other manufacturers?

Profit contribution. What has been the profit contribution of this product to the company? If profits have declined, how are these tied to price? Have selling, promotion, and distribution costs risen out of proportion to sales? Does the product require excessive management time and effort?

Product life cycle. Has the product reached a level of maturity and saturation in the market? Has new technology been developed that poses a threat to the product? Are there more effective substitutes on the market? Has the product outgrown its usefulness? Can the resources used on this product be put to better use?

Customer migration patterns. If the product is deleted, will customers of this product switch to other substitute products marketed by our firm? In total, will profits associated with our line increase due to favorable switching patterns?

HIGHLIGHT 6–6

Advantages of Rejuvenating a Product

Instead of abandoning or harvesting an older, mature product, many companies are looking instead to rejuvenate that product and extend its product life cycle. The advantages of product rejuvenation include the following:

Less Risk. Past experience in all phases of the product's life cycle permits the company to focus on improving business practices instead of formulating completely new, untested methods.

Lower Costs. Most, if not all, of the product's start-up costs are now avoided. Plus, prior experience in both marketing and producing the product makes spending more efficient.

Less Time. Because the beginning stages of product development have already occurred, the time involved in rejuvenating a product is significantly less than a new venture.

Cheaper Market Share. The money new products need to invest to create initial brand recognition as well as the lower costs mentioned above can be saved, used to enhance the product offering, or enable the product to be offered at a lower price.

Higher Profits. Efficiency, brand recognition, superior product quality, and the ability to have a narrow focus all contribute to lower costs and/or increased sales, thus increasing the potential for higher profits.

Source: Reprinted from *Business Horizons,* "Product Rejuvenation: A Less Risky Alternative to Product Innovation," by Conrad Berenson and Iris Mohr-Jackson, November–December 1994, pp. 51–57. © 1994 by the Foundation for the School of Business at Indiana University. Used with permission.

The above factors should be used as guidelines for making the final decision to delete a product. Deletion decisions are very difficult to make because of their potential impact on customers and the firm. For example, eliminating a product may force a company to lay off some employees. There are other factors to consider, such as keeping consumers supplied with replacement parts and repair service and maintaining the goodwill of distributors who have an inventory of the product. The deletion plan should provide for clearing out of stock in question.[31]

Product Improvement

One of the other important objectives of the audit is to ascertain whether to alter the product in some way or to leave things as they are. Altering the product means changing one or more of the product's attributes or marketing dimensions. *Attributes* refer mainly to product features, design, package, and so forth. *Marketing dimensions* refer to such things as price, promotion strategy, and channels of distribution.

It is possible to look at the product audit as a management device for controlling the product strategy. Here, control means feedback on product performance and corrective action in the form of product improvement. Product improvement is a top-level management decision, but the information needed to make the improvement decision may come from the consumer or the middlemen. Suggestions are often made by advertising agencies or consultants. Reports by the sales force should be structured in a way to provide management with certain types of product information; in fact, these reports can be the firm's most valuable product improvement tool. Implementing a product improvement decision will often require the coordinated efforts of several specialists, plus some research. For example, product design improvement decisions involve engineering, manufacturing, accounting, and marketing. When a firm becomes aware that a product's design can be improved, it is not always clear how consumers will react to the various alterations. To illustrate, in blind taste tests, the Coca-Cola Company found that consumers overwhelmingly preferred the taste of a reformulated sweeter new Coke over old Coke. However, when placed on the market in labeled containers, new Coke turned out to be a failure due to consumers' emotional attachments to the classic Coke. Consequently, it is advisable to conduct some market tests in realistic settings.

It would be remiss on our part if the discussion on product improvement was closed without taking into account the benefits associated with benchmarking, especially as they relate to the notion of the extended product.[32] The formal definition of *benchmarking* is the continuous process of measuring products, services, and practices against those of the toughest competitors or companies renowned as leaders. In other words, benchmarking involves learning about best practices from best-performing companies—how they are achieving strong performance. It is an effective tool being used by organizations to improve on existing products, activities, functions, or processes. Major corporations, such as IBM, AT&T, DuPont, Ford, Eastmen Kodak, Miliken, Motorola, and Xerox, all have numerous benchmarking studies in progress. For example, IBM has already performed more than 500 benchmarking studies. Benchmarking can assist companies in many product improvement efforts including (1) boosting product quality, (2) developing more user-friendly products, (3) improving customer order-processing activities, and (4) shortening delivery lead times. In the case of benchmarking, companies can achieve great success by copying others. Thus, by its very nature, benchmarking becomes an essential element in the ongoing product auditing process.

ORGANIZING FOR PRODUCT MANAGEMENT

A firm can organize for managing its products in a variety of ways.[33] Figure 6–3 describes five methods and the types of companies for which they are most useful. Under a *marketing-manager (category management) system,* one individual is responsible for overseeing an entire product line with all the functional areas of marketing reporting to this individual. These include sales, advertising, sales promotion, and product planning. This type of system works well for companies with a line (or lines) of similar products or one dominant product line. The practice of category management has

Figure 6–3   *Five Methods of Organizing for Product Management*

Organization	Characteristics		
	Staffing	Ideal Use	Permanency
Marketing-manager system	Key functional areas of marketing report directly to a senior marketer with considerable authority.	A company makes one product line, has a dominant line, or uses broad category marketing managers.	The system is ongoing.
Products (brand) manager system	There is a layer of middle managers, with each manager focusing on a single product or a group of related products.	A company makes many distinct products, each requiring expertise.	The system is ongoing.
Product-planning committee	Senior executives from various functional areas participate.	The committee should supplement another product organization.	The committee meets irregularly.
New-product manager system	Separate middle managers focus on new products and existing products.	A company makes several existing products and substantial time, resources, and expertise are needed for new products.	The system is ongoing, but new products are shifted to product managers after introduction.
Venture team	An independent group of company specialists guides all phases of a new product's development.	A company wants to create vastly different products than those currently offered, and needs an autonomous structure to aid development.	The team disbands after a new product is introduced, turning responsibility over to a product manager.

Source: Marketing, 5th ed., p. 257 by Joel R. Evans and Barry Berman, © 1992. Reprinted by permission of Prentice-Hall, Inc., Upper Saddle River, NJ.

been advocated as being superior to brand management because one manager oversees all brands within a given line, thus avoiding brand competition. Companies such as PepsiCo, Purex, Eastmen Kodak, and Levi-Strauss use some form of the marketing-manager system.

With the *product (brand) manager system,* there is a middle manager in the organization who focuses on a single product or a small group of new or existing products. Typically, this manager is responsible for everything from marketing research to package design to advertising. There are several drawbacks to the brand manager system. First, brand managers often do not have authority commensurate with their responsibilities. Second, these managers often pay inadequate attention to new products. Third, brand managers are often more concerned with their own brand's profitability than with the profitability of all the organization's brands within a product line. Despite these drawbacks, many companies including RJR Nabisco and Black & Decker have operated under this system type.

A *product-planning committee* is staffed by executives from functional areas, including marketing, production, engineering, finance, and R&D. The committee handles product approval, evaluation, and development on a part-time basis and typically disbands after a product is introduced. The product then becomes the responsibility of a product manager. This method is best used to supplement other methods.

A *new-product manager system* uses separate managers for new and existing products. After a new product is introduced, the new-product manager turns it over to a product manager. This system can be expensive and can cause discontinuity when the product is introduced. However, such firms as General Foods, General Electric, and Johnson & Johnson have used this system successfully.

A *venture team* is a small, independent department consisting of a broad range of specialists who manage a new product's entire development process. The team disbands when the product is introduced. While it can be an expensive method, Xerox, Polaroid, Monsanto, and 3M have used a venture team approach.

Which method to use depends on the diversity of a firm's offerings, the number of new products introduced, the level of innovation, company resources, and management expertise. A combination of product management methods also can be used and many firms find this desirable.

CONCLUSION

This chapter has been concerned with a central element of marketing management—product strategy. The first part of the chapter discussed some basic issues in product strategy, including product definition and classification, product quality and value, product mix and product lines, branding and brand equity, and packaging. The product life cycle was discussed as well as the product audit. Finally, five methods of organizing for product management were presented. Although product considerations are extremely important, remember that the product is only one element of the marketing mix. Focusing on product decisions alone, without consideration of the other marketing mix variables, would be an ineffective approach to marketing strategy.

ADDITIONAL READINGS

Anderson, Erin, and Thomas S. Robertson. "Inducing Multiline Salespeople to Adopt House Brands." *Journal of Marketing*, April 1995, pp. 16–31.

Ansari, Asim; Nicholas Economides; and Avijit Ghosh. "Competitive Positioning in Markets with Nonuniform Preferences." *Marketing Science,* Summer 1994, pp. 248–73.

Bayus, Barry L. "Optimal Pricing and Product Development Policies for New Consumer Durables." *International Journal of Research in Marketing,* June 1994, pp. 249–59.

Cespedes, Frank. "Industrial Marketing: Managing New Requirements." *Sloan Management Review,* Spring 1994, pp. 45–60.

Chaudhuri, Arjun. "Brand Equity or Double Jeopardy?" *The Journal of Product & Brand Management,* 1995, pp. 26–32.

Davis, Scott. "Securing the Future of Your Brand." *The Journal of Product & Brand Management,* 1994, pp. 42–49.

Escover, John L. "Focus: Value." *Business Horizons,* July–August 1994, pp. 47–50.

Kent, Robert J., and Chris T. Allen. "Competitive Interference Effects in Consumer Memory for Advertising: The Role of Brand Familiarity." *Journal of Marketing,* July 1994, pp. 97–105.

Milewicz, John, and Paul Herbig. "Evaluating the Brand Extension Decision." *The Journal of Product & Brand Management,* 3, no. 1 (1994), pp. 39–47.

Nandan, Shiva, and Roger Dickinson. "Private Brands: Major Brand Perspective." *The Journal of Consumer Marketing,* 11, no. 4 (1994), pp. 18–28.

Powell, Thomas C. "Total Quality Management as Competitive Advantage: A Review and Empirical Study." *Strategic Management Journal,* January 1995, pp. 15–37.

Sashi, C. M., and Louis W. Stern. "Product Differentiation and Market Performance in Consumer Goods Industries." *Journal of Business Research,* 1995, pp. 115–27.

Saunders, John, and David Jobber. "Product Replacement: Strategies for Simultaneous Product Deletion and Launch." *Journal of Product Innovation Management,* November 1994, pp. 433–50.

Tatham, Ronald; Jeffrey P. Miller; and Vidyut Vashi. "Product Design and the Pricing Decision: A Sequential Approach." *Journal of the Market Research Society,* January 1995, pp. 5–16.

Zeller, Thomas L., and Darin M. Gillis, "Achieving Market Excellence through Quality: The Case of Ford Motor Company," *Business Horizons,* May–June 1995, pp. 23–31.

Chapter 7
NEW PRODUCT PLANNING
AND DEVELOPMENT

New products are a vital part of a firm's competitive growth strategy. Leaders of successful firms know that it is not enough to develop new products on a sporadic basis.[1] What counts is a climate of product development that leads to one triumph after another. It is commonplace for major companies to have 50 percent or more of their current sales in products introduced within the last 10 years. For example, the 3M Company derives 30 percent of its revenues from products less than four years old.[2] At Rubbermaid, the product development process has evolved to a point where, on average, over 400 new products are developed per year, and products that are five years old or less account for over a third of its $2 billion in annual sales.[3] One should not think the success of this process is limited to just the largest companies. New Pig Corp., a manufacturer and direct marketer of industrial cleaning products, introduced 392 new products in a recent year.[4]

Some additional facts about new products are:

- Many new products are failures. Estimates of new product failures range from 33 percent to 90 percent, depending on industry.[5]
- New product sales grow far more rapidly than sales of current products, potentially providing a surprisingly large boost to a company's growth rate.[6] For example, Mentadent toothpaste, after only 10 months in national distribution had achieved sales of over $91 million for its manufacturer, Cheesebrough-Ponds.[7]
- Companies vary widely in the effectiveness of their new product programs.
- A major obstacle to effectively predicting new product demand is limited vision.[8]
- Common elements appear in the management practices that generally distinguish the relative degree of efficiency and success between companies.[9]

In one recent year, almost 22,000 products were introduced in supermarkets, drugstores, mass merchandisers, and health food stores.[10] Of these, only a small percentage (less than 20 percent) met sales goals. The cost of introducing a new brand in some consumer markets can range from $50 million to hundreds of millions of dollars. To illustrate, Alpo Petfoods spent over $70 million alone in launching a new line of cat food. The Gillette Company spent over $310 million on R&D and promotion costs in introducing its initial line of Sensor razors.[11] In addition to the outlay cost of product failures, there are also opportunity costs. These opportunity costs refer not only to the alternative uses of funds spent on product failures, but also to the time spent in unprofitable product development.

Product development can take many years. For example, Hills Brothers (now owned by Nestle) spent 22 years in developing its instant coffee, while it took General Foods (now owned by Philip Morris) 10 years to develop Maxim. However, the success of one new product is no guarantee that the way will be paved for additional and successful low-cost brand extensions. For example, on the positive side, Gillette was able to leverage the research and monies spent on the original Sensor to successfully develop and launch the Sensor razor for women and the Sensor Excel razor. On the negative side, Maxwell House (Philip Morris), Folgers (Proctor & Gamble), and Nestle are still struggling to develop commercially successful lines of fresh whole bean coffee, having been beaten to the punch by smaller companies such as Millstone Coffee, Inc., and Brothers Gourmet Coffees.[12]

HIGHLIGHT 7–2

Ten Steps in the Development of a New Product Policy

1. Prepare a long-range industry forecast for existing product lines.
2. Prepare a long-range profit plan for the company, using existing product lines.
3. Review the long-range profit plan.
4. Determine what role new products will play in the company's future.
5. Prepare an inventory of company capabilities.
6. Determine market areas for new products.
7. Prepare a statement of new product objectives.
8. Prepare a long-range profit plan, incorporating new products.
9. Assign new product responsibility.
10. Provide for evaluation of new product performance.

Good management, with heavy emphasis on planning, organization, and interaction among the various functional units (e.g., marketing, manufacturing, engineering, R&D), seems to be the key factor contributing to a firm's success in launching new products. The primary reason found for new product failure is an inability on the part of the selling company to match up its offerings to the needs of the customer. This inability to satisfy customer needs can be attributed to three main sources: inadequacy of upfront intelligence efforts, failure on the part of the company to stick close to what the company does best, and the inability to provide better value than competing products and technologies.

NEW PRODUCT POLICY

In developing new products, the first question a marketing manager must ask is: "In how many ways can a product be new?" C. Merle Crawford developed a definition of new products based on the following five different categories:[13]

1. *New-to-the-world products.* Products that are inventions, for example, Polaroid camera, the first car, rayon, the laser printer, in-line skates.
2. *New category entries.* Products that take a firm into a category new to it. Products are not new to the world; for example, P&G's first shampoo, Hallmark gift items, AT&T's Universal Card.
3. *Additions to product lines.* Products that are line extensions, flankers, and so on, to the firm's current markets, for example, Tide Liquid detergent, Bud Light, Apple's Power Mac.
4. *Product improvements.* Current products made better; virtually every product on the market has been improved, often many times.
5. *Repositionings.* Products that are retargeted for a new use or application; a classic case is Arm & Hammer baking soda, which was repositioned several

times as drain deodorant, refrigerator freshener, toothpaste, deodorant, and so on.

The new product categories listed above raise the issue of imitation products, strictly me-too or improved versions of existing products. If a firm introduces a new form of dry beer that is new to them but is identical or similar to those on the market, is it a new product? The answer is yes, as it is new to the firm. Managers should not get the idea that to imitate is bad and to innovate is good, for most of the best-selling products on the market today are improvements over another company's original invention. The best strategy is the one that will maximize company goals. It should be noted that Crawford's categories don't encompass variations such as new to a country, new channel of distribution, packaging improvement, and different resources or method of manufacture, which he considers to be variations of the five categories, especially as they relate to additions to product lines.

A second broader approach to the new product question is the one developed by H. Igor Ansoff in the form of growth vectors.[14] This is the matrix first introduced in Chapter 1 that indicates the direction in which the organization is moving with respect to its current products and markets. It is shown again in Figure 7–1.

Market penetration denotes a growth direction through the increase in market share for present product markets. *Product development* refers to creating new products to replace existing ones. Firms utilizing either market penetration or product development strategies are attempting to capitalize on existing markets and combat competitive entry and/or further market incursions.[15] *Market development* refers to finding new customers for existing products. *Diversification* refers to developing new products and cultivating new markets. Firms utilizing market development and diversification strategies are seeking to establish footholds in new markets and/or preempt competition in emerging market segments.

As shown in Figure 7–1, market penetration and market development strategies utilize present products. A goal of these types of strategies is to either increase frequency of consumption or increase the number of customers utilizing the firm's product(s). A strategic focus is placed on altering the breadth and depth of the firm's existing product lines. Product de-

Figure 7–1 *Growth Vector Components*

Markets	Products	
	Present	**New**
Present	Market penetration	Product development
New	Market development	Diversification

velopment and diversification can be characterized as product mix strategies. New products, as defined in the growth vector matrix, usually require the firm to make significant investments in research and development and may require major changes in its organizational structure. Firms are not confined to pursuing a single direction. For example, Miller Brewing Co. has decided four key strategies should dictate its activities for the balance of the decade, including: (1) building its premium-brand franchises through investment spending, (2) continuing to develop value-added new products with clear consumer benefits, (3) leveraging local markets to build its brand franchise, and (4) building business globally.[16] Success for Miller depends on pursuing strategies that encompass all areas of the growth vector matrix.

It has already been stated that new products are the lifeblood of successful business firms. Thus, the critical product policy question is not whether to develop new products but in what direction to move. One way of dealing with this problem is to formulate standards or norms that new products must meet if they are to be considered candidates for launching. In other words, as part of its new product policy, management must ask itself the basic question: "What is the potential contribution of each anticipated new product to the company?"

Each company must answer this question in accordance with its long-term goals, corporate mission, resources, and so forth. Unfortunately, some of the reasons commonly given to justify the launching of new products are so general that they become meaningless. Phrases such as *additional profits, increased growth,* or *cyclical stability* must be translated into more specific objectives. For example, one objective may be to reduce manufacturing overhead costs by utilizing plant capacity better. This may be accomplished by using the new product as an off-season filler. Naturally, the new product proposal would also have to include production and accounting data to back up this cost argument.

In every new product proposal some attention must be given to the ultimate economic contribution of each new product candidate. If the argument is that a certain type of product is needed to "keep up with competition" or "to establish leadership in the market," it is fair to ask, "Why?" To put the question another way, top management can ask: "What will be the effect on the firm's long-run profit picture if we do not develop and launch this or that new product?" Policymaking criteria on new products should specify (1) a working definition of the profit concept acceptable to top management; (2) a minimum level or floor of profits; (3) the availability and cost of capital to develop a new product; and (4) a specified time period in which the new product must recoup its operating costs and begin contributing to profits.

It is critical that firms not become solely preoccupied with a short-term focus on earnings associated with new products. For example, in the materials market, there has been found to be a 20-year spread between the development and widespread adoption of products, on average.[17] Indeed, an advantage Japanese firms possess is that their management is free from the pressure of steady improvement in earnings per share that plagues American managers who emphasize short-term profits.[18] Japanese managers believe that market share will lead to customer loyalty, which, in turn, will lead to profits generated from repeat purchases. Through a continual introduction of new products, firms will succeed in building share. This share growth will then ultimately result in earnings growth and profitability that will be supported by the stock market in terms of higher share prices over the long term.

NEW PRODUCT PLANNING AND DEVELOPMENT PROCESS

Ideally, products that generate a maximum dollar profit with a minimum amount of risk should be developed and marketed. However, it is very difficult for planners to implement this idea because of the number and nature of the variables involved. What is needed is a systematic, formalized process for new product planning. Although such a process does not provide management with any magic answers, it can increase the probability of new product success. Initially, the firm must establish some new product policy guidelines that include the product fields of primary interest, organizational responsibilities for managing the various stages in new product development, and criteria for making go-ahead decisions. After these guidelines are established, a process such as the one shown in Figure 7–2 should be useful in new product development.

Idea Generation

Every product starts as an idea. But all new product ideas do not have equal merit or potential for economic or commercial success. Some estimates indicate that as many as 60 or 70 ideas are necessary to yield one successful product. This is an average figure, but it serves to illustrate the fact that new product ideas have a high mortality rate. In terms of money, almost three-fourths of all the dollars of new product expense go to unsuccessful products.

The problem at this stage is to ensure that all new product ideas available to the company at least have a chance to be heard and evaluated. Ideas are the raw materials for product development, and the whole planning process depends on the quality of the idea generation and screening process.[19] Since idea generation is the least costly stage in the new product development process (in terms of investment in funds, time, personnel, and escalation of commitment), it makes sense that an emphasis be placed first on recognizing available sources of new product ideas and then on funneling these ideas to appropriate decision makers for screening.

Top management support is critical to providing an atmosphere that stimulates new product activity. Many times, great ideas come from some

Figure 7–2   *The New Product Development Process*

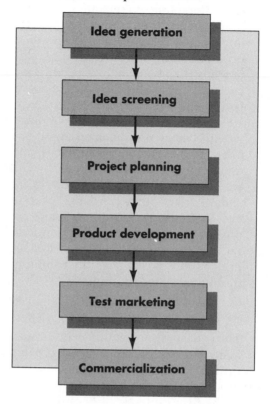

very unusual sources. For example, a successful new snack food was created when product developers looking to make a soft, filled, crunchy snack borrowed technology used by a pet food company to make "bone" snacks with marrowlike centers.[20] A top management structure that is unwilling to take risks will avoid radical, new product and other innovation activities and instead solely concentrate on minor areas of improvement such as line extensions, which more and more are being viewed with growing disinterest by consumers and retailers alike.[21] In order to facilitate top management support, it is essential that new product development be focused on meeting market needs.

Both technology push and market pull research activities play an important role in new product ideas and development. By taking a broad view of customer needs and wants, basic and applied research (technology push) can lead to ideas that will yield high profits to the firm. For example, Compaq bet millions (and won) on PC network servers in the early 1990s even though business customers said they would never abandon their mainframes. In a similar vein, Chrysler forged ahead with the original minivan despite research showing people disliked the odd-looking vehicle.[22] Marketing, on the other hand, is more responsible for gathering and disseminating information gained from customer and other contacts. This information relates mainly to specific features and functions of the product that can be improved upon or market needs that current products are not satisfying. For example, product ideas at Rubbermaid often come from employees roaming the aisles at hardware stores and conversations with family and friends.[23] Both technology push and market pull approaches are essential to the generation of new product ideas.

Some firms use mechanisms such as "out-rotation," outsider involvement, and rewards for boundary-spanning to foster cooperation between design engineers and marketers.[24] Out-rotation involves placing employees in positions that require direct contact with customers, competitors, and other key outside groups. For example, Hewlett-Packard regularly rotates design engineers to retail sales positions on a temporary basis. Other organizations actively involve "outsiders" in planning or reward engineers for making external customer contacts. Regardless of method used, the primary lesson is to keep the communications flow going in all directions throughout the organization.[25]

Idea Screening

The primary function of the idea screening process is twofold: first, to eliminate ideas for new products that could not be profitably marketed by the firm and, second, to expand viable ideas into full product concepts. New product ideas may be eliminated either because they are outside the fields of the firm's interest or because the firm does not have the necessary resources or technology to produce the product at a profit. Generally speaking, the organization has to consider three categories of risk (and their associated risk tolerance) in the idea screening phase prior to reaching a decision. These three risk categories are:[26]

1. *Strategic risk.* Strategic risk involves the risk of not matching the role or purpose of a new product with a specific strategic need or issue of the organization. If an organization feels it necessary to develop certain types of radical innovations or products new to the company in order to carry out long-term strategies, then management must be willing to dedicate necessary resources and time to pursue these type projects.
2. *Market risk.* Market risk is the risk that a new product won't meet a market need in a value-added, differentiated way. As products are being developed, customer requirements change and new technologies evolve. Management must be willing and able to shift its new product efforts to keep pace with change.
3. *Internal risk.* Internal risk is the risk that a new product won't be developed within the desired time and budget. Up front, management must decide

HIGHLIGHT 7–3

Some Sources of New Product Ideas

1. **Customers**
   a. Customer requests
   b. Customer complaints/compliments
   c. Market surveys
   d. Focus groups

2. **Competitors**
   a. Monitoring competitors' developments
   b. Monitoring testing of competitors' products
   c. Monitoring of industry movements

3. **Distribution Channels**
   a. Suppliers
   b. Distributors
   c. Retailers
   d. Trade shows

4. **Research and Engineering**
   a. Product testing
   b. Product enhancement
   c. Brainstorming meetings
   d. Accidental discovery

5. **Other Internal Sources**
   a. Management
   b. Sales force
   c. Employee suggestions
   d. Innovation group meetings
   e. Stockholders

6. **Other External Sources**
   a. Consultants
   b. Academic journals
   c. Periodicals and other press

the level of commitment it will extend in terms of time and budgetary expenditures to adequately ensure the completion of specific projects. Concurrently, progress goals must be established so that "proceed" or "do not proceed" decisions can be reached regarding continuation of projects.

In evaluating these risks, firms should not act too hastily in discounting new product ideas solely because of a lack of resources or expertise. Instead, firms should consider forming joint or strategic alliances with other firms. Potential benefits to be gained from alliances include: (1) increased access to technology, funding, and information; (2) market expansion and greater penetration of current markets; and (3) de-escalated competitive rivalries. Motorola is a company that has prospered by forming numerous joint ventures with both American and foreign companies.[27] Ideas that appear to have adequate profit potential and offer the firm a competitive advantage in the market should be accepted for further study.

Project Planning

This stage of the process involves several steps. It is here that the product proposal is evaluated further and responsibility for the project is assigned to a project team. The proposal is analyzed in terms of production, marketing, financial, and competitive factors. A development budget is estab-

HIGHLIGHT 7–4

Measurements of New Product Performance

Financial Criteria

Return on investment (ROI)
Various profit margin measures
Sales and sales growth
Various profit measures
Payback and payback period
Internal rate of return (IRR)
Return on assets (ROA)
Return on equity (ROE)
Breakeven and breakeven point
Share and market share
Return on sales
Net present value (NPV)

Nonfinancial Criteria

Performance of new products
Market share achieved
Satisfy customer needs
Other market-related benefits
Strategic issues/fit/synergy
Technical aspects of production
Uniqueness of the new products

Source: Reprinted by permission of the publisher from Albert L. Page, "Assessing New Product Development Practices and Performance: Establishing Crucial Norms," *Journal of Product Innovation Management,* September 1993, pp. 273–90. © 1993 by Elsevier Science Inc.

lished, and some preliminary marketing and technical research is undertaken. The product is actually designed in a rough form. Alternative product features and component specifications are outlined. Finally, a project plan is written up, which includes estimates of future development, production, and marketing costs along with capital requirements and manpower needs. A schedule or timetable is also included. Finally, the project proposal is given to top management for a go or no-go decision.

Various alternatives exist for creating and managing the project teams. Two of the better-known methods are the establishment of a skunkworks whereby a project team can work in relative privacy away from the rest of the organization, and a rugby or relay approach whereby groups in different areas of the company are simultaneously working on the project.[28] The common tie that binds these and other successful approaches together is the degree of interaction that develops between the marketing, engineering, production, and other research staff. The earlier in the process that interactive, cooperative efforts begin, the higher the likelihood is that development efforts will be successful. A key component contributing to the success of many companies' product development efforts, relates to the emphasis placed on creating *cross-functional teams* early in the development process. Members from many different departments come together to jointly establish new product development goals and priorities and to also develop new product de-

---

HIGHLIGHT 7–5

Ten Factors Associated with New Product Success

1. *Product superiority/quality.* The competitive advantage the product has by virtue of features, benefits, quality, uniqueness, and so on.
2. *Economic advantage to user.* The product's quality for the customer's money.
3. *Overall company/project fit.* The product's synergy with the company—marketing, managerial, business fit.
4. *Technological compatibility.* The product's technological synergy with the company—R&D, engineering, production fit.

Source: Based on research conducted by Robert G. Cooper, "What Distinguishes the Top Performing New Products in Financial Services," *Journal of Product Innovation Management,* September 1994, pp. 281–99; and "The NewProd System: The Industry Experience," *The Journal of Product Innovation Management,* June 1992, pp. 113–27.

5. *Familiarity to the company.* How familiar or "close to home" the product is to the company's current products and markets (as opposed to being targeted at new customers or markets).
6. *Market need, growth, and size.* The magnitude of the market opportunity.
7. *Competitive situation.* How easy the market is to penetrate from a competitive standpoint.
8. *Defined opportunity.* Whether the product has a well-defined category and established market to enter.
9. *Market-driven process.* The new product process is well planned and executed receiving adequate resources suited to the customer's needs, wants, and buying behavior.
10. *Customer service.* The product is supported by friendly, courteous, prompt,

---

velopment schedules. Frequently, marketing and/or sales personnel are called in to lead these teams.[29]

Product Development

At this juncture the product idea has been evaluated from the standpoint of engineering, manufacturing, finance, and marketing. If it has met all expectations, it is considered a candidate for further research and testing. In the laboratory, the product is converted into a finished good and tested. A development report to management is prepared that spells out in fine detail: (1) the results of the studies by the engineering department; (2) required plan design; (3) production facilities design; (4) tooling requirements; (5) marketing test plan; (6) financial program survey; and (7) an estimated release date.[30]

Test Marketing

Up until now the product has been a company secret. Now management goes outside the company and submits the product candidate for customer approval. Test market programs are conducted in line with the general plans for launching the product. Several of the more commonly utilized forms of test marketing are:[31]

1. *Pseudo sales.* Potential buyers are asked to answer survey questions or pick items off a shelf in a make-believe store. The key factor is that no spending or risk for the consumer takes place.
2. *Controlled sale.* Here the buyer must make a purchase. The sale may be quite formal or informal, but it is conducted under controlled conditions. The product has not been released for regular sale.
3. *Full sale.* In this case, the firm has decided to fully market the product (not so in the above methods). But it wants to do so on a limited basis first, to see if everything is working right. For example, Taco Bell carried out this type of test marketing in 1994, prior to launching its Border Lights menu.[32]
4. *National launch.* Here the firm just launches the product on a national scale and makes adjustments as needed.

The main goal of a test market is to evaluate and adjust, as necessary, the general marketing strategy to be used and the appropriate marketing mix. Additionally, producers can utilize the early interaction with buyers, occurring in test markets, to begin exploration of issues related to the next generation of product development.[33] Especially in cases where new technologies and markets are emerging, firms can benefit greatly from knowledge gained in test markets. Throughout the test market process, findings are being analyzed and forecasts of volume developed. In summary, a well-done test market procedure can reduce the risks that include not only lost marketing and sales dollars but also capital—the expense of installing production lines or building a new factory.[34] Upon completion of a successful test market phase, the marketing plan can be finalized and the product prepared for launch.

Commercialization

This is the launching step. During this stage, heavy emphasis is placed on the organization structure and management talent needed to implement the marketing strategy. Emphasis is also given to following up such things as bugs in the design, production costs, quality control, and inventory requirements. Procedures and responsibility for evaluating the success of the new product by comparison with projections are also finalized.

The Importance of Time

Over the course of the last five years, companies have placed an increasing emphasis on shortening their products' "time to market." *Time to market* can be defined as the elapsed time between product definition and product availability. It has been well documented that companies that can bring their products to market first enjoy a competitive advantage both in terms of profits and market share.[35] Successful time-based innovations can be attributed to the use of short production runs whereby products can be improved on an incremental basis, the use of cross-functional teams, decentralized work scheduling and monitoring, and a responsive system for gathering and analyzing customer feedback.

Several U.S. companies, including Proctor & Gamble, have taken steps to speed up the new product development cycle by giving managers, at the product class and brand family level, more decision-making power. Increasingly, companies are bypassing time-consuming regional test markets, when feasible, in favor of national launches. It is becoming important, more than ever, that firms do a successful job of developing new products right the first time. To accomplish this, companies must have the right people with the right skills and talents in key positions within the new product framework.[36]

CAUSES OF NEW PRODUCT FAILURE

Many new products with satisfactory potential have failed to make the grade. Many of the reasons for new product failure relate to execution and control problems. Below is a brief list of some of the more important causes of new product failures after they have been carefully screened, developed, and marketed.[37]

1. No competitive point of difference and/or unexpected reactions from competitors.
2. Poor positioning.
3. Product was of poor quality.
4. Product didn't deliver on promised benefits.
5. Too little marketing support.
6. Poor perceived price/quality (value) relationship.
7. Faulty estimates of market potential and other marketing research mistakes.
8. Faulty estimates of production and marketing costs.
9. Improper channels of distribution selected.
10. Rapid change in the market (economy) after the product was introduced.

Some of these problems are beyond the control of management; but it is clear that successful new product planning requires large amounts of reliable information in diverse areas. Each department assigned functional responsibility for product development automatically becomes an input to the information system needed by the new product decision maker. For example, when a firm is developing a new product, it is wise for both engineers and marketers to consider both the kind of market to be entered (e.g., consumer, organizational, international) and specific target segments. These decisions will be of paramount influence on the design and cost of the finished good, which will, of course, directly influence price, sales, and profits.

HIGHLIGHT 7–6

Examples of Misfires in Test Marketing

1. **Example:** Proctor & Gamble claims that competitors stole its patented process for Duncan Hines chocolate chip cookies when they saw how successful the product was in test market.

2. **Example:** When Campbell Soup first test marketed Prego Spaghetti Sauce, Campbell marketers say they noticed a flurry of new Ragu ads and cents-off deals that they feel were designed to induce shoppers to load up on Ragu and to skew Prego's test results. They also claim that Ragu copied Prego when it developed Ragu Homestyle spaghetti sauce, which was thick, red, flecked with oregano and basil, and which Ragu moved into national distribution before Prego.

3. **Example:** A health and beauty aids firm developed a deodorant containing baking soda. A competitor spotted the product in a test market, rolled out its own version of the deodorant nationally before the first firm completed its testing, and later successfully sued the product originator for copyright infringement when it launched its deodorant nationally.

4. **Example:** Campbell Soup spent 18 months developing a blended fruit juice called Juiceworks. By the time the product reached the market, three competing brands were already on store shelves. Campbell dropped its product.

5. **Example:** Spurred by its incredible success with Fruit 'N' Juice Bars, Dole worked hard to create a new fruity ice cream novelty product with the same type of appeal. Company officials expected that the product that resulted from this development activity, Fruit and Cream Bars, which it test marketed in Orlando, Florida, would do slightly less well because it was more of an indulgence-type product. However, the test market results were so positive that Dole became the number-one brand in the market within three months. The company consequently shortened the test market to six months. When it rolled out the product, though, the company unhappily found four unexpected entrants in the ice cream novelty category. Due to the intense competition, Fruit and Cream sales fell short of expectations.

Source: G. Churchill, *Basic Marketing Research,* 2nd ed. (Hinsdale, IL: Dryden Press, 1992), p. 150.

Need for Research

In many respects it can be argued that the keystone activity of any new product planning system is research—not just marketing research, but technical research as well. Regardless of the way in which the new product planning function is organized in the company, new product development decisions by top management require data that provide a base for making more intelligent choices. New product project reports ought to be more than a collection of "expert" opinions. Top management has a responsibility to ask certain questions, and the new product planning team has an obligation to generate answers to these questions based on research that provides marketing, economic, engineering, and production information. This need will be more clearly understood if some of the specific questions commonly raised in evaluating product ideas are examined:

1. What is the anticipated market demand over time? Are the potential applications for the product restricted?
2. Can the item be patented? Are there any antitrust problems?
3. Can the product be sold through present channels and sales force? What will be the number of new salespersons needed? What additional sales training will be required?
4. At different volume levels, what will be the unit manufacturing costs?
5. What is the most appropriate package to use in terms of color, material, design, and so forth?
6. What is the estimated return on investment?
7. What is the appropriate pricing strategy?

While this list is not intended to be exhaustive, it serves to illustrate the serious need for reliable information. Note, also, that some of the essential facts required to answer these questions can only be obtained through time-consuming and expensive marketing research studies. Other data can be generated in the engineering laboratories or pulled from accounting records. Certain types of information must be based on assumptions, which may or may not hold true, and on expectations about what will happen in the future, as in the case of "anticipated competitive reaction" or the projected level of sales.

Another complication is that many different types of information must be gathered and formulated into a meaningful program for decision making. To illustrate, in trying to answer questions about return on investment of a particular project, the analyst must know something about (1) the pricing strategy to be used and (2) the investment outlay. Regardless of the formula used to measure the investment worth of a new product, different types of information are required. Using one of the simplest approaches— the payback method (the ratio of investment outlay to annual cash flow)— one needs to estimate the magnitude of the product investment outlay and the annual cash flow. The investment outlay requires estimates of such things as production equipment, R&D costs, and nonrecurring introductory marketing expenditures; the annual cash flow requires a forecast of unit demand and price. For development projects that are dealing with more radical innovations, the difficulty in estimating cash flows in future years is immense due to the uncertainty of demand and competitive reaction(s).[38] In cases where uncertainty exists, more sophisticated analytical methods, including those which incorporate sensitivity analysis, must be utilized.

CONCLUSION

This chapter has focused on the nature of new product planning and development. Attention has been given to the management process required to have an effective program for new product development. It should be obvious to the reader that this is one of the most important and difficult aspects of marketing management. The problem is so complex that, unless management develops a plan for dealing with the problem, it is likely to operate at a severe competitive disadvantage in the marketplace.

ADDITIONAL READINGS

Angeli, Primo. "Thinking Out of the Box: A New Approach to Product Development." *Business Horizons,* May–June 1995, pp. 18–22.

Bailetti, Antonio J., and Paul F. Litva. "Integrating Customer Requirements into Product Design." *The Journal of Product Innovation Management,* January 1995, pp. 3–15.

Duke, Charles R. "Understanding Customer Abilities in Product Concept Tests." *The Journal of Product & Brand Management,* 1994, pp. 48–57.

Dunn, Dan T., Jr., and Claude A. Thomas. "Partnering with Customers." *The Journal of Business & Industrial Marketing* 1994, pp. 34–40.

Gilbert, Joseph T. "Choosing an Innovation Strategy: Theory and Practice." *Business Horizons,* November–December, 1994, pp. 16–22.

Hanna, Nessim; Douglas J. Ayers; Rick E. Ridnour; and Geoffrey L. Gordon. "New Product Development Practices in Consumer Versus Business Products Organizations." *The Journal of Product & Brand Management* 1995, pp. 33–55.

Kamath, Rajan R., and Jeffrey K. Liker. "A Second Look at Japanese Product Development." *Harvard Business Review,* November–December 1994, pp. 154–70.

Kleinschmidt, Elko J. "A Comparative Analysis of New Product Programmes: European versus North American Companies." *European Journal of Marketing,* 1994, pp. 5–29.

Nijssen, Ed J.; Arthur R. L. Arbouw; and Harry R. Commandeur. "Accelerating New Product Development: A Preliminary Empirical Test of a Hierarchy of Implementation." *The Journal of Product Innovation Management,* March 1995, pp. 99–109.

Parker, Glenn M. *Cross-Functional Teams: Working with Allies, Enemies and Other Strangers.* San Francisco, CA: Josey-Bass, 1994.

Rhyne, Lawrence C. "Product Development with a New Technology: Lessons from the America's Cup." *The Journal of Product & Brand Management,* 1994, pp. 39–50.

Schmidt, Jeffrey B. "New Product Myopia." *The Journal of Business & Industrial Marketing,* 1995, pp. 23–33.

Utterback, James M. *Mastering the Dynamics of Innovation: How Companies Can Seize Opportunities in the Face of Technological Change.* Boston, MA: Harvard Business School Press, 1994.

Chapter 8
PROMOTION STRATEGY: ADVERTISING AND SALES PROMOTION

To simplify the discussion of the general subject of promotion, the topic has been divided into two basic categories, personal selling and nonpersonal selling. Personal selling will be discussed in detail in the next chapter, and this chapter will be devoted to nonpersonal selling.

Nonpersonal selling includes all demand creation and demand maintenance activities of the firm other than personal selling. It is mass selling. In more specific terms, nonpersonal selling includes (1) advertising, (2) sales promotion, and (3) publicity. For purposes of this text, primary emphasis will be placed on advertising and sales promotion. Publicity is a special form of promotion that amounts to "free advertising," such as a writeup about the firm's products in a newspaper article. It will not be dealt with in detail in this text.

THE PROMOTION MIX

The promotion mix concept refers to the combination and types of promotional effort the firm puts forth during a specified time period. In developing product strategy, marketers strive for the right mix of promotional elements to make sure that their product is well received.[1] If the product is new, the promotional effort will probably rely heavily on advertising, sales promotion, and publicity in order to: (1) make potential buyers aware of the product; (2) inform these buyers about the benefits associated with the product; (3) convince buyers the product possesses high value; and ;(4) entice buyers to purchase the product. If the product is more established but the objective is to stabilize sales during a weak season, the promotional mix will most likely contain short-term incentives (sales promotion) for people to buy the product immediately. If the product is highly technical and needs a lot of explanation, the promotional mix will probably contain more personal selling, so that potential buyers can ask questions of a salesperson.

HIGHLIGHT 8–1

Some Strengths and Weaknesses of the Major Promotion Elements

Element	Strengths	Weaknesses
Advertising	Efficient for reaching many buyers simultaneously, effective way to create image of the brand, flexible, variety of media to choose from	Reaches many people who are not potential buyers, ads are subject to much criticism, exposure time is usually short, people tend to screen out advertisements, total cost may be high
Personal selling	Salespeople can be persuasive and influential, two-way communication allows for questions and other feedback, message can be targeted to specific individuals	Cost per contact is high, salespeople may be hard to recruit and motivate, presentation skills vary among salespeople
Sales promotion	Supports short-term price reductions designed to stimulate demand, variety of sales promotion tools available, effective in changing short-term behavior, easy to link to other communications	Risks inducing brand-loyal customers to stock up while not influencing others, impact may be limited to short term, price-related sales promotion may hurt brand image, easy for competitors to copy
Publicity	Total cost may be low; media-generated messages seen as more credible than marketer-sponsored messages	Media may not cooperate, heavy competition for media attention, marketer has little control over message

Source: Gilbert A. Churchill, Jr., and J. Paul Peter, *Marketing: Creating Value for Customers* (Burr Ridge, IL: Richard D. Irwin, 1995), p. 543.

As seen by the examples above, a firm's promotion mix is likely to change over time. The mix will need continual altering and adapting to reflect changes in the market, competition, the product's life cycle, and the adoption of new strategies. In essence, the firm should take into account three basic factors when devising its promotion mix: (1) the role of promotion in the overall marketing mix, (2) the nature of the product, and (3) the nature of the market. Highlight 8–1 provides an overview of the major advantages and disadvantages associated with the elements of the promotion mix.

ADVERTISING: PLANNING AND STRATEGY

Advertising seeks to promote the seller's product by means of printed and electronic media. This is justified on the grounds that messages can reach large numbers of people and inform, persuade, and remind them about the firm's offerings. The traditional way of defining advertising is as follows: It is any paid form of nonpersonal presentation of ideas, goods, or services by an identified sponsor.[2]

From a management perspective, advertising is a strategic device for maintaining or gaining a competitive advantage in the marketplace. For example, in a recent year, Proctor & Gamble spent $1.5 billion advertising their products. On an individual brand basis, Ralston Purina spent approximately $62 million solely to advertise their Eveready line of batteries. In total, over $55 billion was spent on media advertising.[3]

For manufacturers and resellers alike, advertising budgets represent a large and growing element in the cost of goods and services. For example, in 1995, Bayer Corp. relaunched its flagship aspirin line in order to (1) educate consumers on the benefits of taking aspirin as a means of warding off heart disease, and (2) fend off competitive actions by private label brands.[4] Bayer spent $40 million on this promotion campaign, an amazing amount considering total annual sales for the Bayer Aspirin line were only $110.5 million prior to the campaign. As part of the seller's promotion mix, advertising dollars must be appropriated and budgeted according to a marketing plan that takes into account such factors as:

1. Nature of the product, including life cycle.
2. Competition.
3. Government regulations.
4. Nature and scope of the market.
5. Channels of distribution.
6. Pricing strategy.
7. Availability of media.
8. Availability of funds.
9. Outlays for other forms of promotion.

Objectives of Advertising

In attempting to evaluate the contribution of advertising to the economic health of the firm, there are at least three different viewpoints on the subject. The generalist viewpoint is primarily concerned with sales, profits, return on investment, and so forth. At the other extreme, the specialist viewpoint is represented by advertising experts who are primarily concerned with measuring the effects of specific ads or campaigns; here primary attention is given to such matters as the Nielsen Index, Starch Reports, Arbitron Index, Simmons Reports, copy appeal, and so forth. A middle view, one that might be classified as more of a marketing management approach, understands and appreciates the other two viewpoints but, in addition, views advertising as a competitive weapon. Emphasis in this approach is given to the strategic aspects of the advertising function. Following are the five major, sequential categories of objectives generally assigned to the advertising function as part of the overall marketing mix:[5]

1. *Create awareness.* Before a new product is introduced, prospective customers are totally unaware of it. Advertising needs to acquaint these customers with the company, product, service, or brand.
2. *Aid comprehension.* Advertising's role is to communicate enough information so some percentage of the aware group recognizes the product's purpose, image, or position; and perhaps, some of its features.

HIGHLIGHT 8-2

The Top 20 Brands in Terms of Media Advertising Spending

Brand, Product, or Service	Parent Company	Measured Ad Spending (in millions)
1. AT&T telephone services	AT&T Corp.	$698
2. Ford cars and trucks	Ford Motor Co.	$549
3. Sears stores	Sears, Roebuck & Co.	$401
4. Kellogg's cereals	Kellogg Co.	$483
5. McDonalds restaurants	McDonalds Corp.	$424
6. Chevrolet cars and trucks	General Motors Corp.	$419
7. Toyota cars and trucks	Toyota Motor Corp.	$374
8. MCI telephone services	MCI Communications Corp.	$325
9. Circuit City stores	Circuit City Stores	$311
10. Chrysler cars and trucks	Chrysler Corp.	$294
11. General Mills cereals	General Mills	$280
12. J. C. Penney stores	J. C. Penney Co.	$276
13. Disney entertainment	Walt Disney Co.	$275
14. Nissan cars and trucks	Nissan Motor Co.	$264
15. Dodge cars and trucks	Chrysler Corp.	$234
16. Honda cars, trucks, and power equipment	Honda Motor Co.	$232
17. Mazda cars and trucks	Mazda Motor Co.	$225
18. Columbia movies and recordings	Sony Corp.	$209
19. Budweiser beer	Anheuser-Busch Cos.	$203
20. Burger King restaurants	Grand Metropolitan	$203

Source: *Advertising Age*, "The Top 200 Brands," May 1, 1995, pp. 33–34. Reprinted with permission from *Advertising Age*, May 1, 1995, © Crain Communications, Inc. All rights reserved.

3. *Induce conviction.* Next, advertising needs to persuade a certain number of people to believe in the product's value.
4. *Develop desire.* Of those who become convinced that the product has high value, some can be moved to desire or want the product.
5. *Produce action.* Finally, after accomplishing all of the preceding steps, some percentage of those who desire the product will take action—request additional information, send in a coupon, visit a store, or buy the product.

Within each category, specific objectives can be formulated that also take into account time and degree of success desired. Figure 8–1 depicts the progression of effects advertising has on its targeted audience—especially for new products. Compared to the large number of people advertising makes aware of the product (base of the pyramid), the number actually motivated to action is usually quite small.

In the long run and often in the short run, advertising is justified on the basis of the revenue it produces. Revenue in this case may refer either to sales or profits. Economic theory assumes that firms are profit maximizers, and the advertising outlays should be increased in every market and medium up to the point where the additional cost of gaining more busi-

Figure 8–1   *The Advertising Pyramid: Five Categories of Advertising Objectives*

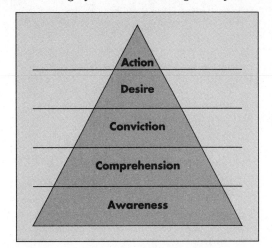

Source: William Arens and Courtland Bovée, *Contemporary Advertising,* 5th ed., p. 214. © Richard D. Irwin. Inc., 1982, 1986, 1989, 1992, and 1994.

ness equals the incremental profits. Since most business firms do not have the data required to use the marginal analysis approach, they usually employ less sophisticated decision-making models. There is also evidence to show that many managers advertise to maximize sales on the assumption that higher sales mean more profits (which may or may not be true).

The point to be made here is that the ultimate objective of the business advertiser is to make sales and profits. To achieve this objective, the actions taken by customers must encompass purchase and continued repurchases of the advertised product. Toward this end, an approach to advertising is needed that provides for intelligent decision making. This approach must recognize the need for measuring the results of advertising, and these measurements must be as valid and reliable as possible. Marketing managers must also be aware of the fact that advertising not only complements other forms of selling but is subject to the law of diminishing returns. This means that for any advertised product, it can be assumed a point is eventually reached at which additional advertising produces little or no additional sales.

ADVERTISING DECISIONS

In line with what has just been said, the marketing manager must make two key decisions. The first decision deals with determining the size of the advertising budget, and the second deals with how the advertising budget should be allocated. Although these decisions are highly interrelated, we deal with them separately to achieve a better understanding of the problems involved. Today's most successful brands of consumer goods were built by

HIGHLIGHT 8–3

Developing Advertising Objectives: Nine Questions

1. Does the advertising aim at *immediate sales?* If so, objectives might be:

   - Perform the complete selling function.
   - Close sales to prospects already partly sold.
   - Announce a special reason for buying now (price, premium, and so forth).
   - Remind people to buy.
   - Tie in with special buying event.
   - Stimulate impulse sales.

2. Does the advertising aim at *near-term sales?* If so, objectives might be:

   - Create awareness.
   - Enhance "brand image."
   - Implant information or attitude.
   - Combat or offset competitive claims.
   - Correct false impressions, misinformation.
   - Build familiarity and easy recognition.

3. Does the advertising aim at building a "long-range consumer franchise? If so, objectives might be:

   - Build confidence in company and brand.
   - Build customer demand.
   - Select preferred distributors and dealers.

   - Secure universal distribution.
   - Establish a "reputation platform" for launching new brands or product lines.
   - Establish brand recognition and acceptance.

4. Does the advertising aim at helping *increase sales?* If so, objectives would be:

   - Hold present customers.
   - Convert other users to advertiser's brand.
   - Cause people to specify advertiser's brand.
   - Convert nonusers to users.
   - Make steady customers out of occasional ones.
   - Advertise new uses.
   - Persuade customers to buy larger sizes or multiple units.
   - Remind users to buy.
   - Encourage greater frequency or quantity of use.

5. Does the advertising aim at some specific step that leads to a sale? If so, objectives might be:

   - Persuade prospect to write for descriptive literature, return a coupon, enter a contest.

heavy advertising and marketing investment long ago.[6] Recently, many marketers have lost sight of the connection between advertising spending and market share. They practice the art of discounting: cutting ad budgets to fund price promotions or fatten quarterly earnings. Companies employing these tactics may benefit in the short term but may be at a severe competitive disadvantage in the long term.

Marketers at some companies, however, know that brand equity and consumer preference for brands drive market share. They understand the balance of advertising and promotion expenditures needed to build brands and gain share, market by market, regardless of growth trends in the product categories where they compete. For example, Proctor & Gamble has built its Jif and Folger's brands from single-digit shares to being among category leaders. In peanut butter and coffee, P&G invests more in advertising and less in discounting than its major competitors. What P&G and other

- Persuade prospect to visit a showroom, ask for a demonstration.
- Induce prospect to sample the product (trial offer).

6. How important are supplementary benefits of advertising? Objectives would be:

- Help salespeople open new accounts.
- Help salespeople get larger orders from wholesalers and retailers.
- Help salespeople get preferred display space.
- Give salespeople an entrée.
- Build morale of sales force.
- Impress the trade.

7. Should the advertising impart information needed to consummate sales and build customer satisfaction? If so, objectives may be to use:

- "Where to buy it" advertising.
- "How to use it" advertising.
- New models, features, package.
- New prices.

- Special terms, trade-in offers, and so forth.
- New policies (such as guarantees).

8. Should advertising build confidence and goodwill for the corporation? Targets may include:

- Customers and potential customers.
- The trade (distributors, dealers, retail people).
- Employees and potential employees.
- The financial community.
- The public at large.

9. What kind of images does the company wish to build?

- Product quality, dependability.
- Service.
- Family resemblance of diversified products.
- Corporate citizenship.
- Growth, progressiveness, technical leadership.

Source: William Arens and Courtland Bovée, *Contemporary Advertising*, 5th ed., p. 217. © Richard D. Irwin, Inc., 1982, 1986, 1989, 1992, and 1994.

smart marketers such as Kellogg, General Mills, Coke, and PepsiCo hold in common is an awareness of a key factor in advertising: consistent investment spending. They do not raid their ad budgets to increase earnings for a few quarters, nor do they view advertising as a discretionary cost.

The Expenditure Question

Most firms determine how much to spend on advertising by one of the following methods:

Percent of sales   This is one of the most popular rule-of-thumb methods, and its appeal is found in its simplicity. The firm simply takes a percentage figure and applies it to either past or future sales. For example, suppose next year's sales are estimated to be $1 million. Using a 2-percent-of-sales criterion, the ad budget would be $20,000. This approach is usually justi-

---

HIGHLIGHT 8–4

Preparing the Advertising Campaign: The Eight-M Formula

Effective advertising should follow a plan. There is no one best way to go about planning an advertising campaign, but, in general, marketers should have good answers to the following eight questions:

1. *The management question:* Who will manage the advertising program?
2. *The money question:* How much should be spent on advertising as opposed to other forms of selling?
3. *The market question:* To whom should the advertising be directed?
4. *The message question:* What should the ads say about the product?
5. *The media question:* What types and combinations of media should be used?
6. *The macroscheduling question:* How long should the advertising campaign be in effect before changing ads or themes?
7. *The microscheduling question:* At what times and dates would it be best for ads to appear during the course of the campaign?
8. *The measurement question:* How will the effectiveness of the advertising campaign be measured and how will the campaign be evaluated and controlled?

---

fied by its advocates in terms of the following argument: (1) advertising is needed to generate sales; (2) a number of cents, that is, the percentage used, out of each dollar of sales should be devoted to advertising in order to generate needed sales; and (3) the percentage is easily adjusted and can be readily understood by other executives. The percent-of-sales approach is popular in retailing.

Per-unit expenditure. Closely related to the above technique is one in which a fixed monetary amount is spent on advertising for each unit of the product expected to be sold. This method is popular with higher priced merchandise, such as automobiles or appliances. For instance, if a company is marketing color televisions priced at $500, it may decide that it should spend $30 per set on advertising. Since this $30 is a fixed amount for each unit, this method amounts to the same thing as the percent-of-sales method. The big difference is in the rationale used to justify each of the methods. The per unit expenditure method attempts to determine the retail price by using production costs as a base. Here the seller realizes that a reasonably competitive price must be established for the product in question and attempts to cost out the gross margin. All this means is that, if the suggested retail price is to be $500 and manufacturing costs are $250, there is a gross margin of $250 available to cover certain expenses, such as transportation, personal selling, advertising, and dealer profit. Some of these expense items are flexible, such as advertising, while others are nearly fixed, as in the case of transportation. The basic problem with this method and the percentage-of-sales method is that they view advertising as a function of sales, rather than sales as a function of advertising.

All you can afford. Here the advertising budget is established as a predetermined share of profits or financial resources. The availability of current revenues sets the upper limit of the ad budget. The only advantage to this approach is that it sets reasonable limits on the expenditures for advertising. However, from the standpoint of sound marketing practice, this method is undesirable because there is no necessary connection between liquidity and advertising opportunity. Any firm that limits its advertising outlays to the amount of available funds will probably miss opportunities for increasing sales and profits.

Competitive parity. This approach is often used in conjunction with other approaches, such as the percent-of-sales method. The basic philosophy underlying this approach is that advertising is defensive. Advertising budgets are based on those of competitors or other members of the industry. From a strategy standpoint, this is a "followership" technique and assumes that the other firms in the industry know what they are doing and have similar goals. Competitive parity is not a preferred method, although some executives feel it is a "safe" approach. This may or may not be true depending in part on the relative market share of competing firms and their growth objectives.

The research approach. Here the advertising budget is argued for and presented on the basis of research findings. Advertising media are studied in terms of their productivity by the use of media reports and research studies. Costs are also estimated and compared with study results. A typical experiment is one in which three or more test markets are selected. The first test market is used as a control, either with no advertising or with normal levels of advertising. Advertising with various levels of intensity are used in the other markets, and comparisions are made to see what effect different levels of intensity have. The marketing manager then evaluates the costs and benefits of the different approaches and intensity levels to determine the overall budget. Although the research approach is generally more expensive than some other models, it is a more rational approach to the expenditure decision.

The task approach. Well-planned advertising programs usually make use of the task approach, which initially formulates the advertising goals and defines the tasks to accomplish these goals. Once this is done, management determines how much it will cost to accomplish each task and adds up the total. This approach is often in conjunction with the research approach.

The Allocation Question

This question deals with the problem of deciding on the most effective way of spending advertising dollars. A general answer to the question is that management's choice of strategies and objectives determines the media and appeals to be used. In other words, the firm's or product division's overall marketing plan will function as a general guideline for answering the allocation question.

From a practical standpoint, however, the allocation question can be framed in terms of message and media decisions. A successful ad campaign has two related tasks: (1) say the right things in the ads themselves and (2) use the appropriate media in the right amounts at the right time to reach the target market.

Message strategy. The advertising process involves creating messages with words, ideas, sounds, and other forms of audiovisual stimuli that are designed to affect consumer (or distributor) behavior. It follows that much of advertising is a communication process. To be effective, the advertising message should meet two general criteria: (1) it should take into account the basic principles of communication, and (2) it should be predicated upon a good theory of consumer motivation and behavior.[7]

The basic communication process involves three elements: (1) the sender or source of the communication; (2) the communication or message; and (3) the receiver or audience. Advertising agencies are considered experts in the communications field and are employed by most large firms to create meaningful messages and assist in their dissemination. Translating the product idea or marketing message into an effective ad is termed *encoding.* In advertising, the goal of encoding is to generate ads that are understood by the audience. For this to occur, the audience must be able to *decode* the message in the ad so that the perceived content of the message is the same as the intended content of the message. From a practical standpoint, all this means is that advertising messages must be sent to consumers in an understandable and meaningful way.

Advertising messages, of course, must be transmitted and carried by particular communication channels commonly known as advertising media. These media or channels vary in efficiency, selectivity, and cost. Some channels are preferred to others because they have less "noise," and thus messages are more easily received and understood. For example, a particular newspaper ad must compete with other ads, pictures, or stories on the same page. In the case of radio or TV, while only one firm's message is usually broadcast at a time, there are other distractions (noise) that can hamper clear communications, such as driving while listening to the radio.

The relationship between advertising and consumer behavior is quite obvious. For many products and services, advertising is an influence that may affect the consumer's decision to purchase a particular product or brand. It is clear that consumers are subjected to many selling influences, and the question arises about how important advertising is or can be. Here is where the advertising expert must operate on some theory of consumer behavior. The reader will recall from the discussion of consumer behavior that the buyer was viewed as progressing through various stages from an

HIGHLIGHT 8–5
Some Relative Merits of Major Advertising Media

Newspapers

Advantages
1. Flexible and timely.
2. Intense coverage of local markets.
3. Broad acceptance and use.
4. High believability of printed word.

Disadvantages
1. Short life.
2. Read hastily.
3. Small "pass-along" audience.

Radio

Advantages
1. Mass use (over 25 million radios sold annually).
2. Audience selectivity via station format.
3. Low cost (per unit of time.)
4. Geographic flexibility.

Disadvantages
1. Audio presentation only.
2. Less attention than TV.
3. Chaotic buying (nonstandardized rate structures).
4. Short life.

Outdoor

Advantages
1. Flexible.
2. Relative absence of competing advertisements.
3. Repeat exposure.
4. Relatively inexpensive.

Disadvantages
1. Creative limitations.
2. Many distractions for viewer.
3. Public attack (ecological implications).
4. No selectivity of audience.

Television

Advantages
1. Combination of sight, sound, and motion.
2. Appeals to senses.
3. Mass audience coverage.
4. Psychology of attention.

Disadvantages
1. Nonselectivity of audience.
2. Fleeting impressions.
3. Short life.
4. Expensive.

Magazines

Advantages
1. High geographic and demographic selectivity.
2. Psychology of attention.
3. Quality of reproduction.
4. Pass-along readership.

Disadvantages
1. Long closing periods (6 to 8 weeks prior to publication).
2. Some waste circulation.
3. No guarantee of position (unless premium is paid).

Direct Mail

Advantages
1. Audience selectivity.
2. Flexible.
3. No competition from competing advertisements.
4. Personalized.

Disadvantages
1. Relatively high cost.
2. Consumers often pay little attention and throw it away.

unsatisfied need through and beyond a purchase decision. The end goal of an advertisement and its associated campaign is to make the consumer feel that, "Hey, this brand is right for me."[8] By doing so, the advertisement will have succeeded in moving the consumer to the trial and repeat purchase stage of the consumer behavior process, which is the end goal of advertising strategy.

The planning of an advertising campaign and the creation of persuasive messages require a mixture of marketing skill and creative know-how. Relative to the dimension of marketing skills, there are some important pieces of marketing information needed before launching an ad campaign. Most of this information must be generated by the firm and kept up to date. Listed below are some of the critical types of information an advertiser should have:

1. *Who* the firms' customers and potential customers are; their demographic, economic, and psychological characteristics; and any other factors affecting their likelihood of buying.
2. *How many* such customers there are.
3. *How much* of the firm's type and brand of product they are currently buying and can reasonably be expected to buy in the short-term and long-term future.
4. *Which* individuals, other than customers and potential customers, *influence* purchasing decisions.
5. *Where* they *buy* the firm's brand of product.
6. *When* they buy, and frequency of purchase.
7. *Which* competitive brands they buy and frequency of purchase.
8. *How* they *use* the product.
9. *Why* they buy particular *types* and *brands* of products.

Media mix. Media selection is no easy task. To start with, there are numerous types and combinations of media to choose from. Below is a list of some of the available advertising media each with its set of options:[9]

1. Television (local or spot, network, cable, public broadcasting, infomercials).
2. Radio (AM, FM, student, public broadcasting, and community stations).
3. Magazines (consumer, specialized business publications, special interest; national, regional, and local).
4. Newspapers (daily, weekly, Sunday, monthly; national, local, and special interest; display, classified, free-standing inserts).
5. Outdoor (billboards, painted buildings, and other structures that carry advertising messages).
6. Transit ("car cards" inside and outside buses and subway trains; posters in and on buses, cars, and trains; and station platform posters).
7. Display (posters around sports stadiums, rinks, racetracks, and public buildings).

8. Other visual outdoor (sky-writing, blimps, and the like).
9. Visual indoor/in-home (calendars, blotters, thermometers, magnets, and the like that carry advertising messages).
10. Direct mail (personal, bulk-rate, and card packs).
11. Throwaways (doorknob hangers, flyers).
12. Point-of-purchase (signage, banners, and handouts in stores and other commercial outlets).
13. Advertising specialties (premiums and gifts such as pens and paper-weights).
14. Trade shows and exhibits.
15. Seminars, training programs, meetings, and open-house events.
16. Audio-visuals (slides, movies, and videos).
17. Audio-cassettes for distribution.
18. Cinema (ads shown in movie theaters).
19. House organs (internal and external newsletters; and periodicals for customers, prospects, and/or employees).
20. Literature (product and application flyers, folders, and brochures; article reprints).
21. Annual reports.
22. Directories and annuals where advertising is sold (Yellow Pages, association member lists).
23. Telemarketing (telephone, fax, and computer bulletin boards).

Of course, each of the media options can be further refined. For example, business magazines can be broken down into individual titles, such as *Forbes, Fortune, Business Week, Worth,* and *Smart Money.* Clearly one dimension of this advertising management problem involves having an overabundance of media to select from. With only four media to choose from, there are 16 possible go or no-go decisions. With 10 media, there would be approximately 1,000 combinations.

Although the number of media and media combinations available for advertising is overwhelming at first glance, four interrelated factors limit the number of practical alternatives:

1. *The nature of the product* limits the number of practical and efficient alternatives. For instance, a radically new and highly complex product could not be properly promoted using billboard advertisements. Instead, the company may choose to develop an *infomercial,* a program-length ad that mixes information and entertainment with sales pitches. Infomercials can either be carried on broadcast media or put on videotapes that are then mailed to targeted customers. Indeed, a growing amount of money is being spent on this medium to promote automobiles and computers.
2. *The nature and size of the target market* also limits appropriate advertising media. For example, it is generally inefficient to advertise goods in mass media publications.

3. *The advertising budget* may restrict the use of expensive media, such as television.

4. *The availability* of some media may be limited in particular geographic areas.

Although these factors reduce media alternatives to a more manageable number, specific media must still be selected. A primary consideration at this point is media effectiveness or efficiency.

In the advertising industry, a common measure of efficiency or productivity is "cost per thousand" or CPMs. This figure generally refers to the dollar cost of reaching 1,000 prospects, and its chief advantage lies in its simplicity and allowance for a common base of comparison between differing media types. The major disadvantage of the use of CPMs also relates to its simplicity. For example, the same commercial placed in two different television programs, having the same viewership and the same audience profile, may very well generate different responses depending on the level of viewer involvement. This "positive effects" theory states that the more viewers are involved in a television program, the stronger they will respond to commercials.[10] In essence, involving programs produce engaged respondents who demonstrate more favorable responses to advertising messages.

Generally, such measures as circulation, audience size, and sets in use per commercial minute are used in the calculation. Of course, different relative rankings of media can occur, depending on the measure used. A related problem deals with what is meant by "effectively reaching" the prospect.[11] *Reach,* in general, is the number of different targeted audience members exposed at least once to the advertiser's message within a predetermined time frame. As important as the number of different people exposed (reach) is the number of times, on average, that they are exposed to an advertisement within a given time period. This rate of exposure is called *average frequency.* Since marketers all have budget constraints, they must decide whether to increase reach at the expense of average frequency or average frequency at the expense of reach. In essence, the marketer's dilemma is to develop a media schedule that both (1) exposes a sufficient number of targeted customers (reach) to the firm's product and (2) exposes them enough times (average frequency) to the product to produce the desired effect. The desired effect can come in the form of reaching goals associated with any or all of the categories of advertising objectives (prospect becomes aware of the product, takes action, etc.) covered earlier in the chapter.

From what has been said so far, it should be clear that advertising decisions involve a great deal of complexity and a myriad of variables. For many executives, until recently, believing in the effectiveness of advertising may have been a matter of faith.[12] Marketing departments might have collected voluminous statistics on television and other media ratings and carefully compared the costs of marketing with total sales. But none of these data

HIGHLIGHT 8–6

Procedures for Evaluating Advertising Programs and Some Services Using the Procedures

Procedures for Evaluating Specific Advertisements

1. *Recognition tests:* Estimate the percentage of people claiming to have read a magazine who recognize the ad when it is shown to them (e.g., Starch Message Report Service).
2. *Recall tests:* Estimate the percentage of people claiming to have read a magazine who can (unaided) recall the ad and its contents (e.g., Gallup and Robinson Impact Service, various services for TV ads as well).
3. *Opinion tests:* Potential audience members are asked to rank alternative advertisements as most interesting, most believable, best liked.
4. *Theater tests:* Theater audience is asked for brand preferences before and after an ad is shown in context of a TV show (e.g., Schwerin TV Testing Service).

Procedures for Evaluating Specific Advertising Objectives

1. *Awareness:* Potential buyers are asked to indicate brands that come to mind in a product category. A message used in an ad campaign is given and buyers are asked to identify the brand that was advertised using that message.
2. *Attitude:* Potential buyers are asked to rate competing or individual brands on determinant attributes, benefits, characterizations using rating scales.

Procedures for Evaluating Motivational Impact

1. *Intention to buy:* Potential buyers are asked to indicate the likelihood they will buy a brand (on a scale from "definitely will not" to "definitely will").
2. *Market test:* Sales changes in different markets are monitored to compare the effects of different messages, budget levels.

Source: Joseph Guiltinan and Gordon Paul, *Marketing Management*, 4th ed., © 1991, New York, McGraw-Hill, Inc., p. 278. Reproduced by permisssion of The McGraw-Hill Companies.

measured what was really important: the incremental sales of a product over and above those that would have happened without advertising. Thanks to a new kind of marketing data, this situation is changing. Single-source marketing data correlates information from actual consumer purchases (available from universal-product-code scanners used in supermarkets and drugstores) with information on the kind of television and other advertising that consumers see or hear. Armed with the results of such analyses, managers can make better decisions regarding advertising effectiveness.

In addition to the use of single-source data, application of quantitative techniques has become quite popular in the area of advertising planning. Linear programming, dynamic programming, heuristic programming, and simulation have been applied to the problem of selecting media schedules, and more comprehensive models of advertising decisions have also been developed. These sophisticated types of applications have enabled advertisers to overcome past problems associated with the use of such simplistic planning tools as GRPs (Gross Rating Points), which fail to differentiate between the importance of reach and frequency.[13] However, although these

---

HIGHLIGHT 8–7

Some Objectives of Sales Promotion

When directed at consumers:

1. To obtain the trial of a product.
2. To introduce a new or improved product.
3. To encourage repeat or greater usage by current users.
4. To bring more customers into retail stores.
5. To increase the total number of users of an established product.

When directed at salespeople:

1. To motivate the sales force.
2. To educate the sales force about product improvements.
3. To stabilize a fluctuating sales pattern.

When directed at resellers:

1. To increase reseller inventories.
2. To obtain displays and other support for products.
3. To improve product distribution.
4. To obtain more and better shelf space.

Source: Steven J. Skinner, *Marketing* 1st ed., p. 542. © 1990 by Houghton Mifflin Company. Adapted with permission.

---

models represent a vast improvement over earlier ones, they must be viewed as an aid in advertising decision making, and not as a replacement for sound managerial decisions and judgment.

SALES PROMOTION

In marketing, the word *promotion* is used in many ways. For instance, it is sometimes used to refer to a specific activity, such as advertising or publicity. In the general sense, promotion has been defined as "any identifiable effort on the part of the seller to persuade buyers to accept the seller's information and store it in retrievable form." However, the term *sales promotion* has a more restricted and technical meaning and has been defined by the American Marketing Association as follows:[14]

> Media and nonmedia marketing pressure applied for a predetermined, limited period of time at the level of consumer, retailer, or wholesaler in order to stimulate trial, increase consumer demand, or improve product availability.

The popularity of sales promotion has been increasing. Since 1983, the promotion–to–advertising expenditure ratio increased from a 57 percent to 43 percent split to a 75 percent to 25 percent level.[15] Dollars spent on trade promotions accounted for about 63 percent of all promotional dollars spent. Reasons for this growth of sales promotion include a shifting emphasis from pull to push marketing strategies by many firms, a widening of the focus of advertising agencies to include promotional services to firms, an emphasis on the part of management towards short-term results, and the emergence of new purchase tracking technology. For example, many supermarket cash registers are now equipped with a device that dispenses coupons to a customer at the point of purchase. The type, variety, and cash amount of the coupon will vary from customer to customer based on their purchases. In essence, it is now possible for the Coca-Cola Company to dispense coupons to only those customers who purchase Pepsi, thus avoiding wasting promotional dollars on already-loyal Coke drinkers.

Push versus Pull Marketing

Push and pull marketing strategies comprise the two options available to firms interested in getting their product into customers' hands. *Push strategies* include all activities aimed at getting products into the dealer pipeline and accelerating sales by offering inducements to dealers, retailers, and salespeople. Inducements might include introductory price allowances, distribution allowances, and advertising-dollar allowances.[16] A *pull strategy*, on the other hand, is one whereby a manufacturer relies mainly on product advertising or consumer sales promotions. These activities are aimed at motivating the consumer to pull the product through the channel.

Several forces and developments have contributed to the increasing use of push marketing strategies by many manufacturers:[17]

1. *Changes in the balance of power between manufacturers and retailers.* Due to the decreasing importance of network television and the increasing use of optical scanning equipment, retailers no longer have to depend on manufacturers for facts. This leads to more power on the part of retailers.
2. *Growth and consolidation of retail package goods businesses.* The growth of regional and national grocery chains such as Safeway and Kroger have led to increasing clout for the retailer. For example, many supermarkets now charge manufacturers a slotting allowance on new products. A *slotting allowance* is a fee manufacturers pay retailers to allocate shelf space to new products.
3. *Low growth rate of the U.S. population.* The U.S. population is growing at only 0.8 percent annually, and growth in per-capita consumption of most mature products is modest. This situation, coupled with excess production capacity, has aggravated competition for market share and the use of price promotions to secure it.[18]
4. *Time constraints of the consumer.* Today's consumer is less interested in shopping, more likely to hold a job, under greater time pressure, and less inclined to prepare a shopping list ahead of a store visit. Hence, today's consumer is more susceptible to prominent displays in the store.[19]
5. *Reduced product differentiation and brand loyalty.* Due to the similarity of many brands and the growing use of sales promotions, consumers are no longer

as brand loyal as they once were. Therefore, more and more sales promotions are needed as an incentive to get the consumer to buy a particular brand. To illustrate, consider the case of domestic car manufacturers. Advertising can no longer be used as a stand-alone promotional strategy to induce consumer automobile purchases. Instead, the manufacturer must also offer additional incentives to the consumer through the dealer including rebates, special option packages, and extended warranties.

Trade Sales Promotions

Trade promotions are those promotions aimed at distributors and retailers of products who make up the distribution channel. The major objectives of trade promotions are to: (1) convince retailers to carry the manufacturer's products; (2) reduce the manufacturer's and increase the distributor's or retailer's inventories; (3) support advertising and consumer sales promotions; (4) encourage retailers to either give the product more favorable shelf space or place more emphasis on selling the product; and (5) serve as a reward for past sales efforts.

Types of dealer sales promotions vary. The most common types are:

1. Point-of-purchase displays including special racks, banners, signs, price cards, and other mechanical product dispensers. For example, an end-of-aisle display for Chips Ahoy cookies would be provided to the retailer by Nabisco.
2. Contests in which organizations and individual salespeople are rewarded for sales efforts.
3. Trade shows that are regularly scheduled events where manufacturers provide information and display products.
4. Sales meetings at which information and support materials are presented to dealers.
5. Push money, which is a form of extra payment given to resellers for meeting specified sales goals.
6. Dealer loaders, which are premiums in the form of merchandise, gifts, or displays given to the reseller for purchasing large quantities of the product.
7. Trade deals, which are price discounts given for meeting certain purchase requirements.
8. Advertising allowances whereby the manufacturer helps to support retailer advertising efforts in which the manufacturer's product is displayed.

Promotions built around price discounts and advertising/other allowances are likely to have higher distributor/retailer participation levels than other type promotions because there is a direct economic incentive attached to the promotion.[20] The importance attached to individual types of promotions may vary by the size of distributor/retailer. For example, small retailers do not consider contests, sweepstakes, and sales quotas as being important to their decision to participate in promotions; getting the full benefit of such promotions is difficult due to their size. Marketers must keep in mind that not all distributors or retailers will have the same reaction to promotions offered. Differences in attitudes need to be carefully considered by the manufacturer when designing and implementing trade promotion programs.

Consumer Promotions

Consumer promotions can fulfill several distinct objectives for the manufacturer. Some of the more commonly sought-after objectives include: (1) inducing the consumer to try the product; (2) rewarding the consumer for brand loyalty; (3) encouraging the consumer to trade up or purchase larger sizes of a product; (4) stimulating the consumer to make repeat purchases of the product; (5) reacting to competitor efforts; and (6) reinforcing and serving as a complement to advertising and personal selling efforts.

Listed below are brief descriptions of some of the most commonly utilized forms of consumer promotion activities.

1. *Sampling.* Consumers are offered regular or trial sizes of the product either free or at a nominal price. For example, Donna Karan Beauty Co. distributed, through Bloomingdales, 10,000 trial kits of a one-month supply of moisturizer, cleanser, and exfoliating masks from their Formula line of skin-care products.[21]

2. *Price deals.* Consumers are given discounts from the product's regular price. For example, Coke and Pepsi are frequently available at discounted prices.

3. *Bonus packs.* Bonus packs consist of additional amounts of the product that a company gives to buyers of the product. For example, manufacturers of disposable razors frequently add additional razors to their packages at no additional charge.

4. *Rebates and refunds.* Consumers, either on the spot or through the mail, are given cash reimbursements for purchasing products. For example, consumers are offered a $3 mail-in rebate for purchasing a Norelco coffee maker.

5. *Sweepstakes and contests.* Consumers can win cash and/or prizes either through chance selection or games of skill. For example, Miller Brewing Co.'s Molson division sponsored a contest where they awarded 200 trips to a Labor Day weekend Ice Polar Beach Party featuring the bands Metallica, Hole, Veruca Soft, and Moist. The party took place at the Arctic Circle.[22]

6. *Premiums.* A premium is a reward or gift that comes from purchasing a product. For example, General Mills gave away Pocahontas patches in boxes of Cheerios cereal and AT&T gave away fax and voice-paging machines to purchasers of their small business systems.

7. *Coupons.* Probably the most familiar and widely used of all consumer promotions, coupons are cents-off or added value incentives. A recent study found that coupon users need to see an average increase of 42 percent in the value of a coupon to try a brand they don't usually buy.[23] That means if a consumer redeems a 50 cents coupon for a frequently used product, it

would require at least a 70 cents coupon to entice that consumer to try another brand. Due to the high incidence of coupon fraud, manufacturers, including Royal Crown Cola and General Mills, are now experimenting with the use of personalized checks as an alternative to coupons. An added advantage of this alternative is a quicker redemption for retailers. As mentioned previously, point-of-purchase coupons are becoming an increasingly efficient way for marketers to target their promotional efforts at specific consumers.

What Sales Promotion Can and Can't Do

Advocates of sales promotion often point to its growing popularity as a justification for the argument that we don't need advertising; sales promotion itself will suffice. Marketers should bear in mind that sales promotion is only one part of a well-constructed overall promotion strategy. While proven to be effective in achieving the objectives listed in the previous sections, there are several compelling reasons why sales promotion should not be utilized as the sole promotional tool. These reasons include sales promotion's inability to: (1) generate long-term buyer commitment to a brand in many cases; (2) change, except on a temporary basis, declining sales of a product; (3) convince buyers to purchase an otherwise unacceptable product; and (4) make up for a lack of advertising or sales support for a product. In addition, promotions can often fuel the flames of competitive retaliation far more than other marketing activities.[24] When the competition gets drawn into the promotion war, the effect can be a significant muting of the sharp sales increases predicted by the initiator of the promotion. Worse yet, promotions can often devalue the image of the promoted brand in the consumer's eyes. To illustrate, General Foods cut back the yearly advertising expenditures on Maxwell House coffee by $60 million in the mid 80s and reallocated the funds to sales promotion activities. Within a year, Folger's coffee dislodged Maxwell House as the largest selling brand.

The dilemma faced by marketers, as shown in Figure 8–2, is how to cut back on sales promotions without losing market share to competitors. In an effort to overcome this problem, some consumer products companies are instituting new pricing policies to try to cut back on the amount of sales promotions used. For example, Proctor & Gamble and General Mills have instituted everyday low-price strategies for many of their products. The intent of this type of policy is to give retailers a lower list price in exchange for the cutting of trade promotions. While the net cost of the product to retailers remains unchanged, retailers are losing promotional dollars that they controlled. In many situations, although trade allowances are supposed to be used for encouraging retail sales, it is not uncommon for retailers to take a portion of the trade allowance money as profit. The rationale behind companies' (such as Proctor & Gamble and General Mills)

Figure 8–2   *The Sales Promotion Dilemma*

Other firms	Our firm	
	Cut back promotions	Maintain promotions
Cut back promotions	**Higher profits for all**	**Market share may go to our firm**
Maintain promotions	**Market share may go to other firms**	**Market share may not change: profits stay low**

Source: George E. Belch and Michael A. Belch, *Introduction to Advertising and Promotion: An Integrated Communications Perspective,* 3rd ed. (Burr Ridge, IL: Richard D. Irwin, 1995), p. 514.

efforts to cut back on trade and other promotions is to: (1) not force brand-loyal customers to pay unusually high prices when a product isn't on special; (2) allow consumers to benefit from a lower average shelf price since retailers will no longer have discretion over the use of allowance dollars; and (3) improve efficiencies in manufacturing and distribution systems because retailers will lose the incentive to do heavy forward buying of discounted items.

In addition to developing pricing policies to cut back on short-term promotions, some consumer products companies are starting to institute *frequency marketing programs* in which they reward consumers for purchases of products or services over a sustained period of time.[25] These programs are not technically considered sales promotions due to their ongoing nature. Frequency marketing originated in 1981 when American Airlines launched its frequent-flyer program with the intention of securing the loyalty of business travelers. Since that time, American has awarded over 14 million free flights. In fact, among all airlines, there are an estimated 34 million individuals holding frequent-flyer cards.

Realizing the success these programs gave to service providers, and more recently to retailers, consumer products companies have begun instituting loyalty programs as well. Nabisco Foods is utilizing a system where it rewards customers for redeeming Nabisco coupons by sending them additional ones; and Dole Foods has linked up with MasterCard in a program where customers get Dole coupons when they purchase a certain amount of Dole products using their MasterCard.[26] The goal of these and similar type programs is to develop sustained customer loyalty through a process of continually rewarding customers for their loyalty to a particular brand.

CONCLUSION

This chapter has been concerned with nonpersonal selling. Remember that advertising and sales promotion are only two of the ways by which sellers can affect the demand for their product. Advertising and sales promotion are only part of the firm's promotion mix, and, in turn, the promotion mix is only part of the overall marketing mix. Thus, advertising and sales promotion begin with the marketing plan and not with the advertising and sales promotion plans. Ignoring this point can produce ineffective and expensive promotional programs because of a lack of coordination with other elements of the marketing mix.

ADDITIONAL READINGS

Aab, Linda; Wesley J. Johnston; and Rita Lohtia. "Building Relationships through Advertising." *Marketing Management,* Summer 1995, pp. 32–38.

Bobinski, George S., Jr., and Gabriel G. Ramirez. "Advertising to Investors: The Effect of Financial-Relations Advertising on Stock Volume and Price." *Journal of Advertising,* December 1994, pp. 13–28.

D'Souza, Giles, and Ram C. Rao. "Can Repeating an Advertisement More Frequently than the Competition Affect Brand Preference in a Mature Market?" *Journal of Marketing,* April 1995, pp. 32–41.

Harrison-Walker, L. Jean. "The Import of Illiteracy to Marketing Communications." *The Journal of Consumer Marketing,* 1995, pp. 50–62.

_____. "The Relative Effects of National Stereotype and Advertising Information on the Selection of a Service Provider: An Empirical Study." *The Journal of Services Marketing,* 1995.

Kent, Robert J. "Competitive Clutter in Network Television Advertising: Current Levels and Advertisers' Response." *Journal of Advertising Research,* January/February 1995, pp. 49–57.

Kline, Barbara, and Janet Wagner. "Information Source and Retail Buyer Decision-Making: The Effect of Product-Specific Buying Experience." *Journal of Retailing,* Spring 1994, pp. 75–88.

Maloney, John C. "Is Advertising Believability Really Important?" *Marketing Management,* 1994, pp. 47–52.

McLeod, Douglas M., and Motoko Kunita. "A Comparative Analysis of the Use of Corporate Advertising in the United States and Japan." *International Journal of Advertising,* December 1994, pp. 137–52.

Pass, Christopher; Brian Sturgess; and Nicholas Wilson. "Advertising, Barriers to Entry, and Competition Policy." *The Journal of Product & Brand Management,* 1994, pp. 51–58.

Rust, Roland T., and Richard W. Oliver. "The Death of Advertising." *Journal of Advertising,* December 1994, pp. 71–77.

Simonson, Itamar; Ziv Carmon; and Suzanne O'Curry. "Experimental Evidence on the Negative Effect of Product Features and Sales Promotions on Brand Choice." *Marketing Science,* Winter 1994, pp. 23–40.

Smith, Kirk H., and Martha Rogers. "Effectiveness of Subliminal Messages in Television Commercials: Two Experiments." *Journals of Applied Psychology,* December 1994, pp. 866–74.

Stautamoyer, Gail L., and Jay Lindquist. "Promotion Decision Models: A State of the Art Review." *Journal of Promotion Management,* 1994, pp. 1–36.

Strong, James T., and Michael F. D'Amico. "Fear Arousal, Prior Product Usage, and Persuasion: An Advertising Study." *The Journal of Marketing Management,* Fall/Winter 1994, pp. 1–7.

Totten, John C., and Martin P. Block. *Analyzing Sales Promotion,* 2nd ed. (Chicago, IL: The Dartnell Corporation, 1994).

Vella, Alexander P. "Marketing a Quality Image." *Public Relations Journal,* October/November 1994, pp. 22–24.

MAJOR FEDERAL AGENCIES INVOLVED IN CONTROL OF ADVERTISING

Agency	Function
Federal Trade Commission	Regulates commerce between states; controls unfair business practices; takes action on false and deceptive advertising; most important agency in regulation of advertising and promotion.
Food and Drug Administration	Regulatory division of the Department of Health, Education, and Welfare; controls marketing of food, drugs, cosmetics, medical devices, and potentially hazardous consumer products.
Federal Communications Commission	Regulates advertising indirectly, primarily through the power to grant or withdraw broadcasting licenses.
Postal Service	Regulates material that goes through the mails, primarily in areas of obscenity, lottery, and fraud.
Alcohol and Tobacco Tax Division	Part of the Treasury Department; has broad powers to regulate deceptive and misleading advertising of liquor and tobacco.
Grain Division	Unit of the Department of Agriculture responsible for policing seed advertising.
Securities and Exchange Commission	Regulates advertising of securities.

Information Source	Description
Patent Office	Regulates registration of trademarks.
Library of Congress	Controls protection of copyrights.
Department of Justice	Enforces all federal laws through prosecuting cases referred to it by other government agencies.

Chapter 9
PROMOTION STRATEGY: PERSONAL SELLING

Personal selling, unlike advertising or sales promotion, involves direct relationships between the seller and the prospect or customer. In a formal sense, personal selling can be defined as a two-way flow of communication between a potential buyer and a salesperson that is designed to accomplish at least three tasks: (1) identify the potential buyer's needs; (2) match those needs to one or more of the firm's products or services; and (3) on the basis of this match, convince the buyer to purchase the product.[1] The personal selling element of the promotion mix can encompass diverse forms of direct interaction between a salesperson and potential buyer including face-to-face, telephone, written, and/or computer communication. The behavioral scientist would most likely characterize personal selling as a type of personal influence. Operationally, it is a complex communication process, one still not fully understood by marketing scholars.

IMPORTANCE OF PERSONAL SELLING

Most businesses find it impossible to market their products without some form of personal selling. To illustrate, vending machines are becoming more popular. The question may be raised about whether or not these machines replaced the salesperson. The answer is both yes and no. In a narrow sense of the word, the vending machine has replaced some retail sales clerks who, for most convenience goods, merely dispensed the product and collected money. On the other hand, vending machines and their contents must be "sold" to the vending machine operators, and personal selling effort must be exerted to secure profitable locations for the machines.

The policies of self-service and self-selection have done much to eliminate the need for personal selling in some types of retail stores. However, the successful deployment of these policies have required manufacturers to do two things: (1) presell the consumer by means of larger advertising and sales promotion outlays, and (2) design packages for their products that would "sell" themselves, so to speak.

The importance of the personal selling function depends partially on the nature of the product. As a general rule, goods that are new, technically complex, and/or expensive require more personal selling effort. The salesperson plays a key role in providing the consumer with information about such products to reduce the risks involved in purchase and use. Insurance, for example, is a complex and technical product that often needs significant amounts of personal selling. In addition, many organizational products cannot be presold, and the salesperson has a key role to play in finalizing the sale. In the pharmaceutical industry, the customer base has grown ever more heterogeneous. As a result, the need for customized messages to meet the individual needs of the differing customer groups has grown more important. One change that has been implemented in the industry to keep company sales forces competitive has been the organization of sales teams.[2] In these teams, salespeople are coupled with technical experts in order to forge strong customer partnerships and add value to the company's product offerings.[3] However, most nationally-branded convenience goods are purchased by the consumer without significant direct assistance from manufacturer or retail store personnel.

The importance of personal selling also is determined to a large extent by the needs of the consumer. In the case of pure competition (a large number of small buyers with complete market knowledge of a homogeneous product), there is little need for personal selling. A close approximation to this situation is found at auctions for agricultural products, such as tobacco or wheat. At the other extreme, when a product is highly differentiated, such as housing, and marketed to consumers with imperfect knowledge of product offerings, personal selling becomes a key factor in the promotion mix. Finally, sellers who differentiate their products at the point of sale will usually make heavy use of personal selling in their promotion mix. For example, automobile buyers are given the opportunity to purchase various extras or options at the time of purchase.

It is important to remember that, for many companies, the salesperson represents the customer's main link to the firm. In fact, to some, the salesperson is the company. Therefore, it is imperative that the company take advantage of this unique link. Through the efforts of the successful salesperson, a company can build relationships with customers that continue long beyond the initial sale. It is the salesperson who serves as the conduit through which information regarding product flaws, improvements, applications, and/or new uses can pass from the customer to the marketing department. To illustrate the importance of using salespeople as an information resource, consider this fact. In some industries, customer information serves as the source for up to 90 percent of new product and process ideas.[4] Along with techniques described in the previous chapter, personal selling provides the push needed to get middlemen to carry new products, increase their amount of goods purchased, and devote more effort in merchandising a product or brand.[5]

The classic relationship between marketing and sales has often entailed confusion and poor communication.[6] Disgruntled salespeople grumble about marketing programs they see as ineffective, while the marketing staff claims mediocre sales are the result of poor execution on the part of the sales force. Salespeople continually complain that they are being asked to serve as the marketing research arm of the organization, being charged with gathering customer information that detracts from their selling efforts. Meanwhile, the marketing staff asserts that rarely, if ever, does the sales staff contribute meaningful information. Regardless of who's right, the results are all too often the same: sales are down and valuable information is lost. It is of critical importance that a synergistic relationship be built between the marketing and the sales function. Toward this end, each function must understand the benefits derived from such an alliance. These benefits include: (1) better targeted marketing programs; (2) more-diverse and accurate marketplace information flows; (3) quicker response times; (4) stronger customer relationships; and (5) above all, improved financial results. Later in the chapter, specific means of improving the sales/marketing relationship will be discussed.

In summary, personal selling is an integral part of the marketing system, fulfilling two vital duties (in addition to the core sales task itself): one for customers and one for companies.[7] First, the salesperson dispenses knowledge to buyers. Lacking relevant information, customers are likely to make poor buying decisions. For example, computer users would not learn about new equipment and new programming techniques without the assistance of data-processing sales representatives. Doctors would have difficulty finding out about new drugs and procedures were it not for pharmaceutical salespeople. Second, salespeople act as a source of marketing intelligence for management. Marketing success depends on satisfying customer needs. If present products don't fulfill customer needs, then profitable opportunities may exist for new or improved products. If problems with a company's product exist, then management must be quickly appraised of the fact. In either situation, salespeople are in the best position to act as the intermediary through which valuable information can be passed back and forth between product providers and buyers.

THE SALES PROCESS

Personal selling is as much an art as it is a science. The word *art* is used to describe that portion of the selling process that is highly creative in nature and difficult to explain. This does not mean there is little control over the personal selling element in the promotion mix. It does imply that, all other things equal, the trained salesperson can outsell the untrained one.

Before management selects and trains salespeople, it should have an understanding of the sales process. Obviously, the sales process will differ according to the size of the company, the nature of the product, the market, and so forth, but there are some elements common to almost all selling situations that should be understood. For the purposes of this text, the term

HIGHLIGHT 9-1

Information the Sales Force Can Obtain from Organizational Customers

a. Problems with current products.

b. Cost-reduction needs of customer.

c. Unmet needs or wishes of customer.

d. Superior features of competitive products.

e. Changes in technology/industry standards.

f. Additions needed for service(s) accompanying the product.

g. Changes in the regulatory environment.

h. Other manufacturers' (competitors') products currently used by customers.

i. Customer's level of satisfaction with products currently used.

j. Product features evaluated by customers in choosing another manufacturer's product.

k. Customer's ideal products according to relevant choice criteria.

l. Customer's criteria for rating products.

m. Customer's order of preference for competing products.

n. Customer's likely demand for products in the future.

Source: Adapted from Geoffrey Gordon, Denise Schoenbachler, Peter Kaminski, and Kimberly Brouchous, "The Use of the Sales Force in the Opportunity Identification Phase of the New Product Development Process," *Journal of Business and Industrial Marketing, (in press).*

sales process refers to two basic factors: (1) the objectives the salesperson is trying to achieve while engaged in selling activities; and (2) the sequence of stages or steps the salesperson should follow in trying to achieve the specific objectives (the relationship-building process).

Objectives of the Sales Force

Much like the concepts covered in the previous chapter, personal selling can be viewed as a strategic means to gain competitive advantage in the marketplace. For example, Dow Chemical Co. includes service representatives as part of their sales team to ensure that customer concerns with present products are addressed and remedied at the same time new business is being solicited.[8] At General Motors, it was the sales force who initially discovered that high levels of customer satisfaction did not result in high levels of customer retention. Rather, they determined the elimination of customer dissatisfaction, regardless of degree, was the driving force behind continued customer loyalty.[9]

In a similar manner, marketing management understands that, while ultimately, personal selling must be justified on the basis of the revenue and profits it produces, there are four major categories of objectives generally assigned to the personal selling function as part of the overall promotion mix.[10] These objectives can be categorized as either image and/or demand-oriented. Although many companies have some interest in image-oriented selling efforts, the primary emphasis is placed on achieving demand-oriented objectives. A brief description of each category follows.

Image-oriented objectives

When personal selling objectives are image-oriented, they usually involve public relations. Public relations, in general, can be considered the use of communication that is designed to foster a favorable image for goods, services, or organizations. Needless to say, when personal selling is utilized as part of a public relations effort, it is initiated and paid for by the sponsoring firm. The specific objectives of image-oriented personal selling efforts can be to utilize the sales force: (1) as public role models in displaying the firm's commitment to ethical behavior through the employment of acceptable sales practices; (2) to portray the firm's upstanding image by having salespeople maintain a good appearance in all customer contacts; and/or (3) to show the firm's commitment to relationship building by having the sales force follow practices aimed at gaining the respect of customers, employees, and other public entities.

Demand-oriented objectives

When personal selling objectives are demand-oriented, the overriding goal is to convert customer interest into first, an initial sale and, subsequently, repeat purchases. To achieve this goal, three major categories of objectives are pursued:

1. *Information provision.* Especially in the case of new products or customers, the salesperson needs to fully explain all attributes of the product or service, answer any questions, and probe for additional questions.
2. *Persuasion.* Once the initial product or service information is provided, the salesperson needs to focus on the following objectives:

   - Clearly distinguish attributes of the firm's products or services from those of competitors.
   - Maximize the number of sales as a percent of presentations.
   - Convert undecided customers into first-time buyers.
   - Convert first-time customers into repeat purchasers.
   - Sell additional or complementary items to repeat customers.
   - Tend to the needs of dissatisfied customers.

3. *After-sale service.* Whether the sale represents a first-time or repeat purchase, the salesperson needs to ensure the following objectives are met:

   - Delivery and/or installation of the product or service that meets or exceeds customer demands.
   - Immediate follow-up calls and visits to address unresolved or new concerns.
   - Reassurance of product or service superiority through demonstrable actions.

The Sales Relationship-Building Process

For many years, the traditional approach to selling emphasized the first-time sale of a product or service as the culmination of the sales process. As emphasized in Chapter 1, the new marketing viewpoint and accompanying approach to personal selling views the initial sale as merely the first step in a long-term relationship-building process, not as the end goal. Long-term relationships between the buyer and seller can be considered partnerships because the buyer and seller have an ongoing, mutually beneficial affiliation, with each party having concern for the other party's well-being.[11] The relationship-building process is designed to meet the objectives listed in the previous section and contains six sequential stages (see Figure 9–1). These stages are: (1) prospecting; (2) planning the sales call; (3) presentation; (4) responding to objections; (5) obtaining commitment/closing the sale; and (6) building a long-term relationship. What follows is a brief description of each of the stages.

Figure 9–1   *The Sales Relationship-Building Process*

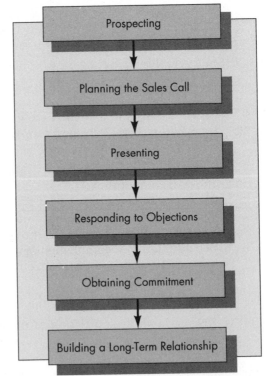

Source: Adapted from material discussed in Barton A. Weitz, Stephen B. Castleberry, and John F. Tanner, *Selling: Building Partnerships,* 2nd ed. (Burr Ridge, IL: Richard D. Irwin, 1995), p. 203.

Prospecting

The process of locating potential customers is called *prospecting*. The prospecting activity is critical to the success of organizations in maintaining or increasing sales volume. Continual prospecting is necessary for several reasons including the fact that customers: (1) switch to other suppliers; (2) move out of the organization's market area; (3) go out of business because of bankruptcy; (4) are acquired by another firm; and/or (5) have only a one-time need for the product or service. In addition, the organization's buying contracts with present customers may be replaced and organizations who wish to grow must increase their customer base. Prospecting in some fields is more important than in others. For example, the stockbroker, real estate agent, or partner in an accounting firm with no effective prospecting plan usually doesn't last long in the business. In these positions, it may take as many as 100 contacts to gain 10 prospects who will listen to presentations from which one to two sales may result. On the other hand, a Proctor & Gamble sales representative in a certain geographic area would likely know all the potential retailers for Crest toothpaste.

The prospecting process usually involves two major activities that are undertaken on a continual, concurrent basis. First, prospects must be located. When names and addresses of prospects are not available, as is usually the case when firms enter new markets or a new salesperson is hired, they can be generated by randomly calling on businesses or households or by employing mass appeals (through advertising). This process is called *random lead* or *blind searching* and usually requires a high number of contacts to gain a sale. A *lead* is a potential prospect that may or may not have the potential to be a true prospect, a candidate, to whom a sale could be made.

For most professional, experienced salespeople, a more systematic approach to generating leads from predetermined target markets is utilized. This approach, aptly named *selected-lead searching*, utilizes existing contacts and knowledge to generate new prospects. In general, the best source of prospects is referrals from satisfied customers.[12] The more satisfied one's customers are, the higher the quality of leads a salesperson will receive from them. Highlight 9–2 lists some common sources of leads and how they are used to generate new contacts.

The second step in the prospecting process involves screening. Once leads are generated, the salesperson must determine whether the prospect is a true prospect. This qualifying process usually entails the gathering of information, which leads to the answering of five questions.

1. Does the lead have a want or need that can be satisfied by the purchase of the firm's products or services?
2. Does the lead have the ability to pay?

HIGHLIGHT 9–2
Common Sources of Sales Leads

Source	How Used
Satisfied customers	Current and previous customers are contacted for additional business and leads.
Endless chain	Salesperson attempts to secure at least one additional lead from each person he or she interviews.
Center of influence	Salesperson cultivates well-known, influential people in the territory who are willing to supply lead information.
Promotional activities	Salesperson ties into the company's direct mail, telemarketing, and shows to secure and qualify leads.
Lists and directories	Salesperson uses secondary data sources, which can be free or fee-based.
Canvassing	Salesperson tries to generate leads by calling on totally unfamiliar organizations.
Spotters	Salesperson pays someone for lead information.
Telemarketing	Salesperson uses phone and/or telemarketing staff to generate leads.
Sales letters	Salesperson writes personal letters to potential leads.
Other sources	Salesperson uses noncompeting salespeople, people in his or her own firm, social clubs, etc., to secure lead information.

Source: Adapted from material discussed in Barton A. Weitz, Stephen B. Castleberry, and John F. Tanner, *Selling: Building Partnerships*, 2nd ed. (Burr Ridge, IL: Richard D. Irwin, 1995), p. 208.

3. Does the lead have the authority to pay?
4. Can the lead be approached favorably?
5. Is the lead eligible to buy?

Depending on the analysis of answers to these questions, the determination of whether a lead is a true prospect can be made. In seeking and qualifying leads, it is important to recognize that responsibility for these activities should not be totally assumed by individual salespeople. Rather, companies should develop a consistent, organized program, recognizing that the job of developing prospects belongs to the entire company not just the sales force.[13]

Planning the sales call

Salespeople will readily admit that their number one problem is getting through the door for an appointment with a prospect.[14] Customers have become sophisticated in their buying strategies. Consequently, salespeople have to be equally sophisticated in developing their selling strategies.[15] A buyer's time is valuable. Without adequate planning, the salesperson may be unable to convince the prospect to entertain a sales call. In addition, lack of planning can lead to the salesperson: (1) covering material in which the buyer has no interest, (2) trying to obtain an order even though that is an unrealistic expectation for the sales call, or (3) striking off into an area that is of no relevance to the buyer. With a clear plan, the salesperson is more likely to gain entry through the buyer's door and win the buyer's respect and commitment. In addition, proper planning helps salespeople meet their call objectives efficiently as well as effectively.

While a full discussion on the topic of planning the sales call is beyond the scope of this text, what follows are brief descriptions of some key areas of knowledge a salesperson should possess prior to embarking on a sales call.

1. They should have thorough knowledge of the company they represent, including its past history. This includes the philosophy of management as well as the firm's basic operating policies.
2. They should have thorough technical and commercial knowledge of their products or product lines. This is particularly true when selling goods. When selling very technical products, many firms require their salespeople to have training as engineers.
3. They should have good working knowledge of competitors' products. This is a vital requirement because the successful salesperson will have to know the strengths and weaknesses of those products that are in competition for market share.
4. They should have in-depth knowledge of the market for their merchandise. *The market* here refers not only to a particular sales territory but also to the general market, including the economic factors that affect the demand for their goods.
5. They should have accurate knowledge of the buyer or the prospect to whom they are selling. Under the marketing concept, knowledge of the customer is a vital requirement. Salespeople can't get close to their customers unless they know what the customers are all about.[16] One of the best ways to seal a relationship is to help a customer solve his/her problems—but first, one has to know what those problems are. Areas of desirable knowledge salespeople should possess include customer applications of the product and customer requirements as they relate to product quality, durability, cost, design, and service. Knowledgeable salespeople should be able to quantify, as well as describe, product benefits to the buyer. Effective selling requires salespeople to understand the unique characteristics of each account, including how the customer will make his/her decision.[17]

Presenting

Successful salespeople have learned the importance of making a good impression. One of the most important ways of improving the buyer's impression is for the salesperson to be well-prepared in the knowledge areas discussed above. Some salespeople actually develop a checklist of things to take to the presentation so that nothing is forgotten. Just as important is the development of good interpersonal skills; they are a key ingredient of effective selling.[18] Salespeople who can adapt their selling style to individual buyer needs and styles have as much as 30 percent stronger overall performance than less flexible counterparts.

While much goes into planning and delivering sales presentations, 14 core principles for presentation success stand out.[19] Successful salespeople:

1. Are prepared.
2. Believe what they have to say is important.
3. Know their call's purpose and make sure it fits the buyer's reality.
4. Identify the fundamental message and associated key points.
5. Know their audience and speak only to issues of concern for them.
6. Summarize at the start of the presentation.
7. Throughout the presentation, continually reinforce ideas and key points.
8. Pay close attention to details when making presentations.
9. Test presentations by performing dry runs.
10. Make their presentation a performance.
11. Remain flexible, being able to adjust the presentation as it evolves.
12. Remain ready for questions.
13. Keep their perspective and enjoy the presentation.
14. Always remember that they are selling, not conversing.

Responding to objections

To assume the buyer will passively listen and positively respond to a sales presentation by placing an immediate order would be folly. Salespeople can expect to hear objections (issues or concerns raised by the buyer) at any time during the presentation and subsequent relationship. Objections can be raised when the salesperson attempts to secure appointments, during the presentation, when the salesperson attempts to obtain commitment, and/or during the after-sale follow-up. Prospects raise many kinds of objections although the following are the most common. The prospect:

1. Has no need for the product or service.
2. Needs more information.
3. Has never done it this way before.
4. Is just not interested.
5. Doesn't understand what is being communicated.
6. Doesn't like the product or service features, the salesperson's company, or even the salesperson him- or herself.
7. Has no money or believes the value does not exceed the cost.
8. Expects a discount or other price concession.
9. Is used to dealing with a competitor.
10. Needs more time to think about the offer.

When sales prospects raise an objection, it is a sign that they are not ready to buy and need an acceptable response to the objection before the buying decision can be made. In response to an objection, the salesperson should not challenge the respondent. Rather, the salesperson's objective should be to present the necessary information so that the prospect is able to make intelligent decisions based on that information.[20] It takes careful

HIGHLIGHT 9–3

Important Topics for Salesperson Training (based on interviews with sales managers)

The following training topics are ranked from 1 (most important) to 14 (least important).

Training Topic	Type of Industry	
	Consumer Goods	Organizational Goods
Company products	1	1
Company policies	3	2
How to sell	2	4
Competitor products	4	3
Competitor policies	6	5
Company strengths and weaknesses	5	6
Company marketing strategy	7	9
Territory management	9	7
Motivation to sell	8	11
Positive attitudes toward firm	13	8
Financial analysis	10	10
Legal matters	12	12
Time management	11	13
Listening	14	14

Source: Albert L. Page, "Assessing New Product Development Practices and Performance: Establishing Crucial Norms," *Journal of Product Innovation Management*, September 1993, pp. 273–90.

thought and preparation to truly respond to objections in an effective manner. To respond to objections, nothing works better than having a positive attitude. Salespeople need to remember that, in most cases, it is not the individual the buyer is objecting to, but rather some other concern related to the product or process.

Obtaining commitment

At some point, if all objections have been resolved, the salesperson must ask for commitment. It's a rare moment when a customer will ask to buy.[21] Consequently, knowing how and when to close a sale is one of a salesperson's most indispensable skills. What follows are some basic guidelines for closing sales.

1. The salesperson should ask for the order as it is the salesperson's, not the customer's responsibility.
2. The salesperson should be persistent as customers usually will not say yes the first time they are asked to commit.
3. The salesperson should review with the customer the benefits and drawbacks associated with saying yes.
4. Once the salesperson asks for the sale, he or she should wait for the customer to respond.

5. After the customer says yes, the salesperson should immediately assure the customer he or she made the right decision.
6. The salesperson should, after commitment has been obtained, show sincere appreciation for the order as well as develop the relationship.

It should be noted that not all sales calls end in commitment, a successful closing. If commitment is not obtained, salespeople should analyze the reasons and determine if: (1) more sales calls are necessary to obtain commitment; or (2) currently, there just does not exist a good match between customer needs and seller offerings. If the salesperson determines more calls are necessary, then he/she should leave the meeting with a clear action plan, which is agreeable to the customer, for the next visit.

Building a long-term relationship

Developing long-term relationships with customers has become increasingly important for salespeople and their firms. It costs substantially more to win a new customer than to keep a current customer—from 5 to 10 times as much.[22] Many marketers continue to overlook the fundamental idea that the longer they keep a customer, the more profitable the customer becomes. The focus of attention and effort on current customers to maximize their satisfaction with an organization is called *aftermarketing*. Successful aftermarketing efforts require many specific activities be undertaken by the salesperson and other organizational members. These activities include:

1. Establishing and maintaining a customer information file.
2. Monitoring order processing.
3. Ensuring initial proper use of the purchased product or service.
4. Providing ongoing guidance and suggestions on the use of the purchased product or service.
5. Analyzing customer feedback and responding quickly to customer questions and complaints.
6. Continually conducting customer satisfaction research and responding to it.

As can be seen by the above discussion, there are no magic secrets of successful selling. The difference between good salespeople and mediocre ones is often the result of training plus experience. Training is no substitute for experience; the two complement each other. The difficulty with trying to discuss the selling job in terms of basic principles is that experienced, successful salespeople will always be able to find exceptions to these principles. Often successful selling seems to defy logic and sometimes, common sense. Trying to program salespeople to follow definite rules or principles in every situation can stifle their originality and creativity.[23] However, six significant factors have been found to contribute most to salesperson failure.[24] These include: (1) poor listening skills; (2) failure to concentrate on top priorities; (3) a lack of sufficient effort; (4) inability to determine customer needs; (5) lack of planning for sales presentations;

and (6) inadequate product/service knowledge. What can be gleaned from these factors is an appreciation of the complex interrelationships existing between company and individual efforts as a prerequisite for sales success.

MANAGING THE SALES AND RELATIONSHIP-BUILDING PROCESS

Every personal sale can be divided into two parts: the part done by the salespeople and the part done for the salespeople by the company. For example, from the standpoint of the product, the company should provide the salesperson with a product skillfully designed, thoroughly tested, attractively packaged, adequately advertised, and priced to compare favorably with competitive products. Salespeople have the responsibility of being thoroughly acquainted with the product, its selling features, and points of superiority, and a sincere belief in the value of the product. From a sales management standpoint, the company's part of the sale involves the following:

1. Efficient and effective sales tools, including continuous sales training, promotional literature, samples, trade shows, product information, and adequate advertising.
2. An efficient delivery and reorder system to ensure that customers will receive the merchandise as promised.
3. An equitable compensation plan that rewards performance, motivates the salesperson, and promotes company loyalty. It should also reimburse the salesperson for all reasonable expenses incurred while doing the job.
4. Adequate supervision and evaluation of performance as a means of helping salespeople do a better job, not only for the company but for themselves as well.

Being a successful sales manager is much different from being a successful salesperson.[25] Reports, budgets, meetings, and other tasks take on new importance as the focus changes from getting an order to running an entire department or division. Indeed, the role of the sales manager can be likened to that of a good coach.[26] The sales manager must possess a variety of skills including those related to: (1) problem solving, (2) interpersonal relations, (3) written and oral communication, (4) persuasion, and (5) technology.[27] The sales manager must continually remind the sales force of the fundamentals, constantly encourage peak efforts, consistently praise effective performance, and, perhaps most importantly, do as much listening as speaking.[28] Simultaneously, the sales manager is charged with developing an effective overall sales plan so that organizational goals can be realized. An important key to maximizing sales productivity and end performance is the ability of the sales manager to give good coaching to the many and not to rely on the individual efforts of the few. With this type responsibility, it is no wonder that good sales managers at large organizations can earn over $170,000 per year.[29]

The Sales Management Task

Since the advent of the marketing concept, a clear-cut distinction has been made between marketing management and sales management. Marketing management refers to all activities in the firm that have to do with satisfying demand. Sales management is a narrower concept dealing with those functions directly related to personal selling. Generally speaking, sales managers are in middle management and report directly to the vice president of marketing. Their basic responsibilities can be broken down into at least seven major areas: (1) developing an effective sales organization for the company; (2) formulating short-range and long-range sales programs; (3) recruiting, training, and supervising the sales force; (4) formulating sales budgets and controlling selling expenses, (5) coordinating the personal selling effort with other forms of promotional activities; (6) maintaining lines of communication between the sales force, customers, and other relevant parts of the business, such as advertising, production, and logistics; and, in some firms, (7) developing sales forecasts and other types of relevant marketing studies to be used in sales planning and control.

Sales managers are line officers whose primary responsibility is establishing and maintaining an active sales organization. In terms of authority, they usually have equivalent rank to that of other marketing executives who manage aspects of the marketing program, such as advertising, product planning, or physical distribution. The sales organization may have separate departments and department heads to perform specialized tasks, such as training, personnel, promotion, and forecasting. Figure 9–2 is an example of such a sales organization.

In other cases, a general marketing manager may have product managers or directors reporting to them. This is common in cases where the firm sells numerous products and each product or product line is handled

Figure 9–2 *An Example of a Sales Organization*

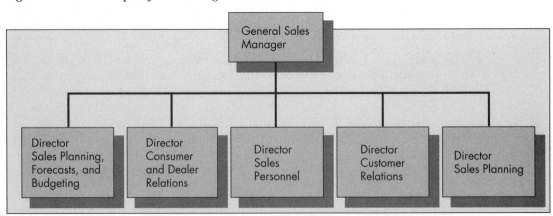

by a separate manager. Another common arrangement is to have sales managers assigned to specific geographic regions or customer groups. This type of specialization enables the sales force to operate more efficiently and effectively by avoiding overlaps.

Toward this end, more and more organizations are embracing the concept of national account management programs. National account management programs allow firms to identify and target their largest and most important customer accounts and provide these accounts with special treatment in marketing administration, and service.[30] Specific sales personnel are assigned to handle each national account regardless of geographic location where individual offices and facilities of the account may reside. National accounts differ from traditional customers in that they tend to have more centralized purchasing processes and purchase a much larger volume of products. National account management programs provide a number of benefits for both the selling organization and the customer. For the selling firm, there is the potential to develop better, closer relationships with the customer, which can give the firm a competitive advantage through increased profit margins, increased communication between the buying and selling firm, and the maintenance of a stable customer base among a firm's national accounts. From the customer's perspective two benefits are that fewer mistakes are likely to occur during processing and servicing orders due to less points of contact with the selling firm and customer needs can be addressed more immediately than if they were processed through more traditional channels.

Regardless of whether national account management or some other method of organizational setup is utilized, it is essential that marketing and sales are closely aligned.[31] As mentioned in previous sections, the sales force is a valuable source of information for designing product/market strategy. Rather than competing, various marketing and sales departments should engage in cooperative efforts. Toward this end, leading organizations are taking steps to better integrate sales and marketing departments including:[32]

1. Setting up compensation systems that rely on the success of multiple departments meeting goals.
2. Making departments responsible for each other.
3. Sending marketing people to work for a time in sales departments and vice versa to help individual personnel understand others' jobs.
4. Holding joint planning meetings.
5. Assigning joint projects.
6. Encouraging communication between departments.
7. Assigning sales managers to head up marketing projects and vice versa.

Controlling the Sales Force

There are two obvious reasons why it is critical that the sales force be properly controlled. First, personal selling can be the largest marketing expense component in the final price of the product. Second, unless the sales force is somehow directed, motivated, and audited on a continual basis, it is likely to be less efficient than it is capable of being. Controlling the sales force involves four key functions: (1) forecasting sales; (2) establishing sales territories and quotas; (3) analyzing expenses; and (4) motivating and compensating performance.

Forecasting sales. Sales planning begins with a forecast of sales for some future period or periods. From a practical standpoint, these forecasts are made on a short-term basis of a year or less, although long-range forecasts of one to five years are made for purposes other than managing the sales force, such as financing, production, and development. Generally speaking, forecasting is the marketing manager's responsibility. In large firms, because of the complexity of the task, it is usually delegated to a specialized unit, such as the marketing research department. Forecast data should be integrated into the firm's marketing decision support system for use by sales managers and other corporate executives. For many companies, the sales forecast is the key instrument in the planning and control of operations.[33]

The sales forecast is an estimate of how much of the company's output, either in dollars or in units, can be sold during a specified future period under a proposed marketing plan and under an assumed set of economic conditions. A sales forecast has several important uses: (1) it is used to establish sales quotas; (2) it is used to plan personal selling efforts as well as other types of promotional activities in the marketing mix; (3) it is used to budget selling expenses; and (4) it is used to plan and coordinate production, physical distribution, inventories, personnel, and so forth.

Sales forecasting has become very sophisticated in recent years, especially with the increased availability of computer hardware and software. It should be mentioned, however, that a forecast is never a substitute for sound business judgment. At the present time there is no single method of sales forecasting known that gives uniformly accurate results with infallible precision. Outlined below are some commonly used sales forecasting methods.[34]

1. *Jury of executive opinion method.* This combines and averages the views of top management representing marketing, production, finance, purchasing, and administration.
2. *Sales-force composite method.* This is similar to the first method in that it obtains the combined views of the sales force about the future outlook for sales. In some companies all salespeople, or district managers, submit estimates of the future sales in their territory or district.
3. *Customer expectations method.* This approach involves asking customers or product users about the quantity they expect to purchase.
4. *Time series analyses.* This approach involves analyzing past sales data and the impact of factors that influence sales (long-term growth trends, cyclical fluctuations, seasonal variations).

5. *Correlation analysis.* This involves measuring the relationship between the dependent variable, sales, and one or more independent variables that can explain increases or decreases in sales volumes.

6. *Other quantitative techniques.* Numerous statistical and mathematical techniques can be used to predict or estimate future sales. Two of the more important techniques are (*a*) growth functions, which are mathematical expressions specifying the relationship between demand and time; and (*b*) simulation models, where a statistical model of the industry is developed and programmed to compute values for the key parameters of the model.

Establishing sales territories and quotas.   The establishment of sales territories and sales quotas represents management's need to match personal selling effort with sales potential (or opportunity). Soundly designed sales territories can improve how the market is served.[35] It is much easier to pinpoint customers and prospects and to determine who should call on them when the market is geographically divided than when the market is considered as a large aggregate of potential accounts. The geographic segments should represent small clusters of customers or prospects within some physical proximity. Implied here is the notion that there are some distinct economic advantages to dividing the market into smaller segments. Salespeople restricted to a geographic area are likely to get more sales in the territory. Instead of simply servicing the "easy" and larger accounts, they are prone to develop small accounts. Of course, there are criteria other than geography for establishing territories. One important criterion is that of product specialization. In this case, salespeople are specialists relative to particular product or customer situations.

The question of managing sales territories cannot be discussed meaningfully without saying something about sales quotas. In general, quotas represent goals assigned to salespeople. As such, quotas provide three main benefits. First they provide incentives for salespeople. For example, the definite objective of selling $500,000 worth of computer equipment is more motivation to most salespeople than the indefinite charge to go out and sell computer equipment. Sales bonuses and commissions based on quotas can also be motivational. Second, quotas provide a quantitative standard against which the performance of individual sales representatives or other marketing units can be measured. They allow management to pinpoint individuals and units that are performing above average and those experiencing difficulty. Third, quotas can be used not only to evaluate salespersons' performance but also to evaluate and control their efforts. As part of their job, salespeople are expected to engage in various activities besides calling on established accounts. These activities might include calling on new accounts, collecting past-due accounts, and planning and developing sales presentations. Activity quotas allow the company to monitor whether salespeople are engaging in these activities to the extent desired.

Figure 9–3   *Ajax Drug Company Sales Activity Evaluation*

	(1)	(2)	(3) Percent (2 ÷ 1)	(4) Weight	(5) Score (3 × 4)
Territory: M Salesperson: Smith					
Functions	**Quota**	**Actual**			
Sales Volume:					
A. Old business	$380,000	$300,000	79	0.7	55.7
B. New business	$ 20,000	$ 20,000	100	0.5	50.0
Calls on prospects:					
A. Doctors	20	15	75	0.2	15.0
B. Druggists	80	60	75	0.2	15.0
C. Wholesalers	15	15	100	0.2	20.0
D. Hospitals	10	10	100	0.2	20.0
				2.0	175.7

Performance Index = 175.7

Sales quotas represent specific sales goals assigned to each territory or unit over a designated time period. The most common method of establishing quotas for territories is to relate sales to forecasted sales potential. For example, if the Ajax Drug Company's territory M has an estimated industry sales potential for a particular product of $400,000 for the year, the quota might be set at 25 percent of that potential, or $100,000. The 25 percent figure represents the market share Ajax estimates to be a reasonable target. This $100,000 quota may represent an increase of $20,000 in sales over last year (assuming constant prices) that is expected from new business.

In establishing sales quotas for its individual territories or sales personnel, management needs to take into account three key factors. First, all territories will not have equal potential and, therefore, compensation must be adjusted accordingly. Second, all salespeople will not have equal ability, and assignments may have to be made accordingly. Some companies adjust quotas up or down depending upon the specific salesperson's: (1) years of experience with the company; (2) past sales performance; and (3) need for organizational resources to support his/her efforts.[36] Third, the sales task in each territory may differ from time period to time period. For instance, the nature of some territories may require that salespeople spend more time seeking new accounts, rather than servicing established accounts, especially in the case of so-called new territories. The point to be made here is that quotas can vary, not only by territory but also by assigned tasks. The effective sales manager should assign quotas not only for dollar sales but also for each major selling function. Figure 9–3 is an example of how this is done for the Ajax Drug Company, where each activity is assigned a quota and a weight reflecting its relative importance.

HIGHLIGHT 9–4

Benefits of Sales-Force Automation

In today's information-driven business environment, companies are looking to their sales force as a vital source of customer information. In a recent survey of sales executives, sales representatives, and information systems managers from large corporations, more than 80 percent admitted to some form of sales-force automation to gather customer data. Pen-based computers (Apple's Newton) and contact databases (ACT! for Windows) are examples of the technology being utilized by salespeople across the globe. Listed below are a few examples of the benefits companies are experiencing from sales-force automation.

I. **Tangible benefits**
   A. Increased time spent with customers/clients.
   B. Higher levels of customer satisfaction.
   C. Increased numbers of promising prospects.
   D. Consistant and prompt follow-up correspondence.
   E. Increased revenue per salesperson.
   F. Increased customer service.
   G. Better time management by both salespeople and managers.
   H. Improved communication within the organization.
   I. Better business results companywide.
   J. Increased favorable exposure of the company name.

II. **Intangible benefits**
   A. Smoother functioning within the company.
   B. Increased employee motivation and satisfaction.
   C. Better trained salespeople and marketing personnel.
   D. More efficient use of field force equipment.
   E. More recent and pertinent information with easier access.
   F. Improved responsiveness to customer and prospect needs.
   G. Enhancement of corporate image.
   H. Corporate differentiation and competitive advantage.
   I. Smoother, more efficient organizational change.
   J. Improved control and understanding of selling and marketing expenses.

Analyzing expenses. Sales forecasts should include a sales expense budget. In some companies, sales expense budgets are developed from the bottom up. Each territorial or district manager submits estimates of expenses and forecasted sales quotas. These estimates are usually prepared for a period of a year and then broken down into quarters and months. The sales manager then reviews the budget requests from the field offices and from staff departments. Expenses may be classified as fixed, semivariable or variable, and direct or indirect. Certain items, such as rent or administrative salaries, are fixed. In field offices, employee compensation is the principal expense, and it may be fixed or semivariable, depending on the plan. Other items, such as travel, samples, or other promotional material, are

---

HIGHLIGHT 9–5

Effort- and Results-Oriented Measures for Evaluating Salespeople

Effort-Oriented Measures

1. Number of sales calls made.
2. Number of MRO calls made.
3. Number of complaints handled.
4. Number of checks on reseller stocks.
5. Uncontrollable lost job time.
6. Number of inquiries followed up.
7. Number of demonstrations completed.

Source: Sales and Marketing Management, "Re-engineering Sales and Marketing with Advanced Information Delivery Systems," pp. S2–14 (Goldberg, April 1995); "SFA: The Newest Orthodoxy," pp. 26–28 (Taylor, February 1993).

Results-Oriented Measures

1. Sales volume (total or by product or model)
2. Sales volume as a percentage of quota.
3. Sales profitability (dollar gross margin or contribution).
4. Number of new accounts.
5. Number of stockouts.
6. Number of distributors participating in programs.
7. Number of lost accounts.
8. Percentage volume increase in key accounts.
9. Number of customer complaints.
10. Distributor sales–inventory ratios.

---

variable in nature. Some expenses are directly traceable to the sale of specific products, such as samples or displays, while other expenses are indirect, as in the case of administrative salaries and rent. Sales commissions and shipping expenses tend to vary in direct proportion to sales, while travel expense and entertainment may not be tied to sales volume in any direct proportion.

It should be understood that selling costs are budgeted much in the same way as manufacturing costs. Selling costs are usually broken down by product lines, sales region, customers, salespersons, or some other unit. Proper budgeting requires a reasonable cost accounting system. From a budgeting standpoint, the firm should use its accounting system to analyze marketing costs as a means of control.

Motivating and compensating performance. The sales manager's personnel function includes more than motivating and compensating the sales force; but from the vantage point of sales-force productivity, these two tasks are of paramount importance. Operationally, it means that the sales manager has the responsibility of keeping the morale and efforts of the sales force at high levels through supervision and motivation. These closely related tasks are accomplished through interaction with the sales force by: (1) spending time in the field visiting customers; (2) communicating on a frequent basis via letters, telephone, or in-person meetings; (3) giving credit and praise for work well done; (4) providing performance feedback on a regular basis; and (5) developing incentive schemes through which greater opportunity for earnings (as in sales contests) or job promotion can be achieved.[37]

HIGHLIGHT 9–6

Characteristics Related to Sales Performance in Different Types of Sales Jobs

Types of Sales Job	Characteristics That Are Relatively Important	Characteristics That Are Relatively Less Important
Trade selling	Age, maturity, empathy, knowledge of customer needs and business methods.	Aggressiveness, technical ability, product knowledge, persuasiveness.
Missionary selling	Youth, hard energy and stamina, verbal skill, persuasiveness.	Empathy, knowledge of customers, maturity, previous sales experience.
Technical selling	Education, product and customer knowledge—usually gained through training, intelligence.	Empathy, persuasiveness, aggressiveness, age.
New business selling	Experience, age and maturity, aggressiveness, persuasiveness, persistence.	Customer knowledge, product knowledge, education, empathy.

Source: Joseph Guiltinan and Gordon Paul, *Marketing Management,* 4th ed. © 1991, New York, McGraw-Hill, p. 3588. Reproduced by permission of The McGraw-Hill Companies.

Compensation is a principal method by which firms are able to recruit, motivate, and retain their sales forces.[38] Devising a compensation plan for a company is a technical matter, but there are some general guidelines in formulating such a plan. First, a firm should be mindful of any modifications necessary to meet its particular needs when adopting another company's compensation plan. Second, the plan should make sense (i.e., should have a logical rationale) to both management and the sales force. Third, the plan should not be so overly complex that it cannot be understood by the average salesperson. Fourth, as suggested in the section on quotas, the plan should be fair and equitable to avoid penalizing the sales force because of factors beyond their control; conversely, the plan should ensure rewards for performance in proportion to results. Fifth, the plan should allow the sales force to earn salaries that permit them to maintain an acceptable standard of living. Sixth, the plan should attempt to minimize attrition by giving the sales force some incentive, such as a vested retirement plan, for staying with the company. Finally, and perhaps most important, the individual compensation plan must be tied to the overall sales and marketing plans.[39]

There are two basic types of compensation: salary and commission. *Salary* usually refers to a specific amount of monetary compensation at an agreed rate for definite time periods. *Commission* is usually monetary compensation provided for each unit of sales and expressed as a percentage of sales. The base on which commissions are computed may be: volume of sales in units of product, gross sales in dollars, net sales after returns, sales volume in excess of a quota, and net profits. Very often, several compensation approaches are combined. For example, a salesperson might be paid

Figure 9–4   *Types of Incentives and Their Possible Performance Outcomes*

Types of Incentives

- Positive feedback on salesperson performance evaluation.
- Company praise (e.g., recognition in a newsletter).
- Bonus (e.g., cash, merchandise, or travel allowances).
- Salary increase.
- Pay for performance for specific new product idea.

- Paid educational allowance.
- Earned time off.
- Fringe benefits.
- Stock options.
- Vested retirement plan.
- Profit sharing.

Performance Outcomes

- Sell a greater dollar volume.
- Increase sales of more profitable products.
- Push new products.
- Push selected items at designated seasons.
- Achieve a higher degree of market penetration by products, kinds of customers, or territories.
- Secure large average orders.

- Secure new customers.
- Service and maintain existing business.
- Reduce turnover of customers.
- Achieve full-line (balanced) selling.
- Reduce direct selling costs.
- Increase the number of calls made.
- Submit reports and other data promptly.

Source: Some of the material was adapted from Gilbert A. Churchill Jr., Neil M. Ford, and Orville C. Walker, *Sales Force Management,* 4th ed. (Homewood, IL: Richard D. Irwin, 1993), p. 575.

a base salary, a commission on sales exceeding a volume figure, and a percentage share of the company's profits for that year.

In addition to straight dollar compensation, there are numerous other forms of incentives that can be used to motivate the sales force. Some of these types of incentives and their potential performance outcomes are listed in Figure 9–4.

CONCLUSION

This chapter has attempted to outline and explain the personal selling aspect of the promotion mix. An emphasis was placed on describing the importance of the relationship-building aspect of the personal selling process. For organizations that wish to continue to grow and prosper, personal selling plays an integral part in the marketing of products and services. As long as production continues to expand through the development of new and highly technical products, personal selling will continue to be an important part of marketing strategy.

ADDITIONAL READINGS

Babakus, Emin; David W. Cravens; Ken Grant; Thomas N. Ingram; and Raymond W. LaForge. "Removing Salesforce Performance Hurdles." *The Journal of Business & Industrial Marketing* 9, no. 3 (1994), pp. 19–29.

Babin, Barry J.; James S. Boles; and William R. Darden. "Salesperson Stereotypes, Consumer Emotions, and Their Impact on Information Processing." *Journal of the Academy of Marketing Science* 23, no. 2 (1995), pp. 94–105.

Dunn, Dan T., Jr., and Claude A. Thomas. "Partnering with Customers." *The Journal of Business & Industrial Marketing* 9, no. 1 (1994), pp. 34–40.

El-Ansary, Adel; Noel B. Zabriske; and John M. Browning. "Sales Teamwork: A Dominant Strategy for Improving Sales Force Effectiveness." *The Journal of Business & Industrial Marketing* 8, no. 3 (1993), pp. 65–72.

Hall, Mark C., and C. P. Rao. "The Impact of Buyer–Seller Relationships on Organizational Purchasing." *The Journal of Marketing Management,* Spring/Summer 1994, pp. 1–10.

Hunt, Shelby D., and Robert M. Morgan. "Relationship Marketing in the Era of Network Competition." *Marketing Management* 3, no. 1 (1994), pp. 19–28.

Jackson, Donald W., Jr., and Stephan S. Tax. "Managing the Industrial Salesforce Culture." *The Journal of Business & Industrial Marketing* 10, no. 2 (1995), pp. 34–47.

Levy, Michael, and Arun Sharma. "Adaptive Selling: The Role of Gender, Age, Sales Experience, and Education." *Journal of Business Research,* September 1994, pp. 39–47.

McIntyre, Roger P., and Martin S. Meloche. "Psychological Determinants of Effective Sales Presentations." *The Journal of Marketing Management,* Fall/Winter 1994, pp. 23–36.

Oliver, Richard L., and Erin Anderson. "An Empirical Test of the Consequences of Behavior- and Outcome-Based Sales Control Systems." *Journal of Marketing,* October 1994, pp. 28–36.

Pettijohn, Charles E., Linda S. Pettijohn; and Albert J. Taylor. "The Relationship between Effective Counseling and Effective Selling Behaviors: An Exploratory Analysis." *The Journal of Consumer Marketing* 12, no. 1 (1995), pp. 5–15.

Pettijohn, Linda S., and Charles E. Pettijohn. "Retail Sales Training: Practices and Prescriptions," *The Journal of Services Marketing* 8, no. 3 (1994), pp. 17–26.

Raymond, Mary Anne, and John F. Tanner, Jr. "The Role and Importance of the Salesperson in Creating a Competitive Advantage." *Journal of Marketing Theory & Practice,* Summer 1994, pp. 126–38.

Shepard, David C., and Rick E. Ridnour. "The Training of Sales Managers: An Exploratory Study of Sales Management Practices." *Journal of Personal Selling & Sales Management,* Winter 1995, pp. 69–74.

Strutton, David; Lou E. Pelton; and James R. Lumpkin. "Personality Characteristics and Salespeople's Choice of Coping Strategies." *Journal of the Academy of Marketing Science* 23, no. 2 (1995), pp. 132–40.

Washburn, Stewart A. "Team Selling." *Journal of Management Consulting,* Fall 1994, pp. 12–22.

Chapter 10
DISTRIBUTION STRATEGY

Channel of distribution decisions involve numerous interrelated variables that must be integrated into the total marketing mix. Because of the time and money required to set up an efficient channel, and since channels are often hard to change once they are set up, these decisions are critical to the success of the firm.

This chapter is concerned with the development and management of channels of distribution and the process of goods distribution in an extremely complex, highly productive, and specialized economy. It should be noted at the outset that channels of distribution provide the ultimate consumer or organizational buyer with time, place, and possession utility. Thus, an efficient channel is one that delivers the product when and where it is wanted at a minimum total cost.

THE NEED FOR MARKETING INTERMEDIARIES

A channel of distribution is the combination of institutions through which a seller markets products to the user or ultimate consumer. The need for other institutions or intermediaries in the delivery of goods is sometimes questioned, particularly since the profits they make are viewed as adding to the cost of the product. However, this reasoning is generally fallacious, since producers use marketing intermediaries because the intermediary can perform functions *more cheaply and more efficiently* than the producer can. This notion of efficiency is critical when the characteristics of our economy are considered.

For example, our economy is characterized by heterogeneity in terms of both supply and demand. In terms of numbers alone, there are nearly 6 million establishments comprising the supply segment of our economy, and there are close to 90 million households making up the demand side. Clearly, if each of these units had to deal on a one-to-one basis to obtain needed goods and services, and there were no intermediaries to collect and disperse assortments of goods, the system would be totally inefficient. Thus, the primary role of intermediaries is to bring supply and demand together in an efficient and orderly fashion.

HIGHLIGHT 10–1

Who Gets What in the Compact Disc Channel of Distribution

	Percentage of Retail Price	Dollar Amount
Record Company	27%	$4.58
Artist	16	2.72
Manufacturer	13	2.21
Wholesaler	9	1.53
Retailer	35	5.94
	100%	$16.98

Source: From *Principles of Marketing*, 3rd ed. by Thomas C. Kinnear and Kenneth L. Bernhardt. Copyright © 1990, 1986 by Scott, Foresman and Company. Reprinted by permission of HarperCollins Publishers.

CLASSIFICATION OF MARKETING INTERMEDIARIES AND FUNCTIONS

There are a great many types of marketing intermediaries, many of which are so specialized by function and industry that they need not be discussed here. Figure 10–1 presents the major types of marketing intermediaries common to many industries. Although there is some overlap in this classification, these categories are based on the marketing functions performed. That is, various intermediaries perform different marketing functions and to different degrees. Figure 10–2 is a listing of the more common marketing functions performed in the channel.

It should be remembered that whether or not a manufacturer utilizes intermediaries to perform these functions, the functions have to be performed by someone. In other words, the managerial question is not whether to perform the functions but who will perform them and to what degree.

CHANNELS OF DISTRIBUTION

As previously noted, a channel of distribution is the combination of institutions through which a seller markets products to the user or ultimate consumer. Some of these links assume the risks of ownership; others do not. Some perform marketing functions while others perform nonmarketing or facilitating functions, such as transportation. The conventional channel of distribution patterns for consumer goods markets are shown in Figure 10–3.

Some manufacturers use a *direct channel*, selling directly to a market. For example, Gateway 2000 sells computers through the mail without the use of other intermediaries. Using a direct channel, called *direct marketing*, increased in popularity as marketers found that products could be sold directly using a variety of media. There media include direct mail, telemar-

Figure 10–1 *Major Types of Marketing Intermediaries*

> **Middleman**—an independent business concern that operates as a link between producers and ultimate consumers or industrial buyers.
>
> **Merchant middleman**—a middleman who buys the goods outright and takes title to them.
>
> **Agent**—a business unit that negotiates purchases, sales, or both but does not take title to the goods in which it deals.
>
> **Wholesaler**—a merchant establishment operated by a concern that is primarily engaged in buying, taking title to, usually storing and physically handling goods in large quantities, and reselling the goods (usually in smaller quantities) to retailers or to industrial or business users.
>
> **Retailer**—a merchant middleman who is engaged primarily in selling to ultimate consumers.
>
> **Broker**—a middleman who serves as a go-between for the buyer or seller. The broker assumes no title risks, does not usually have physical custody of products, and is not looked upon as a permanent representative of either the buyer or the seller.
>
> **Manufacturers' agent**—an agent who generally operates on an extended contractual basis, often sells within an exclusive territory, handles noncompeting but related lines of goods, and possesses limited authority with regard to prices and terms of sale.
>
> **Distributor**—a wholesale middleman especially in lines where selective or exclusive distribution is common at the wholesaler level in which the manufacturer expects strong promotional support: often a synonym for wholesaler.
>
> **Jobber**—a middleman who buys from manufacturers and sells to retailers; a wholesaler.
>
> **Facilitating agent**—a business firm that assists in the performance of distribution tasks other than buying, selling, and transferring title (i.e., transportation companies, warehouses, etc.)

Source: Based on Peter D. Bennett, ed., *Dictionary of Marketing Terms,* 2nd ed. (Chicago: American Marketing Association, 1995).

keting, direct-action advertising, catalog selling, cable selling, on-line selling, and direct selling through demonstrations at home or place of work.

In other cases, one or more intermediaries may be used in the distribution process. For example, Hewlett-Packard sells its computers and printers through retailers such as Best Buy and Office Max. A common channel for consumer goods is one in which the manufacturer sells through wholesalers and retailers. For instance, a cold remedy manufacturer may sell to drug wholesalers who, in turn, sell a vast array of drug products to various retail outlets. Small manufacturers may also use agents, since they do not have sufficient capital for their own sales forces. Agents are commonly used intermediaries in the jewelry industry. The final channel in Figure 10–3 is used primarily when small wholesalers and retailers are involved. Channels with one or more intermediaries are referred to as *indirect channels.*

In contrast to consumer products, the direct channel is often used in the distribution of organizational goods. The reason for this stems from the structure of most organizational markets, which often have relatively few but extremely large customers. Also, many organizational products, such

Figure 10–2 *Marketing Functions Performed in Channels of Distribution*

Buying—purchasing products from sellers for use or for resale.
Selling—the personal or impersonal process whereby the salesperson ascertains, activates, and satisfies the needs of the buyer to the mutual continuous benefit of both buyer and seller.
Sorting—a function performed by intermediaries in order to bridge the discrepancy between the assortment of goods and services generated by the producer and the assortment demanded by the consumer. This function includes four distinct processes: sorting out, accumulation, allocation, and assorting.
Sorting out—a sorting process that breaks down a heterogeneous supply into separate stocks that are relatively homogeneous.
Accumulation—a sorting process that brings similar stocks from a number of sources together into a larger homogeneous supply.
Allocation—a sorting process that consists of breaking a homogeneous supply down into smaller and smaller lots.
Assorting—a sorting process that consists of building an assortment of products for use in association with each other.
Concentration—the process of bringing goods from various places together in one place.
Financing—providing credit or funds to facilitate a transaction.
Storage—maintaining inventories and protecting products to provide better customer service.
Grading—the classifying of a product by examining its quality. It is often done with a program of grade labeling, though individual firms can grade their own products by a private system if they wish, for example, good, better, best.
Transportation—a marketing function that adds time and place utility to the product by moving it from where it is made to where it is purchased and used. It includes all intermediate steps in the process.
Risk-taking—taking on business risks involved in transporting and owning products.
Marketing research—collecting information concerning such things as market conditions, expected sales, consumer trends, and competitive forces.

Source: Based on Peter D. Bennett, ed., *Dictionary of Marketing Terms,* 2nd ed. (Chicago: American Marketing Association, 1995).

as computers, need a great deal of presale and postsale service. Distributors are used in organizational markets when the number of buyers is large and the size of the buying firm is small. As in the consumer market, agents are used in organizational markets in cases where manufacturers do not wish to have their own sales forces. Such an arrangement may be used by small manufacturers or when the market is geographically dispersed. The final channel arrangement in Figure 10–4 may also be used by a small manufacturer or when the market consists of many small customers. Under such conditions, it may not be economical for sellers to have their own sales organization.

SELECTING CHANNELS OF DISTRIBUTION

Given the numerous types of channel intermediaries and functions that must be performed, the task of selecting and designing a channel of dis-

Figure 10–3   *Conventional Channels of Distribution of Consumer Goods*

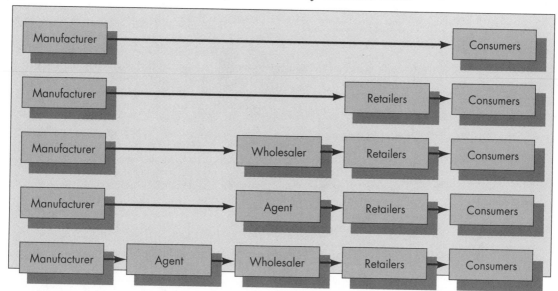

Figure 10–4   *Conventional Channels of Distribution for Organizational Goods*

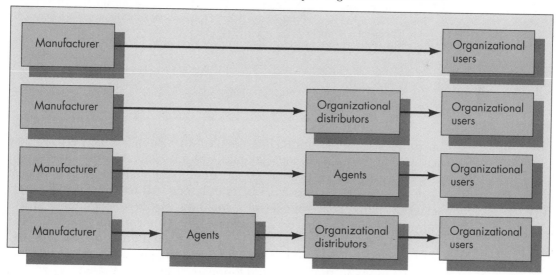

tribution may at first appear to be overwhelming. However, in many industries, channels of distribution have developed over many years and have become somewhat traditional. In such cases, the producer may be limited to this type of channel to operate in the industry. This is not to say that a traditional channel is always the most efficient and that there are no op-

Figure 10–5 *General Considerations in Channel Planning*

1. **Customer characteristics.**
   a. Number.
   b. Geographic dispersion.
   c. Preferred channels and outlets for purchase.
   d. Purchasing patterns.
   e. Use of new channels (e. g., on-line purchasing)
2. **Product characteristics.**
   a. Unit value.
   b. Perishability.
   c. Bulkiness.
   d. Degree of standardization.
   e. Installation and maintenance services required.
3. **Intermediary characteristics.**
   a. Availability.
   b. Willingness to accept product or product line.
   c. Geographic market served.
   d. Marketing functions performed.
   e. Potential for conflict.
   f. Potential for long-term relationship.
   g. Competitive products sold.
   h. Financial condition.
   i. Other strengths and weaknesses.
4. **Competitor characteristics.**
   a. Number.
   b. Relative size and market share.
   c. Distribution channels and strategy.
   d. Financial condition and estimated marketing budget.
   e. Size of product mix and product lines.
   f. Overall marketing strategy employed.
   g. Other strengths and weaknesses.
5. **Company characteristics.**
   a. Relative size and market share.
   b. Financial condition and marketing budget.
   c. Size of product mix and product lines.
   d. Marketing strategy employed.
   e. Marketing objectives.
   f. Past channel experience.
   g. Marketing functions willing to perform.
   h. Other strengths and weaknesses.
6. **Environmental characteristics.**
   a. Economic conditions.
   b. Legal regulations and restrictions.
   c. Political issues.
   d. International and domestic cultural differences and changes.
   e. Technological changes.
   f. Other opportunities and threats.

portunities for innovation, but the fact that such a channel is widely accepted in the industry suggests it is highly efficient. A primary constraint in these cases and in cases where no traditional channel exists is that of *availability* of the various types of middlemen. All too often in the early stages of channel design, executives map out elaborate channel networks only to find out later that no such independent intermediaries exist for the firm's product in selected geographic areas. Even if they do exist, they may not be willing to accept the seller's products. In general, there are six basic considerations in the initial development of channel strategy. These are outlined in Figure 10–5.

It should be noted that for a particular product any one of these characteristics greatly influence choice of channels. To illustrate, highly perishable products generally require direct channels, or a firm with little financial strength may require intermediaries to perform almost all of the marketing functions.

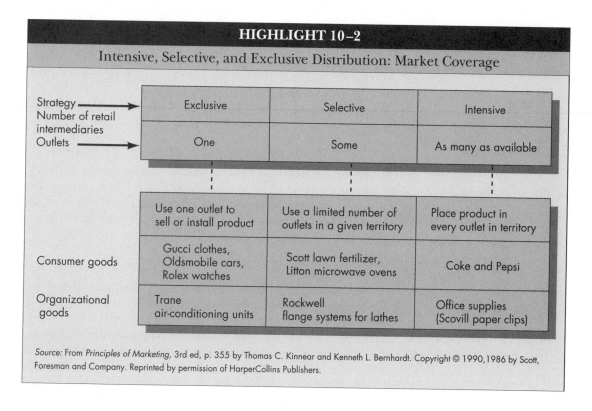

HIGHLIGHT 10–2

Intensive, Selective, and Exclusive Distribution: Market Coverage

	Exclusive	Selective	Intensive
Strategy → Number of retail intermediaries Outlets →	One	Some	As many as available
	Use one outlet to sell or install product	Use a limited number of outlets in a given territory	Place product in every outlet in territory
Consumer goods	Gucci clothes, Oldsmobile cars, Rolex watches	Scott lawn fertilizer, Litton microwave ovens	Coke and Pepsi
Organizational goods	Trane air-conditioning units	Rockwell flange systems for lathes	Office supplies (Scovill paper clips)

Source: From *Principles of Marketing,* 3rd ed, p. 355 by Thomas C. Kinnear and Kenneth L. Bernhardt. Copyright © 1990, 1986 by Scott, Foresman and Company. Reprinted by permission of HarperCollins Publishers.

Specific Considerations

The above characteristics play an important part in framing the channel selection decision. Based on them, the choice of channels can be further refined in terms of (1) distribution coverage required; (2) degree of control desired; (3) total distribution cost; and (4) channel flexibility.

Distribution coverage required

Because of the characteristics of the product, the environment needed to sell the product, and the needs and expectations of the potential buyer, products will vary in the intensity of distribution coverage they require. Distribution coverage can be viewed along a continuum ranging from intensive to selective to exclusive distribution.

Intensive distribution. Here the manufacturer attempts to gain exposure through as many wholesalers and retailers as possible. Most convenience goods require intensive distribution based on the characteristics of the product (low unit value) and the needs and expectations of the buyer (high frequency of purchase and convenience).

Selective distribution. Here the manufacturer limits the use of intermediaries to the ones believed to be the best available. This may be based on the service organization available, the sales organization, or the reputation of the intermediary. Thus, appliances, home furnishings, and better clothing are usually distributed selectively. For appliances, the intermediary's service organization could be a key factor, while for better clothing and home furnishings, the intermediary's reputation would be an important consideration.

Exclusive distribution. Here the manufacturer severely limits distribution, and intermediaries are provided exclusive rights within a particular territory. The characteristics of the product are a determining factor here. Where the product requires certain specialized selling effort and/or investment in unique facilities or large inventories, this arrangement is usually selected. Retail paint stores are an example of such a distribution arrangement.

Degree of control desired

In selecting channels of distribution, the seller must make decisions concerning the degree of control desired over the marketing of the firm's products. Some manufacturers prefer to keep as much control over the policies surrounding their product as possible. Ordinarily, the degree of control achieved by the seller is proportionate to the directness of the channel. One Eastern brewery, for instance, owns its own fleet of trucks and operates a wholly owned delivery system direct to grocery and liquor stores. Its market is very concentrated geographically, with many small buyers, so such a system is economically feasible. However, all other brewers in the area sell through wholesalers or distributors.

When more indirect channels are used, the manufacturer must surrender some control over the marketing of the firm's product. However, attempts are commonly made to maintain a degree of control through some other indirect means, such as sharing promotional expenditures, providing sales training, or other operational aids, such as accounting systems, inventory systems, or marketing research data on the dealer's trading area.

Total distribution cost

The total distribution cost concept has developed out of the more general topic of systems theory. The concept suggests that a channel of distribution should be viewed as a total system composed on interdependent subsystems, and that the objective of the system (channel) manager should be to optimize total system performance. In terms of distribution costs, it generally is assumed that the total system should be designed to minimize costs, other things being equal. The following is a representative list of the major distribution costs to be minimized.

1. Transportation.
2. Order processing.

3. Cost of lost business (an opportunity cost due to inability to meet customer demand).
4. Inventory carrying costs, including:
   a. Storage-space charges.
   b. Cost of capital invested.
   c. Taxes.
   d. Insurance.
   e. Obsolescence and deterioration.
5. Packaging.
6. Materials handling.

The important qualification to the total cost concept is the statement "other things being equal." The purpose of the total cost concept is to emphasize total system performance to avoid suboptimization. However, other important factors must be considered, not the least of which are level of customer service, sales, profits, and interface with the total marketing mix.

Channel flexibility

A final consideration relates to the ability of the manufacturer to adapt to changing conditions. To illustrate, in recent years much of the population has moved from inner cities to suburbs and thus make most of their purchases in shopping centers and malls. If a manufacturer had long-term, exclusive dealership with retailers in the inner city, the ability to adapt to this population shift could have been severely limited.

MANAGING A CHANNEL OF DISTRIBUTION

Once the seller has decided on the type of channel structure to use and selected the individual members, the entire coalition should operate as a total system. From a behaviorial perspective, the system can be viewed as a social system since each member interacts with the others, each member plays a role vis-à-vis the others, and each has certain expectations of the other. Thus, the behaviorial perspective views a channel of distribution as more than a series of markets or participants extending from production to consumption.

Relationship Marketing in Channels

For many years in theory and practice, marketing has taken a competitive view of channels of distribution. In other words, since channel members had different goals and strategies, it was believed that the major focus should be on concepts such as power and conflict. Research interests focused on issues concerning bases of power, antecedents and consequences of conflict, and conflict resolution.

More recently, however, a new view of channels has developed. Perhaps because of the success of Japanese companies in the 1980s, it was recog-

HIGHLIGHT 10–3

Manufacturers and Intermediaries: A Perfect Working Relationship

The Perfect Intermediary

1. Has access to the market that the manufacturer wants to reach.
2. Carries adequate stocks of the manufacturer's products and a satisfactory assortment of other products.
3. Has an effective promotional program—advertising, personal selling, and product displays. Promotional demands placed on the manufacturer are in line with what the manufacturer intends to do.
4. Provides services to customers—credit, delivery, installation, and product repair—and honors the product warranty conditions.

Source: Adapted from William J. Stanton, Michael J. Etzel and Bruce J. Walker, *Fundamentals of Marketing,* 9th ed. © New York, McGraw-Hill, 1991, p. 305. Reproduced by permission of the McGraw-Hill Companies.

5. Pays its bills on time and has capable management.

The Perfect Manufacturer

1. Provides a desirable assortment of products—well designed, properly priced, attractively packaged, and delivered on time and in adequate quantities.
2. Builds product demand for these products by advertising them.
3. Furnishes promotional assistance to its middlemen.
4. Provides managerial assistance for its middlemen.
5. Honors product warranties and provides repair and installation service.

The Perfect Combination

1. Probably doesn't exist.

nized that much could be gained by developing long-term commitments and harmony among channel members. This new view is called *relationship marketing,* which can be defined as "marketing with the conscious aim to develop and manage long-term and/or trusting relationships with customers, distributors, suppliers, or other parties in the marketing environment."[1]

It is well-documented in the marketing literature that long-term relationships throughout the channel often lead to higher-quality products with lower costs. These benefits may account for the increased use of vertical marketing systems.[2]

Vertical Marketing Systems

To this point in the chapter the discussion has focused primarily on conventional channels of distribution. In conventional channels, each firm is relatively independent of the other members in the channel. However, one of the important developments in channel management in recent years is the increasing use of vertical marketing systems.

Vertical marketing systems are channels in which members are more dependent on one another and develop long-term working relationships in

HIGHLIGHT 10–4

Pushing or Pulling through the Channel System

A producer has a special challenge with respect to channel systems: How to ensure that the product reaches the end of the channel. Intermediaries—especially retailers—don't have this problem, since they already control that end of the channel.

The two basic methods of recruiting middlemen are *pushing* and *pulling*.

Pushing a product through the channels means using normal promotion effort—personal selling and advertising—to help sell the whole marketing mix to possible channel

members. This method is common—since these sales transactions are usually between rational, presumably profit-oriented buyers and sellers. The approach emphasizes the importance of building a channel—and securing the wholehearted cooperation of channel members. The producer—in effect—tries to develop a team that will work well together to get the product to the user.

By contrast, pulling means getting consumers to ask intermediaries for the product. This usually involves highly aggressive promotion to final consumers or users—perhaps using coupons or samples—and temporary bypassing of intermediaries. If the promotion works, the intermediaries are forced to carry the product—to satisfy their customers.

Source: Adapted with permission from E. Jerome McCarthy and William D. Perreault, Jr., *Basic Marketing: A Managerial Approach,* 11th ed. (Homewood, IL: Richard D. Irwin, 1993), pp. 428–30.

Figure 10–6 *Major Types of Vertical Marketing Systems*

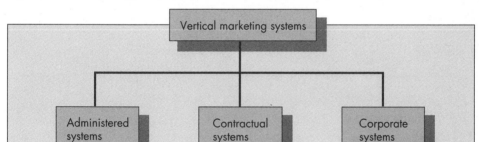

order to improve the efficiency and effectiveness of the system. Figure 10–6 shows the major types of vertical marketing systems, which include administered, contractual, and corporate systems.[3]

Administered systems

Administered vertical marketing systems are the most similar to conventional channels. However, in these systems there is a higher degree of interorganizational planning and management than in a conventional

HIGHLIGHT 10–5

Franchising: An Alternative to Conventional Channels of Distribution

A franchise is a means by which a producer of products or services achieves a direct channel of distribution without wholly owning or managing the physical facilities in the market. In effect, the franchisor provides the franchisee with the franchisor's knowledge, manufacturing, and marketing techniques for a financial return.

Ingredients of a Franchised Business

Six key ingredients should be included within a well-balanced franchise offered to a franchisee. These are given in order of importance:

— **Technical knowledge** in its practical form is supplied through an intensive course of study.
— **Managerial techniques** based on proven and time-tested programs are imparted to the franchisee on a continuing basis, even after the business has been started or taken over by the franchisee.
— **Commercial knowledge** involving pre-scribed methods of buying and selling is explained and codified. Most products to be obtained, processed, and sold to the franchisee are supplied by the franchisor.
— **Financial instruction** on managing funds and accounts is given to the franchisee during the indoctrination period.
— **Accounting controls** are set up by the franchisor for the franchisee.

Source: Partially adapted from Philip D. White and Albert D. Bates, "Franchising Will Remain Retailing Fixture, but Its Salad Days Have Long Since Gone," *Marketing News*, February 17, 1984, p. 14.

— **Protective safeguards** are included in the intensive training of the franchisee for employees and customers, including the quality of the product, as well as the safeguards for assets through adequate insurance controls.

Elements of an Ideal Franchise Program

— **High gross margin.** In order for the franchisee to be able to afford a high franchise fee (which the franchisor needs), it is necessary to operate on a high gross margin percentage. This explains the widespread application of franchising in the food and service industries.
— **In-store value added.** Franchising works best in those product categories where the product is at least partially processed in the store. Such environments require constant on-site supervision—a chronic problem for company-owned stores using a hired manager. Owners simply are willing to work harder over longer hours.
— **Secret processes.** Concepts, formulas, or products that the franchisee can't duplicate without joining the franchise program.
— **Real estate profits.** The franchisor uses income from ownership of property as a significant revenue source.
— **Simplicity.** The most successful franchises have been those that operate on automatic pilot: All the key decisions have been thought through, and the owner merely implements the decisions.

channel. The dependence in these systems can result from the existence of a strong channel leader such that other channel members work closely with this company in order to maintain a long-term relationship. While any level of channel member may be the leader of an administered system, Wal-Mart, Kmart, and Sears are excellent examples of retailers who have established administered systems with many of their suppliers.

Contractual systems

Contractual vertical marketing systems involve independent production and distribution companies entering into formal contracts to perform designated marketing functions. Three major types of contractual vertical marketing systems are the retail cooperative organization, wholesaler-sponsored voluntary chain, and various franchising programs.

In a retail cooperative organization, a group of independent retailers unite and agree to pool buying and managerial resources to improve competitive position. In a wholesaler-sponsored voluntary chain, a wholesaler contracts with a number of retailers and performs channel functions for them. Usually, retailers agree to concentrate a major portion of their purchasing with the sponsoring wholesaler and to sell advertised products at the same price. The most visible type of contractual vertical marketing systems involve a variety of franchise programs. Franchises involve a parent company (the franchisor) and an independent firm (the franchisee) entering into a contractual relationship to set up and operate a business in a particular way. Many products and services reach consumers through franchise systems, including automobiles (Ford), gasoline (Mobil), hotels and motels (Holiday Inn), restaurants (McDonald's), car rentals (Avis), and soft drinks (Pepsi). In fact, some analysts predict that within the next 10 years, franchises will account for 50 percent of all retail sales.

Corporate systems

Corporate vertical marketing systems involve single ownership of two or more levels of a channel. When a manufacturer purchases wholesalers or retailers, it is called *forward integration*. When wholesalers or retailers purchase channel members above them, it is called *backward integration*. Firms may choose to develop corporate vertical marketing systems in order to compete more effectively with other marketing systems, to obtain scale economies and to increase channel cooperation and avoid channel conflict.

CONCLUSION

The purpose of this chapter has been to introduce the reader to the process of distribution of goods in an extremely complex, highly productive, and highly specialized economy. It is important that the reader understand the vital need for marketing intermediaries in such an economy to bring about exchanges between buyers and sellers in a reasonably efficient manner. If the reader appreciates this concept, the major objective of this chapter has been achieved. The chapter also examined conventional channels of distribution for both consumer and organizational goods, and the various types of marketing intermediaries available to a seller. Finally, the selection and management of channels of distribution were discussed.

ADDITIONAL READINGS

Agrawal, Deepak, and Rajiv Lal. "Contractual Arrangements in Franchising: An Empirical Investigation," *Journal of Marketing Research,* May 1995, pp. 213–21.

Anderson, Erin, and Barton Weitz. "The Use of Pledges to Build and Sustain Commitment in Distribution Channels." *Journal of Marketing Research,* February 1992, pp. 18–34.

Berman, Barry. *Marketing Channels.* New York: Wiley, 1996.

Bowersox, Donald J., and M. Bixby Cooper. *Strategic Marketing Channel Management.* New York: McGraw-Hill, 1992.

Boyle, Brett; R. Robert Dwyer; Robert A. Robicheaux; and James T. Simpson. "Influence Strategies in Marketing Channels: Measures and Uses in Different Relationship Structures." *Journal of Marketing Research,* November 1992, pp. 462–73.

Dant, Rajiv, and Patrick L. Schul. "Conflict Resolution Processes in Contractual Channels of Distribution." *Journal of Marketing,* January 1992, pp. 38–54.

Ganesan, Shankar. "Negotiation Strategies and the Nature of Channel Relationships," *Journal of Marketing Research,* May 1993, pp. 183–203.

Purohit, Devavrat, and Richard Staelin. "Rentals, Sales, and Buybacks: Managing Secondary Distribution Channels," *Journal of Marketing Research,* August 1994, pp. 325–38.

Rosenbloom, Bert, *Marketing Channels: A Management View.* 5th ed. Fort Worth: Dryden Press, 1995.

Stern, Louis W., and Adel I. El-Ansary. *Marketing Channels.* 4th ed. Englewood Cliffs, NJ: Prentice Hall, 1992.

Chapter 11

PRICING STRATEGY

One of the most important and complex decisions a firm has to make relates to pricing its products or services. If consumers or organizational buyers perceive a price to be too high, they may purchase competitive brands or substitute products, leading to a loss of sales and profits for the firm. If the price is too low, sales might increase, but profitability may suffer. Thus, pricing decisions must be given careful consideration when a firm is introducing a new product or planning a short- or long-term price change.

This chapter discusses demand, supply, and environmental influences that affect pricing decisions and emphasizes that all three must be considered for effective pricing. However, as will be discussed in the chapter, many firms price their products without explicitly considering all of these influences.

DEMAND INFLUENCES ON PRICING DECISIONS

Demand influences on pricing decisions concern primarily the nature of the target market and expected reactions of consumers to a given price or change in price. There are three primary considerations here: demographic factors, psychological factors, and price elasticity.

Demographic Factors

In the initial selection of the target market that a firm intends to serve, a number of demographic factors are usually considered. Demographic factors that are particularly important for pricing decisions include the following:

1. Number of potential buyers.
2. Location of potential buyers.
3. Position of potential buyers (resellers or final consumers).
4. Expected consumption rates of potential buyers.
5. Economic strength of potential buyers.

These factors help determine market potential and are useful for estimating expected sales at various price levels.

HIGHLIGHT 11-1

The Meaning of Price

Alternative Terms	What Is Given in Return
Price	Most physical merchandise.
Tuition	College courses, education.
Rent	A place to live or the use of equipment for a specific time period.
Interest	Use of money.
Fee	Professional services of lawyers, doctors, consultants.
Fare	Transportation: air, taxi, bus.
Toll	Use of road or bridge, or long-distance phone rate.
Salary	Work of managers.
Wage	Work of hourly workers.
Bribe	Illegal actions.
Commission	Sales effort.

Source: From *Principles of Marketing*, 3rd ed., p. 576, by Thomas C. Kinnear and Kenneth L. Bernhardt. Copyright © 1990, 1986 by Scott, Foresman and Company. Reprinted by permission of HarperCollins Publishers.

Psychological Factors

Psychological factors related to pricing concern primarily how consumers will perceive various prices or price changes. For example, marketing managers should be concerned with such questions as:

1. Will potential buyers use price as an indicator of product quality?
2. Will potential buyers be favorably attracted by odd pricing?
3. Will potential buyers perceive the price as too high relative to the service the product gives them?
4. Are potential buyers prestige oriented and therefore willing to pay higher prices to fulfill this need?
5. How much will potential buyers be willing to pay for the product?

While psychological factors have a significant effect on the success of a pricing strategy and ultimately on marketing strategy, answers to the above questions may require considerable marketing research. In fact, a review of buyers' subjective perceptions of price concluded that very little is known about how price affects buyers' perceptions of alternative purchase offers and how these perceptions affect purchase response.[1] However, some tentative generalizations about how buyers perceive price have been formulated. For example, research has found that persons who choose high-priced items usually perceive large quality variations within product categories and see the consequences of a poor choice as being undesirable. They believe that quality is related to price and see themselves as good judges of product quality. In general, the reverse is true for persons who select low-priced items in the same product categories. Thus, although information on psychological factors involved in purchasing may be difficult to obtain, marketing managers must at least consider the effects of such factors on their desired target market and marketing strategy.[2]

Price Elasticity

Both demographic and psychological factors affect price elasticity. Price elasticity is a measure of consumers' price sensitivity, which is estimated by dividing relative changes in the quantity sold by the relative changes in price:

$$e = \frac{\text{Percent change in quantity demanded}}{\text{Percent change in price}}$$

Although difficult to measure, there are two basic methods commonly used to estimate price elasticity. First, price elasticity can be estimated from historical data or from price/quantity data across different sales districts. Second, price elasticity can be estimated by sampling a group of consumers from the target market and polling them concerning various price/quantity relationships. While both of these approaches provide estimates of price elasticity, the former approach is limited to the consideration of price changes, while the latter approach is often expensive and there is some question as to the validity of subjects' responses. However, even a crude estimate of price elasticity is a useful input to pricing decisions.[3]

SUPPLY INFLUENCES ON PRICING DECISIONS

For the purpose of this text, supply influences on pricing decisions can be discussed in terms of three basic factors. These factors relate to the objectives, costs, and nature of the product.

Pricing Objectives

Pricing objectives should be derived from overall marketing objectives, which in turn should be derived from corporate objectives. Since it is traditionally assumed that business firms operate to maximize profits in the long run, it is often thought that the basic pricing objective is solely concerned with long-run profits. However, the profit maximization norm does not provide the operating marketing manager with a single, unequivocal guideline for selecting prices. In addition, the marketing manager does not have perfect cost, revenue, and market information to be able to evaluate whether or not this objective is being reached. In practice, then, many other objectives are employed as guidelines for pricing decisions. In some cases, these objectives may be considered as operational approaches to achieve long-run profit maximization.

HIGHLIGHT 11–2

Increasing Consumer Prices

Marketers can increase consumer prices in a number of ways. Prices can be increased for the same quantity and quality or maintained for less quantity, less quality, or fewer auxiliary services. Price deals could be reduced or eliminated or interest rates and charges could be increased. Recently, a number of marketers have focused their pricing strategies on the second option, maintaining the same price but offering less quantity. Below are several examples of the use of this strategy.

Brand	Product	It Looks Like	You Pay	But You Get
Knorr	Leek soup and recipe mix	More: Box is 1/2″ deeper	The same	Less: Makes three 8-oz. servings, reduced from four
StarKist	Canned tuna	A bit less: Can is 1/16″ less tall	The same	Less: Weight of tuna reduced by 3/8 oz., or 5.8 percent
Lipton	Instant lemon-flavored tea	The same	The same	Less: Weight reduced by 7.5 percent; company claims it contains same number of servings as before
Brim	Decaffeinated coffee	The same	The same	Less: Weight reduced by 4.2 percent; company claims it contains same number of servings as before

Source: David E. Kalish, "Price Stable, but Products Are Less Filling," *Wisconsin State Journal,* January 6, 1991, p. 1D. Published by permission of the Tribune Media Services.

Research has found that the most common pricing objectives are (1) pricing to achieve a target return on investment; (2) stabilization of price and margin; (3) pricing to achieve a target market share; and (4) pricing to meet or prevent competition.

Cost Considerations in Pricing

The price of a product usually must cover costs of production, promotion, and distribution, plus a profit for the offering to be of value to the firm. In addition, when products are priced on the basis of costs plus a fair profit, there is an implicit assumption that this sum represents the economic value of the product in the marketplace.

Cost-oriented pricing is the most common approach in practice, and there are at least three basic variations: *markup pricing, cost-plus pricing,* and *rate-of-return pricing. Markup pricing* is commonly used in retailing, where a percentage is added to the retailer's invoice price to determine the final selling price. Closely related to markup pricing is cost-plus pricing, where the costs of producing a product or completing a project are totalled and a profit amount or percentage is added on. *Cost-plus pricing* is most often used to describe the pricing of jobs that are nonroutine and difficult to "cost" in advance, such as construction and military weapon development.

HIGHLIGHT 11–3

Basic Break-Even Formulas

The following formulas are used to calculate break-even points in units and in dollars:

$$BEP_{(in\ units)} = \frac{FC}{(SP - VC)}$$

$$BEP_{(in\ dollars)} = \frac{FC}{1 - (VC/SP)}$$

where

FC = Fixed cost
VC = Variable cost
SP = Selling price

If, as is generally the case, a firm wants to know how many units or sales dollars are necessary to generate a given amount of profit, profit (P) is simply added to fixed costs in the above formulas. In addition, if the firm has estimates of expected sales and fixed and variable costs, the selling price can be solved for. (A more detailed discussion of break-even analysis is provided in Section III of this book.)

Rate-of-return or *target pricing* is commonly used by manufacturers. In this method, price is determined by adding a desired rate of return on investment to total costs. Generally, a break-even analysis is performed for expected production and sales levels and a rate of return is added on. For example, suppose a firm estimated production and sales to be 75,000 units at a total cost of $300,000. If the firm desired a before-tax return of 20 percent, the selling price would be (300,000 + 0.20 × 300,000) ÷ 75,000 = $4.80.

Cost-oriented approaches to pricing have the advantage of simplicity, and many practitioners believe that they generally yield a good price decision. However, such approaches have been criticized for two basic reasons. First, cost approaches give little or no consideration to demand factors. For example, the price determined by markup or cost-plus methods has no necessary relationship to what people will be willing to pay for the product. In the case of rate-of-return pricing, little emphasis is placed on estimating sales volume. Even if it were, rate-of-return pricing involves circular reasoning, since unit cost depends on sales volume but sales volume depends on selling price. Second, cost approaches fail to reflect competition adequately. Only in industries where all firms use this approach and have similar costs and markups can this approach yield similar prices and minimize price competition. Thus, in many industries, cost-oriented pricing could lead to severe price competition, which could eliminate smaller firms. Therefore, although costs are a highly important consideration in price decisions, numerous other factors need to be examined.

Product Considerations in Pricing

Although numerous product characteristics can affect pricing, three of the most important are (1) perishability, (2) distinctiveness, and (3) stage in the product life cycle.

Perishability

Goods that are very perishable in a physical sense must be priced to promote sales without costly delays. Foodstuffs and certain types of raw materials tend to be in this category. Products can be considered perishable in two other senses. High fashion, fad, and seasonal products are perishable not in the sense that the product deteriorates but in the sense that demand for the product is confined to a specific time period. Perishability also relates to consumption rate, which means that some products are consumed very slowly, as in the case of consumer durables. Two important pricing considerations here are that (1) such goods tend to be expensive because large amounts of service are purchased at one time; and (2) the consumer has a certain amount of discretionary time available in making replacement purchase decisions.

Distinctiveness

Products can be classified in terms of how distinctive they are. Homogeneous goods are perfect substitutes for each other, as in the case of bulk wheat or whole milk, while most manufactured goods can be differentiated on the basis of certain features, such as package, trademark, engineering design, and chemical features. Thus, few consumer goods are perfectly homogeneous, and one of the primary marketing objectives of any firm is to make its product distinctive in the minds of buyers. Large sums of money are often invested to accomplish this task, and one of the payoffs for such investments is the seller's ability to charge higher prices for distinctive products.

Life cycle

The stage of the life cycle that a product is in can have important pricing implications. With regard to the life cycle, two approaches to pricing are skimming and penetration price policies. A *skimming* policy is one in which the seller charges a relatively high price on a new product. Generally, this policy is used when the firm has a temporary monopoly and in cases where demand for the product is price inelastic. In later stages of the life cycle, as competition moves in and other market factors change, the price may then be lowered. Digital watches and calculators are examples of this. A *penetration* policy is one in which the seller charges a relatively low price on a new product. Generally, this policy is used when the firm expects competition to move in rapidly and where demand for the product is, at least in the short run, price elastic. This policy is also used to obtain large economies of scale and as a major instrument for rapid creation of a mass market. A low price and profit margin may also discourage competition. In later stages of the life cycle, the price may have to be altered to meet changes in the market.

ENVIRONMENTAL INFLUENCES ON PRICING DECISIONS

Environmental influences on pricing include variables that are uncontrollable by the marketing manager. Two of the most important of these are competition and government regulation.

Competition

In setting or changing prices, the firm must consider its competition and how competition will react to the price of the product. Initially, consideration must be given to such factors as:

1. Number of competitors.
2. Size of competitors.
3. Location of competitors.
4. Conditions of entry into the industry.
5. Degree of vertical integration of competitors.
6. Number of products sold by competitors.
7. Cost structure of competitors.
8. Historical reaction of competitors to price changes.

These factors help determine whether the firm's selling price should be at, below, or above competition. Pricing a product at competition (i.e., the average price charged by the industry) is called *going rate pricing* and is popular for homogeneous products, since this approach represents the collective wisdom of the industry and is not disruptive of industry harmony. An example of pricing below competition can be found in *sealed-bid pricing,* where the firm is bidding directly against competition for project contracts. Although cost and profits are initially calculated, the firm attempts to bid below competitors to obtain the job contract. A firm may price above competition because it has a superior product or because the firm is the price leader in the industry.

Government Regulations

Prices of certain goods and services are regulated by state and federal governments. Public utilities are examples of state regulation of prices. However, for most marketing managers, federal laws that make certain pricing practices illegal are of primary consideration in pricing decisions. The list below is a summary of some of the more important legal constraints on pricing. Of course, since most marketing managers are not trained as lawyers, they usually seek legal counsel when developing pricing strategies to ensure conformity to state and federal legislation.

1. Price fixing is illegal per se. Sellers must not make any agreements with *(a)* competitors, or *(b)* distributors concerning the final price of the goods. The Sherman Antitrust Act is the primary device used to outlaw horizontal price fixing. Section 5 of the Federal Trade Commission Act has been used to outlaw price fixing as an "unfair" business practice.
2. Deceptive pricing practices are outlawed under Section 5 of the Federal Trade Commission Act. An example of deceptive pricing would be to mark merchandise with an exceptionally high price and then claim that the lower selling price actually used represents a legitimate price reduction.

3. Price discrimination that lessens competition or is deemed injurious to it is outlawed by the Robinson-Patman Act (which amends Section 2 of the Clayton Act). Price discrimination is not illegal per se, but sellers cannot charge competing buyers different prices for essentially the same products if the effect of such sales is injurious to competition. Price differentials can be legally justified on certain grounds, especially if the price differences reflect cost differences. This is particularly true of quantity discounts.

4. Promotional pricing, such as cooperative advertising, and price deals are not illegal per se; but if a seller grants advertising allowances, merchandising service, free goods, or special promotional discounts to customers, it must do so on proportionately equal terms. Sections 2(d) and 2(e) of the Robinson-Patman Act are designed to regulate such practices so that price reductions cannot be granted to some customers under the guise of promotional allowances.[4]

A GENERAL PRICING DECISION MODEL

From what has been discussed thus far, it should be clear that effective pricing decisions involve the consideration of many factors and, depending on the situation, any of these factors can be the primary consideration in setting price. In addition, it is difficult to formulate an exact sequencing of when each factor should be considered. However, several general pricing decision models have been advanced with the clearly stated warning that all pricing decisions will not fit the framework. Below is one such model, which views pricing decisions as a nine-step sequence.

1. *Define market targets.* All marketing decision making should begin with a definition of segmentation strategy and the identification of potential customers.
2. *Estimate market potential.* The maximum size of the available market determines what is possible and helps define competitive opportunities.
3. *Develop product positioning.* The brand image and the desired niche in the competitive marketplace provide important constraints on the pricing decision as the firm attempts to obtain a unique competitive advantage by differentiating its product offering from that of competitors.
4. *Design the marketing mix.* Design of the marketing mix defines the role to be played by pricing in relation to and in support of other marketing variables, especially distribution and promotional policies.
5. *Estimate price elasticity of demand.* The sensitivity of the level of demand to differences in price can be estimated either from past experience or through market tests.
6. *Estimate all relevant costs.* While straight cost-plus pricing is to be avoided because it is insensitive to demand, pricing decisions must take into account necessary plant investment, investment in R&D, and investment in market development, as well as variable costs of production and marketing.

HIGHLIGHT 11–4

Some Short-Term Price Reduction Tactics

1. Cents-off deals: "Package price is 20¢ off."
2. Special offers: "Buy one, get one free"; "Buy three tires and get the fourth free."
3. Coupons: Store or manufacturer coupons in newspaper, magazines, flyers, and packages.
4. Rebates: Mail-in proof-of-purchase seals for cash or merchandise.
5. Increase quantity for same price: "2 extra ounces of coffee free."
6. Free installation or service for a limited time period.
7. Reduce or eliminate interest charges for a limited time: "90 days same as cash."
8. Special sales: "25 percent off all merchandise marked with a red tag."

7. *Analyze environmental factors.* Pricing decisions are further constrained by industry practices, likely competitive response to alternative pricing strategies, and legal requirements.
8. *Set pricing objectives.* Pricing decisions must be guided by a clear statement of objectives that recognizes environmental constraints and defines the role of pricing in the marketing strategy while at the same time relating pricing to the firm's financial objectives.
9. *Develop the price structure.* The price structure for a given product can now be determined and will define selling prices for the product (perhaps in a variety of styles and sizes) and the discounts from list price to be offered to various kinds of intermediaries and various types of buyers.[5]

While all pricing decisions cannot be made strictly on the basis of this model, such an approach has three advantages for the marketing manager. First, it breaks the pricing decision into nine manageable steps. Second, it recognizes that pricing decisions must be fully integrated into overall marketing strategy. Third, it aids the decision maker by recognizing the importance of both qualitative and quantitative factors in pricing decisions.

CONCLUSION

Pricing decisions that integrate the firm's costs with marketing strategy, business conditions, competition, consumer demand, product variables, channels of distribution, and general resources can determine the success or failure of a business. This places a very heavy burden on the price maker. Modern-day marketing managers cannot ignore the complexity or the importance of price management. Pricing policies must be continually reviewed and must take into account the fact that the firm is a dynamic entity operating in a very competitive environment. There are many ways for money to flow out of a firm in the form of costs, but often there is only one way to bring revenues in and that is by the price–product mechanism.

ADDITIONAL READINGS

Biswas, Abhijit, and Edward A. Blair. "Contextual Effects of Reference Prices in Retail Advertisements." *Journal of Marketing,* July 1991, pp. 1–12.

Kalwani, Manohar U., and Chi Kin Yim. "Consumer Price and Promotion Expectations: An Experimental Study." *Journal of Marketing Research,* February 1992, pp. 90–100.

Lichtenstein, Donald R.; Nancy M. Ridgway; and Richard G. Netemeyer. "Price Perceptions and Consumer Shopping Behavior: A Field Study." *Journal of Marketing Research,* May 1993, pp. 234–45.

Mafzumdar, Tridib, and Sung Youl Jun. "Consumer Evaluations of Multiple versus Single Price Change." *Journal of Consumer Research,* December 1993, pp. 441–50.

Mayhew, Glenn E., and Russell S. Winer. "An Empirical Analysis of Internal and External Reference Prices Using Scanner Data." *Journal of Consumer Research,* June 1992, pp. 62–70.

Monroe, Kent B. *Pricing: Making Profitable Decisions,* 2nd ed. New York: McGraw-Hill, 1990.

Nagle, Thomas T., and Reed K. Holden. *The Strategy and Tactics of Pricing,* 2nd ed. Englewood Cliffs, NJ: Prentice Hall, 1995.

Parker, Philip M. "Price Elasticity Dynamics Over the Adoption Life Cycle." *Journal of Marketing Research,* August 1992, pp. 358–67.

Rajendran, K. N., and Gerard J. Tellis. "Contextual and Temporal Components of Reference Price." *Journal of Marketing,* January 1994, pp. 22–34.

Rao, Akshay R., and Mark E. Bergen. "Price Premium Variations as a Consequence of Buyers' Lack of Information." *Journal of Consumer Research,* December 1992, pp. 412–23.

Urbany, Joel E., and Peter R. Dickson. "Consumer Normal Price Estimation: Market versus Personal Standards." *Journal of Consumer Research,* June 1991, pp. 45–51.

Walters, Rockney G. "Assessing the Impact of Retail Price Promotions on Product Substitution, Complementary Purchase, and Interstore Sales Displacement." *Journal of Marketing,* April 1991, pp. 17–28.

Part D

MARKETING IN SPECIAL FIELDS

CHAPTER 12
THE MARKETING OF SERVICES

CHAPTER 13
INTERNATIONAL MARKETING

Chapter 12
THE MARKETING OF SERVICES

Over the course of the past 15 years, the fastest growing segment of the American economy has not been the production of tangibles but the performance of services. Spending on services has increased to such an extent that today it captures more than 50 cents of the consumer's dollar. Meanwhile, the service sector has also grown steadily in its contribution to the U.S. gross domestic product and now generates 74 percent of the gross domestic product and accounts for 79 percent of all jobs.[1] In addition, the service sector in the United States produces a balance-of-trade surplus of approximately $58 billion annually (versus a deficit of $132 billion for goods) and is expected to be responsible for all net job growth through the year 2005. Over the course of the next decade, the service sector will spawn whole new legions of doctors, nurses, medical technologists, physical therapists, home health aids, and social workers to administer to the needs of an aging population, along with armies of food servers, child-care providers, and cleaning people to cater to the wants of two-income families. Also rising to the forefront will be a swelling class of technical workers, including computer engineers, systems analysts, and paralegals.

Yet, despite its growing size and importance, the service sector remains extraordinarily mismanaged, misunderstood, and mismeasured. The service sector continues to lag behind manufacturing in terms of productivity gains.[2] Further, many Americans still hold the misconception that producing a tangible product is better and more important than providing a service. And finally, the measurement of what constitutes quality service continues to be an issue of great debate. It is for these reasons that we have decided to view services as an important topic that needs to be studied separately from tangible product marketing.

Many marketing textbooks still devote little attention to program development for the marketing of services, especially those in the rapidly changing areas of health care, banking, and travel. This omission is usually based on the assumption that the marketing of products and services is basically the same, and, therefore, the techniques discussed under products apply as well to the marketing of services. Basically, this assumption is true. Whether selling goods or services, the marketer must be concerned with developing a marketing strategy centered around the four controllable decision variables that comprise the marketing mix: the product (or service), the price, the distribution system, and promotion. In addition, the use of marketing research is as valuable to service marketers, as it is to product marketers.

However, because services possess certain distinguishing characteristics, the task of determining the marketing mix ingredients for a service marketing strategy may raise different and more difficult problems than those encountered in marketing products. For example, many consumers believe that all services associated with their credit card are provided by just one company: the bank that they send their payment to. In reality, there are numerous unseen companies, such as First Data Corp. (the largest credit transaction processor), who form the nucleus of the credit card transaction process.

The purpose of this chapter is fourfold. First, the reader will become acquainted with the special characteristics of services and their strategy implications. Second, key concepts associated with providing quality services will be discussed. Third, obstacles will be described that, in the past, impeded and still continue to impede development of services marketing. Finally, current trends and strategies of innovation in services marketing will be explored. Using this approach, the material in the other chapters of the book can be integrated to give a better understanding of the marketing of services.

Before proceeding, some attention must be given to what the authors refer to when using the term *services*. Probably the most frustrating aspect of the available literature on services is that the definition of what constitutes a service remains unclear. The fact is that no common definition and boundaries have been developed to delimit the field of services. The American Marketing Association has defined services as follows:

1. *Service products,* such as a bank loan or home security, that are intangible, or at least substantially so. If totally intangible, they are exchanged directly from producer to user, cannot be transported or stored, and are almost instantly perishable. Service products are often difficult to identify, since they come into existence at the same time they are bought and consumed. They are comprised of intangible elements that are inseparable, they usually involve customer participation in some important way, cannot be sold in the sense of ownership transfer, and have no title. Today, however, most products are partly tangible and partly intangible, and the dominant form is used to classify them as either goods or services (all are products). These common, hybrid forms, whatever they are called, may or may not have the attributes just given for totally intangible services.

2. *Services,* as a term, is also used to describe activities performed by sellers and others that accompany the sale of a product, and aid in its exchange or its utilization (e.g., shoe fitting, financing, an 800 number). Such services are either presale or postsale and supplement the product but do not comprise it. If performed during sale, they are considered to be intangible parts of the product.[3]

The first definition includes what can be considered "almost pure services" such as insurance, banking, entertainment, airlines, health care, telecommunications, and hotels; and the second definition includes such services as wrapping, financing an automobile, and providing warranties on computer equipment and the like because these services exist in connection with the sale of a product or another service. This suggests that marketers of goods are also marketers of services. For example, one could argue that McDonald's is not in the hamburger business. Its hamburgers are actually not very different from those of the competition. McDonalds is in the service business: "You deserve a break today, . . . we do it all for you."[4] In fact, a recent study found that the quality of a company's service can cause it to gain or lose as much as 10 percent in sales revenue.[5] Services, that accompany products, can affect sales in two ways: (1) directly, by enhancing the reliability of product availability; and (2) indirectly, by increasing a buyer's preference for and loyalty to a supplier that provides reliable service with fewer problems.[6] Honda and Merck are prime examples of companies that build their strategies not around products but around deep knowledge of highly developed core service strategies, such as (1) stressing senior management involvement with customers; (2) going all out to resolve customer complaints; and (3) placing an emphasis on retaining current customers.[7]

More and more manufacturers are also exploiting their service capabilities as stand-alone revenue producers.[8] For example, General Motors, Ford, and Chrysler all offer financing services. Ford and General Motors have extended their financial services offerings to include a MasterCard, which offers discounts on purchases of their automobiles. Likewise, Sears introduced the Discover Card, which was positioned as a direct competitor to Visa and MasterCard.

IMPORTANT CHARACTERISTICS OF SERVICES

Services possess several unique characteristics that often have a significant impact on marketing program development. These special features of services may cause unique problems and often result in marketing mix decisions that are substantially different from those found in connection with the marketing of goods. Some of the more important of these characteristics are intangibility, inseparability, perishability, and fluctuating demand, highly differentiated marketing systems, and a client relationship.

Intangibility

The obvious basic difference between goods and services is the intangibility of services, and many of the problems encountered in the marketing of services are due to intangibility. To illustrate, how does an airline make tangible a trip from Philadelphia to San Francisco? These problems are unique to service marketing.

The fact that many services cannot appeal to a buyer's sense of touch, taste, smell, sight, or hearing before purchase places a burden on the marketing organization. For example, hotels that promise a good night's sleep to their customers cannot actually show this service in a tangible way. Obviously, this burden is most heavily felt in a firm's promotional program, but, as will be discussed later, it may affect other areas. Depending on the type of service, the intangibility factor may dictate use of direct channels because of the need for personal contact between the buyer and seller. Since a service firm is actually selling an idea or experience, not a product, it must tell the buyer what the service will do because it is often difficult to illustrate, demonstrate, or display the service in use. For example, the hotel must somehow describe to the consumer how a stay at the hotel will leave the customer feeling well rested and ready to begin a new day. Microsoft and associated computer retailers, in introducing the 'Windows 95' software package, ran a media campaign that focussed on making kids and adults (including small business owners) more comfortable with technology. As customers' comfort level with technology rises and they understand how, for example, the use of computers and particular software can enhance their lives, Microsoft, as well as computer vendors and retailers, expect their willingness to adopt emerging on-line services to also increase.

The above discussion alludes to two strategy elements firms should employ when trying to overcome the problems associated with service intangibility. First, tangible aspects associated with the service should be stressed. For example, advertisements for airlines should emphasize (through text and visuals) the newness of the aircraft, the roominess of the cabin, and the friendliness of the flight attendant. Second, end benefits resulting from completion of the service encounter should be accentuated. In the case of air travel, an individual's ability to make an important meeting or arrive home in time for a special occasion could be the derived benefit.

Inseparability

In many cases, a service cannot be separated from the person of the seller. In other words, the service must often be created and marketed simultaneously. Because of the simultaneous production and marketing of most services, the main concern of the marketer is usually the creation of time and place utility. For example, the bank teller produces the service of receiving a deposit and markets other appropriate bank services at the same time. Many services, therefore, are "tailored" and not mass-produced. Often, because a company's employees are "the company" at the point of contact, they must be given wide latitude and assistance in determining how best to tailor a specific service to meet customer needs.[9]

The implication of inseparability on issues dealing with the selection of channels of distribution and service quality is quite important. Inseparable

HIGHLIGHT 12–1

Ten of the Most Critical Differences between Products and Services

Products	Services
1. The customer owns an object.	1. The customer owns a memory. The experience cannot be sold or passed on to a third party.
2. The goal of producing a product is uniformity—all widgets are alike.	2. The goal of service is uniqueness; each customer and each contact is "special."
3. A product can be put into inventory; a sample can be sent in advance for the customer to review.	3. A service happens at the moment. It cannot be stockpiled or saved to be used at a later date.
4. The customer is an end user who is not involved in the production process.	4. The customer is a coproducer who is a partner in creating the service.
5. One conducts quality control by comparing output to specifications.	5. Customers conduct quality control by comparing expectations to experience.
6. If improperly produced, the product can be pulled off the line or "recalled."	6. If improperly performed, apologies and reparations are the only means of recourse.
7. The morale of production employees is important.	7. The morale of service employees is critical.
8. Customer can determine level of quality by comparing product to other products.	8. Customer can determine level of quality throughout the delivery of the service.
9. Low level of collaboration between the buyer and the seller.	9. High level of collaboration between the buyer and the seller.
10. Greater number and variety of product brands available to customers.	10. Fewer brands of services available to customer.

Source: Ron Zemke, "The Emerging Art of Service Management," *Training,* January 1992, pp. 36–42; and Ralph W. Jackson, Lester A. Neidell, and Dale A. Lunsford, "An Empirical Investigation of the Differences in Goods and Services as Perceived by Organizational Buyers," *Industrial Marketing Management* 24 (1995), pp. 99–108.

services cannot be inventoried, and thus direct sale is the only feasible channel of distribution. Service quality is sometimes unable to be completely standardized due to the inability to completely mechanize the service encounter. However, some industries, through innovative uses of technology, have been able to overcome or, at least, alleviate challenges associated with the inseparability characteristic.

For example, in the financial services industry, automated teller machines (ATMs) and home banking, through use of computers and telephones, have contributed greatly to eliminating the need for the customer to directly interact with a bank teller. Further, many banks are developing computer applications to allow tellers and other service representatives to think like expert problem solvers. These applications allow for platform banking, a means of enabling bank representatives in any location to bring up on a screen all the information the bank has about the customer. Every face-to-face contact with a customer can mean an opportunity to make a sale and, more important, further the relationship with the customer. Of course, the bank representative is still of critical importance as the one who might recognize by the customer's expression or words that this visit is not the appropriate time to be marketing additional services.

In addition to technology, tangible representations of the service can serve to overcome the inseparability problem. For example, in the insurance industry, a contract serves as the tangible representation of the service. The service itself remains inseparable from the seller (insurance provider) but the buyer has a tangible representation of the service in the form of a policy. This enables the use of intermediaries (agents) in the marketing of insurance. Another example would be in the use of a credit card—the card itself is a tangible representation of the service that is being produced and consumed each time the card is being used.

Perishability and Fluctuating Demand

Services are perishable and markets for most services fluctuate either by season (tourism), days (airlines), or time of day (movie theaters). Unused telephone capacity and electrical power; vacant seats on planes, trains, buses, and in stadiums; and time spent by catalog service representatives waiting for customers to reach them all represent business that is lost forever.

The combination of perishability and fluctuating demand has created many problems for marketers of services. Specifically, in the areas of staffing and distribution, avenues must be found to have the services available for peak periods, and new strategies need to be developed to make use of the service during slack periods. Some organizations are attempting to cope with these problems through the use of pricing strategy. *Off-peak pricing* consists of charging different prices during different times or days in order to stimulate demand during slow periods. Discounts given for weekend calling, Saturday night stay-overs, early bird dinners, or winter cruises are all examples of efforts made by service providers to redistribute demand.

Other organizations are dealing with issues related to peak period demand through the use of technology. To illustrate, a well-designed voice mail system allows companies and callers to cut down on missed phone calls, eliminates long waits on hold, and delivers clear, consistent messages. In the catalog industry, automated call routing (ACR) is used to route incoming calls to available service representatives in the order in which they were received. Finally, in the utilities industry, many electric utilities no longer have to generate capacity that will meet peak electrical demand. Instead, they rely on buying unused power from other utilities in other regions of the country.

HIGHLIGHT 12–2

Expectations of Service Customers in Selected Industries

Type of Service	Type of Customer	Principal Expectations
Automobile repair	Consumers	*Be competent.* "Fix it right the first time." *Explain things.* "Explain why you need the suggested repairs—provide an itemized list. *Be respectful.* "Don't treat me like an idiot."
Automobile insurance	Consumers	*Keep me informed.* "I shouldn't have to learn about insurance law changes from the newspaper." *Be on my side.* "I don't want them to treat me like I am a criminal just because I have a claim." *Play fair.* "Don't drop me when something goes wrong." *Protect me from catastrophe.* "Make sure my estate is covered in the event of a major accident." *Provide prompt service.* "I want fast settlement of my claims."
Hotel	Consumers	*Provide a clean room.* "Don't have a deep-pile carpet that can't be completely cleaned . . . You can literally see germs down there." *Provide a secure room.* "Good bolts and a peephole on the door." *Treat me like a guest.* "It is almost like they're looking you over to decide whether or not they're going to let you have a room." *Keep your promise.* "They said the room would be ready at the promised time, but it wasn't."
Property and casualty insurance	Business customers	*Fulfill obligations.* "Pay up." *Learn my business and work with me.* "I expect them to know me and my company." *Protect me from catastrophe.* "They should cover your risk exposure so there is no single big loss." *Provide prompt service.* "Fast claim service."
Equipment repair	Business customers	*Share my sense of urgency.* "Speed of response. One time I had to buy a second piece of equipment because of the huge downtime with the first piece." *Be prepared.* "Have all the parts ready."
Truck and tractor rental/ leasing	Business customers	*Keep the equipment running.* "Need to have equipment working all the time—that is the key." *Be flexible.* "The leasing company should have the flexibility to rent us equipment when we need it." *Provide full service.* "Get rid of all the paperwork and headaches."

Source: A. Parasuraman, Leonard L. Berry, and Valarie A. Zeithaml, "Understanding Customer Expectations of Service," *Sloan Management Review,* Spring 1991, pp. 39–48.

Highly Differentiated Marketing Systems

Although the marketer of a tangible product is not compelled to use an established marketing system, such systems are often available and may be the most efficient. If an established system is not available, the marketer can at least obtain guidelines from the systems used for similar products. In the case of services, however, there may be little similarity between the marketing systems needed and those used for other services. To illustrate, the marketing of banking and other financial services bears little resemblance to the marketing of computer services or telecommunications. The entire area of services marketing, therefore, demands creativity and ingenuity on the part of marketing management. For example, trucking companies are now making arrangements with railways to combine forces on some routes. This form of intermodal transportation allows the trucking companies' customers to take advantage of the cheaper fuel and labor associated with rail transport, coupled with the faster, more reliable service offered by trucks. Likewise, the U.S. Postal Service, due to the heavy volume of mail processed, knows that some of its staff is at work every day of the week. As a result, they instituted Sunday delivery on Express Mail packages to gain an advantage over Federal Express and other private carriers who shut down on Sundays. Conversely, Federal Express, as a result of its efficient delivery processes, is able to now provide same day delivery of packages on Mondays through Fridays.

Client Relationship

In the marketing of a great many services, a client relationship, as opposed to a customer relationship, exists between the buyer and the seller. In other words, the buyer views the seller as someone who has knowledge that is of value to them. Examples of this type of relationship are the physician–patient, college professor–student, accountant–small business owner, and broker–investor. The buyer, many times, abides by the advice offered or suggestions provided by the seller, and these relationships may be of an ongoing nature. Also, since many service firms are client-serving organizations, they may approach the marketing function in a more professional manner, as seen in health care, finance, and legal, governmental, and educational services.

Several recent studies on services marketing by professionals serve to highlight two major challenges professionals face.[10] First, in many cases, fear or hostility is brought to the transaction because the customer is uncertain about how genuine the professional's concern for his or her satisfaction is. For example, many unpleasant reasons exist for consulting doctors, lawyers, bankers, or even visiting a college professor. These could include surgery, being sued, having to take out a loan, or doing poorly on an exam. Second, even high-quality service delivery by the professional can lead to dissatisfied customers. For a physician, the ability to provide high-quality

HIGHLIGHT 12–3

Five Circumstances that Make the Use of Unconditional Guarantees by Professional Service Providers an Effective Marketing Tool

1. *Prices are high.* Fees for management consulting, legal, advertising, and many other types of professional services often run into six figures. By offering compensation for a service failure, the guarantee reduces perceived risk and creates value for clients.
2. *The negative consequences of unsolved problems are high.* Bad service from a restaurant can ruin someone's evening; bad service from a medical center or law firm can ruin someone's life. The greater the client's expected aggravation, expense, and time lost, the greater the guarantee's power.
3. *Services are highly customized.* The professional service firm's past performance with other buyers typically does not provide a reliable indication of how the firm will do with a new product, since different customers are often served in entirely different ways. A guarantee can provide a strong indication of a firm's reliability.
4. *Brand name recognition isn't easily achieved through conventional means.* Marketing opportunities and differentiating characteristics tend to be restricted for professional service firms. An unconditional guarantee can provide such a differentiator, making the firm stand out in potential clients' minds.
5. *Buyer resistance is high.* Clients tend to purchase professional services very cautiously, which sends the firm on long and often fruitless sales efforts. An unconditional guarantee can effectively overcome resistance and close the sale.

Source: Christopher W. L. Hart, Leonard A. Schlessinger, and Dan Maher, "Guarantees Come to Professional Service Firms," *Sloan Management Review,* Spring 1992, pp. 19–29.

medical care may be overshadowed by a brusque, unfriendly personality. For a college professor, the demand on students to only contact or visit him or her during office hours, coupled with students' own hectic work schedules, can diminish the sterling effect of the professor's classroom presentations. It is vitally important that the professional service provider strive to build long-term positive relationships with clients. Highlight 12–3 illustrates the use of unconditional guarantees, which are one way to help build such a relationship.

PROVIDING QUALITY SERVICES

In today's increasing competitive environment, quality service is critical to organizational success. In a study on the importance of service quality, more than 40 percent of all customers surveyed listed poor service as the number one reason for switching to the competition, while only 8 percent listed price.[11] As a result, delivering high quality service is closely linked to profits, cost savings, and market share.[12] Thus, retaining current customers and building their loyalty is of great importance.[13] Unlike products where quality is often measured against standards, service quality is measured against performance.[14] Since services are frequently produced in the presence of a customer, are labor intensive, and are not able to be stored or objectively examined, the definition of what constitutes good service quality can be difficult and, in fact, continually changes in the face of choices.[15] Customers determine the value of service quality in relation to available alternatives and their particular needs. In general, problems in the determination of good service quality are attributable to differences in the expectations, perceptions, and experiences regarding the encounter between the service provider and consumer. These gaps can be classified as:

1. The gap between consumer expectations and management perceptions of the consumer's expectations.
2. The gap between management perceptions of consumer expectations and the firm's service quality specifications.
3. The gap between service quality specifications and actual service quality.
4. The gap between actual service delivery and external communications about the service.

In essence, the customer perceives the level of service quality as being a function of the magnitude and direction of the gap between expected service and perceived service. Management of a company may not even realize that they are delivering poor-quality service due to differences in the way managers and consumers view acceptable quality levels. To overcome this problem and to avoid losing customers, firms must be aware of the determinants of service quality. A brief description of these determinants follows.

1. *Tangibles* include the physical evidence of the service. For example, employees are always visible in a hotel lobby dusting, emptying ash trays, or otherwise cleaning up. Likewise, clean, shiny, up-to-date medical equipment or aircraft are examples of tangible elements.
2. *Reliability* involves the consistency and dependability of the service performance. For example, does a bank or phone company always send out accurate customer statements? Likewise, does the plumber always fix the problem on his/her first visit?
3. *Responsiveness* concerns the willingness or readiness of employees or professionals to provide service. For example, will a physician see patients on the same day they call in to say they are ill? Will a college professor return a student's call the same day?
4. *Assurance* refers to the knowledge and competence of service providers and the ability to convey trust and confidence. This determinant encompasses the provider's name and reputation; possession of necessary skills; and trustworthiness, believability, and honesty. For example, a bank will guarantee same-day loan processing; a doctor is highly trained in a particular specialty.
5. *Empathy* refers to the service provider's efforts to understand the customer's needs and then to provide, as best as possible, individualized service deliv-

ery. For example, flight attendants on a customer's regular route learn what type of beverages the customer drinks and what magazines the customer reads.

Each of the above determinants plays an imporant role in how the customer views the service quality of a firm. Turning service quality into a powerful competitive weapon requires continuously striving for service superiority—consistently performing above the adequate service level and capitalizing on opportunities for exceeding the desired service level. Relentless efforts to continually improve service performance may well be rewarded by improvements in customer attitudes toward the firm: from customer frustration to customer preference to customer loyalty. What should be obvious is that in order to be successful, a service firm must have both an effective means to measure customer satisfaction and dedicated employees to provide high-quality service.

Customer Satisfaction Measurement

As mentioned above, satisfied customers can become loyal customers. Service quality and customer satisfaction are of growing concern to business organizations throughout the world, and research on these topics generally focuses on two key issues: (1) understanding the expectations and requirements of the customer; and (2) determining how well a company and its major competitors are succeeding in satisfying these expectations and requirements.[16]

As such, an organization's approach to measuring service quality through customer satisfaction measurement (CSM) and effectively implementing programs derived from results of such studies can spell the difference between success and failure. Research on Market Leaders' CSMs found they had the following aspects in common.

1. Marketing and sales employees were primarily responsible (with customer input) for designing CSM programs and questionnaires.
2. Top management and the marketing function championed the programs.
3. Measurement involved a combination of qualitative and quantitative research methods that primarily included mail questionnaires, telephone surveys, and focus groups.
4. Evaluations included both the company's and competitor's satisfaction performance.
5. Results of all research were made available to employees, but not necessarily to customers.
6. Research was performed on a continual basis.
7. Customer satisfaction was incorporated into the strategic focus of the company via the mission statement.
8. There was a commitment to increasing service quality and customer satisfaction from employees at all levels within the organization.

The Importance of Internal Marketing

Properly performed customer satisfaction research can yield a wealth of strategic information about customers, the sponsoring company, and competitors. However, service quality goes beyond the relationship between a customer and company. Rather, as shown by the last aspect listed above, it is the personal relationship between a customer and the particular employee that the customer happens to be dealing with at the time of the service encounter that ultimately determines service quality.[17] The importance of having customer-oriented, frontline people cannot be overstated.[18] If frontline service personnel are unfriendly, unhelpful, uncooperative, or uninterested in the customer, the customer will tend to project that same attitude to the company as a whole. The character and personality of an organization reflects the character and personality of its top management.[19] Management must develop programs that will stimulate employee commitment to customer service. In order to be successful, these programs must contain five critical components:

1. A careful selection process in hiring frontline employees. In order to do this, management has to clearly define the skills the service person must bring to the job.[20] For example, Fairfield Inn often considers as many as 25 candidates for each housekeeping or front desk position.[21]
2. A clear, concrete message that conveys a particular service strategy that frontline people can begin to act on. People delivering service need to know how their work fits in the broader scheme of business operations.[22] They need to have a cause because servicing others is just too demanding and frustrating to be done well each day without one.[23]
3. Significant modeling by managers, that is, managers demonstrating the behavior that they intend to reward employees for performing. For example, Virgin Atlantic Airways Chairman Richard Branson regularly travels economy class on his airline to talk to customers and solicit ideas for improvement.[24]
4. An energetic follow-through process, in which managers provide the training, support, and incentives necessary to give the employees the capability and willingness to provide quality service. For example, AT&T Universal Card Services has set up an umbrella organization, aptly called Universal Card University, to give all of its employees a single point of reference in their training.[25]
5. An emphasis on teaching employees to have good attitudes. This type of training usually focuses on specific social techniques, such as eye contact, smiling, tone of voice, and standards of dress.

However, organizing and implementing such programs will only lead to temporary results unless managers practice a strategy of internal marketing. The authors define *internal marketing* as the continual process by which managers actively encourage, stimulate, and support employee commitment to the company, the company's goods and services, and the company's customers. Emphasis should be placed on the word *continual*. Managers who consistently pitch in to help when needed, constantly provide encouragement and words of praise to employees, strive to help employees understand the benefits of performing their jobs well, and emphasize the importance of employee actions on both company and employee results are practitioners of internal marketing. In service marketing, successful internal marketing efforts, leading to employee commitment to service quality, are a key to success.

Federal Express serves as a prime example of the benefits accruing to a company that successfully practices internal marketing.[26] In 1990, Federal Express became the first service organization to win the Malcom Baldrige National Quality Award. The company's motto is "people, service, and profits." Behind its purple, white, and orange planes and uniforms are self-managing work teams, gainsharing plans, and empowered employees seemingly consumed with providing flexible and creative services to customers with varying needs. Federal Express is a high-involvement, horizontally-coordinated organization that encourages employees to use their judgment above and beyond the rulebook.

OVERCOMING THE OBSTACLES IN SERVICE MARKETING

The factors of intangibility and inseparability, as well as difficulties in coming up with objective definitions of acceptable service quality make comprehension of service marketing difficult. However, in view of the size and importance of services in our economy, considerable innovation and ingenuity are needed to make high-quality services available at convenient locations for consumers as well as business people. In fact, the area of service marketing probably offers more opportunities for imagination and creative innovation than does product marketing. Unfortunately, many service firms still lag in the area of creative marketing. Even today, those service firms that have done a relatively good job have been slow in recognizing opportunities in all aspects of their marketing programs. Four reasons, connected to past practices, can be given for the lack of innovative marketing on the part of service marketers: (1) a limited view of marketing; (2) a lack of strong competition; (3) a lack of creative management; and (4) no obsolescence.

Limited View of Marketing

Because of the nature of their service, many firms depended to a great degree on population growth to expand sales. A popular example here is the telephone company, which did not establish a marketing department until 1955. It was then that the company realized it had to be concerned not only with population growth, but also with meeting the needs of a growing population. Increases in educational levels and rises in the standards of living also bring about the need for new and diversified services. A study conducted by *American Demographics* concluded that college-educated householders are much more likely to buy services—from dry cleaning to financial services—than those with less education.[27] As a well-educated, younger generation replaces the less educated, older one, the demand for services should only increase.

Service firms must meet these changing needs by developing new services and new channels, and altering existing channels, to meet the changing composition and needs of the population. For many service industries, growth has come as a result of finding new channels of distribution. For example, some banks and other financial service companies were able to grow and tap into new markets by establishing limited service kiosks in malls and supermarkets. Airlines have successfully brought in a whole new class of travelers by offering advance-purchase discounted fares. Traditionally, users of these fares either drove or utilized other means of transportation in order to reach their destination.

While many service firms have succeeded in adopting a marketing perspective, others have been slow to respond. It was not until deregulation of the telecommunications industry took place in 1984 that the telephone companies began taking a broadened view of marketing. Even today, critics point to the obsession with inventing new technology versus using current technology in meeting customer needs as a weakness of these companies.

Limited Competition

A second major cause of the lack of innovative marketing in many service industries was due to the lack of competition. Many service industries, like banking, railroads, and public utilities have, throughout most of their histories, faced very little competition; some have even been regulated monopolies. Obviously, in an environment characterized by little competition, there was not likely to be a great deal of innovative marketing. However, two major forces have changed this situation. First, in the past two decades the banking, financial services, railroad, cable, airline, and telecommunications industries have all been deregulated in varying degrees. With deregulation has come a need to be able to compete effectively. For example, AT&T was once the sole provider of long-distance telephone service. Now, AT&T has to not only compete against such companies as MCI and Sprint but also against the regional Bell Operating Companies such as Ameritech and US West, who once were part of AT&T. Second, service marketing has taken on an international focus. Today, many foreign companies are competing in domestic service markets. Foreign interests own several banks, many hotels (including Holiday Inn), and shares in major airlines (including Northwest and USAIR). Likewise, American companies are expanding overseas as markets open up. For example, Merrill Lynch & Co. purchased Smith New Court PLC, a large British security firm, in order to become the world's largest stockbrokerage firm.[28]

HIGHLIGHT 12-4

Top 25 Service Corporations

Rank	Company*	Financial Data (in $ millions)	
		Revenues	Profits
1	AT&T	$75,094.0	$4,676.0
2	State Farm Group	38,850.1	(244.3)
3	Prudential Insurance Co. of America	36,945.7	(1,175.0)
4	Citicorp	31,650.0	3,366.0
5	ITT	23,767.0	1,022.0
6	American International Group	22,385.7	2,175.5
7	Metropolitan Life Insurance	22,257.9	80.4
8	GTE	19,944.3	2,444.6
9	United Parcel Service	19,575.7	943.3
10	Federal National Mortgage Assn.	18,572.4	2,131.6
11	Travelers Inc.	18,465.0	1,326.0
12	Cigna	18,392.0	554.0
13	Merrill Lynch	18,233.1	1,016.8
14	Aetna Life & Casualty	17,524.7	467.5
15	BellSouth	16,844.5	2,159.8
16	BankAmerica Corp.	16,531.0	2,176.0
17	Price/Costco	16,480.6	(112.4)
18	AMR (American Airlines)	16,137.0	228.0
19	American Express	15,593.0	1,413.0
20	UAL (United Airlines)	13,950.0	51.0
21	Bell Atlantic	13,791.4	(754.8)
22	Loews	13,515.2	267.8
23	MCI Communications	13,338.0	795.0
24	NYNEX	13,306.6	792.6
25	Nationsbank Corp.	13,126.0	1,690.0

*Some companies listed offer both products and services.

Source: Adapted from "The Fortune 500 Largest U.S. Corporations," *Fortune,* May 15, 1995, p. F-1. Fortune 500, © 1995 Time, Inc. All rights reserved.

Noncreative Management

For many years, the managements of service industries have been criticized for not being progressive and creative. Railroad management was criticized for many years for being slow to innovate. More recently, however, railroads have become leading innovators in the field of freight transportation, introducing such innovations as piggyback service and containerization, and in passenger service, introducing luxury overnight accommodations on trains with exotic names such as the Zephyr. Some other service industries, however, have been slow to develop new services or to innovate in the marketing of their existing services. In fact, as a whole, U.S. firms lag behind their Japanese and German competitors not only in collecting customer satisfaction data, but also in designing services that address customers' functional needs.[29]

No Obsolescence

A great advantage for many service industries is the fact that many services, because of their intangibility, are less subject to obsolescence than goods. While this is an obvious advantage, it has also led some service firms to be sluggish in their approach to marketing. Manufacturers of goods may constantly change their marketing plans and seek new and more efficient ways to produce and distribute their products. Since service firms are often not faced with obsolescence, they often failed to recognize the need for change. This failure has led to wholesale changes in many industries as new operators, who possessed marketing skills, revolutionized the manner in which the service is performed and provided. Many a barbershop and hair dresser have gone out of business due to an inability to compete against hairstyling salons. Many accountants have lost clients to tax preparation services such as H&R Block that specialize in doing one task well and have used technology, including computerized filing services, to their advantage. Likewise, the old, big movie house has become a relic of the past as entrepreneurs realized the advantages to be gained from building and operating theater complexes that contain several minitheaters in or near suburban malls.

THE SERVICE CHALLENGE

Despite traditional thinking and practices on the part of many marketing managers and writers concerning the similarities between the operation of manufacturing and services organizations, the past decade has seen the growth of many innovative ways of meeting the service challenge. The service challenge is the quest to: (1) constantly develop new services that will better meet customer needs; (2) improve upon the quality and variety of existing services; and (3) provide and distribute these services in a manner that best serves the customer. This next section illustrates the challenges facing companies in various service industries and examples of marketing strategies employed by them to meet the service challenge.

Banking

"Banking is vital to a healthy economy. Banks are not." This is the message that a banking expert delivered to an industry group recently.[30] Needless to say, the days when banking was considered a dead-end career, but one that offered stable employment for marketers, is long gone. Perhaps banking best exemplifies the changes that are taking place as service organizations strive to become practitioners of the "marketing concept." Buy or be bought is the new watchword in the banking industry, which is experiencing the biggest wave of consolidation in its history. Experts predict that in the next 10 to 15 years, the United States's 10,200 banks may consolidate into as few as 4,000, a process expedited by the recent clearance for interstate banking.[31] While past bank deals have been mainly predicated on cost savings, today's deals are made to enable surviving banks to effectively compete as major players in the industry.

Banking is becoming an increasingly technology-driven business. The main reason is that more and more financial services, from loans to credit cards, are being marketed through computers and telephones instead of through branches. Banks large enough to afford big technology investments can reach customers nationwide even though their physical franchise may be limited. For example, most consumers possess credit cards from banks they have never physically visited. Further, the advent of new electronic delivery systems (via computer) for consumer and small business banking could, within the next decade, greatly reduce the number of branch banks needed. To prevent a loss of a large portion of their customer base, many of the leading banks, such as Chase Manhattan and Citibank, are aligning themselves with software and hardware manufacturers to develop home banking systems.

Technology is also greatly assisting banks in offering better, more convenient services to their customers. Huntington Bancshare now offers fully automated 24-hour branches in Columbus, Ohio.[32] The branches contain machines that offer video linkups with bank employees at another site. Consumers can apply for loans and mortgages, buy mutual funds, or obtain rate or account information whenever they desire. Likewise, most supermarkets and convenience stores now house ATMs to dispense cash or collect deposits on a 24-hour basis. Banks have also begun extensive promotion campaigns. Numerous banks offer initial low loan rates and run sweepstakes and other seasonal promotions in conjunction with credit card companies that give consumers a chance to win each time they charge a purchase. In addition, many banks now offer affinity cards, such as the NationsBank USAIR card, that allow customers to accumulate frequent flyer miles with each purchase made using the card.

Banks have also learned the value of bundling services. For example, NCNB of Charlotte, North Carolina, offers a Financial Connections account that combines checking, savings, credit card, and auto loan features. Benefits to the customer include free ATM transactions, interest-bearing checking accounts, no-fee credit cards, and the convenience of one-stop banking. In addition, the bank offers preapproved auto loans and cash flow statements. Most banks also offer targeted marketing activities towards senior citizens, which may include discount coupons for entertainment, travel newsletters, and lower monthly minimum required balances.

Competition between banks and other financial institutions will continue to intensify. The banks that survive will be those who have best mastered the art of services marketing. Toward this end, every bank employee must understand the needs and expectations of their customers and then design efficient delivery systems that meet those requirements.[33]

Healthcare

The distribution of healthcare services is of vital concern. In healthcare delivery, the inseparability characteristic presents more of a handicap than in other service industries because users (patients) literally place themselves in the hands of the seller. Although direct personal contact between producer and user is often necessary, new and more efficient means of distribution seem to be evolving.

Up until the past few decades, medical care has been traditionally associated with the solo practice, fee-for-service system. Recently, several alternative delivery systems have been developed, most notably the health maintenance organization (HMO). This type of delivery system stresses the creation of group health care clinics using teams of salaried health practitioners (physicians, pharmacists, technicians, and so forth) that serve a specified, enrolled membership on a prepaid basis. The primary benefits to the customer (patient) from membership in an HMO are: (1) the ability to have all ailments treated at one facility; (2) payment of a fixed fee for services; and (3) the encouragement of preventive versus remedial treatments. The success of the HMO concept in traditional medical care has inspired similar-type programs to be developed for dental and eye care.

As with banking, the hospital segment of the health care industry has become extremely competitive with for-profit hospitals competing amongst themselves and against non-profit organizations. One of the leading hospitals in terms of growth and stock appreciation has been Columbia/HCA (CHCA).[34] In less than three years, CHCA has grown from a hospital chain of around 20 facilities to one of approximately 320. The ultimate goal of CHCA is to own 1,200 to 1,300 hospitals or about 25 percent of the non-government hospitals in the United States. CHCA's success is largely due to its acumen in carrying out operations and marketing strategy. CHCA buys hospitals and, by consolidating activities, gets rid of redundancies, thereby reducing its cost structure. As a result, CHCA can price its services below competition and gain contractual arrangements to service large HMOs. As described by one hospital official, "Columbia/HCA is the self-proclaimed Wal-Mart of health care," offering quality service at an affordable price.

Columbia/HCA is by no means the only hospital that is pursuing innovative strategies. The limitations and competition inherent in taking a broad-based approach to health care marketing led Jewish Hospital of Louisville, Kentucky, to develop a marketing program focused on one specific revenue source: its Emergency Heart Center.[35] This focused approach has allowed Jewish Hospital to survive and thrive. Similarly, Stanford University Medical Center of Palo Alto, California, which also faced increasing competition, decided to emphasize its stroke treatment center as a point of differentiation and successfully developed and utilized a long-term advertising campaign.[36]

In the pharmaceutical field, Chronimed of Minnetonka, Minnesota, has focused on providing great customer service as its avenue to success.[37] The company supplies 100,000 patients across the United States with specialized medications that local pharmacies can't afford to stock. Chronimed's skill is twofold. First, they provide needed drugs by mail to organ transplant recipients and patients with diabetes or AIDS. Second, they employ a team of 50 pharmacists and assistants who provide much-needed information about the medications they dispense, such as details about drug interaction and side effects. As evidenced by the above examples, healthcare companies, regardless of what specific area in which they compete, are becoming more and more market oriented as they try to differentiate their offerings from those of the competition.

Insurance

In recent years, the insurance industry has exploded with new product and service offerings. Not too long ago, customers were faced with limited options in choosing life, hospital, or auto insurance. Now, there is a wide array of insurance policies to choose from, including universal life policies, which double as retirement savings, nursing care insurance, reversible mortgages, which allow people to take equity from their house while still living in it, and other offerings aimed at serving an aging population. To illustrate, Prudential Insurance Company offers a program whereby terminally ill policyholders are allowed to withdraw funds against the face value of their policy while still alive. In addition to insurance services, most insurance companies now offer a full range of financial services including auto loans, mortgages, mutual funds, and certificates of deposit.

Distribution of insurance services has also been growing. The vending machines found in airports for aircraft insurance have been finding their way into other areas. Travel auto insurance is now available in many motel chains and through the American Automobile Association. Group insurance written through employers and labor unions also has been extremely successful. In each instance, the insurance industry has used intermediaries to distribute its services.

Travel

The travel industry, most notably the airlines, has been a leader in the use of technology. Computerized reservation systems allow customers to book plane tickets from home or work. Nearly all airlines are using Internet sites, and United has a destination on CompuServe to dispense flight and fare information. Airlines are in the midst of implementing ticketless travel programs in which passengers purchase tickets, select their seats, and pick up boarding passes and luggage tags at machines resembling ATMs.[38] Technology has also allowed airlines to make strategic pricing decisions through the use of yield management. In yield management, certain seats on aircraft are discounted and certain ones aren't. Through the use of elaborate computer programs, managers are able to determine who their customer segments are and who is likely to purchase airline tickets when and to where.

Despite its success in employing technology to attract additional customers and offered added convenience, the airline industry has operated in somewhat dire straits, plagued by problems associated with overcapacity, high labor costs, and low perceived service quality. The recent period from 1990 through 1995 could be considered the most turbulent ever encountered by U.S. commercial airlines.[39] During this time, some airlines either went out of business (Midway, Eastern, and Pan AM) or were in and out of bankruptcy proceedings (Continental, America West, and TWA); and most others operated at a loss. Fortunately, in late 1995, good news came to the industry in the form of decreased fuel prices, the abandoning of some hub-and-spoke operations, and other events leading to cost decreases.

A notable exception to the fate that befell most carriers is Southwest Airlines, which has finally convinced its peers that a carrier can be consistently profitable by offering cheap fares on short-distance routes.[40] Now, big carriers, such as Continental and United have created their own Southwest look-alikes to supplement their long-haul, full-service, high-fare operations. Southwest's secret to success (which other airlines may or may not be able to imitate) is the high level of employee morale exhibited by everyone associated with the company. This has come as a direct result of upper management's internal marketing efforts.

Recent experiences in the lodging industry point out potential opportunities and pitfalls in service branding strategies.[41] Marriott, one of the most respected names in the lodging industry, is generally regarded as one of the more prestigious hotels. When Marriott decided to enter the lower priced segment of the hotel market, they did so with new brands. By altering the physical appearance and changing the names of their new motels to Courtyard by Marriott, Comfort Inn, and Marriott Resorts, Marriott was able to distinguish between their upscale offerings and those that were moderately priced. Holiday Inn, on the other hand, has experienced difficulty in trying to change from its middle-class image. They created Hampton Inns and Holiday Express for the budget segment, and Crowne Plaza and Embassy Suites for the upscale market. Due to overlapping between segments, Holiday Inn had difficulties in differentiating between the brands, especially in instances when two of the brands were located in the same city. By far, the most confused brand strategy relates to the use of the Ramada name. The Ramada Renaissance is a 16-unit chain of four-star hotels owned and operated in the United States by Ramada International Hotels & Resorts. Concurrently, there exists the 600-unit Ramada Hotel and Inn chain, which is owned and operated by Hospitality Franchise Systems,

---

HIGHLIGHT 12–5

Ten Lessons in Good Services Marketing

1. Customers do not buy your services—they buy solutions to their problems.
2. There are only two conditions under which customers will change their behavior: (*a*) when it's a matter of life and death (and then not in every case); (*b*) if they want to—if they are given a reason to change.
3. The most important parts of employees' contributions to the goals of your organization are being made at their discretion.
4. Management and leadership are exercised outside, not inside the office.

5. Quality service means never having to say "that's not my job."
6. How your employees feel is eventually how your customers will feel.
7. Customers should never be required to restate their request or complain to several employees before having it resolved.
8. If you establish negative expectations for your customers, you will always meet them.
9. The delivery of quality service is never the customer's job.
10. If you are an underdog: only compete in market segments where you have or can develop strengths; avoid head-to-head competition with dominant competitors; emphasize profits rather than volume; and focus on specialization rather than diversification.

Source: Adapted from James H. Donnelly, Jr., *25 Management Lessons from the Customer's Side of the Counter* (Homewood, IL: Irwin Professional Publishing, 1996).

---

a privately held outfit that also manages the Howard Johnson and Days Inn franchises. As a result, much confusion reigns in consumers' minds when asked to define what type of hotel the Ramada name brings to mind. The examples point out the necessity of multiple brands for service marketers when practicing market segmentation.

Implications for Service Marketers

The preceding sections emphasized the use of all components of the marketing mix. Many service industries have been criticized for an overdependence on advertising. The overdependence on one or two elements of the marketing mix is a mistake that service marketers cannot afford. The sum total of the marketing mix elements represents the total impact of the firm's marketing strategy. The slack created by severely restricting one element cannot be compensated by heavier emphasis on another, since each element in the marketing mix is designed to address specific problems and achieve specific objectives.

Services must be made available to prospective users which implies distribution in the marketing sense of the word. The revised concept of the distribution of services points out that service marketers must distinguish conceptually between the production and distribution of services. The problem of making services more widely available must not be ignored.

The above sections also pointed out the critical role of new service development. In several of the examples described, indirect distribution of the service was made possible because "products" were developed that included a tangible representation of the service. This development facilitates the use of intermediaries, because the service can now be separated from the producer. In addition, the development of new services paves the way for companies to expand and segment their markets. With the use of varying service bundles, new technology, and alternative means of distributing the service, companies are now able to practice targeted marketing.

Promotional programs, other than advertising, also play a critical role in service marketing. By running sweepstakes in which contestants were eligible to win prizes each time they used their ATM cards, banks were able to make the public more aware of the ease and convenience of using ATMs. Likewise, no-excuse refunds for poor service have enabled such hotels as Holiday Inn to retain a quality reputation.

CONCLUSION

This chapter has dealt with the complex topic of service marketing. While the marketing of services has much in common with the marketing of products, unique problems in the area require highly creative marketing management skills. Many of the problems in the service area can be traced to the intangible and inseparable nature of services and the difficulties involved in measuring service quality. However, considerable progress has been made in understanding and reacting to these difficult problems, particularly in the area of distribution. In view of the major role services play in our economy, it is important for marketing practitioners to better understand and appreciate the unique problems of service marketing.

ADDITIONAL READINGS

Bitner, Mary Jo; Bernard H. Booms; and Lois A. Mohr. "Critical Service Encounters: The Employee's Viewpoint." *Journal of Marketing,* October 1994, pp. 95–106.

Bowers, Michael R.; John E. Swan; and William F. Koehler. "What Attributes Determine Quality and Satisfaction with Health Care Delivery?" *Health Care Management Review,* Fall 1994, pp. 49–55.

Danaher, Peter J., and Jan Mattsson. "Customer Satisfaction During the Service Delivery Process." *European Journal of Marketing* 28, no. 5 (1994), pp. 5–16.

Day, Ellen, and Hiram C. Barksdale, Jr. "Organizational Purchasing of Professional Services: The Process of Selecting Service Providers." *The Journal of Business & Industrial Marketing* 9, no. 3 (1994), pp. 44–51.

Elliott, Kevin M. "SERVPERF Versus SERVQUAL: A Marketing Management Dilemma." *The Journal of Marketing Management,* Fall/Winter 1994, pp. 56–61.

Fulmer, William E., and Jack S. Goodwin. "So You Want to Be a Superior Service Provider? Start by Answering Your Mail." *Business Horizons,* November/December 1994, pp. 23–26.

Hemmasi, Masoud; Kelly S. Strong; and Steven A. Taylor. "Measuring Service Quality for Strategic Planning and Analysis in Service Firms." *Journal of Applied Business Research,* Fall 1994, pp. 24–34.

Henry, John W. "The Service Employee's Pivotal Role in Organizational Success." *The Journal of Services Marketing* 8, no. 4 (1994), pp. 25–35.

McDougall, Gordon H., and Terrence J. Levesque. "A Revised View of Service Quality Dimensions: An Empirical Investigation." *Journal of Professional Services Marketing* 11, no. 1 (1994), pp. 189–209.

Moore, S. Anne, and Bodo Schlegelmilch. "Improving Service Quality in an Industrial Setting." *Industrial Marketing Management,* February 1994, pp. 83–92.

Ozmont, John, and Edward A. Morash. "The Augmented Service Offering for Perceived and Actual Service Quality." *Journal of the Academy of Marketing Science,* Fall 1994, pp. 352–63.

Rust, Roland; Anthony J. Zahorik; and Timothy L. Keiningham. "Return on Quality (ROQ): Making Service Quality Financially Acceptable." *Journal of Marketing,* April 1995, pp. 58–70.

Tanner, Stephen. "Service Quality as a Strategy." *Journal for Quality & Participation,* December 1994, pp. 58–64.

Taylor, Shirley. "Waiting for Service: The Relationship between Delays and Evaluations of Service." *Journal of Marketing,* April 1994, pp. 56–69.

Taylor, Steven A., and Thomas L. Baker. "An Assessment of the Relationship between Service Quality and Customer Satisfaction in the Formation of Consumers' Purchase Intentions." *Journal of Retailing,* Summer 1994, pp. 163–78.

Truitt, Lawrence J., and Ray Haynes. "Evaluating Service Quality and Productivity in the Regional Airline Industry." *Transportation Journal,* Summer 1994, pp. 21–32.

Walker, James L. "Service Encounter Satisfaction: Conceptualized." *The Journal of Services Marketing* 9, no. 1 (1995), pp. 5–14.

Webster, Cynthia. "Marketing Culture and Marketing Effectiveness in Service Firms." *The Journal of Services Marketing* 9, no. 2 (1995), pp. 6–21.

Chapter 13
INTERNATIONAL MARKETING

A growing number of U.S. corporations have transversed geographical boundaries and become truly multinational in nature. For most other domestic companies, the question is no longer: Should we go international? Instead, the questions relate to when, how, and where the companies should enter the international marketplace. The past 15 years have seen the reality of a truly world market unfold. In today's world, the global economy is becoming almost totally integrated versus 25 percent integrated in 1980 and 50 percent integrated in the early 90s. Primary reasons for previously separated, individual markets evolving to a network of interdependent economies include:

1. The growing influence and economic development of lesser developed countries. In years to come, the real battleground for the two trade powers, the United States and Japan, will take place in the developing world. Containing 80 percent of the world's population and with growth rates nearly double those of industrial nations, these countries have emerged as the "fourth engine in the world economy" (following the United States, Japan, and Europe).[1]
2. The integration of world financial markets. For example, changes in currency exchange rates between the yen and the dollar greatly influence issues relating to import and export activities for all countries.
3. Increased efficiencies in transportation and telecommunication and data communication networks. To illustrate, consider the cases of Eastern Europe, China, and Russia. In these countries, technological advances have allowed the emergence of stock exchanges on which brokers throughout the world can trade.
4. The opening of new markets. For example, recent political events in Vietnam have led to the opening of a market that for decades (since the end of the Vietnam War) was closed to U.S. companies.

Multinational firms invest in foreign countries for the same basic reasons they invest in their own country. These reasons vary from firm to firm, but fall under the categories of achieving offensive or defensive goals. Offensive goals are to: (1) increase long-term growth and profit prospects; (2) maximize total sales revenue; (3) take advantage of economies of scale; and (4) improve overall market position. As many

American markets reach saturation, American firms look to foreign markets as outlets for surplus production capacity, sources of new customers, increased profit margins, and improved returns on investment. The gross domestic product (GDP) of countries such as China, Argentina, Poland, and the Czech Republic are growing at rates two to four times faster than those of the United States, Germany, and Japan.[2] Since the GDP provides the ultimate source for living standard improvements, the implication is that the trend abroad may prove to be a potential boom for the sale of American goods and services abroad. For example, the ability to expand the number of locations of McDonald's restaurants in the United States is becoming severely limited. Yet, Michael Quinlan, chairman and CEO of McDonald's, loves to remind shareholders that, on any given day, only 0.5 percent of the world's population visits McDonald's. This fact illustrates the vast potential markets still open to the company.[3] Indeed, of the 50 most profitable McDonald's outlets, 25 are located in Hong Kong. For PepsiCo, the results are similar. Their restaurant division operates 7,400 Kentucky Fried Chicken, Pizza Hut, and Taco Bell outlets abroad, deriving over $5.6 billion in sales from these foreign locations.

Multinational firms also invest in other countries to achieve defensive goals. Chief among these goals are the desire to: (1) compete with foreign companies on their own turf instead of in the United States; (2) have access to technological innovations that are developed in other countries; (3) take advantage of significant differences in operating costs between countries; (4) preempt competitors' global moves; and (5) not be locked out of future markets by arriving too late. To illustrate, in a recent year, North American sales of Colgate-Palmolive products decreased by 9 percent, an amount attributable in large part to increased competition from a foreign rival, Unilever.[4] Fortunately, Colgate-Palmolive took advantage of worldwide opportunities, increasing global sales by 6 percent to $5.6 billion.

Such well-known companies as Zenith, Pillsbury, A&P, Shell Oil, CBS Records, and Firestone Tire & Rubber are now owned by non-U.S. interests. Since 1980, the share of the U.S. high-tech market held by foreign products has grown from less than 8 percent to close to 25 percent. In such diverse industries as power tools, tractors, television, and banking, U.S. companies have lost the dominant position they once held. By investing solely in domestic operations or not being willing to adapt products to foreign markets, U.S. companies are more susceptible to foreign incursions. For example, there has been a great uproar over Japan's practice of not opening up its domestic automobile market to U.S. companies. However, as of 1996, a great majority of the American cars shipped to Japan still had the steering wheel located on the left side of the vehicle—the opposite of where it should be for the Japanese market.

HIGHLIGHT 13–1

The Largest U.S. Multinationals in Terms of Revenue Derived from Foreign Operations

Company	Revenues ($ million)		Foreign Percent of Total
	Foreign	Total	
1. Exxon	$77,125	$99,683	77.4%
2. General Motors	44,041	154,951	28.4
3. Mobil	40,318	59,621	67.6
4. IBM	39,934	64,052	62.3
5. Ford Motor	38,075	128,439	29.6
6. Texaco	24,760	44,306	55.9
7. CitiCorp	19,703	31,650	62.3
8. Chevron	16,533	38,516	42.9
9. Philip Morris Cos.	16,329	53,776	30.4
10. Proctor & Gamble	15,650	30,296	51.7
11. E. I. du Pont de Nemours	14,322	34,042	42.1
12. Hewlett-Packard	13,522	24,991	54.1
13. General Electric	11,872	60,109	19.8
14. American International Group	11,636	22,442	51.8
15. Coca-Cola	11,048	16,172	68.3
16. Dow Chemical	10,073	20,015	50.3
17. Motorola	9,770	22,245	43.9
18. Xerox	9,678	20,261	47.8
19. United Technologies	8,300	21,197	39.2
20. Digital Equipment	8,274	13,451	61.5

Source: Based on Brian Zajac, "Weak Dollar, Strong Results," *Forbes,* July, 17, 1995, pp. 274–76. Reprinted by permission of Forbes Magazine © Forbes Inc., 1995.

In many ways marketing globally is the same as marketing at home. Regardless of which part of the world the firm sells in, the marketing program must still be built around a sound product or service that is properly priced, promoted, and distributed to a carefully analyzed target market. In other words, the marketing manager has the same controllable decision variables in both domestic and nondomestic markets.

Although the development of a marketing program may be the same in either domestic or nondomestic markets, special problems may be involved in the implementation of marketing programs in nondomestic markets. These problems often arise because of the environmental differences that exist among various countries that marketing managers may be unfamiliar with.

In this chapter, marketing management in an international context will be examined. Methods of organizing international versus domestic markets, international market research tasks, methods of entry strategies into international markets, and potential marketing strategies for a multinational firm will be discussed. In examining each of these areas,

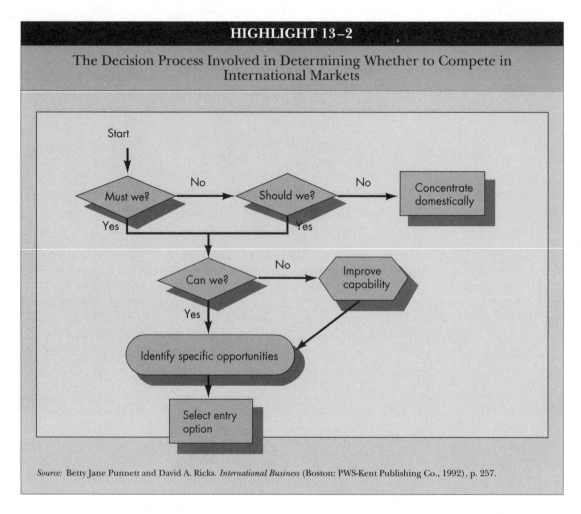

HIGHLIGHT 13–2

The Decision Process Involved in Determining Whether to Compete in International Markets

Source: Betty Jane Punnett and David A. Ricks. *International Business* (Boston: PWS-Kent Publishing Co., 1992), p. 257.

the reader will find a common thread— knowledge of the local cultural environment—that appears to be a major prerequisite for success in each area.

With the proper adaptations, many companies have the capabilities and resources needed to compete successfully in the international marketplace. To illustrate, companies as diverse as Kellogg's, Avon, Eli Lilly, and Sun Microsystems each generates over 40 percent of sales from foreign operations.[5] Smaller companies can also be successful. For example, Nemix, Inc., of Bell Gardens, California, is a franchisee of Church's Fried Chicken with $91 million in annual sales. Small by world standards, this company has succeeded in developing a fully vertical operation in Poland, doing everything from raising chickens to operating restaurants.[6]

ORGANIZING FOR INTERNATIONAL MARKETING

When compared with the tasks it faces at home, a firm attempting to establish an international marketing organization faces a much higher degree of risk and uncertainty. In a foreign market, management is often less familiar with the cultural, political, and economic situation. Many of these problems arise as a result of conditions specific to the foreign country. Managers are also faced with the decisions concerning how to organize the multinational company.

Problems with Entering Foreign Markets

While numerous problems could be cited, attention here will focus on those firms most often face when entering foreign markets.

Cultural misunderstanding

Differences in the cultural environment of foreign countries may be misunderstood or not even recognized because of the tendency for marketing managers to use their own cultural values and priorities as a frame of reference. Some of the most common areas of difference lie in the way dissimilar cultures perceive time, thought patterns, personal space, material possessions, family roles and relationships, personal achievement, competitiveness, individuality, social behavior, and other interrelated issues.[7] Another important source of misunderstandings is in the perceptions of managers about the people with whom they are dealing. Feelings of superiority can lead to changed communication mannerisms.

The tendency to rely on one's own cultural values has been called the major cause of many international marketing problems. For example, the Japanese often say yes when they mean no.[8] They rarely give a direct negative response—even if they want to deny a request or express a negative intent—especially to a foreigner. They are also wary of the common American practice of bringing lawyers to initial meetings. American managers must make the necessary efforts to learn, understand, and adapt to the cultural norms of the managers and customers they deal with in other parts of the world.[9] Failure to do so will result in missed market opportunities. Highlight 13-3 provides further examples of cultural differences that could lead to marketing problems.

On the other hand, companies should not shy away from attempting to enter international markets because conventional wisdom says that products and service will not succeed in some regions purely due to cultural reasons. For example, PepsiCo's Pepsi division entered into a $500 million offensive to try to grab a larger share of the $6 billion Brazilian soft-drink market.[10] Understanding the dramatic changes that had taken place in

HIGHLIGHT 13–3

Examples of Cultural Differences that Could Lead to Marketing Problems

Body Language

- Standing with your hands on your hips is a gesture of defiance in Indonesia.
- Carrying on a conversation with your hands in your pockets makes a poor impression in France, Belgium, Finland, and Sweden.
- When you shake your head from side to side, that means "yes" in Bulgaria and Sri Lanka.
- Crossing your legs to expose the sole of your shoe is really taboo in Muslim countries. In fact, to call a person a "shoe" is a deep insult.

Physical Contact

- Patting a child on the head is a grave offense in Thailand or Singapore, since the head is revered as the location of the soul.
- In an Oriental culture, touching another person is considered an invasion of privacy, while in Southern European and Arabic countries it is a sign of warmth and friendship.

Source: William J. Stanton; Michael J. Etzel; and Bruce J. Walker, *Fundamentals of Marketing*, 9th ed. © 1991, New York, McGraw-Hill, Inc., p. 536. Reproduced by permission of The McGraw-Hill Companies.

Promptness

- Be on time when invited for dinner in Denmark or in China.
- In Latin countries, your host or business associate would be surprised if you arrived at the appointed hour.

Eating and Cooking

- It is rude to leave anything on your plate when eating in Norway, Malaysia, or Singapore.
- In Egypt, it is rude *not* to leave something.
- In Italy and Spain, cooking is done with oil.
- In Germany and Great Britain, margarine and butter are used.

Other Social Customs

- In Sweden, nudity and sexual permissiveness are quite all right, but drinking is really frowned on.
- In Spain, there is a very negative attitude toward life insurance. By receiving insurance benefits, a wife feels that she is profiting from her husband's death.
- In Western European countries, many consumers still are reluctant to buy anything (other than a house) on credit. Even for an automobile, they will pay

Brazil, Pepsi repositioned itself as the choice of a new Brazil. Advertisements for the Pepsi brand feature young people enumerating recent changes in Brazil, such as the new currency and outcomes of recent presidential elections. Does this campaign sound familiar? It should since it's a takeoff on the popular "Pepsi, the choice of a new generation" theme utilized in the United States. Actions taken by PepsiCo's Frito-Lay unit serve as another example of a successful adaptation to cultural differences.[11] In China, Frito-Lay recently introduced its popular Cheetos snack food. The twist to this effort lies in the fact that the Chinese are not big consumers of dairy products. In China, Cheetos are cheeseless, instead consisting of flavors such as "Savory American Cream" and "Zesty Japanese Steak." As a result of these and other adaptations, it's no wonder that PepsiCo ranks among the leaders in the global food and beverage industry.

Political Uncertainty

Governments are unstable in many countries, and social unrest and even armed conflict must sometimes be reckoned with. Other nations are newly emerging and anxious to seek their independence. These and similar problems can greatly hinder a firm seeking to establish its position in foreign markets. For example, firms scaled back their investment plans in Russia due to, among other reasons: (1) a business environment plagued by mobsters; (2) politics badly corrupted by the botched invasion of Chechnya; and (3) an economy troubled by runaway inflation and a plummeting ruble.[12] This is not to say investment in Russia is a poor choice. Rather, in situations like this, caution must be utilized and companies must have a keen understanding of the risks involved in undertaking sizable investments.

Import Restrictions

Tariffs, import quotas, and other types of import restrictions hinder international business. These are usually established to promote self-sufficiency and can be a huge roadblock for the multinational firm. For example, a number of countries, including South Korea, Taiwan, Thailand, and Japan, have placed import restrictions on a variety of goods produced in America, including telecommunications equipment, rice, wood products, automobiles, and produce.[13] In other cases, governments may not impose restrictions that are commonly adhered to in the United States. For example, Chrysler pulled out of a proposed investment deal in China, worth billions of dollars, because the Chinese government refused to protect its right to limit access to technological information. As a result, Mercedes-Benz AG of Germany received the contract.[14]

Exchange Controls and Ownership Restrictions

Some nations establish limits on the amount of earned and invested funds that can be withdrawn from it. These exchange controls are usually established by nations that are experiencing balance-of-payment problems. In addition, many nations have a requirement that the majority ownership of a company operating there be held by nationals. These and other types of currency and ownership regulations are important considerations in the decision to expand into a foreign market. For example, up until 1990, foreign holdings in business ventures in India were limited to a maximum of 40 percent. Once this ban was lifted, numerous global companies such as Sony, Whirlpool, JVC, Grundig, Panasonic, Kellogg's, Levi Strauss, Pizza Hut, and Domino's rushed to invest in this market.[15]

As a result, India holds cash reserves from foreign investment of over $20.5 billion and its economy is growing at a 5.5 percent annual rate.

Economic conditions

As noted earlier, nations' economics are becoming increasingly inter-twined, and business cycles tend to follow similar patterns. However, there are differences, mainly due to political upheaval or social changes, and these may be significant. In determining whether to invest, marketers need to perform in-depth analyses of a country's stage of economic development, the buying power of its populace, and the strength of its currency.[16] For example, when the North American Free Trade Agreement (NAFTA) was signed, many American companies rushed to invest in Mexico, building production facilities and retail outlets. These companies assumed that the signing of the agreement would stabilize Mexico's economy. In the long term, these investments may pay off. However, many companies lost millions of dollars there due to the devaluation of the peso. Indeed, the crash of the peso caused the retail giant Wal-Mart to scale back a $1 billion investment project to open stores throughout Mexico.[17]

Organizing the Multinational Company

There are two kinds of multinational corporations—the multidomestic corporation and the global corporation.[18] The multidomestic company pursues different strategies in each of its foreign markets. Each overseas subsidiary is autonomous. A company's management tries to operate effectively across a series of worldwide positions with diverse product requirements, growth rates, competitive environments, and political risks. Local managers are given the authority and control to make the necessary decisions; however, they are also held responsible for results. In effect, the company competes on a market-by-market basis. Honeywell and General Foods are examples of two American companies that have operated well in this manner.

The global company, on the other hand, pits its entire resources against the competition in an integrated fashion. Foreign subsidiaries and divisions are largely interdependent on both operations and strategy. These "stateless" corporations standardize manufacturing, regularly offer innovative solutions to the market, and seek creative collaborations with other firms to merge complementary skills and gain access to new markets.[19] The global company operates as though the world were one large market, not a series of individual countries. Since there is no one clear-cut way to organize a global company, three alternative structures are normally used: (1) worldwide product divisions, each responsible for selling its own products throughout the world; (2) divisions responsible for all products sold within a geographic area; and (3) a matrix system that combines elements of both these arrangements. Many multinational companies already have structured their organization in a global

HIGHLIGHT 13–4

Leading Global Companies in Selected Industries

Company	Country	Revenues (in $ millions)
Chemicals		
1. E. I. du pont de Nemours	United States	$34,968
2. Hoechst	Germany	30,604
3. BASF	Germany	26,928
Commercial Banks		
1. Deutsche Bank	Germany	33,069
2. Citicorp	United States	31,650
3. Industrial Bank of Japan	Japan	31,072
Electronics		
1. Hitachi	Japan	76,431
2. Matsushita Electrical Industrial	Japan	69,947
3. General Electric	United States	64,687
Food		
1. Philip Morris	United States	53,776
2. Unilever	Britain/Netherlands	45,451
3. Nestlé	Japan	41,626
Rubber, Plastic Goods		
1. Bridgestone	Japan	15,608
2. Goodyear Tire	United States	12,288
3. Michelin	France	12,120
Soaps, Cosmetics		
1. Proctor & Gamble	United States	30,296
2. Henkel	Germany	8,674
3. L'Oreal	France	8,586
Telecommunications		
1. AT&T	United States	75,094
2. Nippon Telephone & Telegraph	Japan	70,844
3. Deutsche Telekom	Germany	41,071
Tobacco		
1. BAT Industries	Britain	22,094
2. Japan Tobacco	Japan	16,961
3. RJR Nabisco Holdings	United States	15,366

Source: Advertising Age, "Numbers for the 90's: Teen Interests Appear to be Universal," July 17, 1995, p. 3; "The Way We Live: The European Women's Cosmetics Landscape," January 16, 1995, p. I-3. Reprinted with permission from Advertising Age, 1995, Copyright Crain Communications, Inc. All rights reserved.

fashion including IBM, Caterpillar, Timex, General Electric, Siemens, and Mitsubishi.

Most companies are realizing the need to take a global approach to managing their businesses. However, recognizing the need and actually implementing a truly global approach are two different tasks. For some companies, industry conditions dictate that they take a global perspective. The ability to actually implement a global approach to managing international operations, however, largely depends on factors unique to the company. Globalization, as a competitive strategy, is inherently more vulnerable to risk than a multidomestic or domestic strategy, due to the relative permanence of the organizational structure once established.[20]

In determining whether or not to globalize a particular business, managers should look first at their industry.[21] Market, economic, environmental, and competitive factors all influence the potential gains to be realized by following a global strategy. Factors constituting the external environment that are conducive to a global strategy are:

1. *Market factors.* Homogeneous market needs, global customers, shortening product life cycles, transferable brands and advertising, and the ability to internationalize distribution channels.
2. *Economic factors.* Worldwide economies of scale in manufacturing and distribution, steep learning curves, worldwide sourcing efficiencies, rising product development costs, and significant differences in host-country costs.
3. *Environmental factors.* Improving communications, favorable government policies, and the increasing speed of technological change.
4. *Competitive factors.* Competitive interdependencies among countries, global moves of competitors, and opportunities to preempt a competitor's global moves.[22]

Many of the reasons given in the first part of the chapter as to why a domestic company should become a multinational can also be used to support the argument that a firm should take a global perspective. This is because the integration of markets is forcing companies that wish to remain successful to not only become multinationals but also to take a global perspective in doing so. In the past, companies had the option of remaining domestic or going multinational due to the separation of markets. This is no longer the case.

There are several internal factors that can either facilitate or impede a company's efforts to undertake a global approach to marketing strategies. These factors and their underlying dimensions are:

1. *Structure.* The ease of installing a centralized global authority and the absence of rifts between present domestic and international divisions or operating units.
2. *Management processes.* The capabilities and resources available to perform global planning, budgeting, and coordination activities, coupled with the ability to conduct global performance reviews and implement global compensation plans.
3. *Culture.* The ability to project a global versus national identity, a worldwide versus domestic commitment to employees, and a willingness to tolerate interdependence among business units.

4. *People.* The availability of employable foreign nationals and the willingness of current employees to commit to multicountry careers, frequent travel, and having foreign superiors.

Overall, whether a company should undertake a multidomestic or global approach to organizing its international operations will largely depend on the nature of the company and its products, how different foreign cultures are from the domestic market, and the company's ability to implement a global perspective. Many large brands have failed in their quest to go global.[23] The primary reason for this failure is rushing the process. Successful global brands carefully stake out their markets, allowing plenty of time to develop their overseas marketing efforts and evolve into global brands.

Indeed, in many cases, firms do not undertake either purely multidomestic or global approaches to marketing. Instead, a hybrid approach is developed whereby these global brands carry with them the same visual identity, the same strategic positioning, and the same advertising. In addition, local characteristics are factored in. For example, Coca-Cola produced two dozen TV commercials for its worldwide effort using the same theme, the same music, and predominately, the same visuals. However, the commercials were in local languages, and local markets were allowed to shoot their own visuals for certain spots. In essence, it was exactly the same campaign, but it was different in every market. Likewise, McDonald's maintains standardized specifications for its equipment technology, customer service, cleanliness, value, and operational systems. Yet, the menus are allowed to vary somewhat from country to country. Regardless of the approach undertaken, management and organizational skills that emphasize the need to handle diversity are the critical factors that determine the long-term success of any company's endeavors in the international marketplace.[24]

PROGRAMMING FOR INTERNATIONAL MARKETING

In this section of the chapter, the major areas in developing an international marketing program will be examined. As was mentioned at the outset, marketing managers must organize the same controllable decision variables that exist in domestic markets. However, many firms that have been extremely successful in marketing in the United States have not been able to duplicate their success in foreign markets.

International Marketing Research

Because the risk and uncertainties are so high, marketing research is equally important (and probably more so) in foreign markets than in domestic markets. Many companies encounter losing situations abroad because they do not know enough about the market.[25] They don't know how to get the information or find the cost of collecting the information too high. To be successful, organizations must collect and analyze pertinent information to support the basic go/no-go decision before getting to the issues addressed by conventional market research. Toward this end, in attempting to analyze foreign consumers and markets, at least four organizational issues must be considered.

Population characteristics

Population characteristics are one of the major components of a market, and significant differences exist between and within foreign countries. If data are available, the marketing manager should be familiar with the total population and with the regional, urban, rural, and interurban distribution. Other demographic variables, such as the number and size of families, education, occupation, and religion, are also important. In many markets, these variables can have a significant impact on the success of a firm's marketing program. For example, in the United States, a cosmetics firm can be reasonably sure of the desire to use cosmetics being common among women of all income classes. However, in Latin America the same firm may be forced to segment its market by upper-, middle-, and lower-income groups, as well as by urban and rural areas. This is because upper-income women want high-quality cosmetics promoted in prestige media and sold through exclusive outlets. In some rural and less prosperous areas, cosmetics must be inexpensive, while in other rural areas women do not accept cosmetics. Even in markets that are small in geographical area, consumers may differ in many of the variables mentioned. Any one or set of such differences may have a strong bearing on consumers' ability and willingness to buy.

Ability to buy

To assess the ability of consumers in a foreign market to buy, four broad measures should be examined: (1) gross national product or per capita national income; (2) distribution of income; (3) rate of growth in buying power; and (4) extent of available financing. Since each of these vary in different areas of the world, the marketing opportunities available must be examined closely.

Willingness to buy

The cultural framework of consumer motives and behavior is integral to the understanding of the foreign consumer. If data are available, cultural values and attitudes toward the material culture, social organizations, the supernatural, aesthetics, and language should be analyzed for their possible influence on each of the elements in the firm's marketing program. It is easy to see that such factors as the group's values concerning acquisition of material goods, the role of the family, the positions of men and women

HIGHLIGHT 13-5
Global and Regional Similarities

Global Teens: The Global Similar Market
(Percent of teens who wear the following types of clothes)

	United States	Europe	Latin America	Asia
Jeans	93%	94%	86%	93%
T-shirt	93	89	59	96
Running shoes	80	70	65	69
Blazer	42	43	30	27
Denim jacket	39	57	41	23

European Women: The Regional Similar Market
(Percent of European women who use the following types of products)

	United Kingdom	Spain	Italy	Germany	France
Deodorant	93%	85%	83%	78%	70%
Fragrances	57	80	62	66	73
Makeup	76	82	80	76	76
Mouthwash	14	11	20	14	7
Skincare products	73	59	68	85	77

Source: Adapted from Jerry Parks, "Numbers for the 90s: Teen Interests Appear to be Universal," *Advertising Age,* July 17, 1995, p. 3; and Jerry Parks, "The Way We Live: The European Women's Cosmetics Landscape," *Advertising Age International,* January 16, 1995, p. I-3.

in society, as well as the various age groups and social classes can have an effect on marketing, because each can influence consumer behavior.

In some areas there appears to be a convergence of tastes and habits, with different cultures becoming more and more integrated into one homogeneous culture, although still separated by national boundaries. This appears to be the case in Western Europe, where consumers are developing into a mass market. This obviously will simplify the task for a marketer in this region. However, cultural differences still prevail among many areas of the world and strongly influence consumer behavior. However, marketing organizations may have to do primary research in many foreign markets to obtain usable information about these issues.

Differences in research tasks and processes.

In addition to the dimensions mentioned above, the processes and tasks associated with carrying out the market research program may also differ from country to country. Many market researchers count on census data for in-depth demographic information. However, in foreign countries there are a variety of problems the market researcher is likely to encounter in using census data. These include:[26]

1. *Language.* Some nations publish their census reports in English. Other countries offer census reports only in their native language; some do not take a census.
2. *Data content.* Data contained in a census will vary from country to country and often omit items of interest to researchers. For example, most foreign nations do not include an income question on their census. Others do not include such items as marital status or education levels.
3. *Timeliness.* The United States takes a census every 10 years. Japan and Canada conduct one every five years. However, some northern European nations are abandoning the census as a data-collection tool and instead are relying on population registers to account for births, deaths, and changes in marital status or place of residence.
4. *Availability in the United States.* If a researcher requires detailed household demographics on foreign markets, the cost and time required to obtain the data will be significant. For example, to get minimal-quality data on Western Europe and Pacific Rim countries might require trips to over 10 different university libraries, as well as to the U.S. Bureau of the Census and the Library of Congress.

Fortunately, research help is on the way. In recent years, both new and established market research firms have begun focusing efforts on collecting relevant information related to foreign country characteristics. Two companies, Lasernet and Disclosure, have begun offering products that provide analyses of financial and economic conditions in emerging markets such as Turkey, Brazil, India, Argentina, Greece, and Pakistan.[27] Further, large market information companies, Information Resources, Inc., (IRI) and Neilson Marketing Research, have both begun pursuing ambitious plans to increase the installation and use of checkout scanning devices in European retail outlets.[28] Sometimes, companies will utilize creative mans to accomplish their foreign information goals. For example, Off-the-Record Research, a San Francisco–based marketing research company that specializes in investment research, employs freelance journalists residing in their native countries to carry out foreign research assignments for U.S. clients. These journalists have in-depth knowledge of their home markets, speak native language(s) fluently, and, most importantly, possess the acumen and skills necessary to provide accurate, unbiased information to their U.S. client companies.

Product Planning for International Markets

International marketing research can help determine whether (1) there is an unsatisfied need for which a new product could be developed to serve a foreign market or (2) there is an unsatisfied need that could be met with an existing domestic product, either as is or adapted to the foreign market. In either case, product planning is necessary to determine the type of product to be offered and whether there is sufficient demand to warrant a foreign market entry.

Most U.S. firms would not think of entering a domestic market without extensive product planning. However, some marketers have failed to do adequate product planning when entering foreign markets. An example of such a problem occurred when American manufacturers began to export refrigerators to Europe. The firms exported essentially the same models sold in the United States. However, the refrigerators were the wrong size, shape, and temperature range for some areas and had weak appeal in others—thus failing miserably. Although adaptation of the product to local conditions may have eliminated this failure, this adaptation is easier said than done. For example, even in the domestic market, overproliferation of product varieties and options can dilute economies of scale. This dilution results in higher production costs, which may make the price of serving each market segment with an "adapted" product prohibitive.

The solution to this problem is not easy. In some cases, changes need not be made at all or, if so, can be accomplished rather inexpensively. In other cases, the sales potential of the particular market may not warrant expensive product changes. For example, Pepsi's Radical Fruit line of juice drinks has been introduced without adaptation on three continents.[29] On the other hand, U.S. companies wishing to market software in foreign countries must undertake painstaking and costly efforts to convert the embedded code from English to foreign languages. This undertaking severely limits the potential markets where individual software products can be profitably marketed. In any case, management must examine these product-related problems carefully prior to making foreign market entry decisions.

International Distribution Systems

The role of the distribution network in facilitating the transfer of goods and titles and in the demand stimulation process is as important in foreign markets as it is at home. Figure 13-1 illustrates some of the most common channel arrangements in international marketing. The continuum ranges from no control to almost complete control of the distribution system by manufacturers.

The channel arrangement where manufacturers have the least control is shown at the left of Figure 13-1. These are the most indirect channels of distribution. Here manufacturers sell to resident buyers, export agents, or export merchants located in the United States. In reality, these are similar to some domestic sales, since all of the marketing functions are assumed by intermediaries.[30]

Manufacturers become more directly involved and, hence, have greater control over distribution when agents and distributors located in foreign markets are selected. Both perform similar functions, except that agents do not assume title to the manufacturers' products, while distributors do.

Figure 13–1 *Common Distribution Channels for International Marketing*

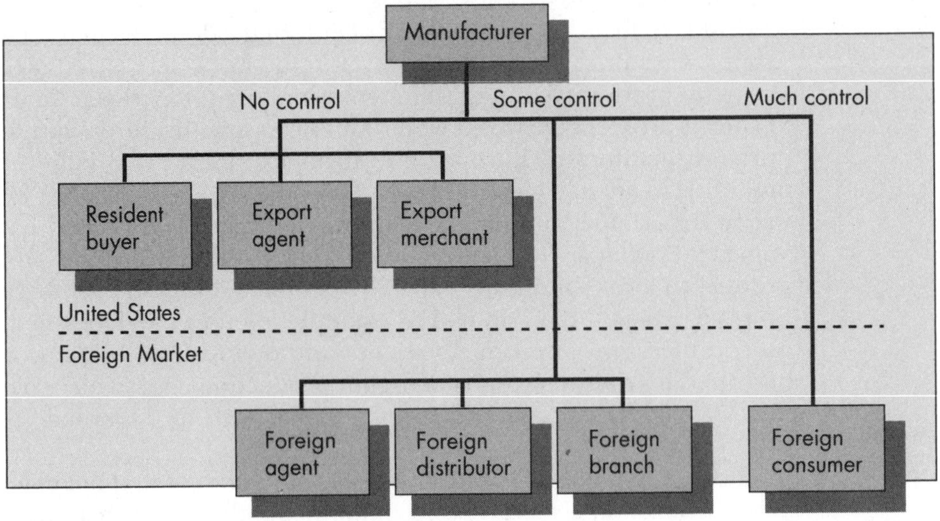

Source: Reproduced from *International Business* by Betty J. Punnett and David A. Ricks, p. 257, with the permission of South-Western College Publishing.

If manufacturers should assume the functions of foreign agents or distributors and establish their own foreign branch, they greatly increase control over their international distribution system. Manufacturers' effectiveness will then depend on their own administrative organization, rather than on independent intermediaries. If the foreign branch sells to other intermediaries, such as wholesalers and retailers, as is the case with most consumer goods, manufacturers again relinquish some control. However, since the manufacturers are located in the market area, they have greater potential to influence these intermediaries. For example, Volkswagen, General Motors, Anheuser- Busch, and Proctor & Gamble have each made substantial investments in building manufacturing facilities in Brazil.[31] These investments allow the companies to begin making direct sales to dealers and retailers in the country.

The channel arrangement that enables manufacturers to exercise a great deal of control is shown at the right of Figure 13-1. Here, manufacturers sell directly to organizational buyers or ultimate consumers. Although this arrangement is most common in the sale of organizational goods, some consumer goods companies have also pursued this arrangement.

Pricing for International Marketing

In domestic markets, pricing is a complex task. The basic approaches used in price determination in foreign markets are the same as those discussed earlier in the chapter on pricing. However, the pricing task is often more complicated in foreign markets because of additional problems associated with tariffs, antidumping laws, taxes, inflation, and currency conversion.[32]

Import duties are probably the major constraint for international marketers and are encountered in many markets. Management must decide whether import duties will be paid by the firm, by the foreign consumer, or shared by both. This and similar constraints may force the firm to abandon an otherwise desirable pricing strategy or may force the firm out of a market altogether.

Another pricing problem arises because of the rigidity in price structures found in many foreign markets. Many foreign intermediaries are not aggressive in their pricing policies. They often prefer to maintain high unit margins at the expense of low sales volume, rather than develop large sales volume by means of lower prices and smaller margins per unit. Many times this rigidity is encouraged by legislation that prevents retailers from cutting prices substantially at their own discretion. These are only a few of the pricing problems encountered by foreign marketers.

However, in some cases foreign pricing policies and customs can give the U.S. marketer a competitive advantage. For example, in Japan, American-style shopping malls with stores such as Toys "R" Us, Talbots, and Virgin Records are able to compete effectively against center-city stores that still adhere to Japanese pricing policies designed to give the retailer huge margins. In fact, U.S. exports to Japan have more than tripled within the last decade and are continuing to grow at a rapid rate (although the balance of trade is still highly skewed in Japan's favor).[33] Clearly, the marketer must be aware of both the constraints and opportunities available in foreign markets.

International Advertising and Sales Promotion

When expanding their operations into the world marketplace, most firms are aware of the language barriers that exist and realize the importance of translating their messages into the proper idiom. However, there are numerous other issues that must be resolved, such as selecting appropriate media and advertising agencies in foreign markets.

There are many problems in selecting media in foreign markets. Often the media that are traditionally used in the domestic market are not available. For example, it was not until recently that national commercial TV became a reality in the former Soviet Union. If media are available, they may be so only on a limited basis or they may not reach the potential buyers. For example, one firm was forced to use sound trucks or roving movie

HIGHLIGHT 13–6

Checklist of Country Selection Criteria for Companies Considering Investment in Eastern Europe

Overall Economic and Political Conditions

- What is the foreign debt service expense as a percentage of hard currency foreign exchange earnings?
- What is the inflation rate? If hyperinflation exists, are appropriate fiscal and monetary policies being implemented to bring it under control?
- How substantial are raw material reserves that can be converted to hard currency?
- Are state subsidies, cheap credits, and tax concessions for state enterprises being phased out?
- Does the government intend to sell stakes in state enterprises to foreign investors?
- Is there an emerging capital market based on real interest rates?
- What progress is being made toward developing a code of company law?
- Is political decision-making authority centralized or fragmented?
- How rapid and sustainable is continued progress toward democracy and a free market economy? Is there any historical tradition to support such trends?

Climate for Foreign Investment

- What percentage ownership may foreign companies have in joint ventures? Is government approval required and, if so, how long does it take to obtain?

Source: John A. Quelch, Erich Joachimsthaler, and Jose Luis Nueno, "After the Wall: Marketing Guidelines for Eastern Europe," *Sloan Management Review,* Winter 1991, p. 85.

- Is private ownership of property recognized?
- Are intellectual property rights upheld?
- Can foreign investors obtain premises easily? Can they own real estate?
- Can an initial capital investment by a foreign company be held in hard currency?
- Can a foreign investor sell its stake in a joint venture?
- Can hard currency be used to pay for imported raw materials or to repatriate profits?
- What is the tax rate on business enterprise profits?

Market Attractiveness

- What is the sales potential in this country?
- Do the country's geographical location and political relations permit it to serve as a gateway to other East European markets?
- How well developed are the necessary managerial and technical skills?
- How skilled is the labor pool? What are labor costs?
- Can continued supply of the raw materials required for production be assured?
- What is the quality of the transportation and telecommunications infrastructure?
- Will Western executives accept being located in the country?
- To what degree have government officials developed a familiarity with Western business practices?

vans to reach potential buyers in the sub-Sahara area of Africa. In addition to the problem of availability, other difficulties arise from the lack of accurate media information. There is no rate and data service or media directory that covers all the media available throughout the world. Where data are available, their accuracy is often questionable.

Another important promotion decision that must be made is the type of agency used to prepare and place the firm's advertisements. Along with the growth in multinational product companies, more multinational advertising agencies are available. Among the top 15 international advertising agencies, less than half are U.S. owned.[34] Alliances and takeovers have served to stimulate growth in the formation of global agencies. For the U.S. company, there are two major approaches to choosing an agency. The first is to use a purely local agency in each area where the advertisement is to appear. The rationale for this approach is that a purely local agency employing only local nationals can better adapt the firm's message to the local culture.

The other approach is to use either a U.S.–based multinational agency or a multinational agency with U.S. offices to develop and implement the ad campaign. For example, the Coca-Cola Company uses one agency to create ads for the 80 nations in which Diet Coke is marketed. The use of these so-called super agencies is increasing (annual growth rates averaging over 30 percent in the last decade). By using global advertising agencies, companies are able to take advantage of economies of scale and other efficiencies. However, global agencies are not without their critics. Many managers believe that small, local agencies in emerging markets take a more entrepreneurial and fresher approach to advertising than do global agencies.[35] Much discussion has developed over which approach is best, and it appears that both approaches can be used successfully by particular firms.[36]

The use of sales promotion can also lead to opportunities and problems for marketers in foreign markets. Sales promotions often contain certain characteristics that are more attractive than other elements of the promotion mix.[37] In less wealthy countries, consumers tend to be even more interested in saving money through price discounts, sampling, or premiums. Sales promotion can also be used as a strategy for bypassing restrictions on advertising placed by some foreign governments. In addition, sales promotion can be an effective means for reaching people who live in rural locations where media support for advertising is virtually nonexistent.

However, laws in some countries place even more restrictions on advertising and sales promotion practices than those found in the United States. For example, Colombia requires substantial proof of claims in comparative advertising and, in Vietnam, foreign companies are charged much higher advertising rates than local companies.[38] In other countries, laws may not permit gifts or premiums to be given, and companies may be required to keep detailed records of promotional transactions. For example, Belgium prohibits sweepstakes and, in Greece, couponing is illegal.[39] In addition, retailers and wholesalers in foreign countries may lack either (1) the appropriate facilities necessary to merchandise the promotional materials or (2) the background to understand how a specific promotion works or explain it to their customers.

ENTRY AND GROWTH STRATEGIES FOR INTERNATIONAL MARKETING

A major decision facing companies who either desire to enter a foreign market or pursue growth within a specific market relates to the choice of a market entry and/or growth strategy. What type of strategy to employ depends upon many factors, including the analysis of market opportunities, company capabilities, the degree of marketing involvement and commitment the company is willing to make, and the amount of risk that the company is able to tolerate.[40] A company can decide to: (1) make minimal investments of funds and resources by limiting its efforts to exporting; (2) make large initial investments of resources and management effort to try to establish a long-term share of international markets; or (3) take an incremental approach whereby the company starts with a low-risk mode of entry that requires the least financial and other resource commitment and gradually increases its commitment over time. All three approaches can be profitable. In general, there are six ways by which a company can initially enter an international market and, subsequently, pursue growth in the international marketplace.

1. **Exporting**. Exporting occurs when a company produces the product outside the final destination and then ships it there for sale. It is the easiest and most common approach for a company making its first international move. Exporting has two distinct advantages. First, it avoids the cost of establishing manufacturing operations in the host country and second, it may help a firm achieve experience-curve and location economies. By manufacturing the product in a centralized location and exporting it to other national markets, the firm may be able to realize substantial scale economies from its global sales volume. This method is what allowed Sony to dominate the global TV market. The major disadvantages related to exporting include: (1) the sometimes higher cost associated with the process; (2) the necessity of the exporting firm to pay import duties or face trade barriers; and (3) the delegation of marketing responsibility for the product to foreign agents who may or may not be dependable.

2. **Licensing.** Companies can grant patent rights, trademark rights, and the right to use technological processes to foreign companies. This is the most common strategy for small and medium-sized companies. The major advantage to licensing is that the firm does not have to bear the development costs and risks associated with opening up a foreign market. In addition, licensing can be an attractive option in unfamiliar or politically volatile markets. The major disadvantages are that: (1) the firm does not have tight control over manufacturing, marketing, and strategy that is required for realizing economies of scale; and (2) there is the risk that the licensed technology may be capitalized on by foreign companies. RCA Corporation, for example, once licensed its color TV technology to a number of Japanese

firms. These firms quickly assimilated the technology and used it to enter the U.S. market.

3. **Franchising.** Franchising is similar to licensing but tends to involve longer-term commitments. Also, franchising is commonly employed by service, as opposed to manufacturing, firms. In a franchising agreement, the franchisor sells limited rights to use its brand name in return for a lump sum and share of the franchisee's future profits. In contrast to licensing agreements, the franchisee agrees to abide by strict operating procedures. Advantages and disadvantages associated with franchising are primarily the same as with licensing except to a lesser degree. In many cases, franchising offers an effective mix of centralized and decentralized decision making.

4. **Joint ventures.** A company may decide to share management with one or more collaborating foreign firms. Joint ventures are especially popular in industries that call for large investments, such as natural gas exploration and automobile manufacturing. Control of the joint venture may be split equally or one party may control decision making. Joint ventures hold several advantages. First, a firm may be able to benefit from a partner's knowledge of the host country's competitive position, culture, language, political systems, and so forth. Second, the firm gains by sharing costs and/or risks of operating in a foreign market. Third, in many countries, political considerations make joint ventures the only feasible entry mode. Finally, joint ventures allow firms to take advantage of a partner's distribution system, technological know-how, and/or marketing skills. For example, General Mills teamed up with CPC International in an operation called International Dessert Partners to develop a major baking and dessert-mix business in Latin America. The venture combines General Mills' technology and Betty Crocker dessert products with CPC's marketing and distribution capabilities in Latin America.[41] The major disadvantages associated with joint ventures are that: (1) a firm may risk giving up control of proprietary knowledge to its partner; and (2) the firm may lose the tight control over a foreign subsidiary needed to engage in coordinated global attacks against rivals.

5. **Strategic alliances.** Although considered by some to be a form of joint venture, we consider strategic alliances to be a distinct entity for two reasons. First, strategic alliances are normally partnerships entered into by two or more firms to gain a competitive advantage on a worldwide, as opposed to local basis. Second, strategic alliances are usually of a much longer-term nature than are joint ventures. In strategic alliances, the partners share long-term goals and pledge almost total cooperation. Strategic alliances can be used to reduce manufacturing costs, accelerate technological diffusion and new product development, and overcome legal and trade barriers.[42] The major disadvantage associated with formation of a strategic alliance is the increased risk for competitive conflict between the partners. Indeed, a recent study showed that strategic alliances have grown at a 25 percent average annual rate, but the median life span of such alliances is only about seven years.[43]

6. **Direct ownership.** Some companies prefer to enter and/or grow in markets either through establishment of a wholly-owned subsidiary or through acquisition. In either case, the firm owns 100 percent of the stock. The advantages to direct ownership are that the firm has: (1) complete control over its technology and operations; (2) immediate access to foreign markets; (3) instant credibility and gains in the foreign country when acquisitions are the mode of entry or growth; and (4) the ability to install its own management team. Of course, the primary disadvantages of direct ownership are the huge costs and significant risks associated with this strategy. These problems may more than offset the advantages depending upon the country entered.

Regardless of the choice of method(s) used to gain entry into and grow within a foreign marketplace, companies must somehow integrate their operations. The complexities involved in operating on a worldwide basis dictate that firms decide on operating strategies. A critical decision that marketing managers must make relates to the extent of adaptation of the marketing mix elements for the foreign country the company operates in. Depending on the area of the world under consideration and the particular product mix, different degrees of standardization/adaptation of the marketing mix elements may take place. As a guideline, standardization of one or more parts of the marketing mix is a function of many factors that individually and collectively affect companies in their decision making.[44] These factors and their resulting influence are:

1. When markets are economically alike, standardization is more practical.
2. When worldwide customers, not countries, are the basis for segmenting markets, a standardization strategy is more effective.
3. The greater the degree of similarity in the markets in terms of customer behavior and lifestyle, the more effective a standardization strategy is.
4. The higher the cultural compatibility of the product across the host countries, the more appropriate is standardization.
5. When a firm's competitive position is similar in different markets, standardization is more practical.
6. When competing against the same adversaries, with similar share position, in different countries, standardization is more appropriate than when competing against purely local companies.
7. Organizational and high-technology products are more suitable for standardization than consumer products.
8. The greater the differences in physical, political, and legal environments between home and host countries, the greater will be the necessary degree of adaptation.
9. The more similar the marketing infrastructure in the home and host countries, the more likely is the effectiveness of standardization.

The decision to adapt or standardize marketing should be made only after a thorough analysis of the product-market mix has been undertaken.

The company's end goal is to develop, manufacture, and market the products best suited to the actual and potential needs of the local (wherever that may be) customer and to the social and economic conditions of the marketplace. There can be subtle differences from country to country and from region to region in the ways a product is used and what customers expect from it.

CONCLUSION

The world is truly becoming a global market. Many companies that avoid operating in the international arena are destined for failure. For those willing to undertake the challenges and risks necessary to become multinational corporations, long-term survival and growth are likely outcomes. The purpose of this chapter was to introduce the reader to the opportunities, problems, and challenges involved in international marketing.

ADDITIONAL READINGS

Ahmed, Sadrudin A., and Alain Astous. "Comparison of Country-of-Origin Effects on Household and Organizational Buyers' Product Perceptions." *European Journal of Marketing* 29, no. 3 (1995), pp. 35–51.

Ambler, Tim. "Reflections in China: Re-Orienting Images of Marketing." *Marketing Management,* Summer 1995, pp. 22–30.

Armstrong, Robert W., and Jill Sweeney. "Industry Type, Culture, Mode of Entry and Perceptions of International Marketing Ethics Problems: A Cross-Culture Comparison." *Journal of Business Ethics,* October 1994, pp. 775–85.

Bartley, Douglas L., and Michael S. Minor. "Why Would a Company Want to Enter a Joint Venture in the Former Soviet Union or Eastern Europe?" *The Journal of Product and Brand Management* 3, no. 2 (1994), pp. 28–36.

Clark, Terry. "National Boundaries, Border Zones, and Marketing Strategy: A Conceptual Framework and Theoretical Model of Secondary Boundary Effects." *Journal of Marketing,* July 1994, pp. 67–80.

Frear, Carol R.; Mary S. Alguire; and Lynn E. Metcalf. "Country Segmentation on the Basis of International Purchasing Patterns." *The Journal of Business & Industrial Marketing* 10, no. 2 (1995), pp. 59–68.

Gripsrud, Geir, and Gabriel Benito. "Promoting Imports from Developing Countries: A Marketing Perspective." *Journal of Business Research,* February 1995, pp. 141–48.

Harrison-Walker, L. Jean. "The Relative Effects of National Stereotype and Advertising Information on the Selection of a Service Provider." *The Journal of Services Marketing* 9, no. 1 (1995), pp. 47–59.

Jarvis, Susan S., and William W. Thompson. "Making Sure Your Canadian Advertisement Does Not Sink Your Sale." *The Journal of Consumer Marketing* 12, no. 2 (1995), pp. 40–46.

Leclerc, France; Bernd H. Schmitt; and Laurette Dube. "Foreign Branding and Its Effects on Product Perceptions and Attitudes." *Journal of Marketing Research,* May 1994, pp. 263–70.

Lugmani, Mushtaq; Ugur Yavas; and Zahir A. Quraeshi. "A Convenience-Oriented Approach to Country Segmentation." *Journal of Consumer Marketing* 11, no. 4 (1994), pp. 29–40.

McDonald, William J. "Developing International Direct Marketing Strategies with a Consumer Decision-Making Content Analysis." *Journal of Direct Marketing,* Autumn 1994, pp. 18–27.

Osland, Gregory E., and Attila Yaprak. "Learning Through Strategic Alliances: Processes and Factors That Enhance Marketing Effectiveness." *European Journal of Marketing* 29, no. 3 (1995), pp. 52–66.

Parameswaran, Ravi, and R. Mohan Pisharodi,. "Facets of Country of Origin Image: An Empirical Assessment." *Journal of Advertising,* March 1994, pp. 43–56.

Roth, Martin. "The Effects of Culture and Socioeconomics on the Performance of Global Brand Image Strategies." *Journal of Marketing Research,* May 1995, pp. 163–75.

Turcq, Dominique. "The Global Impact of Non-Japan Asia." *Long Range Planning,* February 1995, pp. 31–40.

Part E

MARKETING RESPONSE TO A CHANGING SOCIETY

CHAPTER 14
MARKETING MANAGEMENT: SOCIAL AND ETHICAL DIMENSIONS

Chapter 14

MARKETING MANAGEMENT: SOCIAL AND ETHICAL DIMENSIONS

The primary concern of this chapter is the role of marketing in society. While we believe that marketing and the free enterprise system offer the best and most effective system of exchange that has been developed, we also believe that marketers have a responsibility to society that goes beyond the profit objectives of an organization.[1]

In the remainder of this chapter we first investigate the relative power and rights of marketers and consumers. Then we discuss four influences that act a checks and balances to control the power of business in general and marketing in particular. These include legal, political, competitive, and ethical influences.

THE RIGHTS OF MARKETERS AND CONSUMERS

Both marketers and consumers are granted certain rights by society, and both have a degree of power. Overall, many people believe that marketers have considerably more power than consumers. Several years ago, Professor Philip Kotler provided the following list of rights granted to marketers (sellers):

1. Sellers have the right to introduce any product in any size, style, color, and so on, so long as it meets minimum health and safety requirements.
2. Sellers have the right to price the product as they please so long as they avoid discrimination that is harmful to competition.
3. Sellers have the right to promote the product using any resources, media, or message, in any amount, so long as no deception or fraud is involved.
4. Sellers have the right to introduce any buying schemes they wish, so long as they are not discriminatory.
5. Sellers have the right to alter the product offering at any time.
6. Sellers have the right to distribute the product in any reasonable manner.
7. Sellers have the right to limit the product guarantee or postsale services.[2]

While this list is not exhaustive, it does serve to illustrate that marketers have a good deal of power and latitude in their actions.

Since the Consumer Bill of Rights was issued in the early 1960s, consumers have been granted at least four basic rights. First, consumers are granted the *right to safety,* which means the right to be protected against products and services that are hazardous to health and life. Second, consumers are granted the *right to be informed,* which is the right to be protected against fraudulent, deceitful, or misleading advertising or other information that could interfere with making an informed choice. Third, consumers are granted the *right to choose*— the right to have access to a variety of competitive products that are priced fairly and are of satisfactory quality. Finally, consumers are granted the *right to be heard* or the right to be ensured that their interests will be fully and fairly considered in the formulation and administration of government policy. While this list may appear to grant the consumer considerable rights and protection, it has an important weakness: Most of these rights depend on the assumption that consumers are both capable of being and willing to be highly involved in purchase and consumption. In fact, however, many consumers are neither. Young children, many elderly people, and the uneducated poor often do not have the cognitive abilities to process information well enough to be protected. Further, even those consumers who do have the capacity often are not willing to invest the time, money, cognitive energy, and effort to ensure their rights.

The right to choose is also predicated on the assumption that consumers are rational, autonomous, knowledgeable information processors and decision makers. While we believe that most consumers are capable of being so, evidence suggests that consumers often do not behave this way. Further, the right to choose ignores the power of marketing to influence attitudes, intentions, and behaviors. Consumers' needs, wants, and satisfaction may be developed by marketers, for instance. Thus, the assumption of consumer autonomy is not easily supported.

Finally, no matter how much effort consumers exert to ensure they are choosing a good product, they cannot process information that is not available. For example, consumers cannot be aware of product safety risks that are hidden from them.

Overall, then, if there were no other forces in society, marketers might well have more rights and power than consumers do. This is not to say that consumers cannot exert countercontrol on marketers or that consumers do not vary in the degree to which they are influenced by marketers. However, as our society and system of government and exchange evolved, a number of constraints or societal influences on marketing activities have also developed. As shown in Figure 14–1, these include legal, political, competitive, and ethical influences.

Before discussing each of these societal influences, three points should be noted. First, as noted earlier, we believe that marketing and the free

Figure 14–1   *Major Sources of Consumer Protection*

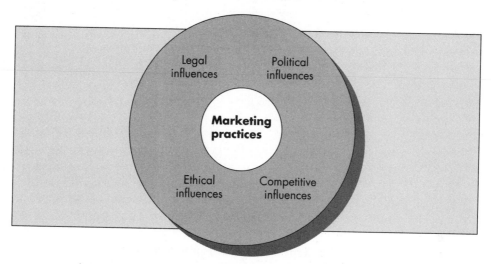

enterprise system offer the best and most effective system of exchange that has ever been developed. This does not mean that the system could not be improved. For example, there is still a large group of poor, uneducated, hungry people in our society who have little chance of improving their lot.

Second, while marketing usually receives the brunt of society's criticism of business, marketing managers are no more or less guilty of wrongdoing than other business executives. Corporate responsibility to society is a shared responsibility of all business executives, regardless of functional field. In addition, marketing executives are no more or less ethical than most other groups in society. Similarly, while business, particularly big business, is commonly singled out for criticism, there is no question that other fields—including medicine, engineering, and law—also have their share of societal problems. Some consumers could also be criticized for the billions of dollars of merchandise that is shoplifted annually, as well as for other crimes against businesses and society.

Third, while some critics of marketing focus on the field in general, many of the problems are confined to a relatively small percentage of firms and practices. Figure 14–2 presents a list of some of the most commonly cited areas of concern, divided into product, promotion, pricing, and distribution issues. Many of these practices are subject to legal influences or constraints.

LEGAL INFLUENCES

Legal influences are federal, state, and local legislation and the agencies and processes by which these laws are upheld. Figure 14–3 presents examples of recent federal legislation designed to protect consumers. Some federal

Figure 14–2   *Some Problem Areas in Marketing*

Product Issues	Pricing Issues
Unsafe products	Deceptive pricing
Poor-quality products	Fraudulent or misleading credit practices
Poor service repair/maintenance after sale	Warranty refund problems
Deceptive packaging and labeling practices	
Promotion Issues	**Distribution Issues**
Deceptive advertising	Sale of counterfeit products and brands
Advertising to children	Pyramid selling
Bait-and-switch advertising	Deceptive in-store selling influences
Anxiety-inducing advertising	
Deceptive personal selling tactics	

legislation is designed to control practices in specific industries (such as food); others are aimed at controlling functional areas (such as product safety).

A variety of government agencies are involved in enforcing these laws and investigating business practices. In addition to state and local agencies, this includes a number of federal agencies, such as those listed in Chapter 1.

Legal influences and the power of government agencies to regulate business and marketing practices grew dramatically in the 1970s; but the 1980s witnessed a decrease in many areas of regulation. In fact, deregulation of business was the major thrust in this period, and government agencies considerably reduced their involvement in controlling business practices. Thus, while legal constraints are an important form of consumer protection, it appears that this influence, at least at the federal level, has diminished somewhat.[3]

POLITICAL INFLUENCES

By *political influences,* we mean the pressure exerted to control marketing practices by various consumer groups. These groups use a variety of methods to influence marketing practices, such as lobbying with various government agencies to enact legislation, boycotting companies for unfair practices, or working directly with consumers in redress assistance and education. Figure 14–4 lists some organizations that are designed to serve consumer interests. These are but a few examples; one tally found over 100 national organizations and over 600 state and local groups concerned with consumerism.

Bloom and Greyser argue that consumerism has reached the mature stage of its life cycle and that its impact has been fragmented.[4] Yet they believe consumerism will continue to have some impact on business, and they

Figure 14-3   *Examples of Consumer-Oriented Legislation*

Year	Legislation	Major Provision of Law
1988	Toxic Substances Control Act Amendment	Provides adequate time for planning and implementation of school asbestos management plans.
1988	Federal Food, Drug and Cosmetic Act Amendment	Bans reimportation of drugs produced in the United States. Places restrictions on distribution of drug samples, bans certain resales of drugs by health care facilities.
1986	Truth in Mileage Act	Amends the Motor Vehicle Information and Cost Savings Act to strengthen, for the protection of consumers, the provisions respecting disclosure of mileage when motor vehicles are transferred.
1986	Petroleum Overcharge Distribution and Restitution Act	Provides for distribution to injured consumers of escrow funds remaining from oil company settlements of alleged price allocation violations under the Emergency Petroleum Allocation of 1973.
1986	Superfund Amendments and Reauthorization Act	Extends and amends the Comprehensive Environmental Response Compensation and Liability Act of 1980. Authorizes appropriations for and revises the EPA Hazardous Substance Response Trust Fund program for financing cleanup of uncontrolled hazardous waste sites.
1986	Anti-Drug Abuse Act	Amends the Food, Drug and Cosmetic Act to revise provisions on regulation of infant formula manufacture.
1986	Processed Products Inspection Improvement Act	Amends the Meat Inspection Act to eliminate USDA continuous inspection requirements for meats, poultry, and egg processing plants for a six-year trial period.
1986	Emergency Response Act	Amends the Toxic Substances Control Act to require the EPA to promulgate regulations pertaining to inspections, development of asbestos management plans, and response actions.
1986	Safe Drinking Water Act Amendments	Amends the Safe Drinking Water Act. Authorizes appropriations for and revises EPA safe drinking water programs, including grants to states for drinking water standards enforcement and groundwater protection programs.
1986	Drug Export Amendments Act	Amends the Food, Drug and Cosmetic Act to remove restrictions on export of human and veterinary drugs not yet approved by FDA or USDA for use in the United States and establishes conditions governing export of such drugs.
1986	Comprehensive Smokeless Tobacco Health Education Act	Provides for public education concerning the health consequences of using smokeless tobacco products. Prohibits radio and television advertising of smokeless tobacco.
1986	Recreational Boating Safety Act Amendment	Enhances boating safety by requiring a report relating to informational displays on gasoline pumps.

Source: John R. Nevin, "Consumer Protection Legislation: Evolution, Structure and Prognosis," Working paper, University of Wisconsin–Madison, Madison, August 1989.

Figure 14-4   *Some Political Groups Concerned with Consumerism*

Broad-Based National Groups	**Special-Interest Groups**
Consumer Federation of America	Action for Children's Television
National Wildlife Federation	American Association of Retired Persons
Common Cause	Group against Smoking and Pollution
Smaller Multi-Issue Organizations	**Local Groups**
National Consumer's League	Public-interest research groups
Ralph Nader's Public Citizen	Local consumer protection offices
	Local broadcast and newspaper consumer "action lines"

Source: Adapted from Paul N. Bloom and Stephen A. Greyser, "The Maturing of Consumerism," *Harvard Business Review,* November–December 1981, pp. 130–39.

offer three strategies for coping with it. First, businesses can try to accelerate the decline of consumerism by *reducing demand* for it. This could be done by improving product quality, expanding services, lowering prices, and toning down advertising claims. Highlight 14–1 describes one company's attempt to reduce demand for consumerism.

Second, businesses can *compete* with consumer groups by having active consumer affairs departments that offer redress assistance and consumer education. Alternatively, a business could fund and coordinate activities designed to "sell" deregulation and other probusiness causes.

Third, businesses can *cooperate* with consumer groups by providing financial and other support. Overall, most of these strategies would likely further reduce the impact and importance of political influences. However, to the degree that following these strategies leads business firms to increase their social responsibility activities in the long run, the consumer could benefit.

COMPETITIVE INFLUENCES

Competitive influences refer to actions of competing firms intended to affect each other and consumers. These actions can be taken in many ways. For example, one firm might sue another firm or point out its alleged fraudulent activities to consumers. Johnson & Johnson frequently took competitors to court to protect its Tylenol brand of pain reliever from being shown in comparative ads. Burger King publicly accused McDonald's of overstating the weight of its hamburgers.

Perhaps the most important consumer protection generated by competition is that it reduces the impact of information from any single firm. In other words, in a marketing environment where there are many active competitors, no single firm can dominate the information flow to consumers. In this sense, conflicting competitive claims, images, information, and offers may help consumers from being unduly influenced by a single firm or brand. Conversely, it may also lead to information overload.

Consumers may also benefit from the development and marketing of better products and services brought about by competitive pressure. Current merger trends and the concentration of various industries may lessen these competitive constraints and societal advantages, however.

ETHICAL INFLUENCES

Perhaps the most important constraints on marketing practices are *ethical influences* and involve *self-regulation* by marketers. Many professions have codes of ethics (see Highlight 14–1), and many firms have their own consumer affairs offices that seek to ensure that the consumer is treated fairly. In addition, some companies have developed a more positive image with consumers by emphasizing consumer-oriented marketing tactics such as offering toll-free hot lines for information and complaints, promoting unit pricing, and supporting social causes.

A difficult problem in discussing ethical constraints is that there is no single standard by which actions can be judged. Laczniak summarizes five ethical standards that have been proposed by various marketing writers:

1. *The Golden Rule:* Act in the way you would expect others to act toward you.
2. *The Utilitarian Principle:* Act in a way that results in the greatest good for the greatest number.
3. *Kant's Categorical Imperative:* Act in such a way that the action taken under the circumstances could be a universal law or rule of behavior.
4. *The Professional Ethic:* Take actions that would be viewed as proper by a disinterested panel of professional colleagues.
5. *The TV Test:* A manager should always ask: "Would I feel comfortable explaining to a national TV audience why I took this action?"[5]

Following these standards could result in many different interpretations of ethical marketing practice. If you doubt this, try applying them to the scenarios in Figure 14–5 and then comparing your answers with those of other readers.

Overall, then, what constitutes ethical marketing behavior is a matter of social judgment. Even in the areas such as product safety, what constitutes ethical marketing practices is not always clear. While at first blush it might be argued that all products should either be completely safe or not be allowed on the market, deeper inspection reveals questions such as How safe? and For whom? For example, bicycles often head the list of the most hazardous products, yet few consumers or marketers would argue that bicycles should be banned from the market. Much of the problem in determining product safety concerns the question of whether the harm done results from an inherent lack of product safety or unsafe use by the consumer.

Figure 14-5 *Marketing Scenarios that Raise Ethical Questions*

Scenario 1

The Thrifty Supermarket Chain has 12 stores in the city of Gotham, U.S.A. The company's policy is to maintain the same prices for all items at all stores. However, the distribution manager knowingly sends the poorest cuts of meat and the lowest-quality produce to the store located in the low-income section of town. He justifies this action based on the fact that this store has the highest overhead due to factors such as employee turnover, pilferage, and vandalism. *Is the distribution manager's economic rationale sufficient justification for his allocation method?*

Scenario 2

The independent Chevy Dealers of Metropolis, U.S.A., have undertaken an advertising campaign headlined by the slogan: "Is your family's life worth 45 MPG?" The ads admit that while Chevy subcompacts are *not* as fuel efficient as foreign imports and cost more to maintain, they are safer according to government-sponsored crash tests. The ads implicitly ask if responsible parents, when purchasing a car, should trade off fuel efficiency for safety. *Is it ethical for the dealers association to use a fear appeal to offset an economic disadvantage?*

Scenario 3

A few recent studies have linked the presence of the artificial sweetener subsugural to cancer in laboratory rats. While the validity of these findings has been hotly debated by medical experts, the Food and Drug Administration has ordered products containing the ingredient banned from sale in the United States. The Jones Company sends all of its sugar-free J.C. Cola (which contain subsugural) to European supermarkets because the sweetener has not been banned there. *Is it acceptable for the Jones Company to send an arguably unsafe product to another market without waiting for further evidence?*

Scenario 4

The Acme Company sells industrial supplies through its own sales force, which calls on company purchasing agents. Acme has found that providing the purchasing agent with small gifts helps cement a cordial relationship and creates goodwill. Acme follows the policy that the bigger the order, the bigger the gift to the purchasing agent. The gifts range from a pair of tickets to a sports event to outboard motors and snowmobiles. Acme does not give gifts to personnel at companies that they know have an explicit policy prohibiting the acceptance of such gifts. *Assuming no laws are violated, is Acme's policy of providing gifts to purchasing agents morally proper?*

Scenario 5

The Buy American Electronics Company has been selling its highly rated System X Color TV sets (21, 19 and 12 inches) for $700, $500, and $300, respectively. These prices have been relatively uncompetitive in the market. After some study, Buy American substitutes several cheaper components (which engineering says may slightly reduce the quality of performance) and passes on the savings to the consumer in the form of a $100 price reduction on each model. Buy American institutes a price-oriented promotional campaign that neglects to mention that the second-generation System X sets are different from the first. *Is the company's competitive strategy ethical?*

Scenario 6

The Smith & Smith Advertising Agency (S & S) has been struggling financially. Mr. Smith is approached by the representative of a small South American country that is on good terms with the U.S. Department of State. He wants S & S to create a multimillion-dollar advertising and public relations campaign that will bolster the image of the country and increase the likelihood that it will receive U.S. foreign aid assistance and attract investment capital. Smith knows the country is a dictatorship that has been accused of numerous human rights violations. *Is it ethical for the Smith & Smith Agency to undertake the proposed campaign?*

Source: Gene R. Laczinak, "Framework for Analyzing Marketing Ethics," *Journal of Macromarketing,* Spring 1983, p. 8.

CONCLUSION

In this chapter we have discussed some of the important relationships between marketers and consumers that involve questions of social responsibility. Overall, while society offers marketers considerable power and latitude in performing marketing tasks, marketers also have a variety of constraints placed on their behavior. These include legal, political, competitive, and ethical influences.

ADDITIONAL READINGS

Akaah, Ishmael P., and Edward A. Riordan. "Judgments of Marketing Professionals about Ethical Issues in Marketing Research: A Replication and Extension." *Journal of Marketing Research* February 1989, pp. 112–20.

Bloom, Paul N.; George R. Milne; and Robert Adler. "Avoiding Misuse of New Information Technologies: Legal and Societal Considerations." *Journal of Marketing,* January 1994, pp. 98–110.

Boedecker, Karl A.; Fred W. Morgan; and Jeffrey J. Stoltman. "Legal Dimensions of Salespersons' Statements: A Review and Managerial Suggestions." *Journal of Marketing,* January 1991, pp. 70–80.

Gundlach, Gregory T., and Patrick E. Murphy. "Ethical and Legal Foundations of Relational Marketing Exchanges." *Journal of Marketing,* October 1993, pp. 35–46.

Heil, Oliver P., and Arlen W. Langvardt. "The Interface between Competitive Signaling and Antitrust Law." *Journal of Marketing,* July 1994, pp. 81–96.

Hunt, Shelby D., and Arturo Z. Vasquez-Parraga. "Organizational Consequences, Marketing Ethics, and Salesforce Supervision." *Journal of Marketing Research,* February 1993, pp. 78–90.

Laczniak, Gene R., and Patrick E. Murphy. *Ethical Marketing Decisions: The Higher Road.* Boston: Allyn and Bacon, 1993.

Smith, N. Craig, and John A. Quelch. *Ethics in Marketing.* Homewood, IL: Richard D. Irwin, 1993.

ANALYZING MARKETING
PROBLEMS AND CASES

HIGHLIGHT 1

A Case for Case Analysis

Cases assist in bridging the gap between classroom learning and the so-called real world of marketing management. They provide us with an opportunity to develop, sharpen, and test our analytical skills at:

—Assessing situations.
—Sorting out and organizing key information.

Source: David W. Cravens and Charles W. Lamb, Jr., *Strategic Marketing: Cases and Applications,* 4th ed. (Homewood, IL: Richard D. Irwin, 1993), p. 95.

—Asking the right questions.
—Defining opportunities and problems.
—Identifying and evaluating alternative courses of action.
—Interpreting data.
—Evaluating the results of past strategies.
—Developing and defending new strategies.
—Interacting with other managers.
—Making decisions under conditions of uncertainty.
—Critically evaluating the work of others.
—Responding to criticism.

The use of business cases was developed by faculty members of the Harvard Graduate School of Business Administration in the 1920s. Case studies have been widely accepted as one effective way of exposing students to the decision-making process.

Basically, cases represent detailed descriptions or reports of business problems. They are usually written by a trained observer who actually had been involved in the firm or organization and had some dealings with the problems under consideration. Cases generally entail both qualitative and quantitative data, which the student must analyze to determine appropriate alternatives and solutions.

The primary purpose of the case method is to introduce a measure of realism into management education. Rather than emphasizing the teaching of concepts, the case method focuses on application of concepts and sound logic to real-world business problems. In this way, the student learns to bridge the gap between abstraction and application and to appreciate the value of both.

The primary purpose of this section is to offer a logical format for the analysis of case problems. Although there is no one format that can be successfully applied to all cases, the following framework is intended to be a logical sequence from which to develop sound analyses. This framework is presented for analysis of comprehensive marketing cases; however, the process should also be useful for shorter marketing cases, incidents, and problems.

A CASE ANALYSIS FRAMEWORK

A basic approach to case analysis involves a four-step process. First, the problem is defined. Second, alternative courses of action are formulated to solve the problem. Third, the alternatives are analyzed in terms of their strengths and weaknesses. And fourth, an alternative is accepted, and a course of action is recommended. This basic approach is quite useful for the student well versed in case analysis, particularly for shorter cases or incidents. However, for the newcomer, this framework may well be inadequate and oversimplified. Thus, the following expanded framework and checklists are intended to aid the student in becoming proficient at case and problem analysis.

1. Analyze and Record the Current Situation

Whether the analysis of a firm's problems is done by a manager, student, or paid business consultant, the first step is to analyze the current situation. This does not mean writing up a history of the firm but entails the type of analysis described below. This approach is useful not only for getting a better grip on the situation but also for discovering both real and potential problems—the central concern of any case analysis.

Phase 1: The environment

The first phase in analyzing a marketing problem or case is to consider the environment in which the firm is operating. The environment can be broken down into a number of different components such as the economic, social, political, and legal areas. Any of these may contain threats to a firm's success or opportunities for improving a firm's situation.

Phase 2: The industry

The second phase involves analyzing the industry in which the firm operates. A framework provided by Michael Porter includes five competitive forces that need to be considered to do a complete industry analysis.[1] The framework is shown in Figure 1 and includes rivalry among existing competitors, threat of new entrants, and threat of substitute products. In addition, in this framework, buyers and suppliers are included as competitors since they can threaten the profitability of an industry or firm.

While rivalry among existing competitors is an issue in most cases, analysis and strategies for dealing with the other forces can also be critical. This is particularly so when a firm is considering entering a new industry and wants to forecast its potential success. Each of the five competitive forces is discussed below.

Rivalry among existing competitors. In most cases and business situations a firm needs to consider the current competitors in its industry in order to develop successful strategies. Strategies such as price competition, advertising battles, sales promotion offers, new product introductions, and increased customer service are commonly used to attract customers from competitors.

In order to fully analyze existing rivalry, it is important to determine which firms are the major competitors and what are their annual sales, market share, growth profile, and strengths and weaknesses. Also, it is useful to analyze their current and past marketing strategies to try to forecast their likely

Figure 1   *Competitive Forces in an Industry*

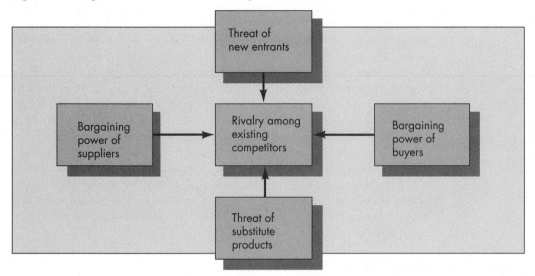

Source: Adapted from Michael E. Porter, "Industry Structure and Competitive Strategy: Keys to Profitability," *Financial Analysts Journal,* July–August 1980, p. 33.

reactions to a change in a competitive firm's strategy. Finally, it is important to consider any trends or changes in government regulation of an industry or changes in technology that could affect the success of a firm's strategy.

Threat of new entrants.   It is always possible for firms in other industries to try to compete in a new industry. New entrants are more likely in industries that have low entry barriers. *Entry barriers* include such things as a need for large financial resources, high brand equity for existing brands in an industry, or economies of scale obtained by existing firms in an industry. Also, existing firms in an industry may benefit from experience curves; that is, their cumulative experience in producing and marketing a product may reduce their per unit costs below those of inexperienced firms. In general, the higher the entry barriers, the less likely outside firms are to enter an industry. For example, the entry barriers for starting up a new car company are much higher than for starting up a new software company.

Threat of substitute products.   In a broad sense, all firms in an industry compete with industries producing substitute products. For example, in cultures where bicycles are the major means of transportation, bicycle manufacturers compete with substitute products such as motor scooters and automobiles. Substitutes limit the potential return in an industry by placing a ceiling on the prices a firm in the industry can profitably charge. The more attractive the price-performance alternative offered by substitutes, the tighter the lid on industry profits. For example, the price of candy, such as Raisinets chocolate-covered raisins, may limit the price Del Monte can charge for "healthy snacks," such as Strawberry Yogurt Raisins.

candy, such as Raisinets chocolate-covered raisins, may limit the price Del Monte can charge for "healthy snacks," such as Strawberry Yogurt Raisins. *Bargaining power of suppliers.* Suppliers can be a competitive threat in an industry because they can raise the price of raw materials or reduce their quality. Powerful suppliers can reduce the profitability of an industry or firm if companies cannot raise their prices to cover price increases by suppliers. Also, suppliers may be a threat because they may forward integrate into an industry by purchasing a firm that they supply or other firms in the industry. *Bargaining power of buyers.* Buyers can compete with an industry by forcing prices down, bargaining for higher quality or more services, and playing competitors off against each other. All of these tactics can lower the profitability of a firm or industry. For example, because Wal-Mart sells such a large percentage of many companies' products, it can negotiate for lower prices than smaller retailers can. Also, buyers may be a threat because they may backward integrate into an industry by purchasing firms that supply them or other firms in the industry.

Phase 3: The firm

The third phase involves analysis of the firm itself not only in comparison with the industry and industry averages but also internally in terms of both quantitative and qualitative data. Key areas of concern at this stage are such factors as objectives, constraints, management philosophy, financial condition, and the organizational structure and culture of the firm.

Phase 4: The marketing strategy

Although there may be internal personnel or structural problems in the marketing department itself that need examination, typically an analysis of the current marketing strategy is the next phase. In this phase, the objectives of the marketing department are analyzed in comparison with those of the firm in terms of agreement, soundness, and attainability. Each element of the marketing mix as well as other areas, like marketing research and decision support systems, is analyzed in terms of whether it is internally consistent, synchronized with the goals of the department and firm, and focused on specific target markets. Although cases often are labeled in terms of their primary emphasis, such as "pricing" or "advertising," it is important to analyze the marketing strategy and entire marketing mix, since a change in one element will usually affect the entire marketing program.

In performing the analysis of the current situation, the data should be analyzed carefully to extract the relevant from the superfluous. Many cases contain information that is not relevant to the problem; it is the analyst's job to discard this information to get a clearer picture of the current situation. As the analysis proceeds, a watchful eye must be kept on each phase to determine (1) symptoms of problems; (2) current problems; and (3) potential problems. Symptoms of problems are indicators of a problem but are not problems in and of themselves. For example, a symptom of a problem may be a decline in sales in a particular sales territory. However, the

---

HIGHLIGHT 2

What Does Case "Analysis" Mean?

A common criticism of prepared cases goes something like this: "You repeated an awful lot of case material, but you really didn't analyze the case." Yet, at the same time, it is difficult to verbalize exactly what *analysis* means—that is, I can't explain exactly what it is, but I know it when I see it!

This is a common problem since the term *analysis* has many definitions and means different things in different contexts. In terms of case analysis, one thing that is clear is that an-

alysis means going beyond simply describing the case information. It includes determining the implications of the case information for developing strategy. This determination may involve careful mathematical analysis of sales and profit data or thoughtful interpretation of the text of the case.

One way of thinking about analysis involves a series of three steps: synthesis, generalizations, and implications. Below is a brief example of this process.

The high growth rate of frozen pizza sales has attracted a number of large food processors, including Pillsbury (Totino's), Quaker Oats (Celeste), American Home Products (Chef Boy-ar-dee), Nestlé (Stouffer's). General Mills (Saluto), and H. J. Heinz (La Pizzeria). The major independents are Jeno's, Tony's, and John's. Jeno's and Totino's are the market leaders, with market shares of about 19 percent each. Celeste and Tony's have about 8 to 9 percent each, and the others have about 5 percent or less.

The frozen pizza market is a highly competitive and highly fragmented market.

In markets such as this, attempts to gain market share through lower consumer prices or heavy advertising are likely to be quickly copied by competitors and thus not be very effective.

Lowering consumer prices or spending more on advertising are likely to be poor strategies. Perhaps increasing freezer space in retail outlets could be effective (this might be obtained through trade discounts). A superior product, for example, better-tasting pizza, microwave pizza, or increasing geographic coverage of the market, may be better strategies for obtaining market share.

Case Material

Synthesis

Generalizations

Implications

Note that none of the three analysis steps includes any repetition of the case material. Rather, they involve abstracting a meaning of the information and, by pairing it with marketing principles, coming up with the strategic implications of the information.

---

problem is the root cause of the decline in sales—perhaps the field representative quit making sales calls and is relying on phone orders only.

The following is a checklist of the types of questions that should be asked when performing the analysis of the current situation.

Checklist for analyzing the current situation

Phase 1: The environment.

2. What are current trends in cultural and social values and how do these affect the industry, firm, or marketing strategy?
3. What are current political values and trends and how do they affect the industry, firm, or marketing strategy?
4. Is there any current or pending federal, state, or local legislation that could change the industry, firm, or marketing strategy?
5. Overall, are there any threats or opportunities in the environment that could influence the industry, firm, or marketing strategy?

Phase 2: The industry.

1. What industry is the firm in?
2. Which firms are the major competitors in the industry and what is their annual sales, market share, and growth profile?
3. What strategies have competitors in the industry been using, and what has been their success with them?
4. What are the relative strengths and weaknesses of competitors in the industry?
5. How much threat is there of new competitors coming into the industry, and what are the major entry barriers?
6. Are there any substitute products for the industry, and what are their advantages and disadvantages compared to this industry's products?
7. How much bargaining power do suppliers have in this industry, and what is its impact on the firm and industry profits?
8. How much bargaining power do buyers have in this industry, and what is its impact on the firm and industry profits?

Phase 3: The firm.

1. What are the objectives of the firm? Are they clearly stated? Attainable?
2. What are the strengths of the firm? Managerial expertise? Financial? Copyrights or patents?
3. What are the constraints and weaknesses of the firm?
4. Are there any real or potential sources of dysfunctional conflict in the structure of the firm?
5. How is the marketing department structured in the firm?

Phase 4: The marketing strategy.

1. What are the objectives of the marketing strategy? Are they clearly stated? Are they consistent with the objectives of the firm? Is the entire marketing mix structured to meet these objectives?
2. What marketing concepts are at issue in the current strategy? Is the marketing strategy well planned and laid out? Is the strategy consistent with sound marketing principles? If the strategy takes exception to marketing principles, is there a good reason for it?
3. To what target market is the strategy directed? Is it well defined? Is the market large enough to be profitably served? Does the market have long-run potential?
4. What competitive advantage does the marketing strategy offer? If none, what can be done to gain a competitive advantage in the marketplace?
5. What products are being sold? What is the width, depth, and consistency of the firm's product lines? Does the firm need new products to fill out its prod-

uct line? Should any product be deleted? What is the profitability of the various products?

6. What promotion mix is being used? Is promotion consistent with the products and product images? What could be done to improve the promotion mix?
7. What channels of distribution are being used? Do they deliver the product at the right time and right place to meet consumer needs? Are the channels typical of those used in the industry? Could channels be made more efficient?
8. What pricing strategies are being used? How do prices compare with similar products of other firms? How are prices determined?
9. Are marketing research and information systematically integrated into the marketing strategy? Is the overall marketing strategy internally consistent?

The relevant information from this preliminary analysis is now formalized and recorded. At this point the analyst must be mindful of the difference between facts and opinions. Facts are objective statements, such as financial data, whereas opinions are subjective interpretations of facts or situations. The analyst must make certain not to place too much emphasis on opinions and to carefully consider any variables that may bias such opinions.

Regardless of how much information is contained in the case or how much additional information is collected, the analyst usually finds that it is impossible to specify a complete framework for the current situation. At this point, assumptions must be made. Clearly, since each analyst may make different assumptions, it is critical that assumptions be explicitly stated. When presenting a case, the analyst may wish to distribute copies of the assumption list to all class members. In this way, confusion is avoided in terms of how the analyst perceives the current situation, and others can evaluate the reasonableness and necessity of the assumptions.

2. Analyze and Record Problems and Their Core Elements

After careful analysis, problems and their core elements should be explicitly stated and listed in order of importance. Finding and recording problems and their core elements can be difficult. It is not uncommon on reading a case for the first time for the student to view the case as a description of a situation in which there are no problems. However, careful analysis should reveal symptoms, which lead to problem recognition.

Recognizing and recording problems and their core elements is most critical for a meaningful case analysis. Obviously, if the root problems are not explicitly stated and understood, the remainder of the case analysis has little merit, since the true issues are not being dealt with. The following checklist of questions is designed to assist you in performing this step of the analysis.

Checklist for analyzing problems and their core elements
1. What is the primary problem in the case? What are the secondary problems?
2. What proof exists that these are the central issues? How much of this proof is based on facts? On opinions? On assumptions?

HIGHLIGHT 3

Understanding the Current Situation through SWOT Analysis

A useful approach for gaining an understanding of the situation an organization is facing at a particular time is called *SWOT analysis*. SWOT stands for the organization's *s*trengths and *w*eaknesses and the *o*pportunities and *t*hreats it faces in the environment. Below are some issues an analyst should address in performing a SWOT analysis.

Potential Internal Strengths

- Core competences in key areas.
- Adequate financial resources.
- Well thought of by buyers.
- An acknowledged market leader.
- Well-conceived functional area strategies.
- Access to economies of scale.
- Insulated (at least somewhat) from strong competitive pressures.
- Proprietary technology.
- Cost advantages.
- Better advertising campaigns.
- Product innovation skills.
- Proven management.
- Ahead on experience curve.
- Better manufacturing capability.
- Superior technological skills.
- Other?

Potential External Opportunities

- Serve additional customer groups.
- Enter new markets or segments.
- Expand product line to meet broader range of customer needs.
- Diversify into related products.
- Vertical integration (forward or backward).
- Falling trade barriers in attractive foreign markets.
- Complacency among rival firms.
- Faster market growth.
- Other?

Potential Internal Weaknesses

- No clear strategic direction.
- Obsolete facilities.
- Subpar profitability because . . .
- Lack of managerial depth and talent.
- Missing some key skills or competences.
- Poor track record in implementing strategy.
- Plagued with internal operating problems.
- Falling behind in R&D.
- Too narrow a product line.
- Weak market image.
- Weak distribution network.
- Below-average marketing skills.
- Unable to finance needed changes in strategy.
- Higher overall unit costs relative to key competitors.
- Other?

Potential External Threats

- Entry of lower-cost foreign competitors.
- Rising sales of substitute products.
- Slower market growth.
- Adverse shifts in foreign exchange rates and trade policies of foreign governments.
- Costly regulatory requirements.
- Vulnerability to recession and business cycle.
- Growing bargaining power of customers or suppliers.
- Changing buyer needs and tastes.
- Adverse demographic changes.
- Other?

Source: Adapted from Arthur A. Thompson, Jr., and A. J. Strickland III, *Strategic Management: Concepts and Cases,* 6th ed. (Homewood, IL: Richard D. Irwin, 1992), p. 88. Reprinted by permission.

3. What symptoms are there that suggest these are the real problems in the case?
4. How are the problems, as defined, related? Are they independent, or are they the result of a deeper problem?
5. What are the ramifications of these problems in the short run? In the long run?

3. Formulate, Evaluate, and Record Alternative Courses of Action

This step is concerned with the question of what can be done to resolve the problem defined in the previous step. Generally, a number of alternative courses of action are available that could potentially help alleviate the problem condition. Three to seven is usually a reasonable number of alternatives to work with. Another approach is to brainstorm as many alternatives as possible initially and then reduce the list to a workable number.

Sound logic and reasoning are very important in this step. It is critical to avoid alternatives that could potentially alleviate the problem, but would create a greater new problem or require greater resources than the firm has at its disposal.

After serious analysis and listing of a number of alternatives, the next task is to evaluate them in terms of their costs and benefits. Costs are any output or effort the firm must exert to implement the alternative. Benefits are any input or value received by the firm. Costs to be considered are time, money, other resources, and opportunity costs, while benefits are such things as sales, profits, goodwill, and customer satisfaction. The following checklist provides a guideline of questions to be used when performing this phase of the analysis.

Checklist for formulating and evaluating alternative courses of action
1. What possible alternatives exist for solving the firm's problems?
2. What limits are there on the possible alternatives? Competence? Resources? Management preference? Social responsibility? Legal restrictions?
3. What major alternatives are now available to the firm? What marketing concepts are involved that affect these alternatives?
4. Are the listed alternatives reasonable, given the firm's situation? Are they logical? Are the alternatives consistent with the goals of the marketing program? Are they consistent with the firm's objectives?
5. What are the costs of each alternative? What are the benefits? What are the advantages and disadvantages of each alternative?
6. Which alternative best solves the problem and minimizes the creation of new problems, given the above constraints?

4. Select and Record the Chosen Alternative and Implementation Details

In light of the previous analysis, the alternative is now selected that best solves the problem with a minimum creation of new problems. It is important to record the logic and reasoning that precipitated the selection of a particular alternative. This includes articulating not only why the alternative was selected but also why the other alternatives were not selected.

No analysis is complete without an action-oriented decision and plan for implementing the decision. The accompanying checklist indicates the type of questions that should be answered in this stage of analysis.

Checklist for selecting and implementing the chosen alternative
1. What must be done to implement the alternative?
2. What personnel will be involved? What are the responsibilities of each?
3. When and where will the alternative be implemented?
4. What will be the probable outcome?
5. How will the success or failure of the alternative be measured?

PITFALLS TO AVOID IN CASE ANALYSIS

Below is a summary of some of the most common errors analysts make when analyzing cases. When evaluating your analysis or those of others, this list provides a useful guide for spotting potential shortcomings.

1. *Inadequate definition of the problem.* By far the most common error made in case analysis is attempting to recommend a course of action without first adequately defining or understanding the problem. Whether presented orally or in a written report, a case analysis must begin with a focus on the central issues and problems represented in the case situation. Closely related is the error of analyzing symptoms without determining the root problem.
2. *The search for "the answer."* In case analysis, there are no clear-cut solutions. Keep in mind that the objective of case studies is learning through discussion and exploration. There is no one "official" or "correct" answer to a case. Rather, there are usually several reasonable alternative solutions.
3. *Not enough information.* Analysts often complain there is not enough information in some cases to make a good decision. However, there is justification for not presenting *all* of the information in a case. As in real life, a marketing manager or consultant seldom has all the information necessary to make an optimal decision. Thus, reasonable assumptions have to be made, and the challenge is to find intelligent solutions in spite of the limited information.
4. *Use of generalities.* In analyzing cases, specific recommendations are necessarily not generalities. For example, a suggestion to increase the price is a generality; a suggestion to increase the price by $1.07 is a specific.
5. *A different situation.* Considerable time and effort are sometimes exerted by analysts contending that "If the situation were different, I'd know what course of action to take" or "If the marketing manager hadn't already fouled things up so badly, the firm wouldn't have a problem." Such reasoning ignores the fact that the events in the case have already happened and cannot be changed. Even though analysis or critcism of past events is necessary in diagnosing the problem, in the end, the present situation must be addressed and decisions must be made based on the given situations.
6. *Narrow vision analysis.* Although cases are often labeled as a specific type of case, such as "pricing," "product," and so forth, this does not mean that

HIGHLIGHT 4

An Operational Approach to Case and Problem Analysis

1. Read the case quickly to get an overview of the situation.
2. Read the case again thoroughly. Underline relevant information and take notes on potential areas of concern.
3. Review outside sources of information on the environment and the industry. Record relevant information and the source of this information.
4. Perform comparative analysis of the firm with the industry and industry averages.
5. Analyze the firm.
6. Analyze the marketing program.
7. Record the current situation in terms of relevant environmental, industry, firm, and marketing strategy parameters.
8. Make and record necessary assumptions to complete the situational framework.

9. Determine and record the major issues, problems, and their core elements.
10. Record proof that these are the major issues.
11. Record potential courses of actions.
12. Evaluate each initially to determine constraints that preclude acceptability.
13. Evaluate remaining alternatives in terms of costs and benefits.
14. Record analysis of alternatives.
15. Select an alternative.
16. Record alternative and defense of its selection.
17. Record the who, what, when, where, how, and why of the alternative and its implementation.

other marketing variables should be ignored. Too often analysts ignore the effects that a change in one marketing element will have on the others.

7. *Realism.* Too often analysts become so focused on solving a particular problem that their solutions become totally unrealistic. For instance, suggesting a $1 million advertising program for a firm with a capital structure of $50,000 is an unrealistic solution.

8. *The marketing research solution.* A quite common but unsatisfactory solution to case problems is marketing research; for example, "The firm should do this or that type of marketing research to find a solution to its problem." Although marketing research may be helpful as an intermediary step in some cases, marketing research does not solve problems or make decisions. In cases where marketing research is recommended, the cost and potential benefits should be fully specified in the case analysis.

9. *Rehashing the case material.* Analysts sometimes spend considerable effort rewriting a two- or three-page history of the firm as presented in the case. This is unnecessary since the instructor and other analysts are already familiar with this information.

10. *Premature conclusions.* Analysts sometimes jump to premature conclusions instead of waiting until their analysis is completed. Too many analysts jump to conclusions upon first reading the case and then proceed to interpret everything in the case as justifying their conclusions, even factors logically against it.

10. *Premature conclusions.* Analysts sometimes jump to premature conclusions instead of waiting until their analysis is completed. Too many analysts jump to conclusions upon first reading the case and then proceed to interpret everything in the case as justifying their conclusions, even factors logically against it.

COMMUNICATING CASE ANALYSES

The final concern in case analysis deals with communicating the results of the analysis. The most comprehensive analysis has little value if it is not communicated effectively. There are two primary media through which case analyses are communicated—the written report and the oral presentation.

The Written Report

Since the structure of the written report will vary by the type of case analyzed, the purpose of this section is not to present a "one and only" way of writing up a case. The purpose of this section is to present some useful generalizations to aid analysts in case writeups.

A good written report starts with an outline that organizes the structure of the analysis in a logical manner. The following is a general outline for a marketing case report.

   I. **Title Page.**
  II. **Table of Contents.**
 III. **Executive Summary. (A one- to two-page summary of the analysis and recommendations)**
  IV. **Situation Analysis.**
       A. *Environment.*
          1. Economic conditions and trends.
          2. Cultural and social values and trends.
          3. Political and legal issues.
          4. Summary of environmental opportunities and threats.
          5. Implications for strategy development.
       B. *Industry.*
          1. Classification and definition of industry.
          2. Analysis of existing competitors.
          3. Analysis of potential new entrants.
          4. Analysis of substitute products.
          5. Analysis of suppliers.
          6. Analysis of buyers.
          7. Summary of industry opportunities and threats.
          8. Implications for strategy development.
       C. *Firm.*
          1. Objectives and constraints.

   2. Financial condition.
   3. Management philosophy.
   4. Organizational structure.
   5. Organizational culture.
   6. Summary of the firm's strengths and weaknesses.
   7. Implications for strategy development.
   D. *Marketing Strategy.*
       1. Objectives and constraints.
       2. Analysis of sales, profits, and market share.
       3. Analysis of target market(s).
       4. Analysis of marketing mix variables.
       5. Summary of marketing strategy's strengths and weaknesses.
       6. Implications for strategy development.
V. Problems Found in Situation Analysis.
   A. *Statement of Primary Problem(s).*
       1. Evidence of problem(s).
       2. Effects of problem(s).
   B. *Statement of Secondary Problem(s).*
       1. Evidence of problem(s).
       2. Effects of problem(s).
VI. Strategic Alternatives for Solving Problems.
   A. *Description of Strategic Alternative 1.*
       1. Benefits of alternative 1.
       2. Costs of alternative 1.
   B. *Description of Strategic Alternative 2.*
       1. Benefits of alternative 2.
       2. Costs of alternative 2.
   C. *Description of Strategic Alternative 3.*
       1. Benefits of alternative 3.
       2. Costs of alternative 3.
VII. Selection of Strategic Alternative and Implementation.
   A. *Statement of Selected Strategy.*
   B. *Justification for Selection of Strategy.*
   C. *Description of Implementation of Strategy.*
VIII. Summary.
IX. Appendices.
   A. *Financial Analysis.*
   B. *Technical Analysis.*

Writing the case report entails filling out the details of the outline in prose form. Of course, not every case report requires all the headings listed above and different headings may be required for some cases. Like any other skill, it takes practice to determine the appropriate headings and approach for writing up particular cases. However, good case reports flow logically from topic to topic, are clearly written, are based on solid situation analysis, and demonstrate sound strategic thinking.

a case or to divide responsibility between team members, simply reading the written report is unacceptable since it encourages boredom and interferes with all-important class discussion.

The use of visual aids can be quite helpful in presenting class analyses. However, simply presenting financial statements contained in the case is a poor use of visual media. On the other hand, graphs of sales and profit curves can be more easily interpreted and can be quite useful for making specific points.

Oral presentation of cases is particularly helpful to analysts for learning the skill of speaking to a group. In particular, the ability to handle objections and disagreements without antagonizing others is a skill worth developing.

CONCLUSION

From the discussion it should be obvious that good case analyses require a major commitment of time and effort. Individuals must be highly motivated and willing to get involved in the analysis and discussion if they expect to learn and succeed in a course where cases are utilized. Persons with only passive interest who perform "night before" analyses cheat themselves out of valuable learning experiences that can aid them in their careers.

ADDITIONAL READINGS

Bernhardt, Kenneth L., and Thomas C. Kinnear. *Cases in Marketing Management.* 6th ed., Burr Ridge, IL: Richard D. Irwin, 1994, chap. 2.

Cravens, David W., and Charles W. Lamb, Jr. *Strategic Marketing Management Cases.* 4th ed. Homewood, IL: Richard D. Irwin, 1993, pp. 94–108.

O'Dell, William F.; Andrew C. Ruppel; Robert H. Trent; and William J. Kehoe. *Marketing Decision Making: Analytic Framework and Cases.* 4th ed. Cincinnati: South-Western Publishing, 1988, chaps. 1–5.

FINANCIAL ANALYSIS FOR MARKETING DECISIONS

FINANCIAL ANALYSIS

Financial analysis is an important aspect of marketing decision making and planning and should be an integral part of marketing problem and case analysis. In this section we present several financial tools that are useful for analyzing marketing problems and cases. First, we investigate break-even analysis, which is concerned with determining the number of units or dollar sales, or both, necessary to break even on a project or to obtain a given level of profits. Second, we illustrate net present value analysis, which is a somewhat more sophisticated tool for analyzing marketing alternatives. Finally, we investigate ratio analysis, which can be a quite useful tool for determining the financial condition of the firm, including its ability to invest in a new or modified marketing program.

Break-Even Analysis

Break-even analysis is a common tool for investigating the potential profitability of a marketing alternative. The *break-even point* is that level of sales in either units or sales dollars at which a firm covers all of its costs. In other words, it is the level at which total sales revenue just equals the total costs necessary to achieve these sales.

To compute the break-even point, an analyst must have or be able to obtain three values. First, the analyst needs to know the selling price per unit of the product (SP). For example, suppose the Ajax Company plans to sell its new electric car through its own dealerships at a retail price of $5,000. Second, the analyst needs to know the level of fixed costs (FC). Fixed costs are all costs relevant to the project that do not change regardless of how many units are produced or sold. For instance, whether Ajax produces and sells 1 or 100,000 cars, Ajax executives will receive their salaries, land must be purchased for a plant, a plant must be constructed, and machinery must be purchased. Other fixed costs include such things as interest, lease payments, and sinking fund payments. Suppose Ajax has totaled all of its fixed costs and the sum is $1.5 million. Third, the analyst must know the variable costs per unit produced (VC). As the name implies, variable costs are those that vary directly with the number of units produced. For example, for each car Ajax produces, there are costs for raw materials and components to build the car, such as batteries, electric motors, steel bodies and tires; there are labor costs for operating employees; these are machine costs, such as electricity and welding rods. Suppose these are totaled by Ajax, and it is determined that the variable costs for each car produced equal $3,500. With this information, the analyst can now determine the break-even point, which is the number of units that must be sold to just cover the cost of producing the cars. The break-even point is determined by dividing total fixed costs by the *contribution margin*. The contribution margin is simply the difference between the selling price per unit (SP) and variable costs per unit (VC). Algebraically,

$$\text{BEP}_{\text{(in units)}} = \frac{\text{Total fixed costs}}{\text{Contribution margin}}$$

$$= \frac{\text{FC}}{\text{SP} - \text{VC}}$$

Substituting the Ajax estimates,

$$\text{BEP}_{\text{(in units)}} = \frac{1,500,000}{5,000 - 3,500}$$

$$= \frac{1,500,000}{1,500}$$

$$= 1000 \ units$$

In other words, the Ajax Company must sell 1,000 cars to just break even (i.e., for total sales revenue to cover total costs).

Alternatively, the analyst may want to know the break-even point in terms of dollar sales volume. Of course, if the preceding analysis has been done, one could simply multiply the $\text{BEP}_{\text{(in units)}}$ times the selling price to determine the break-even sales volume (i.e., 1,000 units $\times$ \$5,000/unit = \$5 million). However, the $\text{BEP}_{\text{(in dollars)}}$ can be computed directly, using the formula below:

$$\text{BEP}_{\text{(in dollars)}} = \frac{\text{FC}}{1 - \dfrac{\text{VC}}{\text{SP}}}$$

$$= \frac{1,500,000}{1 - \dfrac{3,500}{5,000}}$$

$$= \frac{1,500,000}{1 - .7}$$

$$= \$5,000,000$$

Thus, Ajax must produce and sell 1,000 cars, which equals \$5 million sales, to break even. Of course, firms do not want to just break even but want to make a profit. The logic of break-even analysis can easily be extended to include profits (P). Suppose Ajax decided that a 20 percent return on fixed costs would make the project worth the investment. Thus, Ajax would need 20% $\times$ \$1,500,000 = \$300,000 before-tax profit. To calculate how many units Ajax must sell to achieve this level of profits, the profit figure (P) is added to fixed costs in the above formulas. (We will label the break-even point as BEP′ to show that we are now computing unit and sales levels to obtain a given profit level.) In the Ajax example:

$$\text{BEP}'_{\text{(in units)}} = \frac{\text{FC} + \text{P}}{\text{SP} - \text{VC}}$$

$$= \frac{1,500,000 + 300,000}{5,000 - 3,500}$$

$$= \frac{1,800,000}{1,500}$$

$$= 1,200 \text{ units}$$

In terms of dollars,

$$\text{BEP}'(\text{in dollars}) = \frac{\text{FC} + \text{P}}{1 - \dfrac{\text{VC}}{\text{SP}}}$$

$$= \frac{1,500,000 + 300,000}{1 - \dfrac{3,500}{5,000}}$$

$$= \frac{1,800,000}{1 - .7}$$

$$= \$6,000,000$$

Thus, Ajax must produce and sell 1,200 cars (sales volume of $6 million) to obtain a 20 percent return on fixed costs. Analysis must now be directed at determining whether a given marketing plan can be expected to produce sales of at least this level. If the answer is yes, the project would appear to be worth investing in. If not, Ajax should seek other opportunities.

Net Present Value Analysis

The profit-oriented marketing manager must understand that the capital invested in new products has a cost. It is a basic principle in business that whoever wishes to use capital must pay for its use. Dollars invested in new products could be diverted to other uses—to pay off debts, pay out to stockholders, or buy U.S. Treasury bonds—which would yield economic benefits to the corporation. If, on the other hand, all of the dollars used to finance a new product have to be borrowed from lenders outside the corporation, interest has to be paid on the loan.

One of the best ways to analyze the financial aspects of a marketing alternative is *net present value* analysis. This method employs a "discounted cash flow," which takes into account the time value of money and its price to the borrower. The following example will illustrate this method.

To compute the net present value of an investment proposal, the cost of capital must be estimated. The cost of capital can be defined as the required rate of return on an investment that would leave the owners of the firm as well off as if the project was not undertaken. Thus, it is the minimum percentage return on investment that a project must make to be worth undertaking.

There are many methods of estimating the cost of capital. However, since these methods are not the concern of this text, we will simply assume that the cost of capital for the Ajax Corporation has been determined to be 10 percent.[1] Again, it should be noted that once the cost of capital is determined, it becomes the minimum rate of return required for an investment—a type of cutoff point. However, some firms in selecting their new product investments select a minimum rate of return that is above the cost of capital figure to allow for errors in judgment or measurement.

The Ajax Corporation is considering a proposal to market instant developing movie film. After conducting considerable marketing research, sales were projected to be $1 million per year. In addition, the finance department compiled the following information concerning the projects:

New equipment needed	$700,000
Useful life of equipment	10 years
Depreciation	10% per year
Salvage value	$100,000
Cost of goods and expenses	$700,000 per year
Cost of capital	10%
Tax rate	50%

To compute the net present value of this project, the net cash flow for each year of the project must first be determined. This can be done in four steps:

1. Sales − Cost of goods and expenses = Gross income or

$$\$1,000,000 - 700,000 = \$300,000$$

2. Gross income − Depreciation = Taxable income or

$$\$300,000 - 10\% \times 600,000) = \$240,000$$

3. Taxable income − Tax = Net income or

$$\$240,000 - (50\% \times 240,000) = \$120,000$$

4. Net income + Depreciation = Net cash flow or

$$\$120,000 + 60,000 = \$180,000 \text{ per year}$$

Since the cost of capital is 10 percent, this figure is used to discount the net cash flows for each year. To illustrate, the $180,000 received at the end of the first year would be discounted by the factor $1/(+0.10)$, which would be $180,000 \times 0.9091 = \$163,638$; the $180,000 received at the end of the second year would be discounted by the factor $1/(1 + 0.10)^2$ which would be $180,000 \times 0.8264 = \$148,752$, and so on. (Most finance textbooks have present value tables that can be used to simplify the computations.) On the next page are the present value computations for the 10-year project. It should be noted that the net cash flow for year 10 is $280,000 since there is an additional $100,000 inflow from salvage value.

Thus, at a discount rate of 10 percent, the present value of the net cash flow from new product investment is greater than the $700,000 outlay required, and

Year	Net Cash Flow	0.10 Discount Factor	Present Value
1	$ 180,000	0.9091	$ 163,638
2	180,000	0.8264	148,752
3	180,000	0.7513	135,234
4	180,000	0.6830	122,940
5	180,000	0.6209	111,762
6	180,000	0.5645	101,610
7	180,000	0.5132	92,376
8	180,000	0.4665	83,970
9	180,000	0.4241	76,338
10	280,000	0.3855	107,940
Total	$1,900,000		$1,144,560

so the decision can be considered profitable by this standard, Here the *net present value* is $444,560, which is the difference between the $700,000 investment outlay and the $1,144,560 discounted cash flow. The present value ratio is nothing more than the present value of the net cash flow divided by the cash investment. If this ratio is 1 or larger than 1, the project would be profitable for the firm to invest in.

There are many other measures of investment worth, but only one additional method will be discussed. It is the very popular and easily understood "payback method." *Payback* refers to the amount of time required to pay back the original outlay from the cash flows. Staying with the example, the project is expected to produce a stream of cash proceeds that is constant from year to year, so the payback period can be determined by dividing the investment outlay by this annual cash flow. Dividing $700,000 by $180,000, the payback period is approximately 3.9 years. Firms often set a maximum payback period before a project will be accepted. For example, many firms refuse to take on a project if the payback period exceeds five years.

This example should illustrate the difficulty in evaluating marketing investments from a profitability or economic worth standpoint. The most challenging problem is that of developing accurate cash flow estimates because there are many possible alternatives, such as price of the product and channels of distribution, and the consequences of each alternative must be forecast in terms of sales volumes, selling costs, and other expenses. In spite of all the problems, management must evaluate the economic worth of new product decisions, not only to reduce some of the guesswork and ambiguity surrounding marketing decision making, but also to reinforce the the objective of trying to make profitable decisions.

Ratio Analysis

Firms' income statements and balance sheets provide a wealth of information that is useful for marketing decision making. Frequently, this information is included in marketing cases, yet analysts often have no convenient way of interpreting the financial position of the firm to make sound

HIGHLIGHT 1

Selected Present Value Discount Factors

Years	8%	10%	12%	14%	16%	18%
1	.9259	.9091	.8929	.8772	.8621	.8475
2	.8573	.8264	.7972	.7695	.7432	.7182
3	.7938	.7513	.7118	.6750	.6407	.6086
4	.7350	.6830	.6355	.5921	.5523	.5158
5	.6806	.6209	.5674	.5194	.4761	.4371
6	.6302	.5645	.5066	.4556	.4104	.3704
7	.5835	.5132	.4523	.3996	.3538	.3139
8	.5403	.4665	.4039	.3506	.3050	.2660
9	.5002	.4241	.3606	.3075	.2630	.2255
10	.4632	.3855	.3220	.2697	.2267	.1911

marketing decisions. Ratio analysis provides the analyst an easy and efficient method for investigating a firm's financial position by comparing the firm's ratios across time or with ratios of similar firms in the industry or with industry averages.

Ratio analysis involves four basic steps:

1. Choose the appropriate ratios.
2. Compute the ratios.
3. Compare the ratios.
4. Check for problems or opportunities.

1. Choose the appropriate ratios

The five basic types of financial ratios are: (1) liquidity ratios; (2) asset management ratios; (3) profitability ratios: (4) debt management ratios; and (5) market value ratios.[2] While calculating ratios of all five types is useful, liquidity, asset management, and profitability ratios provide information that is most directly relevant for marketing decision making. Although many ratios can be calculated in each of these groups, we have selected two of the most commonly used and readily available ratios in each group to illustrate the process.

Liquidity ratios. One of the first considerations in analyzing a marketing problem is the liquidity of the firm. *Liquidity* refers to the ability of the firm to pay its short-term obligations. If a firm cannot meet its short-term obligations, there is little than can be done until this problem is resolved. Simply stated, recommendations to increase advertising, to do marketing research, or to develop new products are of little value if the firm is about to go bankrupt!

The two most commonly used ratios for investigating liquidity are the *current ratio* and the *quick ratio* (or "acid test"). The current ratio is determined by dividing current assets by current liabilities and is a measure of

HIGHLIGHT 2

Financial Ratios: Where to Find Them

1. *Annual Statement Studies.* Published by Robert Morris Associates, this work includes 11 financial ratios computed annually for over 150 lines of business. Each line of business is divided into four size categories.

2. Dun & Bradstreet provides 14 ratios calculated annually for over 100 lines of business.

3. *The Almanac of Business and Industrial Financial Ratios.* The almanac, published by Prentice Hall, Inc., lists industry averages for 22 financial ratios. Approximately 170 businesses and industries are listed.

4. *The Quarterly Financial Report for Manufacturing Corporations.* This work, published jointly by the Federal Trade Commission and the Securities and Exchange Commission, contains balance-sheet and income-statement information by industry groupings and by asset-size categories.

5. Trade associations and individual companies often compute ratios for their industries and make them available to analysts.

the overall ability of the firm to meet its current obligations. A common rule of thumb is that current ratio should be about 2:1.

The quick ratio is determined by subtracting inventory from current assets and dividing the remainder by current liabilities. Since inventory is the least liquid current asset, the quick ratio deals with assets that are most readily available for meeting short-term (one-year) obligations. A common rule of thumb is that the quick ratio should be at least 1:1.

Asset management ratios. Asset management ratios investigate how well the firm handles its assets. For marketing problems, two of the most useful asset management ratios are concerned with *inventory turnover* and *total asset utilization.* The inventory turnover ratio is determined by dividing sales by inventories.[3] If the firm is not turning its inventory over as rapidly as other firms, it suggests that too many funds are being tied up in unproductive or obsolete inventory. In addition, if the firm's turnover ratio is decreasing over time, it suggests that there may be a problem in the marketing plan, since inventory is not being sold as rapidly as it had been in the past. One problem with this ratio is that, since sales usually are recorded at market prices and inventory usually is recorded at cost, the ratio may overstate turnover. Thus, some analysts prefer to use cost of sales rather than sales in computing turnover. We will use cost of sales in our analysis.

A second useful asset management ratio is total asset utilization. It is calculated by dividing sales by total assets and is a measure of how productively the firm's assets have been used to generate sales. If this ratio is well below industry figures, it suggests that marketing efforts may be relatively less effective than other firms or that some unproductive assets should be disposed of.

Profitability ratios. Profitability is a major goal of marketing and is an important test of the quality of marketing decision making in the firm. Two key profitability ratios are *profit margin on sales* and *return on total assets*. Profit margin on sales is determined by dividing profit before tax by sales. Serious questions about the firm and marketing plan should be raised if profit margin on sales is declining across time or is well below other firms in the industry. Return on total assets is determined by dividing profit before tax by total assets. This ratio is the return on the investment for the entire firm.

2. Compute the ratios

The next step in ratio analysis is to compute the ratios. Figure 1 presents the balance sheet and income statement for the Ajax Home Computer Company. This six ratios can be calculated from the Ajax balance sheet and income statement as follows:

Liquidity ratios:

$$\text{Current ratio} = \frac{\text{Current assets}}{\text{Current liabilities}} = \frac{700}{315} = 2.2$$

$$\text{Quick ratio} = \frac{\text{Current assets} - \text{Inventory}}{\text{Current liabilities}} = \frac{270}{315} = .86$$

Asset management ratios:

$$\text{Inventory turnover} = \frac{\text{Cost of sales}}{\text{Inventory}} = \frac{2{,}780}{430} = 6.5$$

$$\text{Total asset utilization} = \frac{\text{Sales}}{\text{Total assets}} = \frac{3{,}600}{2{,}400} = 1.5$$

Profitability ratio:

$$\text{Profit margin on sales} = \frac{\text{Profit before tax}}{\text{Sales}} = \frac{300}{3{,}600} = 8.3\%$$

$$\text{Return on total assets} = \frac{\text{Profit before tax}}{\text{Total assets}} = \frac{300}{2{,}400} = 12.5\%$$

3. Compare the ratios

While rules of thumb are useful for analyzing ratios, it cannot be overstated that comparison of ratios is always the preferred approach. The ratios computed for a firm can be compared in at least three ways. First, they can be compared over time to see if there are any favorable or unfavorable trends in the firm's financial position. Second, they can be compared with the ratios of other firms in the industry of similar size. Third, they can be compared with industry averages to get an overall idea of the firm's relative financial position in the industry.

Figure 2 provides a summary of the ratio analysis. The ratios computed for Ajax are presented along with the median ratios for firms of similar size in the industry and the industry median. The median is often reported in financial sources, rather than the mean, to avoid the strong effect of outliers.[4]

Figure 1   *Balance Sheet and Income Statement for Ajax Home Computer*

Ajax Home Computer Company
Balance Sheet
March 31, 1990
(in thousands)

Assets		Liabilities and Stockholders' Equity	
Cash	$ 30	Trade accounts payable	$ 150
Marketable securities	40	Accrued	25
Accounts receivable	200	Notes payable	100
Inventory	430	Accrued income tax	40
Total current assets	700	Total current liabilities	315
Plant and equipment	1,000	Bonds	500
Land	500	Debentures	85
Other investments	200	Stockholders' equity	1,500
Total assets	$2,400	Total liabilities and stockholders' equity	$2,400

Ajax Home Computer Company
Income Statement
For the 12-Month Period Ending March 31, 1990
(in thousands)

Sales	$3,600
Cost of sales:	
Labor and materials	2,000
Depreciation	200
Selling expenses	500
General and administrative expenses	80
Total cost	2,780
Net operating income	820
Less interest expense:	
Interest on notes	20
Interest on debentures	200
Interest on bonds	300
Total Interest	520
Profit before tax:	300
Federal income tax (@40%)	120
Net profit after tax	$ 180

4. Check for problems or opportunities

The ratio comparison in Figure 2 suggests that Ajax is in reasonably good shape financially. The current ratio is above the industry figures, although the quick ratio is slightly below them. However, the high inventory turnover ratio suggests that the slightly low quick ratio should not be a problem, since inventory turns over relatively quickly. Total asset utilization is slightly below industry averages and should be monitored closely. This, coupled with the slightly lower return on total assets, suggests that some

Figure 2 *Ratio Comparison for Ajax Home Computer Company*

	Ajax	Industry Firms $1–10 million in Assets	Industry Median
Liquidity ratios:			
Current ratio	2.2	1.8	1.8
Quick ratio	.86	.9	1.0
Asset management ratios:			
Inventory turnover	6.5	3.2	2.8
Total assets utilization	1.5	1.7	1.6
Profitability ratios:			
Profit margin	8.3%	6.7%	8.2%
Return on total assets	12.5%	15.0%	14.7%

unproductive assets should be disposed of. While the problem could be ineffective marketing, the high profit margin on sales suggests that marketing effort is probably not the problem.

CONCLUSION

This section has focused on several aspects of financial analysis that are useful for marketing decision making. The first, break-even analysis, is commonly used in marketing problem and case analysis. The second, net present value analysis, is quite useful for investigating the financial impact of marketing alternatives, such as new product introductions. The third, ratio analysis, is a useful tool sometimes overlooked in marketing problem solving. Performing a ratio analysis, as a regular portion of marketing problem and case analysis, can increase the understanding of the firm and its problems and opportunities.

ADDITIONAL READINGS

Brealey, Richard A., and Stewart C. Myers, *Principles of Corporate Finance*. 4th ed. New York: McGraw-Hill, 1991.

Campsey, B. J., and Eugene F. Brigham. *Introduction to Financial Management*. 2nd ed. Chicago: Dryden Press, 1989.

Day, George, and Liam Fahay. "Valuing Market Strategies." *Journal of Marketing*, July 1988, pp. 45–57.

Jones, Charles P. *Introduction to Financial Management*. Homewood, IL: Richard D. Irwin, 1992.

Ross, Stephen A.; Randolph W. Westerfield; and Jeffrey F. Jaffe. *Corporate Finance*. 3rd ed. Homewood, IL: Richard D. Irwin, 1993.

Section IV

DEVELOPING MARKETING PLANS

Imagine this scenario. After receiving your bachelor's or master's degree in marketing, you are hired by a major consumer goods company. Because you've done well in school, you are confident that you have a lot of marketing knowledge and a lot to offer to the firm. You're highly motivated and are looking forward to a successful career.

After just a few days of work you are called in for a conference with the vice president of marketing. The vice president welcomes you and tells you how glad the firm is that you have joined them. The vice president also says that, since you have done so well in your marketing courses and have had such recent training, he wants you to work on a special project.

He tells you that the company has a new product, which is to be introduced in a few months. He also says, confidentially, that recent new product introductions by the company haven't been too successful. Suggesting that the recent problems are probably because the company has not been doing a very good job of developing marketing plans, the vice president tells you not to look at marketing plans for the company's other products.

Your assignment, then, is to develop a marketing plan for the proposed product in the next six weeks. The vice president explains that a good job here will lead to rapid advancement in the company. You thank the vice president for the assignment and promise that you'll do your best.

How would you feel when you returned to your desk? Surely, you'd be flattered that you had been given this opportunity and be eager to do a good job. However, how confident are you that you could develop a quality marketing plan? Would you even know where to begin?

We suspect that many of you, even those who have an excellent knowledge of marketing principles and are adept at solving marketing cases, may not yet have the skills necessary to develop a marketing plan from scratch. Thus, the purpose of this section is to offer a framework for developing marketing plans. In one sense, this section is no more than a summary of the whole text. In other words, it is an organizational framework based on the text material that can be used to direct the development of marketing plans.

Students should note that we are not presenting this framework and discussion as the only way to develop a marketing plan. While we believe this is a useful framework for logically analyzing the problems involved in developing a marketing plan, other approaches can be used just as successfully.

Often, successful firms prepare much less detailed plans, since much of the background material and current conditions are well known to everyone involved. However, our review of plans used in various firms suggests that something like this framework is not uncommon.

We would like to mention one other qualification before beginning our discussion. Students should remember that one important part of the marketing plan involves the development of a sales forecast. While we have discussed several approaches to sales forecasting in the text, we will detail only one specific approach here.

A MARKETING PLAN FRAMEWORK

Marketing plans have three basic purposes. First, they are used as a tangible record of analysis to investigate the logic involved. This is done to ensure the feasibility and internal consistency of the project and to evaluate the likely consequences of implementing the plan. Second, they are used as roadmaps or guidelines for directing appropriate actions. A marketing plan is designed to be the best available scenario and rationale for directing the firm's efforts for a particular product or brand. Third, they are used as tools to obtain funding for implementation. This funding may come from internal or external sources. For example, a brand manager may have to present a marketing plan to senior executives in a firm to get a budget request filled. This would be an internal source. Similarly, proposals for funding from investors or business loans from banks often require a marketing plan. These would be external sources.

Figure 1 presents a format for preparing marketing plans. Each of the 10 elements will be briefly discussed. We will refer to previous chapters and sections in this text and to other sources where additional information can be obtained when a marketing plan is being prepared. We also will offer additional information for focusing particular sections of the plan as well as for developing financial analysis.

Title Page

The *title page* should contain the following information: (1) the name of the product or brand for which the marketing plan has been prepared—for example, Marketing Plan for Little Friskies Dog Food; (2) the time period for which the plan is designed—for example 1995–96; (3) the person(s) and position(s) of those submitting the plan—for example, submitted by Amy Lewis, brand manager; (4) the persons, group, or agency to whom the plan is being submitted—for example, submitted to

Figure 1   *A Marketing Plan Format*

—Title page
—Executive summary
—Table of contents
—Introduction
—Situational analysis
—Marketing planning
—Implementation and control of the marketing plan
—Summary
—Appendix: Financial analysis
—References

Lauren Ellis, product group manager, and (5) the date of submission of the plan—for example, June 30, 1995.

While preparing the *title page* is a simple task, remember that it is the first thing readers see. Thus, a title page that is poorly laid out, is smudged, or contains misspelled words can lead to the inference that the project was developed hurriedly and with little attention to detail. As with the rest of the project, appearances are important and affect what people think about the plan.

Executive Summary

The *executive summary* is a two- to three-page summary of the contents of the report. Its purpose is to provide a quick summary of the marketing plan for executives who need to be informed about the plan but are typically not directly involved in plan approval. For instance, senior executives for firms with a broad product line may not have time to read the entire plan but need an overview to keep informed about operations.

The executive summary should include a brief introduction, the major aspects of the marketing plan, and a budget statement. This is not the place to go into detail about each and every aspect of the marketing plan. Rather, it should focus on the major market opportunity and the key elements of the marketing plan that are designed to capitalize on this opportunity.

It is also useful to state specifically how much money is required to implement the plan. In an ongoing firm, many costs can be estimated from historical data or from discussions with other executives in charge of specific functional areas. However, in many situations (such as a class project), sufficient information is not always available to give exact costs for every aspect of production, promotion, and distribution. In these cases, include a rough estimate of total marketing costs of the plan. In many ongoing firms, marketing cost elements are concentrated in the areas of promotion and marketing research, and these figures are integrated with those from other functional areas as parts of the overall business plan.

Table of Contents

The table of contents is a listing of everything contained in the plan and where it is located in the report. Reports that contain a variety of charts and figures may also have a table of exhibits listing their titles and page numbers within the report.

In addition to using the table of contents as a place to find specific information, readers may also review it to see if each section of the report is logically sequenced. For example, situational analysis logically precedes marketing planning as an activity, and this ordering makes sense in presenting the plan.

Introduction

The types of information and amount of detail reported in the *introduction* depend in part on whether the plan is being designed for a new or existing product or brand. If the product is new, the introduction should explain the product concept and the reasons why it is expected to be successful. Basically, this part of your report should make the new idea sound attractive to management or investors. In addition, it is useful to offer estimates of expected sales, costs, and return on investment.

If the marketing plan is for an existing brand in an ongoing firm, it is common to begin the report with a brief history of the brand. The major focus here is on the brand's performance in the last three to five years. It is useful to prepare graphs of the brand's performance that show its sales, profits, and market share for previous years and to explain the reasons for any major changes. These exhibits can also be extended to include predicted changes in these variables given the new marketing plan. A brief discussion of the overall strategy followed in previous years also provides understanding of how much change is being proposed in the new marketing plan.

Also useful is to offer a precise statement of the purpose of the report as well as a "roadmap" of the report in the introduction. In other words, tell readers what this report is, how it is organized, and what will be covered in the following sections.

Situational Analysis

The *situational analysis* is not unlike the analysis discussed in Chapter 1 and Section II of this text. The focus remains on the most critical and relevant environmental conditions (or changes in them) that affect the success or failure of the proposed plan. While any aspect of the economic, social, political, legal, or cooperative environments might deserve considerable attention, there is seldom if ever a marketing plan in which the competitive environment does not require considerable discussion. In fact, the competitive environment may be set off as a separate section called *industry analysis*. The strengths and weaknesses of major competitors, their relative market shares, and the success of various competitive strategies are critical elements of the situation analysis.

Section V of the text offers some sources of information for analyzing the competitive environment, such as the *Audits and Surveys National Total-Market Index* and the *Nielson Retail Index*. In addition, trade association publications, *Fortune, Business Week,* and *The Wall Street Journal,* frequently have useful articles on competitive strategies. Firms' annual reports often provide considerable useful information.

HIGHLIGHT 1
Some Questions to Consider in Competitive Analysis

Understanding an industry and the actions of competitors is critical to developing successful marketing plans. Below is a list of some questions to consider when performing competitive analysis. Thinking about these questions can aid the marketing planner in developing better marketing strategies.

1. Which firms compete in this industry, and what is their financial position and marketing capability?
2. What are the relative market shares of various brands?
3. How many brands and models does each firm offer?
4. What marketing strategies have the market leaders employed?

5. Which brands have gained and which have lost market share in recent years, and what factors have led to these changes?
6. Are new competitors likely to enter the market?
7. How quickly do competitive firms react to changes in the market?
8. From which firms or brands might we be able to take market share?
9. What are the particular strengths and weaknesses of competitors in the industry?
10. How do we compare with other firms in the industry in terms of financial strength and marketing skills?

Marketing Planning

Marketing planning is, of course, a critical section of the report. As previously noted, it includes three major elements: marketing objectives, target market(s), and the marketing mix.

Marketing objectives

Marketing objectives are often stated in plans in terms of the percentage of particular outcomes that are to be achieved; for example, 80 percent awareness of the brand in particular markets, increase in trial rate by 30 percent, distribution coverage of 60 percent, increase in total market share by 3 percent over the life of the plan. Similarly, there may also be objective statements in terms of sales units or dollars or increases in these. Of course, the reasons for selection of the particular objectives and rationale are important points to explain.

Target markets

The *target market(s)* discussion explains the customer base and rationale or justification for it. An approach to developing appropriate target markets is contained in Chapter 5 of this text, and a useful source of secondary data for segmenting markets is the *National Purchase Diary Panel.*

This section also includes relevant discussion of changes or important issues in consumer or industrial buyer behavior; for example, what benefits consumers are seeking in this products class, what benefits does the particular brand offer, or what purchasing trends are shaping the market for this product. Discussions of consumer and industrial buyer behavior are contained in Chapters 3 and 4 of this text.

Marketing mix

The marketing mix discussion explains in detail the selected strategy consisting of product, promotion, distribution and price, and the rationale for it. Also, if marketing research has been done on these elements or is planned, it can be discussed in this section.

Product. The product section details a description of the product or brand, its packaging and attributes. Product life-cycle considerations should be mentioned if they affect the proposed plan.

Of critical importance in this discussion is the competitive differential advantage of the product or brand. Here it must be carefully considered whether the brand really does anything better than the competition or is purchased primarily on the basis of image. For example, many brands of toothpaste have fluoride, yet Crest has the largest market share primarily through promoting this attribute of its brand. Thus, does Crest do anything more than other toothpastes, or is it Crest's image that accounts for sales?

Discussion of product-related issues is contained in Chapters 6 and 7, and services are discussed in Chapter 12 of this text. For discussion of marketing plans for products at the international level, see Chapter 13.

Promotion. The promotion discussion consists of a description and justification of the planned promotion mix. It is useful to explain the theme of the promotion and to include some examples of potential ads as well as the nature of the sales force if one is to be used. For mass-marketed consumer goods, promotion costs are clearly significant and need to be considered explicitly in the marketing plan.

Discussion of promotion-related issues is contained in Chapters 8 and 9 of this text. Secondary sources, such as *Standard Rate and Data, Simmons Media/Market Service, Starch Advertising Readership Service,* and the *Nielsen Television Index,* provide useful information for selecting, budgeting, and justifying media and other promotional decisions.

Distribution. The distribution discussion describes and justifies the appropriate channel or channels for the product. This includes types of intermediaries and specifically who they will be. Other important issues concern the level of market coverage desired, cost, and control considerations. In many cases, the channels of distribution used by the firm, as well as competitive firms, are well established. For example, General Motors and Ford distribute their automobiles through independent dealer networks. Thus, unless there is a compelling reason to change channels, the traditional channel will often be the appropriate alternative. However, serious consid-

HIGHLIGHT 2

Stating Objectives: How to Tell a "Good" One from a "Bad" One

For the direction setting purpose of objectives to be fulfilled, objectives need to meet five specifications:

1. An objective should relate to a single, specific topic. (It should not be stated in the form of a vague abstraction or a pious platitude—"we want to be a leader in our industry" or "our objective is to be more aggressive marketers.")
2. An objective should relate to a result, not to an activity to be performed. (The objective is the result of the activity, not the performing of the activity.)
3. An objective should be measurable (stated in quantitative terms whenever feasible).
4. An objective should contain a time deadline for its achievement.
5. An objective should be challenging but achievable.

Consider the following examples:

1. Poor: Our objective is to maximize profits.
   Remarks: How much is "maximum"? The statement is not subject to measurement. What criterion or yardstick will management use to determine if and when actual profits are equal to maximum profits? No deadline is specified.
   Better: Our total profit target in 1996 is $1 million.
2. Poor: Our objective is to increase sales revenue and unit volume.
   Remarks: How much? Also, because the statement relates to two topics, it may be inconsistent. Increasing unit volume may require a price cut, and if demand is price inelastic, sales revenue would fall as unit volume rises. No time frame for achievement is indicated.

Source: Adapted from Arthur A. Thompson, Jr., and A. J. Strickland, *Strategic Management: Concepts and Cases*, 5th ed. (Homewood, IL: Richard D. Irwin, 1990), pp. 23–34.

   Better: Our objective this calendar year is to increase sales revenues from $30 million to $35 million; we expect this to be accomplished by selling 1 million units at an average price of $35.
3. Poor: Our objective in 1996 is to boost advertising expenditures by 15 percent.
   Remarks: Advertising is an activity, not a result. The advertising objective should be stated in terms of what result the extra advertising is intended to produce.
   Better: Our objective is to boost our market share from 8 percent to 10 percent in 1996 with the help of a 15 percent increase in advertising expenditures.
4. Poor: Our objective is to be a pioneer in research and development and to be the technological leader in the industry.
   Remarks: Very sweeping and perhaps overly ambitious; implies trying to march in too many directions at once if the industry is one with a wide range of technological frontiers. More a platitude than an action commitment to a specific result.
   Better: During the 1990s, our objective is to continue as a leader in introducing new technologies and new devices that will allow buyers of electrically powered equipment to conserve on electric energy usage.
5. Poor: Our objective is to be the most profitable company in our industry.
   Remarks: Not specific enough by what measures of profit—total dollars or earnings per share or unit profit margin or return on equity investment or all of these? Also, because the objective concerns how well other companies will perform, the objective, while challenging, may not be achievable.
   Better: We will strive to remain atop the industry in terms of rate of return on equity investment by earning a 25 percent aftertax return on equity investment in 1996.

eration may have to be given to methods of obtaining channel support, for example, trade deals to obtain sufficient shelf space.

Discussion of distribution-related issues is contained in Chapter 10 of this text. Useful retail distribution information can be found in the *Nielsen Retail Index* and the *Audits and Surveys National Total-Market Index.*

Price. The pricing discussion starts with a specific statement of the price of the product. Depending on what type of channel is used, manufacturer price, wholesale price, and suggested retail price need to be listed and justified. In addition, special deals or trade discounts that are to be employed must be considered in terms of their effect on the firm's selling price.

Discussion of price-related issues is contained in Chapter 11. In addition to a variety of other useful information, the *Nielsen Retail Index* provides information on wholesale and retail prices.

Marketing research. For any aspect of marketing planning, there may be a need for marketing research. If such research is to be performed, it is important to justify it and explain its costs and benefits. Such costs should also be included in the financial analysis.

If marketing research has already been conducted as part of the marketing plan, it can be reported as needed to justify various decisions that were reached. To illustrate, if research found that two out of three consumers like the taste of a new formula Coke, this information would likely be included in the product portion of the report. However, the details of the research could be placed here in the marketing research section. Discussion of marketing research is contained in Chapter 2.

Implementation and Control of the Marketing Plan

This section contains a discussion and justification of how the marketing plan will be implemented and controlled. It also explains who will be in charge of monitoring and changing the plan should unanticipated events occur and how the success or failure of the plan will be measured. Success or failure of the plan is typically measured by a comparison of the results of implementing the plan with the stated objectives.

For a marketing plan developed within an ongoing firm, this section can be quite explicit, since procedures for implementing plans may be well established. However, for a classroom project, the key issues to be considered are the persons responsible for implementing the plan, a timetable for sequencing the tasks, and a method of measuring and evaluating the success or failure of the plan.

Summary

This *summary* need not be much different than the executive summary stated at the beginning of the document. However, it is usually a bit longer, more detailed, and states more fully the case for financing the plan.

HIGHLIGHT 3

Some Questions to Consider in Consumer Analysis

Knowledge of consumers is paramount to developing successful marketing plans. Below is a list of questions that are useful to consider when analyzing consumers. For some of the questions, secondary sources of information or primary marketing research can be employed to aid in decision making. However, a number of them require the analyst to do some serious thinking about the relationship between brands of the product and various consumer groups to better understand the market.

1. How many people purchase and use this product in general?
2. How many people purchase and use each brand of the product?
3. Is there an opportunity to reach nonusers of the product with a unique marketing strategy?
4. What does the product do for consumers functionally, and how does this vary by brand?
5. What does the product do for consumers in a social or psychological sense, and how does this vary by brand?
6. Where do consumers currently purchase various brands of the product?
7. How much are consumers willing to pay for specific brands, and is price a determining factor for purchase?
8. What is the market profile of the heavy user of this product, and what percentage of the total market are heavy users?
9. What media reach these consumers?
10. On average, how often is this product purchased?
11. How important is brand image for consumers of this product?
12. Why do consumers purchase particular brands?
13. How brand loyal are consumers of this product?

Appendix—Financial Analysis

Financial analysis is a very important part of any marketing plan. While a complete business plan often includes extensive financial analysis, such as a complete cost breakdown and estimated return on investment, marketing planners frequently do not have complete accounting data for computing these figures. For example, decisions concerning how much overhead is to be apportioned to the product are not usually made solely by marketing personnel. However, the marketing plan should contain at least a sales forecast and estimates of relevant marketing costs.

Sales forecast

As noted, there are a variety of ways to develop sales forecasts. Regardless of the method, however, they all involve trying to predict the future as accurately as possible. It is, of course, necessary to justify the logic for the forecasted figures, rather than offer them with no support.

HIGHLIGHT 4

Some Questions to Consider in Marketing Planning

Below is a brief list of questions to ask yourself about the marketing planning section of the report. Answering them honestly and recognizing both the strengths and weaknesses of your marketing plan should help you improve it.

1. What are the key assumptions that were made in developing the marketing plan?
2. How badly will the product's market position be hurt if these assumptions turn out to be incorrect?
3. How good is the marketing research?
4. Is the marketing plan consistent? For example, if the plan is to seek a prestige position in the market, is the product priced, promoted, and distributed to create this image?

5. Is the marketing plan feasible? For example, are the financial and other resources (such as a distribution network) available to implement it?
6. How will the marketing plan affect profits and market share, and is it consistent with corporate objectives?
7. Will implementing the marketing plan result in competitive retaliation that will end up hurting the firm?
8. Is the marketing mix designed to reach and attract new consumers or increase usage among existing users or both?
9. Will the marketing mix help to develop brand-loyal consumers?
10. Will the marketing plan be successful not just in the short run but also contribute to a profitable long-run position?

One basic approach to developing a sales forecast is outlined in Figure 2. This approach begins by estimating the total number of persons in the selected target market. This estimate comes from the market segmentation analysis and may include information from test marketing and from secondary sources, such as *Statistical Abstracts of the United States*. For example, suppose a company is marketing a solar-powered watch that is designed not only to tell time but to take the pulse of the wearer. The product is targeted at joggers and others interested in aerobic exercise. By reviewing the literature on these activities, the marketing planner, John Murphy, finds that the average estimate of this market on a national level is 60 million persons and is growing by 4 million persons per year. Thus, John might conclude that the total number of people in the target market for next year is 64 million. If he has not further limited the product's target market and has no other information, John might use this number as a basis for starting the forecast analysis.

The second estimate John needs is the annual number of purchases per person in the product's target market. This estimate could be quite large for such products as breakfast cereal or less than one (annual purchase per person) for such products as automobiles. For watches, the estimate is likely to be much less than one since people are likely to buy a new watch

HIGHLIGHT 5

Some Questions to Consider in Implementation and Control

Implementation and control of a marketing plan require careful scheduling and attention to detail. While some firms have standard procedures for dealing with many of the questions raised below, thinking through each of the questions should help improve the efficiency of even these firms in this stage of the process.

1. Who is responsible for implementing and controlling the marketing plan?
2. What tasks must be performed to implement the marketing plan?
3. What are the deadlines for implementing the various tasks, and how critical are specific deadlines?

4. Has sufficient time been scheduled to implement the various tasks?
5. How long will it take to get the planned market coverage?
6. How will the success or failure of the plan be determined?
7. How long will it take to get the desired results from the plan?
8. How long will the plan be in effect before changes will be made to improve it based on more current information?
9. If an ad agency or other firms are involved in implementing the plan, how much responsibility and authority will they have?
10. How frequently will the progress of the plan be monitored?

only every few years. Thus John might estimate the annual number of purchases per person in the target market to be .25. Of course, as a careful marketing planner, John would probably carefully research this market to refine this estimate. In any event, multiplying these two rough numbers gives John an estimate of the *total potential market,* in this case, 64 million times .25 equals 16 million. In other words, if next year alone John's company could sell the watch to every jogger or aerobic exerciser who is buying a watch, the company could expect sales to be 16 million units.

Of course, the firm cannot expect to sell every jogger a watch for several reasons. First, it is unlikely to obtain 100 percent market coverage in the first year, if ever. Even major consumer goods companies selling convenience goods seldom reach the entire market in the first year and many never achieve even 90 percent distribution. Given the nature of the product and depending on the distribution alternative, John's company might be doing quite well to average 50 percent market coverage in the first year. If John's plans call for this kind of coverage, his estimate of the total available market would be 16 million times .5, which equals 8 million.

A second reason why John's plans would not call for dominating the market is that his company does not have the only product available or wanted by this target market. Many of the people who will purchase such a watch will purchase a competitive brand. He must, therefore, estimate the product's likely market share. Of all the estimates made in developing a

Figure 2 *A Basic Approach to Sales Forecasting*

Total number of people in target markets *(a)*	*a*
Annual number of purchases per person *(b)*	× *b*
Total potential market *(c)*	= *c*
Total potential market *(c)*	*c*
Percent of total market coverage *(d)*	× *d*
Total available market *(e)*	= *e*
Total available market *(e)*	*e*
Expected market share *(f)*	× *f*
Sales forecast (in units) *(g)*	= *g*
Sales forecast (in units) *(g)*	*g*
Price *(h)*	× *h*
Sales forecast (in dollars) *(i)*	= *i*

sales forecast, this one is critical, since it is a reflection of the entire marketing plan. Important factors to consider in developing this estimate include: (1) competitive market shares and likely marketing plans; (2) competitive retaliation should the product do well; (3) differential advantage of the product, such as lower price; (4) promotion mix and budget relative to competitors; and (5) market shares obtained by similar products in the introductory year.

Overall, suppose John estimates the product's market share to be 5 percent, since other competitive products have beat his company to the market and because the company's differential advantage is only a slightly more stylish watch. In this case, the sales forecast for year one would be 8 million times .05, which equals 400,000 units. If the manufacturer's selling price was $50, then the sales forecast in dollars would be 400,000 times $50, which equals $20 million.

This approach can also be used to extend the sales forecast for any number of years. Typically, estimates of most of the figures change from year to year, depending on changes in market size, changes in distribution coverage, and changes in expected market shares. The value of this approach is that it forces an analyst to carefully consider and justify each of the estimates offered, rather than simply pulling numbers out of the air. In developing and justifying these estimates, many of the sources listed in Section V provide a good place to start searching for information—for example, *Selling Areas Marketing Inc.* (SAMI) data.

Estimates of marketing costs

A complete delineation of all costs, apportionment of overhead, and other accounting tasks are usually performed by other departments within a firm. All of this information, including expected return on investment from implementing the marketing plan, is part of the overall business plan.

However, the marketing plan should at least contain estimates of major marketing costs. These include such things as advertising, sales-force training and compensation, channel development, and marketing research. Estimates may also be included for product development and package design.

For some marketing costs, reasonable estimates are available from sources such as *Standard Rate and Data*. However, some cost figures, such as marketing research, might be obtained from asking various marketing experts for the estimated price of proposed research. Other types of marketing costs might be estimated from financial statements of firms in the industry. For example, Morris's *Annual Statement Studies* offers percentage breakdowns of various income statement information by industry. These might be used to estimate the percentage of the sales-forecast figure that would likely be spent in a particular cost category.

References

This section contains the sources of any secondary information that was used in developing the marketing plan. This information might include company reports and memos, statements of company objectives, and articles or books used for information or support of the marketing plan.

References should be listed alphabetically using a consistent format. One way of preparing references is to use the same approach as is used in marketing journals. For example, the format used for references in *Journal of Marketing* articles is usually acceptable.

CONCLUSION

Suppose you're now back sitting at your desk faced with the task of developing a marketing plan for a new product. Do you believe that you might have the skills to develop a marketing plan? Of course, your ability to develop a quality plan will depend on your learning experiences during your course work and the amount of practice you've had; for example, if you developed a promotion plan in your advertising course, it is likely that you could do a better job on the promotion phase of the marketing plan. Similarly, your experiences in analyzing cases should have sharpened your skills at recognizing problems and developing solutions to them. But inexperience (or experience) aside, hopefully you now feel that you understand the process of developing a marketing plan. You at least know where to start, where to seek information, how to structure the plan, and what are some of the critical issues that require analysis.

ADDITIONAL READINGS

Abratt, Russell; Maria Beffon; and John Ford. "Relationship between Marketing Planning and Annual Budgeting." *Marketing Intelligence & Planning* 12, no. 1 (1994), pp. 22–28.

Cohen, William A. *The Marketing Plan.* New York: John Wiley & Sons, 1995.

Goetsch, Hal. "Are Marketing Plans Passé? Does the Sun Rise? *Marketing News,* December 5, 1994, pp. 4–5.

Hartman, John W. "Unplanned Events Wreak Havoc on Business Plans." *Business Marketing,* February 1994, p. 10.

Hudson, Phil. "Communicate Your Marketing Plan." *Bank Marketing,* October 1994, p. 64.

Lehmann, Donald R., and Russell S. Winer. *Analysis for Marketing Planning.* 3rd ed., Burr Ridge, IL: Richard D. Irwin, 1994.

Manaktala, Vin. "Marketing: The Seven Deadly Sins." *Journal of Accountancy,* September 1994, pp. 67–72.

Rifken, Glenn. "Information Technology: The Client/Server Challenge." *Harvard Business Review,* July–August 1994, pp. 9–10.

Shark, Alan R. "Orchestrating a Strategic Marketing Plan. *Association Management,* November 1994, pp. 46–59.

Stephens, Nancy J. "Plan First." *Manager's Magazine,* November 1994, pp. 6–9.

Weber, John A. "Using Purchase Influence Niching for Better Focus in Industrial Marketing Plans." *Industrial Marketing Management,* December 1994, pp. 419–38.

Weylman, C. Richard. "Making Sure Your Marketing Plan Becomes Reality." *National Underwriter,* January 2, 1995, p. 18.

Section V
SECONDARY DATA SOURCES

In analyzing and presenting cases and developing marketing plans, it is often very useful for analysts to use secondary data, data from outside sources, as a means of supporting their recommendations or conclusions. These data can be located in most business libraries or from on-line service providers. The purpose of this section is to list and briefly describe some of the key data sources that are available to analysts. The references are listed under nine specific headings: selected periodicals (journals and magazines), general marketing information sources, selected marketing information services, selected retail trade publications, financial information sources, basic U.S. statistical sources, general business and industry sources, indexes and abstracts, and on-line marketing information services.[1] Due to the newness and complexity of using on-line services, a brief explanation accompanies this section.

SELECTED PERIODICALS

Advertising Age
American Demographics
American Economist
Bank Marketing
Brandweek
Business America
Business Economics
Business Horizons

Business Marketing
Business & Professional Ethics Journal
Business Quarterly
Business and Society Review
Business Week
California Management Review

CASE WESTERN RESERVE JOURNAL OF INTERNATIONAL

Columbia Journal of World Business
Conference Board Record
Direct Marketing
Distribution
Forbes
Fortune

Global Trade
Harvard Business Review
Health Marketing Quarterly Inc.
Industrial Marketing Management
Industry Week

INFORMATION RESOURCES MANAGEMENT JOURNAL
INFORMATION STRATEGY: THE EXECUTIVE'S JOURNAL

Journal of the Academy of Marketing Science
Journal of Advertising
Journal of Advertising Research
Journal of Asia-Pacific Business
Journal of Business Ethics

Journal of Business and Industrial Marketing
Journal of Business Research
Journal of Business Strategy
Journal of Business-To-Business Marketing

JOURNAL OF CONSUMER MARKETING

Journal of Consumer Research

JOURNAL OF DIRECT MARKETING

Journal of East-West Business
Journal of Euromarketing

Journal of Experimental Psychology
Journal of Food Products Marketing

JOURNAL OF FORECASTING

Journal of Global Marketing
Journal of Hospitality Marketing
*Journal of Hospitality & Leisure
    Marketing*
*Journal of International Business
    Studies*

*Journal of International Consumer
    Marketing*
Journal of Macro Marketing
Journal of Marketing
*Journal of Marketing and Public
    Policy*
Journal of Marketing Channels

JOURNAL OF MARKETING FOR HIGHER EDUCATION
JOURNAL OF MARKETING MANAGEMENT

Journal of Marketing Research

JOURNAL OF MARKETING THEORY & PRACTICE

*Journal of Multinational
    Financial Management*
*Journal of NonProfit & Public
    Sector Marketing*

*Journal of Personal Selling and
    Sales Management*
*Journal of Pharmaceutical
    Marketing Management*

JOURNAL OF PRODUCT & BRAND MANAGEMENT
JOURNAL OF PRODUCT INNOVATION MANAGEMENT

*Journal of Professional Services
    Marketing*
Journal of Promotion Management
Journal of Psychology

*Journal of Restaurant &
    Foodservice Marketing*
Journal of Retailing

JOURNAL OF SERVICES MARKETING
JOURNAL OF TRAVEL RESEARCH

*Journal of Travel & Tourism
    Marketing*
Marketing (Maclean Hunter)
Marketing and Media Decisions
Marketing Briefing
Marketing Communications
Marketing In Action
Marketing Information Guide
Marketing Insights
Marketing News
Marketing Perspectives

Market Research Facts & Trends
Market Research Society
Marketing Science
Marketing Times
Michigan Business Review
*Michigan State University
    Business Topics*
Money
Nations Business
Organizational Dynamics

QUARTERLY JOURNAL OF BUSINESS & ECONOMICS

Sales Management   *Sales and Marketing Management*

SMART MONEY

Strategic Management Journal   *The Review of Business and*
Survey of Current Business   *Economic Research*
The Journal of Business   *Time*
                                       Worth

SELECTED PERIODICALS

GENERAL MARKETING INFORMATION SOURCES

Commercial Atlas and Marketing Guide. Skokie, IL: Rand-McNally. Statistics on population, principal cities, business centers, trading areas, sales and manufacturing units, transportation data, and so forth.

Editor and Publisher "Market Guide." Market information for 1,500 American and Canadian cities. Data include population, household, gas meters, climate, retailing, and newspaper information.

Guide to Consumer Markets. New York: The Conference Board. This useful annual compilation of U.S. statistics on the consumer marketplace covers population, employment, income, expenditures, production, and prices.

Market Guide. New York. This guide compiles market data for over 1,600 U.S. and Canadian newspaper cities.

Marketing Economic Guide. New York: Marketing Economics Institute. Statistics in this guide are similar to those published in *Sales and Marketing Management.* Data covers 1,500 U.S. cities, 3,100 counties, and all metro areas.

Marketing Information Guide. Washington, D.C.: Department of Commerce. Annotations of selected current publications and reports, with basic information and statistics on marketing and distribution.

Milutinovich, J. S. "Business Facts for Decision Makers: Where to Find Them." *Business Horizons,* March–April 1985, pp. 63–80.

Population and Its Distribution: The United States Markets. J. Walter Thompson Co. New York: McGraw-Hill. A handbook of marketing facts selected from the U.S. Census of Population and the most recent census data on retail trade.

Sales and Marketing Management. (Formerly *Sales Managment,* to October 1975.) This valuable semimonthly journal includes four useful annual statistical issues: *Survey of Buying Power* (July); *Survey of Buying Power, Part II* (October); *Survey of Industrial Purchasing Power* (April); *Survey of Selling Costs* (January). These are excellent references for buying income, buying power index, cash income, merchandise line, manufacturing line, and retail sales.

Small Business Bibliography Series. U.S. Small Business Administration. Concise annotated bibliographies of subjects of interest to a small business owner.

Standard Directory of Advertisers. National Register Publishing Co. Directory of 17,000 companies that advertise nationally, arranged by industry with alphabetical index.

The Dartnell Sales Manager's Handbook. Dartnell Corporation. A practical one-volume reference work for concise information about the sales policies and practices of American companies.

SELECTED MARKETING INFORMATION SERVICES

Audits and Surveys National Total-Market Index. Contains information on various product types, including total market size, brand market shares, retail inventory, distribution coverage, and out of stock.

Directory of U.S. and Canadian Marketing Surveys and Services. C. H. Kline & Co. Contains a list of almost 3,000 marketing reports and continuing services available from 191 consulting firms.

Dun & Bradstreet Market Identifiers. Relevant marketing information on over 4.3 million establishments for constructing sales prospect files, sales territories, sales territory potentials, and isolating potential new customers with particular characteristics.

FINDEX, The Directory of Market Research Reports, Studies and Surveys. Bethesda, MD: Cambridge Information Group. This publication provides a directory of more than 10,000 research reports produced by 500 top U.S. and international research firms.

Handbook of Marketing Research. Amsterdam: European Society for Opinion and Marketing Research. Provides a list of European market research societies and organizations, arranged by country.

International Directory of Published Market Research. London. Contains almost 7,000 published market research studies. Over 100 countries are represented.

Membership Roster and International Buyer's Guide to Marketing Services. Chicago. Provides a list of AMA members that contains an index by affiliation for each member.

National Purchase Diary Panel (NPD). Monthly purchase information based on the largest panel diary in the United States with detailed brand, frequency of purchase, characteristics of heavy buyers, and other market data.

Nielson Retail Index. Contains basic product turnover data, retail prices, store displays, promotional activity, and local advertising based on a national sample of supermarkets, drugstores, and mass merchandisers.

Nielson Television Index. Well-known index that provides estimates of the size and nature of the audience for individual television programs.

Selling Areas Marketing, Inc. Reports on warehouse withdrawals of various food products in each of 42 major markets covering 80 percent of national food sales.

Simmons Media/Marketing Service. Provides cross-referencing of product usage and media exposure for magazine, television, newspaper, and radio based on a strict national probability sample.

Standard Rate and Data. Nine volumes on major media that include a variety of information in addition to prices for media in selected markets.

Starch Advertising Readership Service. Measures the reading of advertisements in magazines and newspapers and provides information on overall readership percentages, readers per dollar, and rank when grouped by product category.

SELECTED RETAIL TRADE PUBLICATIONS

American Druggist (monthly), The Hearst Corporation, 959 Eighth Avenue, New York, NY 10019.

Auto Chain Store Magazine (ACS) (monthly), Babcox Publications, Inc., 11 South Forge Street, Akron, OH 44304.

Body Fashions & Intimate Apparel (monthly), Harcourt Brace Jovanovich Publications, 757 Third Avenue, New York, NY 10017.

C. Store Business (10 times/year), Maclean Hunter Media, 1351 Washington Boulevard, Stamford, CT 06902.

Catalog Showroom Business (monthly), Gralla Publications, 1515 Broadway, New York, NY 10036.

Catalog Showroom Merchandiser (monthly), CSM Marketing, Inc., 1020 West Jericho Turnpike, Smithtown, NY 11787.

Chain Drug Review (biweekly), Racher Press, Inc., 1 Park Avenue, New York, NY 10016.

Chain Store Age —Executive Edition (monthly), Lebhar-Friedman, Inc., 425 Park Avenue, New York, NY 10022.

Chain Store Age —General Merchandise Edition (monthly), Lebhar-Friedman, Inc., 425 Park Avenue, New York, NY 10022.

Chain Store Age —Supermarkets Edition (monthly), Lebhar-Friedman, Inc., 425 Park Avenue, New York, NY 10022.

CompetitivEdge (monthly), National Home Furnishings Association, 405 Merchandise Mart, Chicago, IL 60654.

Consumer Electronics Monthly (monthly), CES Publishing Corporation, 135 West 50th Street, New York, NY 10020.

Convenience Store Merchandiser (monthly), Associated Business Publications, Inc., 41 East 42nd Street, New York, NY 10017.

Convenience Store News (monthly, with additional issues in March, April, August, and October), BMT Publications, Inc., 254 West 31st Street, New York, NY 10001.

Daily News Record (daily), Fairchild Publications, 7 East 12th Street, New York, NY 10003.

Decorating Retailer (monthly), National Decorating Products Association, 1050 North Lindbergh Boulevard, St. Louis, MO 63132.

Decorative Products World (monthly, except January), 2911 Washington Avenue, St. Louis, MO 63103.

Direct Marketing (monthly), Hoke Communications, Inc., 224 Seventh Street, Garden City, NY 11530.

Discount Merchandiser (monthly), Schwartz Publications, 2 Park Avenue, New York, NY 10016.

Discount Store News (biweekly except May and December), Lebhar-Friedman, Inc., 425 Park Avenue, New York, NY 10022.

Discount Store News (biweekly except May and September), Lebhar-Friedman, Inc., 425 Park Avenue, New York, NY 10022.

Drug Store News (biweekly), Lebhar-Friedman, Inc., 425 Park Avenue, New York, NY 10022.

Drug Topics (biweekly), Medical Economics Company, Inc., 680 Kinderkamack Road, Oradell, NJ 07649.

Earnshaw's Infants Girls Boys Wear Review (monthly), Earnshaw Publications, Inc., 393 Seventh Avenue, New York, NY 10001.

Electronics Retailer (monthly, except combined issues in January–February, and June–July), Fairchild Publications, 7 East 12th Street, New York, NY 10003.

Floor Covering Weekly (weekly), Hearst Business Communications, Inc., 645 Steward Avenue, Garden City, NY 11530.

Food Merchandising for Nonfood Retailers (quarterly), Lehbar-Friedman, Inc., 425 Park Avenue, New York, NY 10022.

Furniture/Today (biweekly), Communications/Today Ltd., 200 S. Mai Street, High Point, NC 27261.

Garden Supply Retailer (monthly), The Miller Publishing Company, 2501 Wayzata Blvd., Minneapolis, MN 55440.

Giftware Business (monthly), Gralla Publications, 1515 Broadway, New York, NY 10036.

Hardware Age (monthly), Chilton Company, Chilton Way, Radnor, PA 19089.

Hardware Merchandiser (monthly), The Irving-Cloud Publishing Company, 7300 North Cicero Avenue, Lincolnwood, IL 60646.

Home & Auto (semimonthly except November and December), Harcourt Brace Jovanovich Publications, 757 Third Avenue, New York, NY 10017.

Home Center (monthly), Vance Publishing Corporation, 300 West Adams, Chicago, IL 60606.

Housewares (semimonthly plus January, July, and December issues), Harcourt Brace Jovanovich Publications, 757 Third Avenue, New York, NY 10017.

Lawn & Garden Marketing (10 times annually), Intertec Publishing Corporation, 9221 Quivira Road, Overland Park, KS 66212.

Mart (monthly), Morgan-Grampian Publishing Co., 2 Park Avenue, New York, NY 10016.

Men's Wear (semimonthly), Fairchild Publications, 7 East 12th Street, New York, NY 10003.

Merchandising (monthly), Gralla Publications, 1515 Broadway, New York, NY 10036.

NARDA News (monthly), NARDA, Inc., 2 North Riverside Plaza, Chicago, IL 60606.

Nation's Restaurants News (biweekly), Lebhar-Friedman, Inc., 425 Park Avenue, New York, NY 10022.

National Jeweler (bimonthly), Gralla Publications, 1515 Broadway, New York, NY 10036.

National Mall Monitor (bimonthly), National Mall Monitor, 2280 U.S. 19 North, Suite 264, Clearwater, FL 33575.

National Petroleum News (*NPN*) (monthly), Hunter Publishing Company, 950 Lee Street, Des Plaines, IL 60016.

Non-Foods Merchandising (monthly), Charleson Publishing Co., 124 East 40th Street, New York, NY 10016.

Non-Store Marketing Report (biweekly), Maxwell Sroge Publishing, Inc., Sroge Building, 731 North Cascade Avenue, Colorado Springs, CO 80903.

Outdoor Retailer (bimonthly), Pacifica Publishing Corporation, 31652 Second Avenue, South Laguna, CA 92677.

Private Label (monthly), E. W. Williams Publishing Co., 80–88th Avenue, New York, NY 10011.

Professional Furniture Merchant (monthly), Vista Publications, Inc., 9600 W. Sample Road, Coral Springs, FL 33065.

Progressive Grocer (monthly), Maclean Hunter Media, 1351 Washington Boulevard, Stamford, CT 06901.

Restaurants & Institutions (semimonthly), Cahners Publishing Co., 221 Columbus Avenue, Boston, MA 02116.

Retail Control (monthly except April–May, and June–July when bimonthly), NRMA—Financial Executives Division, 100 West 31st Street, New York, NY 10001.

Retailing Home Furnishings (weekly), Fairchild Publications, 7 East 12th Street, New York, NY 10003.

Shopping Center World (monthly), Communications Channels, Inc., 6255 Barfield Road, Atlanta, GA 30328.

Sporting Goods Business (monthly), Gralla Publications, 1515 Broadway, New York, NY 10036.

Sporting Goods Dealer (monthly), The Sporting News Publishing Company, 1212 North Lindbergh Boulevard, St. Louis, MO 63132.

Sports Retailer (monthly), National Sporting Goods Association, 1699 Wall Street, Mt. Prospect, IL 60056.

Stores (monthly), National Retail Merchants Association, 100 W. 31st Street, New York, NY 10001.

Supermarket Business (monthly), Fieldmark Media, Inc., 25 West 43rd Street, New York, NY 10036.

Supermarket News (weekly), 71 West 35th Street, Suite 1600, New York, NY 10001.

Teens and Boys Magazine (monthly), 71 West 35th Street, Suite 1600, New York, NY 10001.

Tire Review (monthly), Babcox Publications, 11 South Forge Street, Akron, OH 44304.

Toys Hobbies & Crafts (monthly except June), Harcourt Brace Jovanovich Publications, 1 East First Stret, Duluth MN 55802.

Video Store (monthly), Hester Communications, Inc., 1700 East Dyer Road, Suite 250 Santa Ana, CA 92705.

Visual Merchandising & Store Design (monthly), Signs of the Times Publishing Company, 407 Gilbert Avenue, Cincinnati, OH 45202.

Women's Wear Daily (daily), Fairchild Publications, 7 East 12th Street, New York, NY 10003.

FINANCIAL INFORMATION SOURCES

Almanac of Business and Industrial Financial Ratios. Prentice Hall. Provides financial and operating ratios for about 160 industries.

Annotated Bibliography of Corporate Finance. Toronto: Macmillan Company of Canada. Classified, annotated bibliography on the theory and practice of corporate finance. Includes 26 subject sections from corporate finance in general to international financial management.

Annual Statement Studies. Robert Morris Associates. Provides financial and operating ratios for about 300 lines of businesses.

Blue Line Investment Survey. Quarterly ratings and reports on 1,000 stocks; analysis of 60 industries and special situations analysis (monthly); supplements on new developments and editorials on conditions affecting price trends.

Commercial and Financial Chronicle. Variety of articles and news reports on business, government, and finance. Monday's issue lists new securities, dividends, and called bonds. Thursday's issue is devoted to business articles.

Dun's Review. Dun & Bradstreet. This monthly includes very useful annual financial ratios for about 125 lines of business.

Encyclopedia of Banking and Finance. Boston: Bankers Publishing Co. One-volume encyclopedia covers the whole area of banking and finance.

Expenses in Retail Business. NCR Corp. Includes operating ratios for over 17 lines of retail businesses.

Fairchild's Financial Manual of Retail Stores. Information about officers and directors, products, subsidiaries, sales, and earnings for apparel stores, mail order firms, variety chains, and supermarkets.

Federal Reserve Bulletin. Board of Governors of the Federal Reserve System. The "Financial and Business Statistics" section of each issue of this monthly bulletin is the best single source for current U.S. banking and monetary statistics.

Financial Executive. Financial Executives Institute. Includes articles for the financial manager.

Financial Planning. Atlanta: International Association of Financial Planning. Provides articles on a wide range of topics of interest to financial planners.

Financial Studies of the Small Business. Financial Research Associates. Includes financial and operating ratios for 50 lines of small businesses.

Financial World. Articles on business activities of interest to investors, including investment opportunities and pertinent data on firms, such as earnings and dividend records.

Industry Norms and Key Business Ratios. Dun & Bradstreet Credit Services.

Mergers & Acquisitions. Information for Industry. Contains lists of rosters of U.S. mergers and acquisitions and of joint ventures and cooperation agreements.

Moody's Bank and Finance Manual; Moody's Industrial Manual; Moody's Municipal & Government Manual; Moody's Public Utility Manual; Moody's Transportation

Manual; Moody's Directors Service. Brief histories of companies and their operations, subsidiaries, officers and directors, products, and balance sheet and income statements over several years.

Moody's Bond Survey. Moody's Investors Service. Weekly data on stocks and bonds, including recommendations for purchases or sale and discussions of industry trends and developments.

Moody's Handbook of Widely Held Common Stocks. Moody's Investors Service. Weekly data on stocks and bonds, including recommendations for purchases or sale and discussions of industry trends and developments.

Quarterly Financial Report for Manufacturing, Mining, and Trade Corporations. U.S. Federal Trade Commission. U.S. Government Printing Office. Details quarterly income statement/balance sheet data and financial/operating ratios classified by industry.

Security Owner's Stock Guide. Standard & Poor's Corp. Standard & Poor's rating, stock price range, and other helpful information for about 4,200 common and preferred stocks.

Security Price Index. Standard & Poor's Corp. Price indexes, bond prices, sales, yields, Dow Jones averages, and so on.

Standard Corporation Records. Standard & Poor's Corp. Published in looseleaf form, offers information similar to Moody' manuals. Use of this extensive service facilitates buying securities for both the individual and the institutional investor.

Yearbook on Corporate Mergers, Joint Ventures, and Corporate Policy. Cambridge Corporation. Arranged by industry and often includes date, price, the business of the acquired company, sales or earnings, and price/earnings ratio.

BASIC U.S. STATISTICAL SOURCES

American Statistics Index. Congressional Information Service. Detailed, descriptive guide and index to statistics published by all government agencies, congressional committees, and statistics-producing programs.

Business Service Checklist. Department of Commerce. Weekly guide to Department of Commerce publications, plus key business indicators.

Business Statistics. Department of Commerce. (supplement to *Survey of Current Business.*) History of the statistical series appearing in the *Survey.* Also included are source references and useful explanation notes.

Census Catalog and Guide. Provides a listing of the programs and services of the Census Bureau. Lists reports, diskettes, microfiche, and maps.

Census of Agriculture. Department of Commerce. Data by states and counties on livestock, farm characteristics, and values.

Census of Manufacturers. Department of Commerce. Industry statistics, area statistics, subjects reports, location of plants, industry descriptions arranged in standard industrial classification, and a variety of ratios.

Census of Mineral Industries. Department of Commerce. Similar to *Census of Manufacturers.* Also includes capital expenditures and employment and payrolls.

Census of Retail Trade. Department of Commerce. Compiles data for states, SMSAs, counties, and cities with populations of 2,500 or more by kind of business. Data include number of establishments, sales, payroll, and personnel.

Census of Selected Services. Department of Commerce. Includes data on hotels, motels, beauty parlors, barber shops, and other retail service organizations.

Census of Transportation. Passenger Transportation Survey, Commodity Transportation Survey, Travel Inventory and Use Survey, Bus and Truck Carrier Survey.

Census Tract Reports. Department of Commerce. Bureau of Census. Detailed information on both population and housing subjects.

Census of Wholesale Trade. Department of Commerce. Similar to *Census of Retail Trade*—information is for wholesale establishment.

County and City Data Book. Department of Commerce. Summary statistics for small geographical areas.

Current Business Reports. Department of Commerce. Reports monthly department stores sales of selected items.

Economic Indicators. U.S. Council of Economic Advisors. Source for statistical tables and charts of basic economic indicators.

Economic Report of the President. Transmitted to the Congress, January (each year), together with the *Annual Report* of the Council of Economic Advisers. Statistical tables relating to income, employment, and production.

Federal Reserve Bulletin. Washington, DC: Federal Reserve System Board of Governors. Published monthly, this publication is an important source of financial data, including statistics on banking activity, interest rates, savings, the index of industrial production, an index of department store sales, prices, and international trade and finance.

Handbook of Basic Economic Statistics. Economic Statistics Bureau of Washington, DC. Current and historical statistics on industry, commerce, labor, and agriculture.

Handbook of Cyclical Indicators. Washington, DC: U.S. Department of Commerce. Published monthly, this publication contains at least 70 indicators of business activity designed to serve as a key to general economic conditions.

Merchandising, "Statistical and Marketing Report." New York: Billboard Publications. This annual report, contained in the March issue, includes statistical information related to sales, shipments, imports, exports, and more for certain consumer durables, including home electronics and major appliances.

Predicasts Basebook. Predicasts, Inc. Comprehensive, 29,000 time series, arranged by a modified 7-digit SIC number and includes statistics for economic indicators.

Predicasts Forecasts. Predicasts, Inc. Reports short- and long-range forecast statistics for basic economic indicators and for individual industries/products. Each forecast includes date and page reference.

Social Indicators. U.S. Bureau of the Census. Includes statistics and charts for a variety of U.S. social conditions and trends.

Standard & Poor's Corporate Records. New York: Standard & Poor's Corporation. *Corporate Records* provides current financial statistics for companies as well as background information and news items.

Standard & Poor's Industry Surveys. New York: Standard & Poor's Corporation. These surveys provide analyses of all major domestic industries, including outlooks for the industry, trends and problems, and statistical tables and charts. A basic analysis is published yearly and offers a comparative company analysis of the leading companies in an industry. Current analyses are published three times per year and include important developments and available statistics for the industry, market, and company, as well as investment outlook for the industry.

Standard & Poor's Statistical Service. New York: Standard & Poor's Corporation. This publication presents monthly statistical data (current and historical) for several areas, including banking and finance, production and labor, and income and trade.

Statistical Abstract of the United States. Department of Commerce. Summary statistics in industrial, social, political, and economic fields in the United States. It is augmented by the *Cities Supplement, The County Data Book,* and *Historical Statistics of the United States.*

Statistical Reference Index. Congressional Information Service. Selective guide to American statistical publications available from sources other than the U.S. government.

Statistical Service (Standard & Poor's Corp. Reports coverage of current and basic statistics arranged in three parts: the white current statistics gives latest annual figures; the yellow monthly issue provides latest figures covering the current year; and the basic statistics section.

Statistics of Income: Corporation Income Tax Returns. Internal Revenue Service. Balance sheet and income statement statistics derived from corporate tax returns.

Statistics of Income: U.S. Business Tax Returns. Internal Revenue Service. Summarizes financial and economic data for proprietorships, partnerships, and small business corporations.

Statistics Sources. Gale Research. Provides a guide to general sources for statistics on industrial, business, social, education, financial, and other subjects.

Survey of Current Business. Department of Commerce. Facts on industrial and business activity in the United States and statistical summary of national income and product accounts. A weekly supplement provides an up-to-date summary of business.

U.S. Industrial Outlook. U.S. Bureau of Industrial Economics, Department of Commerce. Contains information on recent trends and outlook in 250 individual industries.

GENERAL BUSINESS AND INDUSTRY SOURCES

Aerospace Facts and Figures. Aerospace Industries Association of America.

Almanac of the Canning, Freezing, Preserving Industries. E. E. Judge & Sons. Includes general industry information and a directory of the industry.

America's Corporate Families: The Billion Dollar Directory. Dun & Bradstreet. Similar to *Million Dollar Directory.*

Annual Statistical Report. American Iron and Steel Institute.

Appliance. Dana Chase Publications. Includes statistical reviews, purchasing directory, and general information.

Beverage Industry. Magazines for Industry, Inc. Publishes a separate Annual Manual in three segments: relevant statistics, manual of operations, and a buyer's guide.

Bibliographic Guide to Business and Economics. Boston: G. K. Hall. A comprehensive author/title/subject listing of all business and economic materials cataloged during one year by the Library of Congress and the Research Libraries of the New York Public Library.

Business Information Sources. Daniells. University of California Press. A book complete with bibliographies representing almost every aspect of business.

Chemical Marketing Reporter. Schnell Publishing. Includes lengthy, continuing list: "Current Prices of Chemicals and Related Materials."

Computerworld. Computerworld, Inc. Last December issue includes "Review and Forecast," an analysis of computer industry's past year and the outlook for the next year.

Construction Review. Department of Commerce. Current statistics on construction put in place, costs, and employment.

Directory of Corporate Affiliations. National Register Publishing Co. Lists over 4,000 major American parent companies' line of business, approximate sales, number of employees, ticker symbol, top officers, subsidiaries, divisions and/or affiliates.

Directory of Industry Data Sources. Information Access Co. Provides a listing of industry-intensive data for United States, Canada, and Europe.

Distribution Worldwide. Chilton Co. Special annual issue, *Distribution Guide,* compiles information on transportation methods and wages.

Drug and Cosmetic Industry. Drug Markets, Inc. Separate publication in July, *Drug and Cosmetic Catalog,* provides list of manufacturers of drugs and cosmetics and their respective products.

Electronic News Financial Fact Book & Directory. Fairchild Publications. A detailed financial manual covering electronic companies; includes a ranked list of top companies.

Electronic World. January and February issues include two-part statistical report on expenditures, construction, and other categories by region; capacity; sales; and financial statistics for the electrical industry.

Encyclopedia of Business Information Sources. Paul Wasserman et al., eds., Gale Research Company. A detailed listing of primary subjects of interest to managerial personnel, with a record of sourcebooks, periodicals, organizations, directories, handbooks, bibliographies, and other sources of information on each topic. Two vols., nearly 17,000 entries in over 1,600 subject areas.

Forest Industries. Miller Freeman Publications, Inc. The March issue includes "Forest Industries Wood-Based Panel," a review of production and sales figures for selected wood products; extra issue in May includes a statistical review of the lumber industry.

Implement and Tractor. Intertec Publishing Corporation. January issue includes equipment specifications and operating data for farm and industrial equipment. November issue includes statistics and information on the farm industry.

Industry Surveys. Standard & Poor's Corp. Continuously revised analysis of leading industries (40 industries made up of 1,300 companies). Current analysis contains interim operating data of investment comment. Basic analysis features company ratio comparisons and balance sheet statistics.

Kline Guide to the Chemical Industry. 4th ed. C. H. Kline & Co. An economic analysis of the chemical industry.

Middle Market Directory. Dun & Bradstreet. Inventories approximately 18,000 U.S. companies with an indicated worth of $500,000 to $999,999, giving officers, products, standard industrial classification, approximate sales, and number of employees.

Million Dollar Directory. Dun & Bradstreet. Lists U.S. companies with an indicated worth of $1 million or more, giving officers and directors, products, standard industrial classification, sales, and number of employees.

Modern Brewery Age. Business Journals, Inc. February issue includes a review of sales and production figures for the brewery industry. A separate publication, *The Blue Book,* issued in May, compiles sales and consumption figures by state for the brewery industry.

Motor Vehicle Facts & Figures. Manufacturers Association of the United States. Contains statistics on automobile and truck production, sales and registrations, ownership and usage, economic and social impact of the automobile.

National Petroleum News. McGraw-Hill, Inc. May issue includes statistics on sales and consumption of fuel oils, gasoline, and related products. Some figures are for 10 years, along with 10-year projections.

Operating Results of Department and Specialty Stores. National Retail Merchants Association.

Packaging. Cahners Publishing Co. Industry publication that includes special annual issues "Packaging Encyclopedia" and "Buyer's Guide and Directory."

Paper Trade Journal. Vance Publishing Corp. Includes: Financial Review: North America's Paper Industry Outlook, Who's Who in North America Papermaking, and general industry information.

Petroleum Facts and Figures. American Petroleum Institute.

Poor's Register of Corporations, Directors, and Executives of the United States and Canada. Standard & Poor's Corp. Divided into two sections. The first gives officers, products, sales range, and number of employees for about 30,000 corporations. The second gives brief information on executives and directors.

PROMPT. Predicasts, Inc. Predicasts Overview of Markets and Technology. A continuing abstracting index to worldwide articles of 28 industries.

Publishers Weekly. R. R. Bowker Co. Includes general discussions of the industry, an annual summary and highlights publication, and industry statistics.

Quick-Frozen Foods. Harcourt Brace Jovanovich Publications. October issue includes "Frozen Food Almanac" providing statistics on the frozen food industry by product.

Retail Trade. Provides a survey of retail sales, retail inventories, purchases, gross margins, and accounts receivable by type of retail store and form of legal organization.

Statistical Sources. Paul Wasserman et al., eds. Gale Research Corp., 4th ed., 1974. A subject guide to industrial, business, social, educational, financial data, and other related topics.

The Super Market Industry Speaks. Super Market Institute.

Vending Times. February issue includes "The Buyers Guide," a special issue providing information on the vending industry; June issue includes "The Census of the Industry," a special issue containing statistics on the vending industry.

Who Owns Whom: North America. Dun & Bradstreet. A directory of U.S. and Canadian parent companies listing their subsidiaries and associates outside the United States or Canada.

INDEXES AND ABSTRACTS

Accountants Digest. L. L. Briggs. A digest of articles appearing currently in accounting periodicals.

Accountants Index. American Institute of Certified Public Accountants. An index to books, pamphlets, and articles on accounting and finance.

Accounting Articles. Commerce Clearing House. Loose-leaf index to articles in accounting and business periodicals.

Advertising Age Editorial Index. Crain Communications, Inc. Index to articles in *Advertising Age.*

American Statistical Index. Congressional Information Service. A comprehensive two-part annual index to the statistical publications of the U.S. government.

Applied Science & Technology Index. (Formerly *Industrial Arts Index* to 1958). H. W. Wilson Co. Reviews over 300 periodicals relevant to the applied sciences, many of which pertain to business.

Battelle Library Review. (Formerly *Battelle Technical Review* to 1962.) Battelle Memorial Institute. Annotated bibliography of books, reports, and articles on automation and automatic processes.

Bulletin of Public Affairs Information Service. Public Affairs Information Service, Inc. (Since 1915—annual index.) A selective list of the latest books, pamphlets, government publications, reports of public and private agencies, and periodicals relating to economic conditions, public administration, and international relations.

Business Education Index. McGraw-Hill Book Co. (Since 1940—annual index.) Annual author and subject index of books, articles, and theses on business education.

Business Index. Los Altos, Calif.: (Microfilm Reel) Information Access Co. An index that includes 650 business periodicals or selected articles from nonbusiness journals.

Business Periodicals Index. H. W. Wilson Co. A subject index to the disciplines of accounting, advertising, banking, general business, insurance, labor, management, and marketing.

Business Publications Index and Abstracts. Prepared by Management Contents. Gale Research Co. A two-part monthly subject/author index to all articles in over 700 English language business/management periodicals, plus some proceedings, study courses, and a few books.

Canadian Business Index. Toronto: Micromedia Ltd. An index to 150 Canadian periodicals and a few newspapers.

Catalog of United States Census Publication. Washington, DC: Department of Commerce, Bureau of Census. Indexes all available Census Bureau data. Main divisions are: agriculture, business, construction, foreign trade, government, guide to locating U.S. census information.

Computer and Information Systems. (Formerly *Information Processing Journal* to 1969.) Cambridge Communications Corporation.

Conference Board. Cumulative Index. A subject index to a wide range of studies, pamphlets, and articles in the areas of: consumer research, corporate relations, economic and policy analysis, human resources, international business management, and management functions.

Cumulative Index of NICB Publications.. The National Industrial Conferences Board. Annual index of NICB books, pamphlets, and articles in the area of management of personnel.

Current Contents: Social & Behavioral Sciences. Institute for Scientific Information. A collection of tables of contents from 1,300 periodicals in the social and behavioral sciences. Business, finance, economics, management, and many other related areas of sociology and social issues are covered.

Engineering Index Monthly. Engineering Information, Inc. A subject list of abstracts, significant technological periodicals, and other literature.

Financial Times Index. Financial Times Business Information, Ltd. A three-part index for corporate information in the United States and worldwide, including institutions, associations, and so on.

Funk and Scott Index Europe. Predicasts, Inc. Indexes articles on U.S. companies, products, and industries from over 750 business, industrial, and financial periodicals. Includes a third section of articles arranged by region and country.

Funk and Scott Index International. Predicasts, Inc. Indexes articles on foreign companies and industries from over 1,000 foreign and domestic periodicals and documents.

Funk and Scott Index United States. Predicasts, Inc. Indexes articles on U.S. companies, products, and industries from over 750 business, industrial, and financial periodicals.

Guide to U.S. Government Publications. McLean, VA, Documents Index. Annotated guide to publications of various U.S. government agencies.

International Abstracts in Operations Research. Operations Research Society of America.

International Journal of Abstracts of Statistical Methods in Industry. The Hague, Netherlands: International Statistical Institute.

Management Contents. A collection of tables of contents for a selection of over 300 business/management journals.

Management Information Guides. Gale Research Company. Bibliographical references to information sources for various business subjects.

Management Review. American Management Association.

Monthly Catalog of U.S. Government Publications. U.S. Government Printing Office. Continuing list of federal government publications.

Monthly Checklist of State Publications. U.S. Library of Congress, Exchange and Gift Division. Record of state documents received by Library of Congress.

National Newspaper Index. An assortment of citations to articles and news appearing in leading newspapers nationwide.

New York Times Index. New York. Very detailed index of all articles in the *Times,* arranged alphabetically with many cross-references.

Psychological Abstracts. American Psychological Association.

Public Affairs Information Service. Public Affairs Information Service, Inc. A selective subject list of books, pamphlets, and government publications covering business, banking, and economics as well as subjects in the area of public affairs.

Reader's Guide to Periodical Literature. H. W. Wilson Co. Index by author and subject to selected U.S. general and nontechnical periodicals.

Research Index. Dorking, Surrey, England: Business Surveys, Ltd. Indexes news of financial interest on industries and companies, appearing in over 100 British (and a few European) trade and economics journals as well as several newspapers.

Sociological Abstracts. American Sociological Association.

The Wall Street Journal Index. Dow Jones & Company, Inc. An index of all articles in *The WSJ* grouped in two sections: corporate news and general news.

ON-LINE MARKETING INFORMATION SERVICES

"Going on-line" is another way to say the analyst (user) is utilizing one computer to connect to another one. Users go on-line to communicate with others via computers. In this section, the focus is on connecting the user's computer with other computers to retrieve market-related information. There is a wealth of information available on-line, and analysts should become familiar with this valuable tool. When a user goes on-line, he/she is tapping into the "information superhighway." Technically, there is not one information highway but, in reality, many that transverse the electronic information universe. For example, Compuserve could be considered an information highway as it is a route to various information sources. Additionally, the user can connect to the Internet via Compuserve. The Internet is analogous to a superhighway while Compuserve may be considered a secondary highway. They are distinct, however. Compuserve will take the user to information sources that the Internet will not and vice versa. Additionally, they may both take the user to the same information source but get one there in a different fashion.

There are numerous options for going on-line. For obtaining market information, there are three main options: Consumer on-line services, professional on-line services and the Internet. Each of these will be discussed below. This section concludes with a description of some of the more useful on-line information sources.

Consumer On-Line Services

Consumer on-line services are readily available to virtually anyone who has access to a computer and a modem. The most popular consumer on-line services are American Online, Compuserve, and Prodigy. Generally for a monthly fee, subscribers have access to a wide range of services ranging from electronic shopping to participation in electronic forums. These services also provide access to multiple sources of market information. Users can acquire information on individual companies, markets, and industries, as well as on the economy as a whole. Often there is an additional charge for the search and/or retrieval of information. The consumer on-line services provide access to some powerful databases available in professional on-line services such as DIALOG. The primary advantage of consumer on-line services is ease of use. Graphical interfaces make searching more intuitive and less challenging. However, these services cannot provide the depth and breadth of information that professional on-line services can. Additionally, they may be more expensive to use. Consumer on-line services are recommended for infrequent and/or exploratory research needs.

Professional On-Line Services

Professional on-line services provide access to multiple proprietary databases. Examples of some of the more popular services include DIALOG, Lexis-Nexis, Dow Jones News/Retrieval, and NewsNet. These services are essentially database supermarkets containing more than 10,000 individual, commercial databases. For example, DIALOG offers access to about 400 different industry-specific databases. Global searches can be performed that will search for keywords in multiple databases at the same time. To use a professional on-line service, the user needs to set up an account with the service provider. To be economically justifiable, the user's information needs should be extensive and frequent. The interfaces are generally not as user-friendly as consumer on-line services and training is recommended to maximize one's searching/retrieval skills.

The Internet

The Internet is the backbone of the much-hyped information highway. Essentially, the Internet is a network of computer networks. Thousands of networks and millions of users worldwide are connected to the Internet. As a result, the amount of information available is staggering and also frustratingly difficult to sort through. Technically, the Internet is not owned and operated by any single entity, as are consumer and professional on-line services. Therefore, there is considerably less consistency among the information sites reachable through the Internet. Several tools exist to help bring order to the Internet. Search protocols such as Archie and Gopher greatly ease the daunting task of searching the Internet for information. A more recent development is the World Wide Web (WWW). The WWW is a system that provides a graphical interface for the Internet and also provides a simplified way to navigate the Internet through what is called *hypertext*. The WWW is the most user-friendly way to search the Internet, and search devices such as *Yahoo* greatly assist the search for and retrieval of information.

Currently, the Internet is primarily a communication tool as opposed to a powerful research source for market information. Much of the market information available through the Internet is, in reality, the same as that available through professional on-line services. The Internet merely serves as a different route to access these databases. However, the Internet holds great potential to be an excellent information resource in the future. As it stands now, the Internet is better suited as a source for academic and scientific research. In addition, the Internet is very useful for accessing information and databases in other countries around the world.

Sources of On-line Information

A few of the more common on-line information sources are listed below.[2] For each, the reader will find a brief description of the source and the "on-line-site". Remember, the list provides only a small sampling of the numerous information sources available on-line. Once on-line, the user is destined to find many more.

Business database plus

This database contains over 1 million full-text articles published over the last five years in business magazines, trade journals, and industry newsletters. Searches can be performed by titles, keywords, subjects, and publication information. *Business Database Plus* is available through Compuserve.

ClariNet

ClariNet is a network of news groups on the Internet. These news groups are professionally-based discussion forums that provide constantly updated details regarding industries and companies. Information on ClariNet can be found on the WWW.

Company News

Company News allows the user to seach the newswires for stories relating to any company. The stories are derived from the Dow Jones News Retrieval Service and are updated continuously during every business day. This database is a good source of current information but the stories only go back one week. This database can be found on Prodigy.

Computer Database Plus

This database serves as an excellent source of information on the computer and other technology industries. It contains full-text articles and abstracts from leading technology periodicals. This database can be found on Ziffnet for Compuserve.

DIALOG

DIALOG is a professional on-line server that offers access to hundreds of different industry-specific and general business databases. An example of one these databases is PTS Promt (Predicasts Report on Technology and Markets). PTS Promt contains detailed information on virtually all manufacturing and service industries, from computers, electronics, and telecommunications to chemicals, food, pharmaceuticals, and finance. It contains market forecasts, in addition to company-specific information. DIALOG is available through Knight-Ridder Information, Inc.

EDGAR

EDGAR is the database of filings from the U.S. Securities and Exchange Commission (SEC). It is indexed by company and contains electronic versions of all SEC filings for each company.

Industry Net

This database is a good place to start a search on company-specific information and is located on the WWW. It contains links to many sources of industry information and is an Internet service.

InfoSeek

InfoSeek is a WWW service that provides access to numerous professional on-line databases Searches can be performed on various wire services such as AP, Reuters, Newswire, and so on, as well as on diverse computer and health periodicals. In addition, InfoSeek can search news groups pertaining to various subjects on the Internet. Many of the professional on-line data services now have access sites on the WWW.

International Company Information

This collection of databases contains extensive information on the largest companies in each individual country including their products, earnings, size, and more. This service is available through Compuserve.

Chapter Notes

Chapter 1

1. See Reinhard Angelmar and Christian Pinson, "The Meaning of Marketing," *Philosophy of Science,* June 1975, pp. 208–14.

2. Peter D. Bennett, *Dictionary of Marketing Terms* 2nd ed. (Chicago: American Marketing Association, 1995), p. 166.

3. Gilbert A. Churchill, Jr., and J. Paul Peter, *Marketing: Creating Value for Customers* (Burr Ridge, IL: Richard D. Irwin, 1995), p. 7.

4. Much of this section is based on J. H. Donnelly, Jr., J. L. Gibson, and J. M. Ivancevich, *Fundamentals of Management,* 9th ed. (Burr Ridge, IL: Richard D. Irwin, 1995), chap. 7.

5. For a detailed discussion on this topic, see Gary Hamal and C. K. Prahalad, "Competing for the Future," *Harvard Business Review,* July/August 1994, pp. 122–28.

6. For a discussion on this issue, see H. Igor Ansoff, "Comment on Henry Mintzberg's Rethinking Strategic Planning," *Long Range Planning,* June 1994, pp. 31–32.

7. Joe Dodson, "Strategic Repositioning through the Customer Connection," *The Journal of Business Strategy,* May/June 1991, pp. 4–7.

8. For a discussion on this topic, see D. Keith Denton, "Creating a System for Continuous Improvement," *Business Horizons,* January/February 1995, pp. 16–20.

9. Frederick F. Reichheld, "Loyalty and the Renaissance of Marketing," *Marketing Management* 2, no. 4 (1994), pp. 10–21.

10. G. S. Day, K. E. Jocz, and H. P. Root, "Domains of Ignorance: What We Most Need to Know," *Marketing Management,* Winter 1992, pp. 9–14.

11. For a discussion of this issue, see Christopher Rodrigues, "Think Local," *International Management,* January/February 1994, p. 52.

12. For a discussion of this topic see Susan Changler, "Where Sears Wants America to Shop Now," *Business Week,* June 12, 1995, p. 39; and Leah Rickard, "Troubled Kmart Follows the Blue Light," *Advertising Age,* May 29, 1995, p. 67.

13. Neil Weinberg, "Digital Faces Challenging Climb to Reach PC Heights," *Computerworld,* May 1, 1995, p. 41.

14. Peter Lorange and Johan Roos, "Why Some Strategic Alliances Succeed and Others Fail," *The Journal of Business Strategy,* January/February 1991, pp. 25–30.

15. For a discussion of the benefits and problems associated with the strategic planning process, see Henry Mintzberg, "The Fall and Rise of Strategic Planning," *Harvard Business Review,* January/February 1994, pp. 107–14; and F. Paul Carlson, "The Long and Short of Strategic Planning," *The Journal of Business Strategy,* May/June 1990, pp. 15–19.

16. The process may differ depending on the type of organization or management approach, or both. For certain types of organizations, one strategic plan will be sufficient. Some manufacturers with similar product lines or limited product lines will develop only one strategic plan. However, organizations with widely diversified product lines and widely diversified markets may develop strategic plans for units or divisions. These plans usually are combined into a master strategic plan.

17. Jean Voight, "Demystifying the Mission Statement," *Nonprofit World,* January/February 1994, pp. 29–32.

18. For a discussion of this topic, see Gerald E. Ledford, Jr., Jon R. Wendenhof, and James T. Strahely, "Realizing a Corporate Philosophy," *Organizational Dynamics,* Winter 1995, pp. 4–19; and Stephan Cummings and John Davies, "Mission, Vision, Fusion," *Long Range Planning,* December 1994, pp. 147–50.

19. Martin Vander Weyer, "Mission Improvable," *Management Today,* September 1994, pp. 66–68.

20. Philip Kotler and Gary Armstrong, *Principles of Marketing,* 6th ed. (Englewood Cliffs, NJ: Prentice Hall, 1994), chap. 2.

21. Peter Drucker, "The Theory of Business," *Harvard Business Review,* September/October 1994, pp. 95–104.

22. Darrell Rigby, "Managing the Management Tools," *Planning Review,* September/October 1994, pp. 20–24.

23. Philip Kotler, *Marketing Management: Analysis, Planning, Implementation and Control,* 8th ed. (Englewood Cliffs, NJ: Prentice Hall, 1994), chap. 3.

24. Norton Paley, "A Sign of Intelligence," *Sales & Marketing Management,* March 1995, pp. 30–31.

25. For a discussion of this issue, see William B. Werthre, Jr. and Jeffrey L. Kerr, "The Shifting Sands of Competitive Advantage," *Business Horizons,* May/June 1995, pp. 11–17.

26. For examples related to this topic, see Allan J. Magrath, "Finding New Ways to Add Value," *Sales & Marketing Management,* March 1994, pp. 23–24.

27. Peter Drucker, *Management: Tasks, Responsibilities, Practices* (New York: Harper & Row, 1974), pp. 77–89; Kotler, *Marketing Management,* chap. 3.

28. George S. Day, "Continuous Learning about Markets," *California Management Review,* Summer 1994, pp. 9–31.

29. Much of the following discussion is based on Drucker, *Management,* pp. 79–87.

30. Martha H. Peak, "More Than Syntax," *Academy of Management Review,* January 1993, p 1.

31. P. Doyle, "Setting Business Objectives and Measuring Performance," *European Management Journal,* June 1994, pp. 123–32.

32. Donald K. Yee, "Pass or Fail? How to Grade Strategic Progress." *The Journal of Business Strategy,* May/June 1990, pp. 10–14.

33. For a discussion of this topic, see Thomas Renda, "Are Your Organization and Business Strategies at Odds?" *Supervisory Management,* March 1994, pp. 10, 12.

34. Noel B. Zabriskie and Alan B. Huellmantel, "Marketing Research as a Strategic Tool," *Long Range Planning,* February 1994, pp. 107–18.

35. Originally discussed in the classic H. Igor Ansott, *Corporate Strategy* (New York: McGraw-Hill, 1965).

36. For complete coverage of this topic, see Michael E. Porter, *Competitive Advantage: Creating and Sustaining Superior Performance* (New York: The Free Press, 1985). Material in this section is based upon discussions contained in Steven J. Skinner, *Marketing,* 2nd ed. (Boston: Houghton Mifflin Co., 1994), pp. 48–50, and Thomas A. Bateman and Carl P. Zeithaml, *Management Function & Strategy,* 2nd ed. (Homewood, IL: Irwin, 1993), pp. 152–53.

37. For a complete discussion of this topic see Michael Treacy and Fred Wiersema, *The Discipline of Market Leaders* (Reading, MA: Addison-Wesley, 1995), and Michael Treacy and Fred Wieserma, "How Market Leaders Keep Their Edge," *Fortune,* February 6, 1995, pp. 88–98.

38. N. Venkatramen and J. C. Camillus, "Exploring the Concept of 'Fit' in Strategic Management," *Academy of Management Review,* July 1984, pp. 513–25; H. Mintzberg and J. A. Waters, "Of Strategies, Deliberate and Emergent," *Strategic Management Journal,* July–September 1985, pp. 257–72.

39. For a discussion of this topic, see D. Aaker, "Managing Assets and Skills: The Key to a Sustainable Competitive Advantage," *California Management Review,* Winter 1989, pp. 99–106; Jeffrey Pfeffer, "Competitive Advantage Through People," *California Management Review,* Winter 1994, pp. 9–28; Thomas C. Powell, "Total Quality Management as Competitive Advantage: A Review and Empirical Study," *Strategic Management Journal,* January 1995, pp. 15–37.

40. For a discussion of how channel relations can create a competitive advantage, see Robert Buzzell and Gwenn Ortmeyer, "Channel Partnerships Streamline Distribution," *Sloan Management Review,* Spring 1995, pp. 85–95.

41. There are several portfolio models; each has its detractors and supporters. The interested reader should consult Richard G. Hamermesh and Roderick E. White, "Manage Beyond Portfolio Analysis," *Harvard Business Review,* January–February 1984, pp. 103–9, and J. A. Seeger, "Revising the Images of BCG's Growth/Share Matrix," *Strategic Management Journal,* January–March 1984, pp. 93–97.

42. See Alexander Hiam, "Exposing Four Myths of Strategic Planning," *The Journal of Business Strategy,* September/October 1990, pp. 23–28, for a discussion of this topic.

43. Shlomo Maital, "Adapting the Unknowable," *Across the Board,* June 1994, pp. 59–60.

44. R. A. Linneman and H. E. Klein, "Using Scenarios in Strategic Decision Making," *Business Horizons,* January–February 1985, pp. 64–74.

45. Philip Kotler, *Marketing Management: Analysis, Planning, Implementation, and Control,* 8th ed. (Englewood Cliffs, NJ: Prentice-Hall, 1994), p. 13.

46. For a more complete discussion of customer service and the mission statement, see Richard Germain and M. Bixby Cooper, "How a Customer Mission Statement Affects Company Performance," *Industrial Marketing Management,* February, 1990, pp. 47–54, and Harvey N. Shycon, "Improved Customer Service: Measuring the Payoff," *The Journal of Business Strategy,* January/February 1992, pp. 13–17.

47. David A. Heenan, "Why the U.S. Government Should Go to Bat for Business," *The Journal of Business Strategy,* March/April 1990, pp. 46–48.

48. For a discussion of this issue and other mistakes marketers frequently make, see Kevin J. Clancy and Robert S. Shulman, "Breaking the Mold," *Sale & Marketing Management,* January 1994, pp. 82–84.

49. See D. W. Cravens and S. S. Shipp, "Market-Driven Strategies for Competitive Advantage," *Business Horizons,* January–February 1991, pp. 53–61, for a discussion of the relationship between strategic and market planning.

50. For a discussion of this topic, see Gavin Chalcroft, "Like All Good Things, Strategic Planning Takes a Little Time," *Brandweek,* February 20, 1995.

51. George S. Day and David B. Montgomery, "Diagnosing the Experience Curve," *Journal of Marketing,* Spring 1983, pp. 44–58.

52. P. Rajan Varadarajan, Terry Clark, and William M. Pride, "Controlling the Uncontrollable: Managing Your Market Environment," *Sloan Management Review,* Winter 1992, pp. 39–47.

53. Reed E. Nelson, "Is There Strategy in Brazil?" *Business Horizons,* July–August 1992, pp. 15–23.

54. Peter S. Davis and Patrick L. Schill, "Addressing the Contingent Effects of Business Unit Strategic Orientation on the Relationship between Organizational Context and Business Unit Performance," *Journal of Business Research,* 1993, pp. 183–200.

55. J. Scott Armstrong and Roderick J. Brodie, "Effects of Portfolio Planning Methods on Decision Making: Experimental Results," *International Journal of Research in Marketing,* January 1994, pp. 73–84.

56. Michel Roberts, "Times Change But Do Business Strategies?" *Journal of Business Strategy,* March–April 1993, pp. 12–15.

57. Donald L. McCabe and V. K. Narayanan, "The Life Cycle of the PIMS and BCG Models," *Industrial Marketing Management,* November 1991, pp. 347–52.

Chapter 2

1. Peter D. Bennett, Ed., *Dictionary of Marketing Terms,* 2nd ed. (Chicago: American Marketing Association, 1995), p. 77.

2. See Gilbert A. Churchill, Jr., *Marketing Research: Methodological Foundations,* 6th ed. (Fort Worth, TX: Dryden Press, 1995), chap. 2.

3. Peter D. Bennett, ed., *Dictionary of Marketing Terms,* 2nd ed., (Chicago: American Marketing Association, 1995), pp. 169–70.

4. For a complete discussion of these issues, see Robert F. Hartley, *Marketing Mistake,* 4th ed. (New York: John Wiley & Sons, 1989), pp. 221–36.

5. For a discussion of the role of trust in marketing researcher and marketing manager relationships, see Christine Moorman, Rohit Deshpande, and Gerald Zaltman, "Factors Affecting Trust in Market Research Relationships," *Journal of Marketing,* January 1993, pp. 81–101.

6. For a discussion of some general problems in marketing research, see Alan G. Sawyer and J. Paul Peter, "The Significance of Statistical Significance Testing in Marketing Research," *Journal of Marketing Research,* May 1983, pp. 122–33.

Chapter 3

1. A. H. Maslow, *Motivation and Personality* (New York: Harper & Row. 1954); also see James F. Engel, Roger D. Blackwell and Paul W. Miniard, *Consumer Behavior,* 8th ed. (Fort Worth, TX: Dryden Press, 1995, chap. 5, for further discussion of need recognition.

2. For a detailed review of research on external search, see Sharon E. Beatty and Scott M. Smith, "External Search Effort: An Investigation Across Several Product Categories," *Journal of Consumer Research,* June 1987, pp. 83–95. Also see Narasimhan Srinivasan and Brian T. Ratchford, "An Empirical Test of a Model of External Search for Automobiles," *Journal of Consumer Research,* September 1991, pp. 233–42; and Julie L. Ozanne, Merrie Brucks and Dhruv Grewal, "A Study of Information Search Behavior During the Categorization of New Products," *Journal of Consumer Research,* March 1992, pp. 452–63.

3. For further discussion of information processing, see J. Paul Peter and Jerry C. Olson, *Consumer Behavior and Marketing Strategy,* 4th ed. (Burr Ridge, IL: Richard D. Irwin, 1996), Chap. 3.

4. For a summary of research on attitude modeling, see Blair H. Sheppard, Jon Hartwick, and Paul R. Warshaw, "The Theory of Reasoned Action: A Meta-Analysis of Past Research with Recommendations for Modification and Future Research," *Journal of Consumer Research,* December 1988, pp. 325–43.

5. For further discussion of postpurchase feelings, see Richard L. Oliver, "Cognitive, Affective, and Attribute Bases of the Satisfaction Response," *Journal of Consumer Research,* December 1993, pp. 418–30; Haim Mano and Richard L. Oliver, "Assessing the Dimensionality and Structure of the Consumption Experience: Evaluation, Feeling, and Satisfaction," *Journal of Consumer Research,* December 1993, pp. 451–66.

6. See William O. Bearden and Michael J. Etzel, "Reference Group Influence on Product and Brand Purchase Decisions," *Journal of Consumer Research,* September 1982, pp. 183–94; and Terry L. Childers and Akshay R. Rao, "The Influence of Familial and Peer-Based Reference Groups on Consumer Decisions," *Journal of Consumer Research,* September 1992, pp. 198–211.

7. See Rosann L. Spiro, "Persuasion in Family Decision Making," *Journal of Consumer Research,* March 1983, pp. 393–402.

8. See Janet Wagner and Sherman Hanna, "The Effectiveness of Family Life Cycle Variables in Consumer Expenditure Research," *Journal of Consumer Research.* December 1983, pp. 281–91. Also see Charles M. Schanninger and William D. Danko, "A

Conceptual and Empirical Comparison of Alternative Household Life Cycle Models," *Journal of Consumer Research,* March 1993, pp. 580–94.

9. Russell W. Belk, "Situational Variables and Consumer Behavior," *Journal of Consumer Research* December 1975, pp. 156–64. Also see Jacob Hornik, "Situational Effects on the Consumption of Time," *Journal of Marketing,* Fall 1982, pp. 44–55; C. Whan Park, Easwer S. Iyer, and Daniel C. Smith, "The Effects of Situational Factors on In-Store Grocery Shopping Behavior: The Role of Store Environment and Time Available for Shopping," *Journal of Consumer Research,* March 1989, pp. 422–33; Mary Jo Bitner, "Servicescapes: The Impact of Physical Surroundings on Customers and Employees," *Journal of Marketing,* April 1992, pp. 57–71.

Chapter 4

1. This discussion is based on Gilbert A. Churchill, Jr. and J. Paul Peter, *Marketing: Creating Value for Customers* (Burr Ridge, IL: Austen Press/Irwin, 1995), pp. 270–71. Also see Michele D. Bunn, "Taxonomy of Buying Decision Approaches," *Journal of Marketing,* January 1993, pp. 38–56.

2. This discussion is based on Eric N. Berkowitz, Roger A. Kerin, Steven W. Hartley, and William Rudelius, *Marketing,* 4th ed. Richard D. Irwin, (Burr Ridge, IL: 1994) p. 184.

3. For research on influence strategies in organizational buying, see Gary L. Frazier and Raymond Rody, "The Use of Influence Strategies in Interfirm Relationships in Industrial Product Channels," *Journal of Marketing,* January 1991, pp. 52–69; Julia M. Bristor, "Influence Strategies in Organizational Buying," *Journal of Business-to-Business Marketing,* 1993, pp. 63–98.

4. For research on the role of organizational climate in industrial buying, see William J. Qualls and Christopher P. Puto, "Organizational Climate and Decision Framing: An Integrated Approach to Analyzing Industrial Buying Decisions," *Journal of Marketing Research,* May 1989, pp. 179–92.

Chapter 5

1. Russell I. Haley, "Benefit Segmentation: A Decision-Oriented Research Tool," *Journal of Marketing,* July 1968, pp. 30–35; Russell I. Haley, "Benefit Segmentation—20 Years Later," *Journal of Consumer Marketing,* 1983, pp. 5–13; Russell I. Haley, "Benefit Segments: Backwards and Forwards," *Journal of Advertising Research,* February–March 1984, pp. 19–25.

2. Roger J. Calantone and Alan G. Sawyer. "The Stability of Benefit Segments," *Journal of Marketing*

Research, August 1978, pp. 395–404; also see James R. Merrill and William A. Weeks, "Predicting and Identifying Benefit Segments in the Elderly Market," in *AMA Educator's Proceedings,* ed. Patrick Murphy et al. (Chicago: American Marketing Association, 1983), pp. 399–403; Wagner A. Kamakura, "A Least Squares Procedure for Benefit Segmentation with Conjoint Experiments," *Journal of Marketing Research,* May 1988, pp. 157–67; Michel Wedel and Jan-Benedict E. M. Steenkamp, "A Clusterwise Regression Method for Simultaneous Fuzzy Market Structuring and Benefit Segmentation." *Journal of Marketing Research,* November 1991, pp. 385–96.

3. John L. Lastovicka, John P. Murry, Jr., and Eric Joachimsthaler, "Evaluating the Measurement Validity of Lifestyle Typologies with Qualitative Measures and Multiplicative Factoring," *Journal of Marketing Research,* February 1990, pp. 11–23.

4. This discussion is taken from J. Paul Peter and Jerry C. Olson, *Consumer Behavior and Marketing Strategy,* 3rd ed. (Homewood, IL: Richard D. Irwin, 1993), pp. 557–58.

5. See Al Ries and Jack Trout, *Positioning: The Battle for Your Mind* (New York: Warner Books, 1981); Al Ries and Jack Trout, *Marketing Warfare* (New York: McGraw-Hill, 1986).

Chapter 6

1. Material for this section is based on discussions contained in Louis E. Boone and David L. Kurtz, *Contemporary Marketing,* 8th ed. (Fort Worth, TX: Dryden, 1995), chap. 2; Gilbert A. Churchill, Jr. and J. Paul Peter, *Marketing: Creating Value for Customers,* (Burr Ridge, IL: Irwin, 1995), chap. 1, p. 634; James H. Donnelly, James L. Gibson, and John M. Ivancevich, *Fundamentals of Management,* 9th ed. (Burr Ridge, IL: Irwin 1995), p. 501; Joseph M. Juran, "Made in the U.S.A.: A Renaissance in Quality," *Harvard Business Review,* July–August 1993, pp. 42–47, 50; and Valerie A. Zeithaml, "Consumer Perceptions of Price, Quality, and Value: A Means End Model and Synthesis of Evidence," *Journal of Marketing,* April 1988, pp. 35–48.

2. Paul D. Larson, "Buyer–Supplier Co-operation, Product Quality, and Total Costs," *International Journal of Physical Distribution & Logistics Management,* 1994, pp. 4–10.

3. For a discussion on this topic, see Andrew J. Bergman, "What the Marketing Professional Needs to Know about ISO 9000 Series Registration," *Industrial Marketing Management,* 1994, pp. 367–70.

4. Yoram Wind and Henry J. Claycamp, "Planning Product Line Strategy: A Matrix Approach," *Journal of Marketing,* January 1976, p. 2.

5. Ibid.

6. The material for this section comes from Glenn L. Urban and Steven H. Star, *Advanced Marketing Strategy* (Englewood Cliffs, NJ: Prentice Hall, 1991), chap. 16.

7. For a detailed discussion of this topic, see Anne Perkins, "Product Variety Beyond Black," *Harvard Business Review,* November–December 1994, pp. 13–14; and "Perspectives: The Logic of Product-Line Extensions," *Harvard Business Review,* November–December 1994, pp. 53–62.

8. Mats Urde, "Brand Orientation—A Strategy for Survival," *Journal of Consumer Marketing,* 1994, pp. 18–32.

9. James Lowry, "Survey Finds Most Powerful Brands," *Advertising Age,* July 11, 1988, p. 31.

10. Peter H. Farquhar, "Strategic Challenges for Branding," *Marketing Management,* 1994, pp. 8–15.

11. Peter D. Bennett, ed., *Dictionary of Marketing Terms,* 2nd ed. (Chicago: American Marketing Association, 1995), p. 27.

12. Terance Shimp, *Promotion Management and Marketing Communications,* 2nd ed. (Hinsdale, IL: Dryden Press, 1990), p. 67.

13. David A. Aaker and Kevin Lane Keller, "Consumer Evaluations of Brand Extensions," *Journal of Marketing,* January 1990, pp. 27–41.

14. For a discussion of dual branding, see Akshay R. Rao and Robert W. Ruekert, "Brand Alliances as Signals of Product Quality," *Sloan Management Review,* Fall 1994, pp. 87–96.

15. Aaker and Keller, "Consumer Evaluations of Brand Extensions."

16. For a detailed discussion of brand equity, see David Aaker, *Managing Brand Equity* (New York and London: The Free Press, 1991).

17. For a complete discussion of this topic, see Geoffrey L. Gordon, Roger J. Calantone, and C. A. di Benedetto, "Brand Equity in the Business-to-Business Sector: An Exploratory Study," *The Journal of Product & Brand Management,* 1993, pp. 4–16.

18. For a more detailed discussion, see Elaine Underwood, "Something for Everyone," *Brandweek,* September 7, 1992, pp. 18–24.

19. Joe Berry, "National Brands on the Rebound, but the War Is Far from Over," *Brandweek,* February 27, 1995, pp. 17–18.

20. For a discussion on the growth of private label brands, see Hillary Miller, "Store Brands Are Looking Good," *Beverage Industry,* April 1995, pp. 60–61; Marcia Mogelonsky, "When Stores Become Brands," *American Demographics,* February 1995, pp. 32–36; and Dawn Wilensky, "Store Brands Take Paramount Importance as Retailers Scale Back National Brands," *Discount Store News,* May 16, 1994, pp. 24–27.

21. Gary Levin, "No Global Private Quake—Yet," *Advertising Age—International Supplement,* January 16, 1995, p. I–26.

22. Jeffrey D. Zbar, "Industry Trends Hold Private-Label Promise," *Advertising Age,* April 3, 1995, p. 31.

23. Pam Weisz, "Contac Looks for Relief in Redesign," *BrandWeek,* February 6, 1995, p. 18.

24. Karen Benezra, "Frito Bets 'Reduced' Pitch Is in the Chips," *Brandweek,* January 23, 1995, p. 18.

25. Thomas Hine, "Why We Buy," *Worth,* May 1995, pp. 80–83.

26. Note that the labeling of the new product features, new uses, and new markets curves is arbitrary. In other words, any of the three may result in the highest sales and profits depending on the product and situation.

27. For an overview of issues concerning the product life cycle, see George Day, "The Product Life Cycle: Analysis and Application Issues," *Journal of Marketing,* Fall 1981, pp. 60–67. This is the introductory article to a special section dealing with the product life cycle.

28. For a discussion of problems related to this issue, see Geoffrey L. Gordon, Roger J. Calantone, and C. Anthony di Benedetto, "Mature Markets and Revitalization Strategies: An American Fable," *Business Horizons,* May–June 1991, pp. 39–50.

29. Barry L. Bayus, "Are Product Life Cycles Really Getting Shorter?" *Journal of Product Innovation Management,* September 1994, pp. 300–308.

30. Glenn Rifken, "Product Development: The Myth of the Short Life Cycle," *Harvard Business Review,* July–August 1994, p. 11.

31. For further discussion of product deletion decisions, see George J. Avlonitis, "Product Elimination Decision Making: Does Formality Matter?" *Journal of Marketing,* Winter 1985, pp. 41–52.

32. The discussion on benchmarking is based on Stanley Brown, "Don't Innovate—Imitate," *Sales & Marketing Management,* January 1995, pp. 24–25; Charles Goldwasser, "Benchmarking: People Make the Process," *Management Review,* June 1995, pp. 39–43; and L. S. Pryor and S. J. Katz, "How Benchmarking Goes Wrong (and How to Do It Right)," *Planning Review,* January–February 1993, pp. 6–14.

33. This section is based on Joel R. Evans and Barry Berman, *Marketing,* 6th ed. (New York: Macmillan, 1994), pp. 359–61; Micheal J. Zenor, "The Profit Benefits of Category Management," *Journal of Marketing Research,* May 1994, pp. 202–13; John M. McCann, "Why Category Management Fails: Look to the MIS/Marketing Gap," *Brandweek,* January 16, 1995, p. 18; Tracy Carlson, "Brand Burnout," *Brandweek,* January 17, 1994, pp. 22–30; and Linda Gorchels, "Traditional Product Management Evolves," *Marketing News,* January 30, 1995, p. 4.

Chapter 7

1. Michael Barrier, "Innovation as a Way of Life," *Nation's Business,* July 1994, pp. 18–25.

2. "Face Value: The Mass Production of Ideas, and Other Impossibilities," *The Economist,* March 18, 1995, p. 72.

3. For a complete discussion of Rubbermaid's successes in new product development, see Tim Stevens, "Where the Rubbermaid Meets the Road," *Industry Week,* March 20, 1995, pp. 14–18; and Marshall Loeb, "How to Grow a New Product Every Day," *Fortune,* November 14, 1994, pp. 167–68.

4. Theodore B. Kinni, "New-Product Hog Heaven," *Industry Week,* March 20, 1995, pp. 31–37.

5. Pam Weisz, "1994's New Products Winners and Sinners, a la Consumer Panels," *Brandweek,* December 12, 1994, pp. 22–24.

6. Merrill S. Brenner, "Tracking New Products: A Practitioner's Guide," *Research-Technology Management,* November/December 1994, pp. 36–40.

7. Pam Weisz, "Gary Frazier," *Brandweek,* November 14, 1994, p. 58.

8. Thomas T. Semon, "Forecasting Demand for New Products Always Difficult," *Marketing News,* March 27, 1995, p. 10.

9. R. G. Cooper, C. J. Easingwood, S. Edgett, E. J. Kleinschmidt, and C. Storey, "What Distinguishes the Top Performing Products in Financial Services," *The Journal of Product Innovation Management,* September 1994, pp. 281–99.

10. Greg Erickson, "New Package Makes a New Product Complete," *Marketing News,* May 8, 1995, p. 10.

11. Pam Weisz, "The Razor's Edge," *Brandweek,* April 24, 1995, pp. 26–32; and Mark Maremont and Paula Dwyer, "How Gillette Is Honing Its Edge," *Business Week,* September 28, 1992, pp. 60–65.

12. Zina Mouhkheiber, "Oversleeping," *Forbes,* June 15, 1995, pp. 78–79.

13. The material on the five categories of new products is from C. Merle Crawford, *New Products Management,* 4th ed. (Burr Ridge, IL: Richard D. Irwin, 1994), pp. 9–11.

14. H. Igor Ansoff, *Corporate Strategy* (New York: McGraw-Hill, 1965), pp. 109–10.

15. For a discussion of firm objectives in developing new products, see Vijay Mahajan and Jerry Wind, "New Product Models: Practice, Shortcomings and Desired Improvements," *The Journal of Product Innovation Management,* June 1992, pp. 128–39.

16. Richard Stroup, "Growing in a Crowded Market Requires Old and New Strategies," *Brandweek,* August 22, 1994, p. 19.

17. Thomas Eager, "Bringing New Materials to Market," *Technology Review,* February/March 1995, pp. 42–49.

18. For a discussion of Japanese product development practices, see R. B. Kennard, "From Experience: Japanese Product Development Processes," *The Journal of Product Innovation Management,* September 1991, pp. 184–88.

19. For a detailed discussion of the idea generation and screening process, see Linda Rochford and Thomas Wotruba, "New Product Development Under Changing Economic Conditions," *Journal of Business & Industrial Marketing,* 1993, pp. 4–12; and Linda Rochford, "Generating and Screening New Product Ideas," *Industrial Marketing Management,* November 1991, pp. 287–96.

20. For a discussion of some unusual idea sources, see Mark Sebell, "Examining the New Product Ideation Process," *Visions,* July 1995, pp. 16–17; and George Gruenwald, "Some New Products Spring from Unsystematic Process," *Marketing News,* May 8, 1995, p. 4.

21. Jonathan Prinz, "Extending Your Brand? Consider What's at Stake," *Brandweek,* April 4, 1994, p. 17.

22. These two examples came from Justin Martin, "Ignore Your Customers," *Fortune,* May 1, 1995, pp. 121–26.

23. Where Do They Get All Those Ideas?" *Machine Design,* p. 40, January 26, 1995.

24. This section is based on Daryl McKee, "An Organizational Learning Approach to Product Innovation," *The Journal of Product Innovation Management,* September 1992, pp. 232–45.

25. George Gruenwald, "Great New Product! Fills a Need! Never Goes to Market!" *Marketing News,* March 13, 1995, p. 7.

26. The discussion on risk is from Thomas D. Kuczmarski and Arthur G. Middlebrooks, "Innovation Risk & Reward," *Sales & Marketing Management,* February 1993, pp. 44–51.

27. For a more complete discussion on the advantages and disadvantages or strategic alliances, see Richard N. Cardozo, Shannon H. Shipp, and Kenneth J. Roering, "Proactive Strategic Partnerships: A New Business Markets Strategy," *The Journal of Business and Industrial Marketing,* Winter 1992, pp. 51–63; Frank K. Sonnenberg, "Partnering: Entering the Age of Cooperation," *Journal of Business Strategy,* May/June 1992, pp. 49–52; Godfrey Devlin and Mark Bleackley, "Strategic Alliances—Guidelines for Success," *Long Range Planning,* 1988, pp. 18–23; Charles W. Joiner, "Harvesting American Technology—Lessons from the Japanese Garden," *Sloan Management Review,* Summer 1989, pp. 61–68; Richard P. Neilson, "Cooperative Strategies in Marketing," *Harvard Business Review,*

July–August 1987, pp. 61–68; and Pedro Nueno and Jan Oosterveld, "Managing Technology Alliances," *Long Range Planning*, 1988, pp. 11–17.

28. James Quinn, "Managing Innovation: Controlled Chaos," *Harvard Business Review*, May–June 1985, pp. 73–84; and Hirotaka Takeuchi and Ikujiro Nonaka, "The New New Product Development Game," *Harvard Business Review*, January–February 1986, pp. 137–46.

29. For a discussion of this issue, see Eric M. Olson; Orville C. Walker, Jr.; and Robert W. Ruekert, "Organizing For Effective New Product Development: The Moderating Role of Product Innovativeness," *Journal of Marketing*, January 1995, pp. 48–62; and Cristopher Meyer, "How the Right Measures Help Teams Excel," *Harvard Business Review*, May–June 1994, pp. 95–97.

30. For a detailed discussion on these stages, see Karl T. Ulrich and Steven D. Eppinger, *Product Design and Development* (New York: McGraw-Hill, 1995); and Glen Rifken, "Product Development: Emphatic Design Helps Understand Users Better," *Harvard Business Review*, March–April 1994, pp. 10–11.

31. The material on test marketing is from: C. Merle Crawford, *New Products Management*, 4th ed. (Burr Ridge, IL: Richard D. Irwin, 1994), chaps. 17 and 18.

32. "Taco Bell to Roll 'Border Lights' Lower-Fat Menu," *Nation's Restaurant News*, February 13, 1995, p. 2.

33. Patricia W. Meyers and Gerald A. Athaide, "Strategic Mutual Learning Between Producing and Buying Firms During Product Innovation," *The Journal of Product Innovation Management*, September 1991, pp. 155–69.

34. For an in-depth discussion of test marketing, see Kevin J. Clancy; Robert S. Shulman; and Marianne Wolf, *Simulated Test Marketing: Technology for Launching Successful New Products* (Lexington, MA: Lexington Books, 1995).

35. For a discussion of this issue, see Christina Brown and James Lattin, "Investigating the Relationship between Time in Market and Pioneering Advantage, *Management Science*, October 1994, pp. 1361–69; Robin Peterson, "Forecasting for New Product Introduction," *Journal of Business Forecasting*, Fall 1994, pp. 21–23; and Tracy Carlson, "The Race Is On," *Brandweek*, May 9, 1994, pp. 22–27.

36. Sandra S. Donovan, "It's People Who Get New Products to market Fast," *Research-Technology Management*, September/October 1994, pp. 12–13.

37. For a discussion of reasons why products fail, see Betsy Spellman, "Big Talk, Little Dollars," *Brandweek*, January 23, 1995, pp. 21–29.

38. For a discussion of the pitfalls associated with using traditional financial techniques to evaluate new product decisions, see George T. Haley and Stephen M. Goldberg, "Net Present Value Techniques and Their Effects on New Product Research," *Industrial Marketing Management*, June 1995, pp. 177–90.

Chapter 8

1. This discussion is adapted from material contained in Gilbert A. Churchill, Jr., and J. Paul Peter, *Marketing: Creating Value for Customers*, (Burr Ridge, IL: Richard D. Irwin, 1995), chap. 18.

2. Peter D. Bennett, ed., *Dictionary of Marketing Terms* (Chicago: American Marketing Association, 1988), p. 4.

3. For a description of ad spending by leading companies and brands, see "The Top 200 Brands," *Advertising Age*, May 1, 1995, pp. 33–34.

4. Pam Weisz, "Mayer Sets $40M, 'Wonder Drug' Position to Weather Rough Seas," *Brandweek*, May 1, 1995.

5. Material for this section is largely based on the discussion of advertising tasks and objectives contained in William Arens and Courtland Bovée, *Contemporary Advertising*, 5th ed. (Burr Ridge, IL: Richard D. Irwin, 1994), chap. 7.

6. Much of the material for this section is based on Phillip Jones, "Ad Spending: Maintaining Market Share," *Harvard Business Review*, January–February 1990, pp. 38–42; and James C. Schroer, "Ad Spending: Growing Market Share," *Harvard Business Review*, January–February 1990, pp. 44–48.

7. For a complete discussion of message strategy, see Arens and Bovée, *Contemporary Advertising*.

8. For a discussion of developing effective advertising, see Jeffrey F. Durgee, "Qualitative Methods for Developing Advertising That makes Consumers Feel, 'Hey, That's Right For Me'," *The Journal of Consumer Marketing*, Winter 1990, pp. 15–21.

9. The list is from Stuart C. Rogers, "How to Create Advertising That Works," *The Journal of Business & Industrial Marketing*, 1995, pp. 20–33.

10. Kevin J. Clancy, "CPMs Must Bow to Involvement Measurement," *Advertising Age*, January 20, 1992, p. 26.

11. For more comprehensive coverage of this topic, see George E. Belch and Michael A. Belch, *Introduction to Advertising and Promotion: An Integrated Communications Perspective*, 3rd ed. (Burr Ridge, IL: Richard D. Irwin, 1995), chap. 12.

12. The discussion of single-source data is based on Magid M. Abraham and Leonard M. Lodish, "Getting the Most Out of Advertising and Promotion," *Harvard Business Review*, May–June 1990, pp. 50–60.

13. For a discussion of problems inherent in the use of GRPs, see Peter R. Dickson, "GRP: A Case of a Mistaken Identity," *Journal of Advertising Research,* February/March 1991, pp. 55–59.

14. Peter D. Bennett, ed., *Dictionary of Marketing Terms* 2nd ed. (Chicago: American Marketing Association, 1995), p. 253.

15. George E. Belch and Michael A. Belch, *Introduction to Advertising and Promotion, An Integrated Communications Perspective,* 3rd ed. (Burr Ridge, IL: Richard D. Irwin, 1995), p. 478.

16. Definition of push marketing and its activities is from Arens and Bovée, *Contemporary Advertising,* p. G–17.

17. For a fuller explanation of the pros and cons associated with push marketing strategies, see Betsy Spellman, "Trade Promotion Redefined," *Brandweek,* March 13, 1995, pp. 25–34; and John McManus, " 'Lost' Money Redefined as 'Found' Money Won't Connect the Disconnects," *Brandweek,* March 25, 1995, p. 16.

18. Robert D. Buzzell, John A. Quelch, and Walter J. Salmon, "The Costly Bargain of Trade Promotion," *Harvard Business Review,* March–April 1990, pp. 141–48.

19. Ibid.

20. This discussion is based on Donald R. Glover, "Distributor Attitudes Toward Manufacturer-Sponsored Promotions," *Industrial Marketing Management,* August 1991, pp. 241–49.

21. Elaine Underwood, "Karan Sets Massive Sampling Blitz for Formula Skincare," *Brandweek,* May 1, 1995, p. 14.

22. Ira Teinowitz, "Promotions Fly High for Coors, Molson," *Advertising Age,* May 22, 1995, p. 38.

23. Coupons At Right Price Can Torpedo Brand Loyalty," *Advertising Age,* May 18, 1992, p. 52.

24. For a further discussion of the dangers involved in using sales promotions, see John P. Jones, "The Double Jeopardy of Sales Promotions," *Harvard Business Review,* September–October 1990.

25. For a discussion of this topic, see Murray Raphel, "Frequent Shopper Clubs: Supermarkets' Newest Weapon," *Direct Marketing,* May 1995, pp. 18–20; Richard G. Barlow, "Five Mistakes of Frequency Marketing," *Direct Marketing,* March 1995, pp. 16–17; and Alice Cuneo, "Savvy Frequent-Buyer Plans Build on a Loyal Base," *Advertising Age,* March 20, 1995, pp. S-10–11.

26. Kerry J. Smith, "Dole Charges into Stores with MasterCard," *Promo,* May 1995, pp. 1, 6.

Chapter 9

1. Warren Keegan, Sandra Moriarty, and Thomas Duncan, *Marketing,* 2nd ed. (Englewood Cliffs, NJ: Prentice Hall, 1994), p. 654.

2. For a discussion of innovative selling practices in the pharmaceutical industry, see Jeremy Walsh, "The Sales Manager's Nightmare Is Really a Wake-Up Call," *Medical Marketing & Media,* May 1994, pp. 22–30.

3. Cathy Hyatt Hills, "Making the Team," *Sales & Marketing Management,* February 1992, pp. 54–57.

4. Eric von Hipple, "The Sources of Innovation," *The McKinsey Quarterly,* Winter 1988, pp. 72–79.

5. Terance A. Shimp, *Promotion Management and Marketing Communication,* 2nd ed. (Chicago, IL: Dryden Press, 1990), p. 602.

6. This section is based on Philip Carpenter, "Bridging the Gap Between Marketing and Sales," *Sales & Marketing Management,* March 1992, pp. 28–31.

7. Material for this discussion came from Ronald B. Marks, *Personal Selling: An Interactive Approach,* 5th ed. (Boston, MA: Allyn and Bacon, 1994), pp. 12–13.

8. John Tschol, "Sales Has a Role in Keeping Customers," *The American Salesman,* April 1995, pp. 10–12.

9. Robert E. Hall, "The Dirty Half Dozen," *Sales & Marketing Management,* February 1995, pp. 76–78.

10. Material for the discussion of objectives is adapted from Joel R. Evans and Barry Berman, *Marketing,* 6th ed. (New York: Macmillan, 1994), pp. 640–42.

11. Unless otherwise noted, the discussion on the relationship-building process is based largely on material contained in Barton A. Weitz, Stephen B. Castleberry, and John F. Tanner, Jr., *Selling: Building Partnerships,* 2nd ed. (Burr Ridge, IL: Richard D. Irwin, 1995); and Rolph Anderson, *Essentials of Personal Selling: The New Professionalism,* (Englewood Cliffs, NJ: Prentice Hall, 1995). For an in-depth discussion of this topic, readers should consult these references.

12. Lee Boyan, "How to Get Referrals," *Agri Marketing,* February 1995, p. 40.

13. For a discussion of this topic, see John R. Graham, "The Sales Edge: Prospecting," *American Salesman,* July 1994, pp. 16–21.

14. John R. Graham, "Motivate the Prospect," *Manager's Magazine,* April 1995, pp. 29–30.

15. Fiona Gibb, "The New Sales Basics," *Sales & Marketing Management,* April 1995, p. 81.

16. For a discussion of relationship selling, see Barry J. Farber and Joyce Wycoff, "Relationships: Six Steps to Success," *Sales & Marketing Management,* April 1992, pp. 50–58.

17. John P. Kirwin, Jr., "The Precision Selling Payoff," *Sales & Marketing Management,* January 1992, pp. 59–61.

18. Interpersonal Skills Key to Sales Performance," *Canadian Manager,* December 1994, p. 16.

19. Material for this discussion is from Thomas Leech, "Getting It Right the First Time," *Sales & Marketing Management*, March 1995, p. 49.

20. Alan Test, "Answering the Price Objection," *American Salesman*, June 1994, pp. 11–13.

21. Material for the discussion on closing guidelines is drawn from "Don't Forget to Ask for the Sale," *Sales & Marketing Management*, June 1995, p. 37.

22. Terry G. Vavra, "Selling after the Sale," *Bank Marketing*, January 1995, pp. 27–30.

23. For a review of research findings regarding factors that are predictive of salespeople's performance, see Gilbert A. Churchill, Jr., Neil M. Ford, Steven W. Hartley, and Orville C. Walker, Jr., "The Determinants of Salesperson Performance: A Meta-Analysis," *Journal of Marketing Research*, May 1985, pp. 87–93.

24. For a detailed discussion of this topic, see Thomas N. Ingram, Charles H. Schwepker, Jr., and Don Hutson, "Why Salespeople Fail," *Industrial Marketing Management*, August 1992, pp. 225–30; and Thomas N. Ingram and Keun S. Lee, "Sales Force Commitment and Turnover," *Industrial Marketing Management*, May 1990, pp. 149–54.

25. Bill Kelley, "From Salesperson to Manager: Transition and Travail," *Sales & Marketing Management*, February 1992, pp. 32–36.

26. For a discussion of this topic, see Saul W. Gellerman, "The Tests of a Good Salesperson," *Harvard Business Review*, May–June 1990, pp. 64–69.

27. William J. Stanton, Richard H. Buskirk, and Rosann L. Spiro, *Management of a Sales Force*, 9th ed. (Burr Ridge, IL: Richard D. Irwin, 1995), pp. 319–20.

28. Michael Kelley, "Replace Sales Management with Sales Leadership," *Marketing News*, June 19, 1995, p. 10.

29. "Income in Sales/Marketing Management Exceeds $250,000," *The American Salesman*, May 1995, pp. 22–24.

30. The discussion on national account management is from James S. Boles, Bruce K. Pilling, and George W. Goodwyn, "Revitalizing Your National Account Marketing Program, *The Journal of Business & Industrial Marketing* 9, no. 1 (1994), pp. 24–33.

31. Stanton, Buskirk, and Spiro, *Management of a Sales Force*, 9th ed. (Burr Ridge, IL: Richard D. Irwin, 1995), p. 38.

32. The list of integration activities is from Ginger Trumfio, "Are You on Par?" *Sales & Marketing Management*, April 1995, pp. 89–99.

33. For additional discussion on the use of sales force automation and other technological systems in sales management, see "Productivity Gains Are Up Another Notch," *Sales & Marketing Management*, September 1992, pp. 110–12; Thayer C. Taylor, "The Future," *Sales & Marketing Management*, June 1992, pp. 47–55; "Software Directory Update," *Sales & Marketing Management*, June 1992, pp. 58–60; "Sales Automation Faces Hard Times," *Sales & Marketing Management*, April 1992, p. 115; and "The Simple ABCs of SFA: The Customer Comes First," *Sales & Marketing Management*, March 1992, pp. 84–85.

34. Based on a survey by the National Industrial Conference Board: "Forecasting Sales," *Studies in Business Policy*, No. 106.

35. Much of the discussion in this section is based on material contained in Gilbert A. Churchill, Jr., Neil M. Ford, and Orville C. Walker, Jr., *Sales Force Management*, 4th ed. (Burr Ridge, IL: Richard D. Irwin, 1993), and Stanton, Buskirk, and Spiro, *Management of a Sales Force*.

36. For additional discussions, see David J. Good and Robert W. Stone, "How Sales Quotas Are Developed," *Industrial Marketing Management*, February 1991, pp. 51–55.

37. For a complete discussion of the skills and policies utilized by sucessful sales leaders in motivating salespeople, see David W. Cravens, Thomas N. Ingram, Raymond W. LaForge, and Clifford E. Young, "Hallmarks of Effective Sales Organizations," *Marketing Management*, Winter 1992, pp. 57–66; Thomas R. Wortruba, John S. Mactie, and Jerome A. Colletti, "Effective Sales Force Recognition Programs," *Industrial Marketing Management*, February 1991, pp. 9–15; and Dr. Ken Blanchard, "Reward Salespeople Creatively," *Personal Selling Power*, March, 1992, p. 24.

38. For a discussion of this and other means by which companies can recruit, motivate, and retain salespeople, see Jeffrey K. Sager, "Recruiting and Retaining Committed Salespeople," *Industrial Marketing Management*, May 1991, pp. 99–103; and Jeffrey K. Sager, "How to Retain Salespeople," *Industrial Marketing Management*, May 1990, pp. 155–60.

39. Robert G. Head, "Restoring Balance to Sales Compensation," *Sales & Marketing Management*, August 1992, pp. 48–53.

Chapter 10

1. Peter D. Bennett, *Dictionary of Marketing Terms*, 2nd ed. (Chicago: American Marketing Association, 1995), p. 242.

2. For further discussion of relationship marketing, see Jan B. Heide, "Interorganizational Governance in Marketing Channels," *Journal of Marketing*, January 1994, pp. 71–85; Robert M. Morgan and Shelby D. Hunt, "The Commitment-Trust Theory of Relationship Marketing," *Journal of Marketing*, July

1994, pp. 20–38; Manohar U. Kalwani and Narakesari Narayandas, "Long-Term Manufacturer-Supplier Relationships: Do They Pay Off for the Supplier Firm?" *Journal of Marketing*, January 1995, pp. 1–16.

3. This section is based on Donald J. Bowersox and M. Bixby Cooper, *Strategic Marketing Channel Management* (New York: McGraw-Hill, 1992), pp. 104–7; Bert Rosenbloom, *Marketing Channels: A Management View*, 4th ed. (Hinsdale, IL: Dryden Press), pp. 440–65; Eric N. Berkowitz, Roger A. Kerin, Steven W. Hartley, and William Rudelius, *Marketing*, 3rd ed. (Homewood, IL: Richard D. Irwin, 1992), pp. 387–90.

Chapter 11

1. Kent B. Monroe, "Buyers' Subjective Perceptions of Price," *Journal of Marketing Research*, February 1973, pp. 70–80; also see Donald R. Lichtenstein and Scot Burton, "The Relationship between Perceived and Objective Price—Quality." *Journal of Marketing Research*, November 1989, pp. 429–43.

2. For research concerning the effects of price and several other marketing variables on perceived product quality, see Akshay R. Rao and Kent B. Monroe, "The Effect of Price, Brand Name, and Store Name on Buyers' Perceptions of Product Quality: An Integrative Review," *Journal of Marketing Research*, August 1989, pp. 351–57; William B. Dodds, Kent B. Monroe, and Dhruv Grewal, "Effects of Price, Brand, and Store Evaluations on Buyers' Product Evaluations," *Journal of Marketing Research*, August 1991, pp. 307–19.

3. For further discussion of price elasticity see Stephen J. Hoch, Byung-Do Kim, Alan L. Montgomery, and Peter Rosi, "Determinants of Store-Level Price Elasticity," *Journal of Marketing Research*, February 1995, pp. 17–29.

4. For further discussion of legal issues involved in pricing, see Louis W. Stern and Thomas L. Eovaldi, *Legal Aspects of Marketing Strategy* (Englewood Cliffs, NJ: Prentice Hall, 1984), chap. 5.

5. Frederick E. Webster, *Marketing for Managers* (New York: Harper & Row, 1974), pp. 178–79; also see Thomas T. Nagle and Reed K. Holden, *The Strategy and Tactics of Pricing* (Englewood Cliffs, NJ: Prentice Hall, 1995); Kent B. Monroe, *Pricing: Making Profitable Decisions*, 2nd ed. (New York: McGraw-Hill, 1990).

Chapter 12

1. Much of the material for this introduction came from Ronald Henkoff, "Service Is Everybody's Business," *Fortune*, June 27, 1994, pp. 48–60; and Tim R. Smith, The Tenth District's Expanding Service Sector," *Economic Review*, Third Quarter 1994, pp. 55–66.

2. Gustavo A. Vargas and Ghasem H. Manoocheri, "An Assessment of Operations in U.S. Service Firms," *International Journal of Operations & Production Management*, 1995, pp. 24–37.

3. Peter D. Bennett, ed., *Dictionary of Marketing Terms* 2nd ed., (Chicago, American Marketing Association, 1995), p. 261.

4. Carolyn R. Fryer, "What's Different About Services Marketing," *Journal of Services Marketing*, Fall 1991, pp. 53–58.

5. Harry N. Shycon, "Improved Customer Service Measuring the Payoff," *The Journal of Business Strategy*, January/February 1992, pp. 13–17.

6. Ibid.

7. For a discussion of customer service in product companies, see A. Lynn Daniel, "Overcome the Barriers to Superior Customer Service," *The Journal of Business Strategy*, January/February 1992, pp. 18–24; and James Brian Quinn, Thomas L. Doorley, and Penny C. Paquette, "Beyond Products: Services-Based Strategies," *Harbard Business Review*, March–April 1990, pp. 58–67.

8. James Brian Quinn, Jordan J. Baruch, and Penny C. Paquette, "Exploiting the Manufacturing-Service Interface," *Sloan Management Review*, Summer 1988, pp. 45–56.

9. Craig Cina, "Five Steps to Service Excellence," *The Journal of Services Marketing*, Spring 1990, pp. 39–47.

10. For a full discussion of problems faced in marketing professional services, see Christopher W. L. Hart, Leonard A. Schlesinger, and Don Maher, "Guarantees Come to Professional Service Firms," *Sloan Management Review*, Spring 1992, pp. 19–29; Gabriel R. Bitran and Johannes Hoech, "The Humanization of Service: Respect at the Moment of Truth," *Sloan Management Review*, Winter 1990, pp. 89–96; and Betsy D. Gelb, Samuel V. Smith, and Gabriel M. Gelb, "Service Marketing Lessons from the Professionals," *Business Horizons*, September–October 1988, pp. 29–34.

11. Frank Sonnenberg, "Service Quality Forethought, Not Afterthought," *The Journal of Business Strategy*, September/October 1989, pp. 54–57.

12. Susan J. Devlin and H. K. Dong, "Service Quality from the Customer's Pespective," *Marketing Research* 6, no. 1 (1995), pp. 4–13.

13. Joan O. Fredericks and James M. Salter II, "Beyond Customer Satisfaction," *Management Review*, May 1995, pp. 29–32.

14. The material in this section draws from research performed by Leonard L. Berry, Valerie A. Zeithaml, and A. Parasuraman, "Quality Counts in Services, Too," *Business Horizons*, May–June 1985, pp.

44–52; A Parasuraman, Valerie A. Zeithaml, and Leonard L. Berry, "A Conceptual Model of Service Quality and Its Implications for Future Research," *Journal of Marketing,* Fall 1985, pp. 41–50; Leonard L. Berry, A. Parasuraman, and Valerie A. Zeithaml, "The Service-Quality Puzzle," *Business Horizons,* September–October 1988, pp. 35–43; Stephen W. Brown and Teresa A. Swartz, "A Gap Analysis of Professional Service Quality," *Journal of Marketing,* April 1989, pp. 92–98; Leonard L. Berry, Valerie A. Zeithaml, and A. Parasuraman, "Five Imperatives for Improving Service Quality," *Sloan Management Review,* Summer 1990, pp. 29–38; A. Parasuraman, Leonard L. Berry, and Valerie A. Zeithaml, "Understanding Customer Expectations of Service," *Sloan Management Review,* Spring 1991, pp. 39–48; and Leonard L. Berry, *On Great Service: A Framework for Action,* (New York: The Free Press, 1995).

15. Rick Berry, "Define Service Quality So You Can Deliver it," *Best's Review,* March 1995, p. 68.

16. Material for this section is drawn from John T. Mentzer, Carol C. Bienstock, and Kenneth B. Kahn, "Benchmarking Satisfaction," *Marketing Management,* Summer 1995, pp. 41–46; and Alan Dutka, *AMA Handbook for Customer Satisfaction: A Complete Guide to Research, Planning & Implementation,* (Lincolnwood, IL: NTC Books, 1994). For detailed information on this topic, readers are advised to consult these sources.

17. William A. Sheldon, "Gaining the Service Quality Advantage," *The Journal of Business Strategy,* March/April 1988, pp. 45–48.

18. Much of the material for this section was taken from Karl Albrecht and Ron Zemke, *Service America* (Homewood, IL: Dow-Jones Irwin, 1985); and Ron Zemke and Dick Schaaf, *The Service Edge 101 Companies That Profit from Customer Care* (New York: New American Library, 1989).

19. Charles E. Cox, "18 Ways to Improve Customer Service," *HR Magazine,* March 1992, pp. 69–72,

20. Chip R. Bell and Kristen Anderson, "Selecting Super Service People," *HR Magazine,* February 1992, pp. 52–54.

21. James A. Schlesinger and James L. Heskett, "Breaking the Cycle of Failure in Services," *Sloan Management Review,* Spring 1991, pp. 17–28.

22. Leonard L. Berry and A. Parasuraman, "Services Marketing Starts from Within," *Marketing Management,* Winter 1992, pp. 25–34.

23. Ibid.

24. Leonard L. Berry and A. Parasuraman, "Prescriptions for a Service Quality Revolution in America," *Organizational Dynamics,* Spring 1992, pp. 5–15.

25. Bob O'Neal, "World-Class Service," *Executive Excellence,* September 1994, pp. 11–12.

26. This example is from David E. Bowen and Edward E. Lawler III, "The Empowerment of Service Workers: What, Why, How, and When," *Sloan Management Review,* Spring 1992, pp. 31–39.

27. Judith Waldrop, "Spending by Degree," *American Demographics,* February 1990, pp. 22–26.

28. "Merrill Lynch Buying British Firm, Will Be World's Largest Stockbroker," *Chicago Tribune,* July 22, 1995, sec. 2, pp. 1, 3.

29. Howard Schlossberg, "Study: U.S. Firms Lag in Using Customer Satisfaction Data," *Marketing News,* June 1992, p. 14.

30. Andrew E. Serwer, "The Competition Heats Up in Online Banking," *Fortune,* June 26, 1995, pp. 18–19.

31. Material on bank consolidations is from Kelly Holland, "Why Banks Keep Bulking Up," *Business Week,* July 31, 1995, pp. 66–67; and Amy Dunkin, "Investing in a Bank-Eat-Bank World," *Business Week,* July 31, 1995, pp. 92–93.

32. Chad Rubel, "Banks Should Show That They Care for Consumers," *Marketing News,* July 3, 1995, p. 4.

33. Tom Harvey, "Quality: The Only Profit Strategy," *Bank Marketing,* January 1995, pp. 43–46.

34. Material for the discussion of Columbia/HCA was provided courtesy of *Off the Record Research,* a San Francisco–based institutional investment research company.

35. Henry C. Wagner, David Fleming, W. Glynn Mangold, and Raymond W. LaForge, "Relationship Marketing in Health Care," *Journal of Health Care Marketing,* Winter 1994, pp. 42–47.

36. Kelly Shriver, "Providers Have to Tailor Ads to Consumer Needs," *Modern Healthcare,* February 13, 1995, p. 86.

37. John Labate, "Chronimed," *Fortune,* February 20, 1995, p. 118.

38. Elaine Underwood, "Airlines Continue Flight to E-Ticketing," *Brandweek,* May 8, 1995, p. 3.

39. Peter L. Ostrowski, Terrence V. O'Brien, and Geoffrey L. Gordon, "Determinants of Service Quality in the Commercial Airline Industry: Differences Between Business and Leisure Travelers," *Journal of Travel & Tourism Marketing* 3, no. 1 (1994), pp. 19–47.

40. Stanley Ziemba, "Nimble Discount Airline Outpacing Wannabes," *Chicago Tribune,* July 3, 1995, pp. D1, 3.

41. Material for the discussion on the lodging industry came from Elaine Underwood, "Joined at the Hip," *Adweek's Marketing Week,* June 1, 1992, pp. 22–23; and Sak Onkvisit and John L. Shaw, "Service Marketing: Image, Branding, and Competition," *Business Horizons,* January–February 1989, pp. 13–18.

Chapter 13

1. Karen Pennar, "America: Losing Out on Exports," *Business Week,* July 31, 1995, p. 30.

2. Louis S. Richman, "Global Growth Is on a Tear," *Fortune,* March 20, 1995, pp. 108–14.

3. Material on McDonald's and PepsiCo is from Jeanne Whitman, "McDonald's Cooks Worldwide Growth," *Advertising Age International,* July 17, 1995, p. I-4.

4. Pat Sloan, "U.S. Business Is Key to Colgate's Future," *Advertising Age,* December 19, 1994, p. 4.

5. Brian Zajac, "Weak Dollar, Strong Results," *Forbes,* July 17, 1995, pp. 274–76.

6. Jason Vogel, "Chicken Diplomacy," *Financial World,* March 14, 1995, pp. 46–49.

7. For a full explanation on cultural differences, see Rose Knotts, "Cross-Cultural Management: Transformations and Adaptations," *Business Horizons,* January–February 1989, pp. 29–33.

8. "In Japan, if Your Prospect Says Yes, Don't Start Celebrating Yet," *Marketing News,* February 5, 1990, p. 18.

9. For a further discussion of the influence of foreign culture, see Naoko Oikawa and John F. Tanner, Jr., "The Influence of Japanese Culture on Business Relationships and Negotiations," *The Journal of Services Marketing,* Summer 1992, pp. 67–74; and Sergey Frank, "Global Negotiations," *Sales & Marketing Management,* May 1992, pp. 64–69.

10. Claudia Penteado, "Pepsi's Brazil Blitz," *Advertising Age,* January 16, 1995, p. 12.

11. Karen Benezra, "Fritos 'Round the World'," *Brandweek,* March 27, 1995, pp. 32, 35.

12. Material for this section is from Craig Mellow, "Russia: Making Cash from Chaos," *Fortune,* April 17, 1995, pp. 145–51; and Peter Galuszka, "And You Think You've Got Tax Problems," *Business Week,* May 29, 1995, p. 50.

13. William J. Holstein and Laxmi Nakarmi, "Korea," *Business Week,* July 31, 1995, pp. 56–63; and Paul Magnusson and Blanca Riemer, "Carla Hills, Trade Warrior," *Business Week,* January 22, 1990, pp. 50–56.

14. John Templeton and David Woodruff, "How Mercedes Trumped Chrysler in China," *Business Week,* July 31, 1995, pp. 50–51.

15. Mir Magbool Alam Khan, "Enormity Tempts Marketers to Make a Passage to India," *Advertising Age International,* May 15, 1995, p. I–12.

16. Gilbert A. Churchill and J. Paul Peter, *Marketing: Creating Value for Customers,* (Burr Ridge, IL: Richard D. Irwin, 1995), p. 99.

17. Christopher Power, "Second Thoughts on Going Global," *Business Week,* March 13, 1995, pp. 48–49; and Carla Rapoport and Justin Martin, "Retailers Go Global," *Fortune,* February 20, 1995, pp. 102–8.

18. This section was taken from James F. Bolt, "Global Competitors: Some Criteria for Success," *Business Horizons,* January–February 1988, pp. 34–41.

19. For further discussion on global marketing, see Michael R. Czinkota and Ilkka A. Ronkainen, "Global Marketing 2000: A Marketing Survival Guide," *Marketing Management,* Winter 1992, pp. 37–45.

20. For a complete discussion of the risks associated with pursuing a global strategy, see Barrie James, "Reducing the Risks of Globalization," *Long Range Planning,* February 1990, pp. 80–88.

21. This section is based on George S. Yip, Pierre M. Loewe, and Michael Y. Yoshino, "How to Take Your Company to the Global Market," *Columbia Journal of World Business,* Winter 1988, pp. 37–48.

22. Ibid.

23. "Brands Fight Back Against Private Labels," *Marketing News,* January 16, 1995, pp. 8–9.

24. For a more complete discussion of both sides of the multidomestic versus global debate, see Julian Birkinshaw, "Encouraging Entrepreneurial Activity in Multidomestic Corporations," *Business Horizons,* May–June 1995, pp. 32–38; Robert N. Lussier, Robert W. Baeder, and Joel Corman, "Measuring Global Practices: Global Strategic Planning Through Company Situation Analysis," *Business Horizons,* September–October 1994, pp. 56–62; and Milton Leontides, "The Japanese Art of Managing Diversity," *The Journal of Business Strategy,* March/April 1991, pp. 30–36.

25. The introductory material on foreign research is based on Michael R. Czintoka, "Take a Shortcut to Low-Cost Global Research," *Marketing News,* March 13, 1995, p. 3.

26. Donald B. Pittenger, "Gathering Foreign Demographics Is No Easy Task," *Marketing News,* January 8, 1990, pp. 23, 25.

27. Bristol Voss, "Painting Portraits of Emerging Markets," *Journal of Business Strategy,* May–June 1994, pp. 6–7.

28. Cyndee Miller, "New Battleground Looms for IRI and Neilson," *Marketing News,* April 25, 1994, pp. 1, 3.

29. Debbie Klosky, "Pepsi, Coke Usher in New Age in Spain," *Advertising Age,* June 5, 1995, p. 45.

30. The manufacturer does have slightly more control over the export agent than the resident buyer or export merchant, since the export agent does not take title to the goods.

31. Ian Katz, "It's Carnival Time for Investors," *Business Week,* March 13, 1995, p. 53.

32. For a more complete discussion of issues affecting pricing in foreign markets, see James K. Weekly, "Pricing in Foreign Markets: Pitfalls and Opportunities," *Industrial Marketing Management,* April 1992, pp. 173–79.

33. Robert Neff, "The Japanese Have a New Thirst for Imports," *Business Week,* June 5, 1995, pp. 52–53.

34. Laurel Wentz, "Publicis-FCB Leads Euro-networks," *Advertising Age,* June 12, 1989, p. 36.

35. Kathleen Barnes, "Nestlé Exec Criticizes Sluggish Global Shops," *Advertising Age,* November 13, 1989.

36. For a discussion on this topic, see R. Blackwell, R. Ajami, and K. Stephan, "Winning the Global Advertising Race: Planning Globally, Acting Locally," *Journal of International Consumer Marketing* 3, no. 2 (1991), pp. 97–120; and J. H. Holmes, "Toward More Effective International Advertising," *Journal of International Consumer Marketing* 3, no. 1 (1990), pp. 51–65.

37. This discussion is based on John Burnett, *Promotion Management,* (Boston: Houghton-Mifflin Co., 1993), chap. 19.

38. Todd Pruzan, "Emerging Markets: A Mixed Bag of Promise and Pitfalls," *Advertising Age International,* May 15, 1995, pp. I12–I14.

39. Jean-Pierre Jeanett and H. David Hennessey, *Global Marketing Strategies,* 3rd ed. (Boston: Houghton-Mifflin Co., 1995), p. 489.

40. The material for this section on market entry and growth approaches is based on Philip R. Cateora, *International Marketing,* 8th ed. (Burr Ridge, IL: Richard D. Irwin, 1993), pp. 325–34; Charles W. L. Hill, *International Business: Competing in the Global Marketplace* (Burr Ridge, IL: Richard D. Irwin, 1994), pp. 402–8; and William M. Pride and O. C. Ferrell, *Marketing: Concepts and Strategy,* 9th ed. (Boston: Houghton-Mifflin Co., 1995), pp. 111–14.

41. General Mills Teams Up with CPC in Latin America," *Food Engineering,* March 1995, p. 25.

42. Bruce A. Walters, Steve Peters, and Gregory G. Dess, "Strategic Alliances and Joint Ventures: Making Them Work," *Business Horizons,* July/August 1994, pp. 5–10.

43. Joel Bleeke and David Ernst, "Is Your Strategic Alliance Really a Sale?" *Harvard Business Review,* January–February 1995, pp. 97–105.

44. Material in this section is based on Subhash C. Jain, "Standardization of International Marketing Strategy: Some Research Hypotheses," *Journal of Marketing,* January 1989, pp. 70–79.

Chapter 14

1. This chapter is based on J. Paul Peter and Jerry C. Olson, *Consumer Behavior and Marketing Strategy,* 4th ed. (Burr Ridge, Homewood, IL: Richard D. Irwin, 1996), chap. 20.

2. Phillip Kotler, "What Consumerism Means for Marketers," *Harvard Business Review,* May–June 1972, pp 48–57. Also see Joseph V. Anderson, "Power Marketing: Its Past, Present, and Future," *Journal of Consumer Marketing,* Summer 1987. pp. 5–13.

3. For complete discussions of legal influences on marketing, see Louis W. Stern and Thomas L. Eovaldi, *Legal Aspects of Marketing Strategy* (Englewood Cliffs, NJ: Prentice Hall, 1984); Robert J. Posch Jr., *The Complete Guide to Marketing and the Law* (Englewood Cliffs, NJ: Prentice Hall, 1988).

4. Paul N. Bloom and Stephen A. Greyser, "The Maturing of Consumerism," *Harvard Business Review,* November–December 1981, pp. 130–39; also see Paul N. Bloom and Ruth Belk Smith, *The Future of Consumerism* (Lexington, MA: Lexington Books, 1986).

5. Gene R. Laczniak, "Framework for Analyzing Marketing Ethics," *Journal of Macromarketing,* Spring 1983, pp. 7–18; also see Donald P. Robin and R. Eric Reidenbach, "Social Responsibility, Ethics, and Marketing Strategy: Closing the Gap between Concept and Application," *Journal of Marketing,* January 1987, pp. 44–58; Jerry R. Godsby and Shelby D. Hunt, "Cognitive Moral Development and Marketing," *Journal of Marketing,* January 1992, pp. 55–68. Oswald A. J. Mascarenhas, "Exoner-ating Unethical Marketing Executive Behav-iors: A diagnostic Framework," *Journal of Marketing,* April 1995, pp. 43–57.

Section II

1. Michael E. Porter, *Competitive Strategy* (New York: Free Press, 1980). Also see Michael E. Porter, *Competitive Advantage: Creating and Sustaining Superior Performance* (New York: Free Press, 1985); Michael E. Porter, *The Competitive Advantage of Nations* (New York: Free Press, 1990).

Section III

1. For methods of estimating the cost of capital, see Charles P. Jones, *Introduction to Financial Management* (Homewood, IL: Richard D. Irwin, 1992), chap. 14.

2. See Eugene F. Brigham, *Fundamentals of Financial Management* (Hinsdale, IL: Dryden Press, 1986).

3. It is useful to use average inventory rather than a singe end-of-year estimate if monthly data are available.

4. For a discussion of ratio analysis for retailing, see Joseph B. Mason and Morris L. Mayer, *Modern Retailing: Theory and Practice,* 6th ed. (Homewood, IL: Richard D. Irwin, 1993), chap. 8.

Section V

1. Some of the listed references included in this section were adapted excerpts from: Gilbert A. Churchill, Jr., *Marketing Research: Methodological Foundations,* 5th ed. (Chicago: Dryden Press, 1991); Barry Berman and Joel R. Evans, *Retailing Management,* 5th ed. (New York: Macmillan, 1992); William Davidson, Daniel J. Sweeney, and Robert Stampfl, *Retailing Management,* 5th ed. (New York: John Wiley & Sons, 1984); and Lorna M. Daniells, *Business Information Sources: Revised Edition* (Berkeley, CA: University of California Press, 1985).

2. Information for the discussion of on-line services is from Fredrick Elkind and Amelia Kassel, "A Marketer's Guide for Navigating the Information Superhighway," *Marketing News,* July 31, 1995, pp. 2, 7; Neil Randall, "Find Everything . . . Do Anything . . . ONLINE," *PC Computing,* March 1995, pp. 112–23; Jack M. Germain, "Finding Hard-Core Business Information on the Internet," *The Traveler's Guide to the Information Highway,* (Emeryville, CA: Ziff-Davis, 1994); John December and Neil Randall, *The Worldwide Web Unleashed,* (Indianapolis, IN: SAMS Publishing, 1994).

Name
Index

Subject
Index